Theatricality as Medium

SAMUEL WEBER

Theatricality as Medium

Fordham University Press *New York* 2004

Library of Congress Cataloging-in-Publication Data

Weber, Samuel, 1940–
    Theatricality as medium / Samuel Weber.—1st ed.
      p.   cm.
    Includes bibliographical references and index.
    ISBN 0-8232-2415-5 (hardcover) — ISBN 0-8232-2416-3 (pbk.)
  1. Theater—Philosophy.   I. Title.
    PN2039.W36   2004
    792′.01—dc22   2004021850

Printed in the United States of America
07 06 05 04   5 4 3 2 1
First edition

In Memory of

Axel Manthey (1945–1995)

and

Jacques Derrida (1930–2004)

Contents

Preface

THIS BOOK has had a long period of gestation and a hybrid history. It goes back, first, to a fascination with texts, "fictional" or not, in which the reader is called upon to play an active part. This summons is surely coextensive with all reading in the strong sense. But certain texts render the awareness of this possibility more accessible than others. From Sterne to Kafka, Kierkegaard to Derrida, Freud to Lacan, a transformative involvement of the reader is required in order for the text "itself" to function—just as an "audience" is required for a representation to be "theatrical." The second source was less academic and developed from the experience of working as a dramaturge in German productions of theater and opera during the 1980s and 1990s. Unlike the director, stage designer, or actors, the dramaturge, like the academic, is primarily concerned with texts. Whereas the academic tends to be guided by a notion of a long-lasting, if not eternal *truth*, however, the goal of a theatrical production is far more ephemeral, more localized, and more singular. If, as the O.E.D. speculates, the word *truth* derives from the Old English word for *truce*, this etymological filiation remains palpable today in the process of theatrical staging: its result resembles a temporary *truce* between warring factions rather than a peace treaty of long duration. It can therefore differ from performance to performance and in any case rarely outlives them.

This experience contrasts with certain aspects of "scholarly" life, where belief in a durable truth often functions as the tenet of a secular faith. In providing an alternative perspective to this faith, "theatricality" offers another perspective from which to approach the relation of institutions, interpretation, and media investigated in my previous work. For *theatricality*—which is not the same as theater, although also not separable from it—spans the gap dividing "old" and "new" media in ways whose investigation and reflection can illuminate the cultural, social, and political transformations currently underway.

Although this book thus results from a history involving both academic and theatrical experiences, the texts it brings together were written almost exclusively for academic occasions. Although initially conceived as independent studies, a common set of concerns that gradually emerged links the different texts in various ways. At the center of their concerns stands the tension between the effort to reduce the *theatrical medium* to a *means* of meaningful representation by enclosing its space within an ostensibly self-contained narrative, and the resistance of this medium to such reduction. Theatricality resists the reduction to a meaningful narrative by virtue of its ability to signify. This ability associates it with what is called "language." As the most ubiquitous of signifying media—a pleonasm insofar as *all* media are such through signifying—language demonstrates the priority of the signifying function over that of representation. In so doing, far from reducing the materiality and corporeality of theater, it marks their irreducibility. This is what Walter Benjamin interprets as baroque "allegory," and it is why he links it to theater in the form of the German "mourning play." In its allegorical dimension, the process of signifying always leaves something *out* and something *over*: an excess that is also a deficit, or, as Derrida has formulated it, a "remainder"—*un reste*. It is the irreducibility of this remainder that, ultimately, renders language *theatrical*, and theatricality *significant*.

The essays collected in this volume repeat and rehearse certain chapters in the emergence of this significance, while exploring some of its ramifications. They make no claim to completeness and remain as aleatory as their subject matter. Whether or not they leave anything in their wake will have to depend on the readings to which they give rise.

• • •

As work on this book has been in progress for well over a decade, it is impossible to acknowledge adequately or completely the many helpful suggestions I have received. Memory retains the most recent of these, whereas older ones tend to be assimilated over the years so that one forgets that they initially came from elsewhere. My apologies therefore in advance to those whose names deserve to be mentioned here but are not.

This book would almost certainly never have been published without the insight and involvement of Helen Tartar, whose dedication and support have been a constant source of encouragement. Largely due to her interventions, as well as those of Ela Kotkowska, the original manuscript has become far more readable. My friend and former colleague Haun Saussy also gave generously of his time in suggesting revisions and corrections. Jennifer Bajorek and Nicholas Müller-Schöll were discerning readers; Rodolphe Gasché gave valuable suggestions at various points. A word of thanks is also due the Wooster Group, who kindly made available a taped recording of their unforgettable production of O'Neill's *Emperor Jones*. Although I was unable to include a discussion of this staging here, their approach to theater and media certainly informs my notion of "theatricality" throughout.

A debt of a different kind is due Klaus Zehelein, currently Director of the Stuttgart Opera; his invitation to work with the Frankfurt Opera in the 1980s allowed me to experience the theatrical process from behind the scenes. A determining aspect of that experience was the opportunity to work on several theater and opera productions, as *dramaturg*, with the director and stage designer Axel Manthey. I gratefully dedicate this volume to his to memory.

Finally, a unique word of thanks is due my wife, Arlette. Her experience in television production provided me with an invaluable perspective on the relation of "theatricality" to media. Beyond that, her patience and understanding made this book possible.

Although I have tended to modify existing translations or retranslate, I have often used and learned from the published English versions, to which I remain greatly indebted.

Prior Publication

PORTIONS OF the chapters in this book have been published in the following books and journals.

Chapter 1: "Replacing the Body: An Approach to the Question of Digital Democracy," in Marcel Henaff and Tracy Strong, eds., *Public Space and Democracy* (Minneapolis: University of Minnesota Press, 2001), pp. 172–88.

Chapter 2: "Family Scenes: Some Preliminary Remarks on Domesticity and Theatricality," *SAQ* (*The South Atlantic Quarterly*), 98, no. 3, *Domestic/Tragedy*, special issue ed. Julie Carlson (1999): 22–28.

Chapter 4: "Breaching the Gap: Lacan's *Ethics of Psychoanalysis* and the Question of the Tragicomic," in Mark Poster, ed., *Literature and Politics* (Columbia University Press: New York, 1992).

Chapter 9: "Critical Theory and the Task of Reading (Adorno)," *New German Critique*, no. 81 (Fall 2000): 83–106. Reprinted in A. Rubin and N. Gibson, eds., *Theodor Adorno: A Critical Reader* (Oxford: Basil Blackwell, 2002), pp. 379–99.

Chapter 10: "Psychoanalysis and Theatricality," *Parallax* 6, no. 3 (2000): 29–48. In German in *Riss*, 1999.

Chapter 11: "The Virtual Reality of Theater," in *100 Years of Cruelty* (Sydney: Power Publications, 2000), pp. 7–32.

Chapter 12: "Double-Take: Acting and Writing in Genet's '*L'Étrange Mot d'* . . . ,'" *Yale French Studies* 91 (1997), ed. Scott Durham, pp. 28–48.

Chapter 13: "La Théâtralité dans le cinema: Considérations préliminaires," trans. André Loiselle, *L'Annuaire théâtral* 30 (Fall 2001), *Entre théâtre et cinéma*, 13–23.

Chapter 14: "War, Terrorism, Spectacle: The Towers and the Caves," *Grey Room* 07 (Cambridge: MIT Press, 2002), pp. 14–23. Reprinted in *Medium Cool*, ed. A. McNamara and Peter Krapp, *SAQ (The South Atlantic Quarterly)*, 101, no. 3 (Summer 2002): 449–58. In German as "Türme und Höhlen: Das Theater des Terrorismus und das gute Gewissen Amerikas," *Lettre international* 58 (Autumn 2002): 18–22.

Chapter 15: "Responding: Interview with Simon Morgan-Wortham and Gary Hall," in *Medium Cool*, ed. A. McNamara and Peter Krapp, *SAQ (The South Atlantic Quarterly)*, 101, no. 3 (Summer 2002): 695–724.

Theatricality as Medium

Introduction:
Theatricality as Medium

THE ESSAYS that compose this book seek to respond to
two sets of questions.

First, how does it come about, and what does it signify, that, in an
age increasingly dominated by electronic media, notions and practices
that could be called "theatrical," far from appearing merely obsolete,
seem to gain in importance? In other words, given that the medium
of theater and the effect of theatricality presuppose, as one of their
indispensable preconditions, some sort of real, immediate, physical
presence, and given that the status and significance of such presence
has been rendered increasingly problematic by the advent of the "new
media," with their powerful "virtualizing" effects, one might expect
to find that practices relating to theater and theatricality would tend
to diminish progressively in scope and significance. Yet the contrary
appears to be the case. Theatrical practices, attitudes, even organizations seem to proliferate, in conjunction with if not in response to the
new media. Why is this happening, and what are its possible consequences?

The notions of "theater" and "theatricality" are anything but self-
evident or unambiguous. They have a vexed and complex history,
and only by articulating some of the major traits and tendencies of this
history can we begin to investigate the renewed significance these
terms are acquiring today. This brings me to the second set of questions to which I seek to respond.

Second, how has theater been conceptualized in the West? I limit
myself here to the Western European tradition and its sequels, not
because non-Western theater and theatrical practices lack importance,
on the contrary. Non-Western theatrical practices have played a decisive and determining role throughout the long history of Western

1

theater. In the twentieth century, they have inspired a critical reevaluation of this history, most conspicuously in playwrights and theatrical thinkers such as Brecht, Artaud, Deleuze, Barthes, and Derrida. This rethinking has a much longer history, however. It emerges perhaps most significantly in the early part of the nineteenth century, in what might be called the "aftermath" of the Hegelian philosophical system and the culmination of thought it entails—in a writer-thinker such as Kierkegaard, for example—and it continues to mark the work of many of the most radical writer-thinkers of that century, such as Marx and Nietzsche, to name just the most obvious and influential. In the wake of the exhaustion of a conceptual tradition based on a certain notion of identity, reflexivity, and subjectivity, *theater* and *theatricality* emerge as names for an alternative that begins to articulate itself in the writings of these thinkers, although it certainly has far more complex a progeny than this limited list would seem to suggest. To understand just how a certain questioning of theater and theatricality could assume this function in the nineteenth century, we must first examine that *against* which such thinkers and dramaturges were reacting. In this emergence of theatrical language, figures, and concerns, it becomes clear that a battle is being fought to redefine the meaning and value of words such as *theater* and *theatricality*, and that this battle has a very long history. It reaches back at least as far as Plato and Aristotle, in whose work the question of theater as medium is posed, but only to be rapidly disposed of in a way that was to determine much of the history—the thought and practice—of theater in the West. This tendency continues, even and perhaps especially today, to extend its influence in the world dominated by electronic media that have developed out of these same traditions. It is thus crucial to elaborate, as precisely as possible, just what the determining characteristics of this systematic conception of theater are, in order to discern alternatives to it, alternatives that have their own "history," which is quite distinct from that associated with "mainstream" versions. We will discover that an alternative approach to the dominant Western concept of theater is already at work *within* the elaboration of the mainstream concept. It is not something simply imposed upon it from without, but accompanies it from the start—which is to say, from the initial efforts of Western metaphysics to appropriate theater for its purposes.

To understand what is at stake in this effort of appropriation, one need only return to a well-known and often-discussed fact: The term *theater* has the same etymology as the term *theory*, from the Greek word *thea*, designating a place from which to observe or to see. The fact that theater, like television today, has always involved much more than simply seeing only makes this privileging of sight all the more significant, and questionable.[1] The valorization of sight over the other senses, especially hearing, which is implied in the currency of words such as *theory* and *theater*, but also *television*, often results from the desire to secure a position, from a distance that ostensibly permits one to view the object in its entirety while remaining at a safe remove from it. This desire for exteriority and control has always felt both threatened by and attracted to a certain conception of theater. I will briefly discuss several instances of this ambivalent tendency, one quite old and the others relatively recent.

The Cave

The first is the famous scene of the cave in Plato's *Republic*. This scene, designed to illustrate the limitations of ordinary human existence insofar as it is not enlightened by a philosophical perspective, involves the staging of a scenario with strong, if negative, theatrical connotations:

> "Picture men dwelling in a sort of subterranean cavern with a long entrance open to the light on its entire width. Conceive them as having their legs and necks fettered from childhood, so that they remain in the same spot, able to look forward only, and prevented by the fetters from turning their heads. Picture further the light from a fire burning higher up and at a distance behind them, and between the fire and the prisoners and above them a road along which a low wall has been built, as the exhibitors of puppet shows have partitions before the men themselves, above which they show the puppets."
>
> "All that I see," he said.
>
> "See also, then, men carrying past the wall implements of all kinds that rise above the wall, and human images and shapes of animals as well, wrought in stone and wood and every material, some of these bearers presumably speaking and others silent."
>
> "A strange image you speak of," he said, "and strange prisoners."

"Like to us," I said. "For, to begin with, tell me, do you think that these men would have seen anything of themselves or of one another except the shadows cast from the fire on the wall of the cave that fronted them?"

"How could they," he said, "if they were compelled to hold their heads unmoved through life?"

"And again, would not the same be true of the objects carried past them?"

"Surely."

"If then they were able to talk to one another, do you not think that they would suppose that in naming the things that they saw they were naming the passing objects?"

"Necessarily."

"And if their prison had an echo from the wall opposite them, when one of the passers-by uttered a sound, do you think that they would suppose anything else than the passing shadow to be the speaker?"

"By Zeus, I do not," said he.

"Then in every way such prisoners would deem reality to be nothing else than the shadows of the artificial objects"

"Quite inevitably," he said. (514b–515c)[2]

The cave here is a particular kind of theater, it is true, or a particular interpretation of theater, but it is unmistakably a theater nonetheless. Two traits mark the setting as being *also* a theater. First, the reader is invited to "picture" a defined, limited place. This placement—the arrangement of the place, the positioning of the people and things in it—is constitutive of what is taking place there. This is the first characteristic of a theater: the events it depicts are not indifferent to their placement. The second trait is the no less constitutive role of spectators. A theatrical scene is one that plays to others, called variously "spectators" or, in this case, more properly "audience," since in the cave "vision" and "visibility" are by no means the only media of perception involved. They are not the only media, but they are placed in a dominant, if problematic, position.

What is characteristic of Plato's parable of the cave, however, is that the protagonists are above all *spectators*. And spectators of a very distinct kind: they are not merely fixed in place, but riveted to their posts. They are "prisoners," although—and this is what makes the scene so modern in many ways—they are prisoners unaware of their imprisonment. They do not know where they are, and hence they do not know how and who they are.

But where, precisely, are they? They are in a particular kind of "home theater": dwelling in a subterranean cavern (*katageiōi oikēsei spēlaiōdei*): at home in a place defined by a certain vacuity, a hollow place under the earth. A place that is profound, interior, and yet precisely not self-contained. Indeed, the cave may be said to be a prison to the very extent that it is not self-contained. Just this lack of self-containment distinguishes the spatial character of the setting. The cave or cavern is described as having "a long entrance" that is "open to the light on its entire width." What is distinctive about this "prison" enclosure is that it is not entirely closed. Rather, it appears to be open to the outside. Indeed, its cavernous hollowness suggests that it itself is an outside that has been enclosed by a kind of container. Like every "place," however, it remains in contact with an outside that it excludes.

So much for the curious place, or *setting*, of the cave. What of its inhabitants? What is most pertinent for our concerns is that the much-celebrated blindness of the cave dwellers is bound up with their being bound into place. The cave dwellers do not understand what they see, not because they are blind or in any other way intrinsically deficient, but because they are bound—unable to get up and move about, and thereby to experience the *relativity* of their point of view. Their positions are fixed and stable, but the very stability of their point of view prevents them from seeing it *as situationally conditioned*. They have never known any other position, or situation, and therefore are not aware of the relations that frame the situation from which they see. Lack of alternative experience and force of habit make what they see and hear seem entirely natural, in the sense of being self-evident and self-contained.

Yet this cavern is by no means simply a natural setting: It conflates nature and culture. Deep in the earth, it is chthonic; but in its organization it is fabricated, technical, cultivated. The cavern is a theater in which the spectators observe a highly organized, "staged" spectacle, which, however, they take to be utterly self-contained. "Shadows" are apprehended as "reality." The lighting in this home theater is both natural and artificial. The space is illuminated by the glare of a fire, a "natural" phenomenon, but one that has been carefully set up and thus is also the result of artifice. This natural-technical source of light is placed so that, given the immobility of the spectators, it remains invisible. As in a theater when the lights have been dimmed, the stage is lit by lights that themselves remain out of sight.

This carefully staged scene is explicitly compared to a "puppet" show. The comparison is significant, since—as we will see later on in this book[3]—even today puppets exemplify the aspect of theatricality which has caused it to be regarded with suspicion by a certain humanistic tradition: its heterogeneity. On one side, an audience of spectators is locked in place, indeed, chained to their positions (they cannot move their heads . . .) vis-à-vis "implements of all kinds . . . and human images and shapes of animals" being carried past the wall, upon which they cast shadows or silhouettes. This shadow play suggests certain Javanese puppets, which cast shadows on a screen, to the accompaniment of gamelan music. But in Javanese puppet shows the audience is free to move about, free to pass to the other side of the "screen," to experience the "reality" of theater as relativity and as surface, an experience that seems hardly compatible with the reductive dichotomy of "appearance" versus "reality."

Even in Plato's scenario, that dichotomy is not unequivocal. In the commentary that articulates and accompanies the scene, a third instance can be distinguished, though it remains in the shadows. Not all the inhabitants of the cave are passively fixed in their seats: there are also "men carrying past the wall" those "implements" and figures. Those "men," who are responsible for the movement of the silhouettes, exercise a function situated somewhere between artists and stagehands. What is their ontological or, for that matter, political status? How do they relate to that spellbound, enthralled audience of spectator-prisoners? How do they relate to the organization and significance of the "spectacle" itself?

Plato does not respond to these questions, though his own scenario stages, and thus implicitly raises, them. The question of theater and theatricality thereby remains unaddressed by the ontological condemnation Plato reserves for emphatically mimetic practices. But that condemnation sets the scene, as it were, for all successive attempts to determine the precise place—ontologically, epistemologically, ethically, politically—of theater and its "special" effects, including spectators and actors, stages and their "props," lighting, sound, and perhaps *effectiveness* in general. Insofar as one proceeds from a presumption of self-identity and self-presence, all departures from their putative self-enclosure—and theater entails just such a departure—are to be vigilantly controlled, if not condemned. Theater marks the spot where the spot reveals itself to be an ineradicable macula, a stigma or stain that cannot be cleansed or otherwise rendered transparent, diaphanous.

This irreducible opacity defines the quality of theater as *medium*.[4] When an event or series of events *takes place* without reducing the place it "taken" to a purely neutral site, then that place reveals itself to be a "stage," and those events become theatrical happenings. As the gerund here suggests—and this will be a recurrent topic of discussion throughout this book—such happenings never take place once and for all but are ongoing. This in turn suggests that they can neither be contained within the place where they unfold nor entirely separated from it. They can be said, then, in a quite literal sense, to *come to pass*. They take place, which means in a particular place, and yet simultaneously also *pass away*—not simply to disappear but to happen somewhere *else*. Out of the dislocations of its repetitions emerges nothing more or less than the *singularity of the theatrical event*. Such theatrical singularity haunts and taunts the Western dream of self-identity.[5]

In the Western tradition, here exemplified not so much by the scenario of the cavern as by its explicit interpretation, the desire for self-identity informs the condemnation of theater. It is the desire to occupy a place from which one can take everything in, first and foremost visually, but also orally and audibly, that renders the theater and theatricality so terribly suspect. For theatrical space, like the cavern, allows no simple extraterritoriality. Yet, to reside "in" it is to be most distant from it—from its "truth," its "reality." Which perhaps is why, following Plato's scenario at least, those who seek to address theater *as theater*, to explore its *theatricality*, must be prepared to suffer the most severe consequences. As the text of the *Republic* makes clear, the basis of most existing political communities, as distinct from those that would be desirable, involves confounding theater with nature or, more precisely, with things themselves. In the modern period, such "naturalness" is often attributed to or absorbed into "history." The shifting attribution changes little, so long as the attribute—that of self-contained meaningfulness, that is, of self-identity—remains essentially unchanged.

The alternative to theater and its shadows is portrayed by Plato as the liberating if painful ascent into the open and natural light of the sun. In the world above, the world of ideas and of truth, space need no longer be localized, for what counts is never a particular place but rather the ubiquity of daylight itself. No shadows or obscurities, no echoes, projections, or simulacra: only light as it is and things as they are, in and of themselves: such is the dream of a liberation that would leave behind the cavernous nightmare of theater in which enslavement appears as freedom.

Plato thus dreams of exchanging the cave, its fire and shadows, for the bright sunlight and its direct, if dazzling illumination. But the example of Socrates remains as a stern reminder of what it can cost to defy, not just habit and custom, but the desire for stability from which they draw much of their force. The scenario of the cave dwellers displays the desire of those who have either never known or cannot admit the possibility of change. The formation and maintenance of communities, of polities, Socrates seems to suggest, may depend above all on the power of this desire: the desire to *remain*, to remain the *same*, to survive in the *same place*, if necessary until the end of time. It is this desire that makes the cave dwellers such willing spectators— and prisoners. To *stay* the same, the story seems to say, is to *see* the same, even while seeing others: that is, to see shadows as though they were real persons, stage props as though they were things in themselves, a stage as though it were a world. And thus to confound "reality" with self-identity and thereby to misconstrue the relationality of one's own place and position in a world that cannot simply be surveyed by those who inhabit it.

Theater is thus, from the very beginnings of what, for convenience, we continue to call "Western" thought, considered to be a place not just of dissimulation and delusion but, worse, self-dissimulation and self-delusion. It is a place of fixity and unfreedom, but also of fascination and desire. A prison, to be sure, but one that confines through assent and consensus rather than through constraint and oppression. Theater, in short, is that which challenges the "self" of self-presence and self-identity by reduplicating it in a seductive movement that never seems to come full circle.

The Stage

Millennia after Plato, a resolutely modern philosopher introduces his most influential and perhaps most innovative thought by resorting to a familiar comparison:

A performative utterance will, for example, be in a peculiar way hollow or void if said by an actor on the stage, or if introduced in a poem, or spoken in soliloquy. This applies in a similar manner to any and every utterance—a sea-change in special circumstances. Language in such circumstances is in special ways—intelligibly—used not seriously, but in many ways parasitic upon its normal use—ways which fall under the doctrine of the etiolations of language. All this we are excluding from consideration. Our performative utterances, felicitous or not, are to be understood as issued in ordinary circumstances.[6]

Examples are never chosen fortuitously, and the one that J. L. Austin invokes in order to illustrate the constitutive negative precondition of his notion of a "performative" speech act is exemplary in more ways than one. It also stands in a significant relationship to Plato's cave scenario. In both texts, a certain theatricality serves as the quintessence of what is both most normal and most anomalous. In Austin's language, theater is the epitome of the *extra-ordinary* "circumstances" that must be excluded if language is to be analyzed as a "performative" speech *act*. Such an argumentative strategy presupposes that language outside of theater is being or can be used seriously, whereas theatrical *acting* on a stage imposes itself as the most striking instance of nonserious, "parasitic" language use. The seriousness or integrity of an "act" or "action" is thus to be clearly demarcated from its "parasitical" cognate: from theatrical acting. Why?

For reasons and in terms that recall those of the Platonic cave. True, there is no "cave" here, but when it is recited on a stage, language creates a kind of "cave" or, more precisely, a "hollow or void." The intentional meaning, which in "ordinary circumstances" is directed at a more or less self-contained object, is undercut on the stage, hollowed out by the ambivalent dynamics of repetition, which Derrida has analyzed, precisely in respect to this passage, as "iterability."[7] An actor on a stage simply repeats, recites, reproduces his "lines," his "part," which therefore must be seen in the context of a different network of relations from that which one would expect in "ordinary" language use. For Austin, the nonserious theatrical use of language is dependent—"parasitical"—upon what is considered to be its serious, nontheatrical use, just as for Plato the repetition (or mimesis) of an object is dependent upon the object in and of itself, prior to all such repetition or mimesis. "Play-acting" is the quintessence of nonserious behavior and, once again, seems defined by a relationality that cannot be reduced to the dichotomous structure and self-enclosed trajectory usually associated with unambiguous "intention" and its undivided "goal." By contrast, the reciting of lines on stage involves a process of repetition that can never be entirely self-contained, insofar as its horizon is determined by an audience of spectators and not simply by the communication of a message. In short, the horizon of specifically theatrical performance can never be enclosed or comprehended by the kind of "act"—speech or other—to which Austin appeals. "Ordinary" English makes this distinction when it discriminates between *acting* and *act* or *action*. It should be noted, however, that even the word *act* is equivocal, often connoting—or infected by—the very lack of "seriousness" that Austin attributes to "parasitic" theatricality. ("It's all an act.")

But the fact that Austin, in his theatrical reference, resorts to the particular spatial figure "hollow or void" points to what is perhaps the most significant aspect of the theatrical with which we will be concerned. It entails the intrusion of spatiality within the process of localization: the fact that the process of being situated has to include (spatial) relationships that it cannot enclose or integrate. From the ontological and axiological position first systematized by Plato, such a situation can only be considered negative, as a lack or deficiency, as "parasitical." Can it be avoided? Austin has little doubt that it can, at least in principle. But when the parasitical and theatrical become the guiding principle of society as a whole, the critique takes on a very different tone. We turn now to another, very different but not unrelated formulation of this traditional, Platonic condemnation.

The Show

It is difficult to imagine a figure further removed—culturally, institutionally, linguistically—from Austin than his contemporary Guy Debord, whose major work, *The Society of the Spectacle*, was published in 1967. Debord, co-founder of the Situationist International, places his notion of "spectacle" (or "show") at the center of a comprehensive post-Marxist critique of bourgeois capitalist society. The spectacle, he argued, "asserts that all human life, which is to say all social life, is mere appearance," whereas an authentic critique should "expose it as a visible negation of life."[8] Debord thus seeks to "expose" the "spectacle" or "show" as the consequence of a capitalist social system directed toward the production of "commodities." What distinguishes his critique from previous Marxist theory is its emphasis on seduction rather than on constraint. As we have seen, this is also a trait of the Platonic critique of theatricality: theater is dangerous because it induces assent. (This aspect also resonates in Austin's notion of the "parasitical.")

The major traits of Debord's critique can be stated in four assertions. (1) The spectacle is both *social* and *global* in scope.[9] It does not merely "express" the capitalist system: it "justifies" it (§6). (2) The spectacle implies a spectator whose role is essentially passive and alienated (§30). (3) The medium of the spectacle is "the autonomous image" (§2). (4) Despite its "global" reach, the spectacle is based on the "separation" and "isolation" of the individual spectator (§13, §§25–28). "The spectacle thus unites what is separate, but . . . only in its separateness" (p. 22).

All of these features are inscribed in the conception of theatricality already encountered in Plato's description of the cavern. Above all, the spectacle "turns reality on its head" (§14, p. 14) by causing "a world that is no longer directly perceptible to be seen" (§18, p. 17), by transforming "mere images . . . into real beings" (ibid.). Images and representations usurp the role of "reality" and threaten "life." As a correlative, the role of the spectator is one of alienated passivity. Like Plato's cave dweller, the spectator is locked into place by a system that produces a high degree of acquiescence. Constraint imposes itself through consensus. Debord, in a formulation that is both resolutely contemporary and at the same time profoundly Platonic, asserts that "the spectacle is a permanent opium war," whose seductive power depends on the way it links the desire to survive with "deprivation":

> The spectacle is a permanent opium war waged to make it impossible to distinguish goods from commodities, or true satisfaction from a survival that increases according to its own logic. Consumable survival *must* increase, in fact, because it continues to enshrine deprivation. The reason there is nothing *beyond* augmented survival, and no end to its growth, is that survival itself belongs to the realm of dispossession: it may gild poverty, but it cannot transcend it. (§44, pp. 30–31)

Debord, in his critique of the spectacle, is thus condemning the-ater—but it is a certain kind of theater, one that, as already for Plato, presents itself as a nontheatrical "reality." At the same time, this con-ception of theater leaves room for another kind of spectacle or, per-haps, another reading of spectacle, which would not regard it as a mere surrogate (for) reality. For Debord, this involves another kind of "game" (*jeu*), one that would build upon certain traits of the society of spectacle in a way Debord seems not to want to acknowledge. One of those traits has to do with the change in the sense of "place" brought about by commodity production and consecrated by the spectacle:[10] "Just as the accumulation of commodities mass-produced for the abstract space of the market inevitably shattered all regional and legal barriers . . . so too it was bound to dissipate the indepen-dence and quality of *places*. The power to homogenize is the heavy artillery that has battered down all Chinese walls" (§165, p. 120).

Commodity production undermines the integrity of place by sub-mitting it to the universalizing, "homogenizing" law of value. But another development of this destabilizing of place is also conceivable:

> The same history that threatens this twilight world is capable of subjecting space to a directly experienced time. The proletarian revolution is that *critique of human geography* whereby individuals and communities must construct places and events commensu-rate with the appropriation, no longer just of their labor, but of their total history. By virtue of the resulting mobile space of play, and by virtue of freely chosen variations in the rules of the game, the independence of places will be rediscovered without any new exclusive tie to the soil, and thus too the authentic *journey* will be restored to us, although with authentic life un-derstood as a journey containing its whole meaning within itself. (§178, p. 126)

Debord's formulation here once again underscores his affinity with the Platonic critique of theatricality already discussed. "Subjecting space to a directly experienced time" raises the question of "place" as the dialectical result of the intrusion of time into space. But however "mobile" Debord wishes those places to be, their motion is still to be oriented by a goal: that of a "total history." The "rules of the game" that preside over the "mobility of places" are informed by the ideal of a certain *self-containment*, as a "journey containing its whole meaning within itself." This ideal of containment, however, is ultimately incompatible with the theatrical dimension of the spectacle as Debord describes it: "The world the spectacle holds up to view is at once *here* and *elsewhere*" (§37, p. 26). This "at once" constitutes the challenge of theatricality to every system of thought based on the priority of identity and self-presence.

Presenting

One of the most powerful articulations of that challenge is to be found in the writings of Jacques Derrida. In "The Double Session," a reading of Mallarmé elaborates an alternative to the more traditional—Platonic—subordination of mimesis to truth construed in terms of self-presence. This alternative is described as a peculiar type of "closure of Metaphysics," peculiar because it does not simply "close" but also, in a repetitive re-marking, opens a different sort of space and place, a sort of "dis-location."[11] This dislocated space "takes place" simultaneously as the written text of Mallarmé and as the theatricality of the performance it describes, comments upon, interprets, and quotes (the libretto). In his reading of the network of texts involved—not just the published text of Mallarmé, but its precursors, including the libretto of the Mime—Derrida provides an account of theatrical performance that in certain ways recalls that of Debord, but without succumbing to the nostalgia for a self-present "life" or "reality" that would both antedate and ground theatrical mimesis as its "authentic" origin and foundation. Drawing his key terms from the texts he reads, Derrida singles out Mallarmé's use of "hymen" in the following passage:

> in a hymen (from which the Dream proceeds), vice-ridden yet sacred, between desire and fulfillment, perpetration and its memory: here anticipating, there remembering, in the future, in the past, under a false appearance of the present. (p. 209)

> Dans un hymen (d'où procède le Rêve), vicieux mais sacré, entre le désir et l'accomplissement, la perpétration et son souvenir: ici devançant, là remémorant, au futur, au passé, sous une apparence fausse de présent. (p. 237)

Whereas Mallarmé's formulation at the end of this passage, "under a false appearance of the present," would seem to inscribe itself in the "illusionist" conception of theater we have found at work from Plato to Debord, Derrida argues that it is both possible and compelling to read Mallarmé's text as deconstructing the duality of appearance and reality to which this formulation seems to appeal: "The hymen, consummation of differences [*des différents*], . . . confounds itself with that from which it seems to be derived" (pp. 212/241), producing in Mallarmé what Derrida describes as "a simulacrum of Platonism or of Hegelianism . . . separated from what it simulates only by a barely perceptible veil, of which one could just as well say that it passes already-unnoticed—between Platonism and itself, between Hegelianism and itself. In between enter[s] [*Entre*] the text of Mallarmé and itself" (pp. 207/235).

The awkward expedient to which I have resorted to translate the single French word *entre* in this passage—"in between enter[s]"—has the virtue of calling attention to what is decisive in Derrida's reading, here and elsewhere. In Austinian terms, one might have said that his discourse moves from a constative to a performative mode, were not the notion of "performative" subject to the very logic here being put into question by being put into play. It is therefore more precise to say that, in repeating and remarking the ambiguity of the word *entre* in Mallarmé's text, a word that can be read as both adverb ("between") and verb ("enter"), Derrida moves from a purely "theoretical" discourse, describing an object independent of it, to a "theatrical" mode of (re)writing that *stages* (dislocates) what it also recites: the theatrical movement of Mallarmé's writing. It should also be noted that if *entre* is read as a verb here, its syntactical placement at the start of the phrase makes it into an injunction rather than a simple indicative: "*Let* Mallarmé's text *enter.*" This indeed is what happens more and more explicitly from this moment on, both in this particular text of Derrida and in his writing in general. In the almost four decades since this essay was published, Derrida's writing has not ceased to demonstrate and explore, with increasing explicitness and variety, its own theatrical quality as a "staging" or *mise en scène*, rather than as an essentially constative reading of something held to exist independently of it.[12]

A text that does not merely "reproduce" and yet also does not simply "create" or "produce." Its object is situated in an unusual and complicated relationship to its "pretext." It is involved in an operation that, like the "hymen," exposes the interval "between" texts and in so doing allows something else to "enter" the stage or scene: a certain theatricality, which has as its grammatical hallmark the *present participle*.

Why the present participle? For two interrelated reasons, at least. First, because its "presence" is suspended, as it were, in and as the interval linking and separating that which is presented from the presentation "itself." The "presence" of the present participle is thus bounded, or defined, by the convergence of its articulation with that which it articulates. But in thus being defined by its own redoubling—and this is the second reason—it is also constituted by and as a series of repetitions, each of which is separated from the others and yet is also bound to them in the sequence. Already in *Mimique* Mallarmé resorts to this tense where he must articulate that "false appearance of the present" as "ici devançant, là remémorant, au futur, au passé." In short, something is going on that is more than just a false appearance. The *appearing* of the present participle is the grammatical index of those disjunctive "goings-on" that make the "present" into a "tense" in the most intense sense: "coming before" (*devançant*) or anticipating (the future) by "remembering" (the past).

If theatrical performance does not simply reproduce or accomplish something that exists in and of itself or that is at least intrinsically self-contained, the reiterative openness of the present participle is always both ahead of and behind itself, an ambiguity that in English is condensed in the preposition "after." As present participle the present is "after" itself, in hopeless self-pursuit. From this point of view, it can be designated as "false" with respect to a notion of truth as self-presence. But at the same time it can be understood as being more truly "pre-sent," in the etymological sense of being placed *before* itself as well as before "spectators," who, from this standpoint, are anything but merely "passive," although they occupy a position that calls for impassiveness rather than for expressiveness.

What is curious about the present participle is the way it is both very close and yet irreducibly remote. Since it never adds up to a whole and always remains a part, the participation it entails follows a trajectory like that of the ballerina in another text of Mallarmé. Her pirouette, as Derrida shows, revolves incessantly around a center that is displaced with each turn, never coming full circle, never adding up to a whole nor even to a simple step forward.[13] If the ballerina's pirouette is eminently theatrical, it is because its complex movement winds up going nowhere, if going somewhere is understood in the sense of that "authentic journey" described by Debord.

Derrida is, of course, aware of the curious status of the present participle, to which he refers explicitly at various times in this text. Yet these references do not explicitly discuss or dwell on either its incidence in the texts of Mallarmé that he cites or his own use of it.[14] In most cases, the present participle is assimilated to an oppositional pair that appears as part and parcel of the logic that has to be deconstructed:

> As soon as a mirror is interposed in some way, the simple opposition of activity and passivity, like that of producing [*produire*] and product, or also all the present and past participles (imitating/imitated, signifying/signified, structuring/structured, etc.) become ineffective and formally too weak to dominate the graphics of the hymen, its spider web and the play of its eyelids. (pp. 224/253)

But can the significance of the present participle be contained or comprehended within a "simple opposition," which would place it in a certain symmetry with other participles? Or does something happen to "presence" when it is articulated as a *participle* that exceeds the bounds of such an opposition?

There is an earlier allusion to the present participle in this text, which could have been the occasion for a more prolonged reflection on its status, especially since it links this "tense" to one of the major figures of Derrida's reading of Mallarmé: the fold (*pli*). Derrida is arguing that the traditional notion of truth as self-presence undoes itself in the phenomenological insistence on truth as an appearing, "in the ambiguity or the duplicity of the presence of the present, of its *appearance*—that which appears *and* its appearing [*ce qui apparaît et son apparaître*]—in the *fold* of the present participle (pp. 192/219).

How this "fold" of the present participle might relate to all the other folds that Derrida remarks in his reading of Mallarmé is a question that remains in abeyance throughout this particular text, although it goes on to engender increasingly powerful and conspicuous effects in virtually all his subsequent writings.[15] Heidegger himself, of course, has little patience with or interest in theater, a point to which I shall return later.[16] Nevertheless, in the essay to which Derrida here alludes, what he does elaborate about the fold or, rather, about the "twofold" quality of the present participle bears significant implications for its relation to theatricality.

Parting With

In his essay "Moïra," Heidegger discusses a text by Parmenides, Fragment VIII, lines 34–41, which he reads as an elaboration of the more celebrated dictum, Fragment III, usually translated as "Thinking and Being are the same." Heidegger introduces his commentary on Fragment VIII by noting that, although it seems simply to repeat and amplify the more famous assertion in Fragment III, there is a significant shift in the manner in which Parmenides articulates the relation between thinking and being:

> Above all else, we should observe that [Fragment VIII, lines 34ff], which thinks this relationship more profoundly, speaks of *ēon* and not of *einai* as does Fragment III. As a result the impression results, understandably, that what Fragment VIII addresses is not the to-be [*Sein*] but being [*Seienden*]. But in the noun *ēon* Parmenides in no way thinks being in itself [*das Seiende an sich*] wherein everything [*das Ganze*], including thinking, belongs, insofar as it is a being. Just as little does *ēon* mean *einai* in the sense of the to-be for itself, as though the thinker sought to demarcate the non-sensuous way of the to-be from the being as sensuous [entity]. The *ēon*, the being [*das Seiend*], is rather thought in the twofold split [*Zwiefalt*] of the to-be and being, and spoken participially, without the grammatical concept on its own being able to attain to the knowledge of language.[17]

Heidegger thus dismisses the ability of the "grammatical concept" of the "participle" "on its own" to "attain to the knowledge of language." Nevertheless, although mere grammar may not be enough, it seems hardly accidental that the problem that will occupy Heidegger throughout this essay and much of his philosophical work—the ontological difference and relationship between "the to-be" and "beings"—is linked here to the present participle, in the form of a gerund, *das Seiend*, which is both singular and general at once. This "at once," however, distinguishes the "two-fold" structure of the to-be and being, *Sein* and *Seiendes*, from that of a mere duality or opposition, since what is decisive is the emergence of a third term, *das Seiend*, to designate the way-of-being as a *singular event*. The key distinction here is that between *Seiendes*, the entity in general, and *das Seiend*, the singularization of being as an event or happening.

In English, by contrast, the three terms employed by Heidegger—*Sein, Seiendes, Seiend*—tend to be rendered by the "same" word, *being*. There would thus seem to be a loss of differentiation in the inability of English to distinguish *Sein*, verbal infinitive noun, from *Seiendes*, participial noun, as well as from their singularization as *das Seiend*. But perhaps this linguistic impoverishment of English with respect to German can become a resource, a "chance," insofar as it offers no other choice than to articulate this singularization of being through what appears to be a *repetition* of the same word, in which the ostensible tautology both dissimulates and deploys the difference at the heart of sameness—the *tautos*. If, however, the singularization of being were to turn out to be inseparable from just such a process of repetition, then the inability of English to "get its act together" by proffering the series of ostensibly self-contained nouns that German has at its disposal, far from being (!) merely a deficiency, could open a perspective that Heidegger's native language, by dint of its very lexical and morphological richness, tends to obscure. Were this the case, the comparison between the respective linguistic resources of German and English would remain a helpful, if not indispensable condition of any such interpretation. The lexical paucity of English, in its limited ability to name "being" and its modes, would assume significance only through the comparison with (Heidegger's) German.

To sum up: *das Seiend*, Heidegger's decisive "third" term in the discussion of Parmenides, names "being" as a singular event or happening. The contribution of English, lacking equivalent nouns, would be to foreground a certain *repetition* as that which splits or transfixes the twofold—the to-be and beings—into the always singular way of being, *das Seiend*, that is its effect. The two German turns of phrase usually used to describe this split—"Sein *des* Seienden" (the to-be *of* beings) and "Seiendes *im* Sein" (being *in* the to-be)—are, Heidegger notes, unsatisfactory makeshifts, since both the genitive "des" and the inclusive "in" tend to "hide" rather than disclose the way in which the two-fold *unfolds*. What thereby unfolds is a singularity that has the attributes of a process (being) and at the same time is *localized* (*das Seiend*) without being identifiable as a substance or entity (a *Seiendes*).

Thus, despite the tendency of Heidegger to downplay the significance of the grammatical form "on its own" to accede to the meaning of to-be, his effort to articulate the "twofold" of being leads him to resort to the present participle and in particular to its nominal, gerundive forms. The fact that, perhaps even more insistently than Derrida, Heidegger again and again recurs to the present participle and the gerund when he has to formulate the event of being places his disclaimer in a singular light. To be sure, a purely grammatical category is "on its own"—*eigens*—insufficient to explain anything, much less the complex and ambivalent event of being with which Heidegger is concerned. Nevertheless, the present participle and gerund recur too regularly at decisive junctures in his texts not to be indicative of a problem that deserves further attention.

The fact that it is a form of the gerund, *das "Seiend,"* that, as Heidegger writes, "in its ambiguity names the twofold," (38) tells us something, in return, about the significance of the gerund and the present participle. The notion of "participle," etymologically, comes from *participium*, which in Latin signifies "a sharing, partaking." The Latin word in turn is a translation of the Greek *metokhē*, derived from the verb *methexis*, used by Plato to describe the manner in which entities "partake" or "participate" in the absolutes, the "ideas" that determine their qualities. But already these discussions of *methexis* indicate the close and for Plato problematical link between *participation* and *partitioning*, which is why Parmenides criticizes the notion in the dialogue of that name (*Parmenides*, 130c–131a). The same problem will crop up with respect to *mimēsis*, of which Aristotle, in the *Metaphysics* (987b), declares *methexis* to be nothing more than a verbal variant.

In order to share and partake, there must, however, be a concomitant dividing or divesting, a *parting* or, perhaps more precisely, a departing, a taking leave, a *partitioning* in order to *im-part*. All of this is uncannily condensed in the English phrase *parting with*. The "with" suggests that parting entails a departure, not simply as the dissolving of a relationship, but rather as a singular way of (re)constituting one. To remain in relation *with* precisely *by parting* is, however, one of the distinctive traits of the "spectacle," as Debord recognized, albeit primarily from a critical-nostalgic point of view: "The spectacle thus unites what is separate, but it unites it only *in its separateness*" (§29).[18] Heidegger would of course reject any such assimilation, positive or negative, of the twofold to theater or the theatrical, however strongly his conception of truth as *alētheia*, as self-dissimulation—concealing through revealing—seems to move in such a direction. As we shall see in Chapter 2, he will explicitly reject the related possibility of assimilating what he calls the clearing, *Lichtung*, to a theatrical stage, with "constantly raised curtain." And yet his image itself suggests there is more to the matter than a simple rejection (or acceptance) could account for. Why should a "curtain" in front of a stage be "constantly raised"—or constantly lowered, for that matter? Heidegger's effort to dismiss the stage by invoking a constant curtain suggests, by its very incommensurability with even the most rudimentary "ontic" experience of theater, that the simple *opposition* of raising and lowering will be no more appropriate to theater than to truth as *alētheia*. What if it were not the presence or absence of the curtain, no more than that of the to-be of beings, that was at stake in this negative figure, but rather its *folds*? Might not the ambivalent ambiguity of the present participle turn out to be a singularly powerful linguistic *and theatrical* medium for articulating such a self-dissimulating parting-with?

The split with which Heidegger is concerned here, in his reading of Parmenides, is that between "thinking" and "being"—in Greek, between *noein* and *ēon*, which he renders as "the twofold of oncoming and the ongoing [*Anwesen und Anwesendem*]" (p. 41). Like Derrida's *arrivant*, Heidegger's twofold has as its destiny never fully to arrive at its destination. Its *Geschick* is to suffer *Mißgeschick*.[19] As the *Anwesen des Anwesenden*, the "oncoming of the ongoing," it is neither one nor the other but their singular duplicity. It is not *two* folds, but rather the crease of a *singularly single fold*, enfolding and exposing its constitutive difference from itself.

Such singular duplicity, however, requires a no less singular process of being received, "collected," discerned. It must, as Heidegger puts it, be *brought forward*.[20] The medium of such bringing forth Heidegger conceives to be the *muthos*, *Sage*: which is not just myth or legend, but at the same time also and perhaps above all a saying (*Sagen*), which in "calling" "brings-to-appearing."[21] Such "calling" calls *forth* only by also calling *for* a receiving, perceiving, discerning instance. Yet any such instantiation arrests the complex and conflicting movement of the twofold, which only discloses itself through self-concealment:

> The destiny [*Geschick*] of the disclosing of the twofold hands over the oncoming (*ta eonta*) to the everyday apprehension of the mortal.
>
> How does this destined handing-over happen? Only through the way the twofold as such, together with its unfolding, remains concealed. Hence, self-concealment prevails in disclosure. (p. 51)

This kind of self-concealment affects not so much what appears as the way it appears. More precisely, what is concealed is precisely the *way*, in the double sense of trajectory and of manner. The "way" or trajectory is dissimulated by appearing as an event that seems simply to take *place*, in a single, self-identical place or, better, in a series of such places. Such a semblance, however, would reduce what Heidegger calls *saying* to a series of discrete statements, as in a narrative, for instance. It would construe *muthos*, not as a kind of saying, but rather as *plot*, in the sense of the word found in Aristotle's *Poetics*, namely, a sequence of events with beginning, middle, and end, adding up to an integrated, meaningful whole. Heidegger does not speak of this explicitly, to be sure, but it seems consonant with his description of the self-dissimulation of the twofold, which he identifies, on the one hand, with the reduction of language to *naming*, and on the other, with the locating of the named in an unequivocal *place*. Heidegger formulates this as follows:

> The usual saying of mortals, insofar as they do not attend to the oncoming [*Anwesen*], becomes the saying of names in which the pronouncement [*Verlautbarung*] and the immediately graspable figure of the word . . . predominate.
>
> And where the usual . . . mode of discerning [*Vernehmen*], speaking out of the words, comes upon rising and falling, it recurs to the "this as well as that" of emerging and passing-away. The place, *topos*, is never attended to as placement [*Ortschaft*], as which the twofold offers a home to the oncoming of the ongoing [*dem Anwesen des Anwesenden*]. The meaning of mortals, in preferring the this-as-well-as-that, follows only the each-and-always-distinctness of places [*Plätze*]. (pp. 50–51)

Heidegger's language suggests why he would be so little at home—or perhaps, so uncannily at home—with theater or theatricality. However riven he construes the twofold of being and beings to be, he still envisages the possibility of being "at home" in it or with it, of giving it a *Heimat*. But what becomes of such an "offer" in a world where, as Debord observes, "the spectator feels at home nowhere, for the spectacle is everywhere" (§30)? In being everywhere, the spectacle transforms each everywhere into *somewhere else*, into another scene. Heidegger attempts to dismiss this other scene by reducing it to the neutral simultaneity of the "this-as-well-as-that," which is to say, to a constant stream of places that are "always different" from one another—and yet, in their in-difference, always the same. Debord's position is not so very removed from that of Heidegger, since he too suggests that the capitalist commodity-spectacle always amounts to, returns to, the same. But he insists that in so doing it remains split, never simply taking place here and now.

The divided character of such taking place constitutes the quintessence of the theatrical scene, which is never just a place or series of places, making room for the orderly sequence of a narrative plot leading to a meaningful conclusion. Since no narrative sequence succeeds in framing or enclosing such places it traverses, it winds up being partitioned by them; in concluding, it gestures toward other scenes, which remain inconclusive, even and especially where the sequence ends or stops. With respect to such a sequence, it is not always easy to get one's bearings or to take a stand.

Linking Pearls

Taking a stand, having or finding firm ground under one's feet, has surely constituted one of the oldest concerns of Western modernity.[22] It is not surprising, therefore, that at its very beginnings Western theater should have staged precisely this concern and explored its vicissitudes in the fate of a king whose very name, far from concealing the complex and conflictual folding discussed by Heidegger, flaunts it. Oedipus, "swollen foot," made his name a public word by finding the word or noun that "solved" the riddle of the Sphinx and liberated Thebes from its scourge, only to reveal that the greatest dangers do not always come from without. Having supplied the name of a species that seemed to subsume the paradoxes of the Sphinx—paradoxes that describe a creature who has "two, three, and four legs," who speaks with a "single voice" and yet moves most rapidly on two feet and most slowly on four—Oedipus suffered a fate that demonstrates what can happen when the Heideggerian twofold deploys itself under feet that are trying to move.

We will have occasion to explore certain effects of this deployment later in this book.[23] For now, however, it is time to bring this introduction to a provisional conclusion by taking a very brief look at another sort of theatrical performance, one that sheds light on the ambivalent attitude that has dominated the Western approach to theater almost from its very beginnings, although never without being contested and challenged. In contrast to what I will have occasion to designate a "mythological" approach to theater, epitomized in the *Poetics* of Aristotle—a theater that is understood to be essentially a vehicle for the presentation of a coherent, meaningful story—the theatrical performance I wish to discuss, although it includes a narrative element, is not essentially dependent on a story to produce its effects. To quote Heidegger's "Moïra" one last time, such theater is concerned with "the manner in which the Word speaks, rather than the words' individual pronouncements" (p. 51).

I refer to a performance of Peking Opera, given in Beijing in August 1999, a few weeks before the celebration of the fiftieth anniversary of the successful culmination of the Communist Revolution in China. Some sixty years earlier, Bertolt Brecht, in an article entitled "On Chinese Drama and the Alienation Effect," provided the following account of a similar scene performed by a Peking Opera company in Moscow:

> A young woman, the daughter of a fisherman, is shown standing and rowing in an imaginary boat. To steer it, she uses an oar that barely reaches to her knees. The current becomes faster; she finds it more difficult to keep her balance. . . . Each of the girl's movements is as familiar as a picture; each bend of the river is known before the boat comes to it. This feeling is produced in the audience by the manner in which the actress plays the scene; it is she who makes the occasion seem so memorable.[24]

The contrast described here by Brecht, between "standing and rowing" and hence between land and water, is one of the recurring situations of Peking Opera, part of its scenic repertoire. Since the movements performed by the actress are "as familiar as a picture," Brecht emphasizes that it is "the manner in which the actress plays the scene" that "makes the occasion seem so memorable." Elsewhere, he discusses how Chinese theater (and this could be extended to other Asiatic theaters as well) operates with a defined repertoire of gestures and situations, which are presented in infinitely varied and singular ways.[25] What therefore "happens" on the stage is not the communication of something new, in the sense of content, but the variation of something familiar through its repetition. Repetition thus emerges as a visible, audible, and constitutive element of the theatrical medium. To vary Heidegger's observation, it is not so much *what* is said or shown as the *way* that showing takes place. Or rather, since the stage of the Peking Opera is largely empty, the way that place is constituted as a scene.

The scene is set, as it were, through the contrast of water and land that recurs so often in Peking Opera. Where there is land, one can hope to take a stand, to acquire and maintain a certain stability. The joy and relief of sighting land is inseparable from the conception of the "voyage of life" that we find in Debord, who invokes it as a contrast to the spectacle. As a "journey," rather than a spectacle, life can be seen as "containing its whole meaning within itself," he writes.[26] By contrast, the theatricality of the scene described by Brecht does not derive from the desire for such a journey, but rather from the ability to cope with the water's current. The oar "that barely reaches to her knees" forces the body of the woman to bend as she rows. Bending to channel one's movements while rowing is very different from trying to take a stand, or trying to conduct the journey to its successful conclusion, where it can display its "whole meaning within itself." If such meaning is truly "within itself," that is, within the narrative sequence that makes it "whole," then the movements of the body on (or off) the stage can at best be means toward attaining that end or, as Aristotle insists, to presenting the whole story, the *muthos*, and through it the meaningful action upon which all tragedy is based, its *praxis*.

Western audiences have been encouraged to expect the display of such meaning and to demand it from theater and from art in general. This is why theatrical writers from Brecht to Artaud to Genet have all recognized the need to change, not just the habits of stagecraft, but those of spectatorship as well. As Brecht put it, once again with respect to Chinese theater: "What appears particularly important for us in Chinese theater is its efforts to produce a true art of beholding [*eine wahre Zuschaukunst*]." This "art" presupposes an awareness of the rules and repertoire, since this alone permits each performance to be evaluated in its singularity.[27]

Although such knowledge is, as Brecht writes, required for a "full appreciation" of the "art" of Chinese theater, a more general kind of comparison can be no less illuminating for those whose theatrical experience is primarily "Western." One obvious point of departure for such a cross-cultural comparison would be the respective function of "plot" in mainstream Western theater and Peking Opera. In the latter, and presumably in Chinese and Asian theater generally, the importance of plot is closer to that assumed by "myth" in the practice of the Attic tragedians than to that first systematized by Aristotle's theoretical reflections on that practice in his *Poetics*, even though the latter has continued to dominate, not just theater in the West, but also the newer media of film and television. The primary interest of Peking Opera is not to present a meaningful action through a coherent plot, but rather to use both action and plot to foreground the significance of the performance. This alters the function of both narrative and its staging. In the program of a contemporary Peking Opera company, the Liyuan Theater,[28] this is described as follows: "The plot structure of Beijing Opera is often characterized as 'linking pearls with a thread.' Here the 'thread' refers to the general plot of the play, while the 'pearls' are the specific scenes of the play. Each scene is an integral part of the play. On the other hand, it has its own sub-plot and can be staged separately" (p. 21).

This suggests that the scenic "pearls" can be separated from, and are therefore not entirely dependent upon, the "thread." Judging from the performance I saw, such independence could well be described as "situational"—with the proviso that "situation" here includes not merely the actions represented on stage but their presentation as well. The latter deploys its own significance, one that is neither separable from nor reducible to an extra-theatrical, referential "plot."

The scene I want to discuss is taken from a sequence entitled "Autumn River." The story thread tells of a student, Pan Bizheng, who has failed his examination, falls in love with a beautiful young nun, Chen Miaochang, who lives in a convent directed by Pan's aunt. When the aunt learns about their relationship, she forces Pan to leave without saying goodbye to Chen. Chen finds the courage to forsake the convent in pursuit of Pan. Reaching the banks of the Autumn River, she desperately searches for a means of crossing it. Here is how the program of the Liyuan Theater sums up this scene: "She happens to meet an elderly boatman, who turns out to be a jocular person. Having understood thoroughly why the girl is in such a hurry, the old boatman takes it easy and enjoys teasing the girl. Having had enough fun [with] her, the kind-hearted old man helps the girl catch up with the big ship Pan Bizheng has boarded" (pp. 47–48).

So much for the "story." In its deliberately stereotypical manner, it is hardly the kind of *muthos* that Aristotle recommended as suitable for tragedy. But of course this is no tragedy, and that is part of the point: the Peking Opera and Asian theater generally are neither *tragic* nor even "dramatic" in the sense these terms have acquired in Western theater. The decision to privilege "tragedy" as exemplary of theater in general is a distinctively Western one, even if, as we shall see, the actual tragedies to which Aristotle refers in the *Poetics*, above all those of Sophocles, do not necessarily conform to his interpretation of them. One of the ways in which "Autumn River" is not "tragic" is in its refusal to focus upon the fate of one or two noble individuals. Not that its "characters" are not "noble": they belong to the aristocracy, even if not necessarily to its ruling class. But already at the level of the plot they do not function primarily as "individuals," even though the story is a love story. These lovers make no claim to be interesting or autonomous "individuals," for the same reason that the "plot" does not provide the performance with its necessary coherence or meaning. Meaning is not separable from the way in which it is staged; indeed, it can be said to inhere in the staging of a certain type of performance, even if the latter is not unrelated to the story that frames it. But this story is no more equivalent to the scenic "situation" that is staged than a paraphrase is equivalent to the poem it paraphrases. To demonstrate the difference between the two, it is first necessary to describe the situation more closely.

It is that of a journey undertaken by Chen in the hopes of finding Pan. But the fascination of the scene—in which Chen finds the boatman, boards the ferry, and makes her way across the river to its distant shore—derives, not from the notion of a journey that might be completed, for instance, with the reuniting of the lovers, but rather from the deployment of a different kind of *desire*, involving separation rather than than fulfillment. "Autumn River" stages one of the ways in which separation is experienced, traversed, negotiated—but never simply overcome or forgotten. It is separation, then, that sets the scene for an unforgettable exhibition of theatricality.

The scene begins with a brief musical prelude, in which the timbre of the instruments—wood blocks and cymbals being struck in rhythmic patterns—almost seems to "embody" the separation itself, in the very "hollowness" of the sounds. As with Plato's cave, "hollowness" is a hallmark of theater, which itself is a "hollow" space—"shallow," "void," Austin calls in. Such hollowness marks separation as a kind of inner space rather than an interval in-between. Theater takes place in the hollow of this separation, which it deploys and to which it responds.[29]

Scenically, such a response is not restricted to its most explicit manifestations, as in the cries of Chen and the boatman's answer: It is already at work in the gliding movement with which she first "enters" the scene. Taking tiny but regular steps, she appears to glide onto the stage rather than to walk across it. This gliding motion has a double effect: First, it does not appear as the *act* of an individual but rather *bears* her along in a movement that has its origin elsewhere.[30] Of course, this impression presupposes the consummate training and athletic skill required of such performers. But if the aim of such art is self-dissimulation, that is perhaps because its effectiveness cannot be measured in terms of individual prowess, even if Brecht seems to formulate his admiration for this theater in such terms. For the performers in this scene do not appear primarily as individuals. Neither passive nor active in the Western sense, they demonstrate, quite literally, a *way of being-moved* that confounds such oppositions. The skill of the performer allows a movement to be deployed that can never be reduced to the property or product of an individual *qua individual*.

How different seem the movements alluded to by the riddle of the Sphinx, or by Oedipus's not so proper name "swollen feet." Just as that name consists not of "proper" but of "common nouns," so too Oedipus finds his way blocked at that fatal crossroads. Lethal violence alone allows him to remove the obstacle and resume his way to Thebes, making his way to power and glory, but also toward destitution and death. In contrast to Chen and the boatman, Oedipus does not allow himself to *be moved*—and in the process is driven all the more ineluctably toward his destructive destiny.

On the stage of the Liyuan Theater, by contrast, Chen is soon joined by another gliding figure, that of the boatman. With one long oar as his sole prop, this rustic figure glides onto the stage in his (invisible) boat, suggested by the way he holds and moves the oar, as well as by the parallel, lateral movement of his feet, while his upper body remains rigid and unbending. With the suggested movement of the boat, there is inevitably that of the water itself, "visible" only in its effects: the rhythmic swaying of the man's body, rigid as it leans against the pole. The boatman seems to sway in the water, going nowhere, yet constantly moving. Such going-nowhere-while-moving constitutes much of the magic of this scene, making it an exemplary allegory of theatricality as the staging of separation. It is, in a way that Heidegger perhaps would not have endorsed, a "*sway* of being," one that is not compelled to try to take a stand but is content to *respond* rather than to impose and resist.

With the boatman's swaying, water invisibly enters the scene, taking (its) place less "on" than *as* the stage. A bantering dialogue follows, in which the boatman urges a hesitant, timorous Chen to take the leap, give up the security of the land and entrust herself to the boat, the water, and his skill. He holds the sole prop, the oar, and extends it to her so that she can hold onto it and use it to steady herself while timorously trying to climb into the boat. What ensues is a remarkable "ballet" of standing, swaying, and almost falling, in which the relation of land and sea, stability and precariousness, is demonstrated through bodily gestures indicating the fear of losing one's balance. At the same time, the fear of falling (into the water) compels Chen to seek a different sort of equilibrium, one that no longer looks to *terra firma* but rather responds to the never entirely predictable rise and fall of the waves.

This is the true and memorable "drama" of this scene: not the search to be reunited with one's beloved, but the fearful dependence upon the support of the "land" and the courage to search for another kind of balance, a balance and movement that is defined in terms of responsiveness, rather than in those of stability and security, much less of spontaneity.

It is this ballet of balance, expressed, not just in Chen's movements, but above all in the way they interact with those of the boatman, that constitutes the exquisite theatricality of this scene, which, in our context at least, can be read, witnessed, seen, and heard as an allegory of theatricality as *medium*—not as a medium of representation, but as a medium that redefines activity as reactivity, and that makes its peace, if ever provisionally, with separation.

The choreography of that balancing act is the result, not of the doings of a single performer, simply, but of the remarkable interaction of the two: boatman and noblewoman, separated by gender, age, class, costume, habit, and culture, and yet *in their separation linked* through the reciprocity of their movements. That reciprocity here has little to do with synergy is perhaps clearest when Chen barely avoids falling into the water by bouncing and balancing up and down to the same rhythm as the boatman, responding to the current of the river. Reciprocity has more to do with the interplay of distinct rhythms than with the identity of the persons involved. After her near-fall, Chen recovers her balance and reaches the boat, where she and the boatman bob up and down together, but always inversely, in the shared but separate movements that constitute their common rhythm—and situation.

Having thus finally boarded the boat, their next problem is to launch it by freeing it from its moorings, in which it is presumably all the more deeply mired due to the added weight of its new passenger. Although launching the boat is, of course, the task of the boatman, his effort, which is at first unsuccessful, evokes frantic responses in his passenger. The rocking of the two figures shakes the boat precariously before it finally becomes unstuck and is launched. Fear of falling is never absent, no more than is desire itself; both are orchestrated by the skilful interplay of the two performers.

This ability to *respond* to the fear of falling by a complex meshing of movements defines, not just the actions of the individual figures, but the very theater that stages them. The gestures here suggest a response to the twofold that assumes its duplicity rather than seeking to arrest or control it by assigning it a name, as Oedipus does in responding to the riddle of the Sphinx. As we shall have occasion to see, Sophocles' Theban plays show how this response resolves the riddle only by displacing the secret it signifies and thereby setting the stage for a series of new and destructive events. The staging of "Autumn River" demonstrates how theater can be the medium of a displacement or dislocation that opens other *ways*, not bound to arrive at a final destination—or at least, not too soon. Theater thus emerges as a powerful medium of the *arrivant*.

• • •

This mediality of theater as *arrivant* will be in question, from various vantage points, in the following chapters. Theater is a medium that, from Plato and Aristotle to the present, has been regarded with suspicion, fear, and contempt—but also with fascination and desire—by a tradition seeking at all costs to keep the ground from slipping out from under its feet. The twists and turns of this medium, in its theory as well as its practice, are perhaps even more acute today, when the notion of "media" has becomes more ubiquitous and more elusive than ever before.

What we call "theater" and, even more, "theatricality" provides an instructive arena for the examination of those "twists and turns." "Multimedia" long before the word became a cliché, Western theater has long occupied an uneasy position between "art" and "entertainment," between discovery and manipulation, and this situation has not changed. The following chapters seek to examine a few strands in that history, without making the slightest claim at completeness, whose very possibility the history of theater calls into question. Some of the forms in which this question recurs, throughout the different readings that constitute the individual chapters, are: How does the consideration of theater as a representational genre, a form of art, relate to the understanding of it as a *medium?* Can a medium be a genre? Is theater primarily or predominantly an "art"? Is a "play" a "work"? Is "theater" synonymous, as is often supposed, with "dramatic"? Does it depend upon plot and character? And, above all, what does attention to the old medium of theater tell us about the "new media"? Is theater as medium an end, a beginning, or both at once?[31]

1

Theatrocracy; or, Surviving the Break

T H E   R E L A T I O N between theater and politics has a long and vexed history. Of all the "arts," theater most directly resembles politics insofar as traditionally it has been understood to involve the assemblage of people in a shared space. But the audience in the theater differs from the members of a political grouping: its existence is limited in time, whereas a polity generally aspires to greater duration. Theater acknowledges artificiality and artifice, whereas political communities are often construed in terms of a certain naturalness, an association underscored by the etymology of the word *nation*—deriving from Latin *nasci*, to be born.[1] Political entities have historically derived their legitimacy from their ability to promote what is shared and common—a "commonwealth"—whereas theater tends frequently to the extreme and to the exceptional.[2] Politics is supposed to involve an appeal to reason, whereas theater frequently appeals unabashedly to desire and emotion. Finally, perhaps most important of all, politics as generally practiced claims to be the most effective means of regulating or at least controlling conflict, whereas theater flourishes by exacerbating it. Yet both the thinkers of politics and its practitioners have recognized a need to come to terms with theater, lest it wind up dictating its terms to them.

One of the earliest and most illuminating articulations of this strained relation between politics and theatricality is to be found in book 3 of Plato's *Laws*. As has often been noted, not the least significant of the paradoxes that mark Plato's work is that such an eminently theatrical writer should have so profoundly mistrusted the political effects of theatricality. In the passage I am referring to from the *Laws*, the main speaker, called simply "The Athenian," discusses the reasons for the decline of his city. He identifies as a major issue the way in which political communities respond to *fear*. Formerly, he recalls, his countrymen had been able to resist the onslaught of the Persians only because of two interrelated factors, both involving fear: fear of the enemy and of the consequences of defeat, and "that other fear instilled by subjection to preexisting law," which allowed them to turn mere fear into disciplined resistance (699c).³ The Athenian concludes his historical review, however, with an ominous, if at first enigmatic, observation. Noting the obvious differences in the respective political histories of the Athenians and the Persians—how the latter "reduced the commonality to utter subjection, whereas we encouraged the multitude toward unqualified liberty"—the Athenian asserts that such differences notwithstanding, "our fate has, in a way, been the same as that of the Persians" (699e). Megillus, one of his interlocutors, is understandably puzzled and asks for clarification. In response, the Athenian, somewhat surprisingly, invokes the history of *music* as an exemplary illustration of how liberty can degenerate into license and bring about the collapse of a state of law. In times gone by, he remembers,

> our music was divided into several kinds and patterns. . . . These and other types were definitely fixed, and it was not permissible to misuse one kind of melody for another. The competence to take cognizance of these rules, to pass verdicts in accord with them, and, in case of need, to penalize their infraction was not left, as it is today, to the catcalls and discordant outcries of the crowd, nor yet to the clapping of applauders; the educated made it their rule to hear the performances through in silence and for the boys, their attendants, and the rabble at large, there was the discipline of the official's rod to enforce order. Thus, the bulk of the populace was content to submit to this strict control in such matters without venturing to pronounce judgment by its clamors.
>
> Afterward, in the course of time, an unmusical license set in with the appearance of poets who were men of native genius, but ignorant of what is right and legitimate in the realm of the Muses. Possessed by a frantic and unhallowed lust for pleasure, they contaminated laments with hymns and paeans with dithyrambs, actually imitated the strains of the flute on the harp, and created a universal confusion of forms. . . . By compositions of such a kind and discourse to the same effect, they naturally in-

spired the multitude with contempt of musical law, and a conceit of their own competence as judges. Thus our once silent
audiences have found a voice, in the persuasion that they understand what is good and bad in art; the old sovereignty of the
best, aristocracy, has given way to an evil "sovereignty of the
audience," a theatrocracy [*theatrokratia*]. (700–701a)⁴

"Theatrocracy" as the rule of the audience, which is to say, of a more
or less contingent, more or less temporary assemblage, is, for the
Athenian, worse even than democracy, which is far from his favorite
form of government:

If the consequences had been even a democracy, no great harm
would have been done, so long as the democracy was confined
to art, and composed of free men. But, as things are with us,
music has given occasion to a general conceit of universal
knowledge and contempt for law, and liberty has followed in
their train. . . .

So the next stage of the journey toward liberty will be refusal
to submit to the magistrates, and on this will follow emancipation from the authority and correction of parents and elders;
then . . . comes the effort to escape obedience to the law, and
when that goal is all but reached, contempt for oaths, for the
plighted word, and all religion. The spectacle of the Titanic
nature of which our old legends speak is reenacted; man returns
to the old condition of a hell of unending misery. (701a–c)

A democracy, although obviously not the political form of choice
for the Athenian, would at least have respected certain "confines": it
would have been "confined to art," and it would have confined its
demos to "free men," thus excluding (but also presupposing, for its
freedom) women and slaves. What is so frightening and fearful about
theatrocracy, by contrast, is that it appears to respect no such limits.
And how, after all, can there be a *polis*, or anything political, without
limits and confinement?⁵ It is the established system of such demarca-
tions, epitomized here by the organization of music into fixed genres
and types, that is progressively dissolved by a practice that mixes
genres and finally leaves no delimitation untouched or unquestioned.
The driving force of such a development seems at first glance to be
hedonistic, and so it is usually read. But the mere fact that the "lust

for pleasure" is qualified as being "frantic and unhallowed" suggests that here, no less than in their military struggles, the Athenians are driven as much by fear as by desire: or, rather, that fear and desire may turn out to be very difficult to separate. As Socrates observes in the *Philebus*: "In laments and tragedies and comedies—and not only in those of the stage but in the whole tragicomedy of life—as well as on countless other occasions, pains are mixed with pleasures" (50b).[6] The mixing of pleasures has as its privileged site the stage, the place and medium of theater, but the danger, here and elsewhere, is that such mixing will not confine itself to a single place but rather will be driven, almost by nature, to transgress all places, limits, and laws.[7] Like theater itself, the theatrocratic usurpation of the rule of law is driven as much by fear as by pleasure. At the same time, this drive appears to be associated with an acoustical rather than simply a visual medium: song, dance, and music break down most effectively the sense of propriety and the barriers that are its condition, giving the "silent" majority a voice and producing a hybrid music bordering on noise.[8]

The emergence of theatrocracy thus necessarily and essentially involves what today we would call "multimedia." The reference to *theater* acquires special significance against this background. The theater that is being referred to—indirectly, via the notion of "theatrocracy"—is clearly not that of tragedy or comedy, which will furnish Aristotle with his canonical instances, and yet it is still designated as theater. As already noted, the Greek word *theatron* designates the place from which one sees. The notion of theatrocracy retains this reference to a specific place or site, but it is disrupted, disorganized by the different media that converge upon it. Curiously, the "rule" of the *theatron* seems to entail the absence of all stable rules. The theater emerges as an open-air version of the Platonic cave. It is a place where one comes and goes, and yet where one is not free in one's movements.

What results, then, is described by the Athenian in a judgment that has lost little of its resonance in the thousands of years since Plato: "Everybody knows everything, and is ready to say anything; the age of reverence is gone, and the age of irreverence and licentiousness has begun."[9] From Plato to the present, this verdict has served to condemn "the media."

Even Walter Benjamin, who, in contrast to his colleagues of the Frankfurt Institute for Social Research, did not have a predominantly negative view of the media, did not hesitate to designate "theatro-cracy" as the enemy of all innovation and change. But, in a character-istic departure from traditional moralistic critiques, he added the decisive nuance that theatrocracy is especially dangerous when it be-comes the alibi of a "criticism" that invokes the "false, dissimulating totality" of the "audience" (*Publikum*) as the ultimate and unques-tioned criterion. Benjamin's condemnation of "theatrocracy," while ostensibly echoing the Platonic critique, is diametrically opposed to it. What Benjamin finds dangerous is not the appeal to the "audience" but the pretense that the addressee of that appeal is one and the same, monolithic, unchangeable, natural. Such fetishization—in the Marx-ian (and perhaps also Freudian) sense—of the audience justifies a criti-cism that is in fact an apology for existing power relations. By treating the audience as monolithic and immutable, such criticism tends to universalize and perpetuate a relation of forces whose relativity it de-nies and obscures. For Benjamin, the potentiality of theatrical specta-tors is not to be found in their staying the same, but in their possibility for change.

This possibility, however, is precisely what concerned Plato. His concern indicates that he recognizes a similar potential in theater, al-though he valorizes it negatively: the potential of disturbing and trans-forming the established order, traditional authority, and the hierarchies it entails. It is this potential that leads Plato, through the figure of the Athenian, to forge the word *theatrocracy*.

Having thus designated the danger, the question now becomes: Wherein does its power lie? We can already surmise that the answer will have something to do with the nature of the theatrical site and the way it influences the perceptions and behavior of those who fall under its sway. As we will see, for Plato the fascinating power of the theatrocracy is marked by a resurgence of *thauma*, the wonder that draws and holds one's gaze, and whose powerful fascination is there-fore very difficult to control.

The consequences of this "thaumatic" aspect of theatrocracy emerge more clearly in book 7 of the *Laws* that I want to discuss briefly, from book 7. In it, the Athenian sketches another nightmare scenario, this time drawn not from the history of Athens but from its contemporary life, thereby illustrating the depths of political degrada-tion into which his city has descended:

A magistrate has just offered sacrifice in the name of the public when a choir, or rather a number of choirs, turn up, plant themselves not at a remote distance from the altar, but, often enough, in actual contact with it, and drown the solemn ceremony with sheer blasphemy, harrowing the feelings of their audience with their language, rhythms, and lugubrious strains, and the choir which is most successful in plunging the city which has just offered sacrifice into sudden tears is adjudged the victor. Surely, our vote will be cast against such a practice. (800c–d)[10]

Public rites are disturbed by itinerant choirs, who lack all respect for constituted authority and who show this lack of respect through their very movement, refusing to stay "at a remote distance from the altar but often enough" entering "in actual contact with it."[11] Through such proximity, the voices of these moving masses can "drown" out the "solemn ceremony," just as the noise of the audience overwhelms the voices of reason and competence in theatrocracy.

If we reflect on just what elicits condemnation in these two passages, we come to two conclusions. First, theatrocracy, which replaces aristocracy and is not even democratic, is associated with the dissolution of universally valid laws and consequently with the destabilization of the social space that those laws both presuppose and help maintain. The rise of theatrocracy subverts and perverts the unity of the *theatron* as a social and political site by introducing an irreducible and unpredictable *heterogeneity*, a multiplicity of perspectives and a cacophony of voices. This disruption of the *theatron* goes together, it seems, with a concomitant disruption of *theory*, which is to say, of the ability of *knowledge* and *competence* to localize things, keep them in their proper place and thus to contribute to social stability.

It should be remembered, however, that theatrocracy does not originate in the audience but rather in those poets and composers "of native genius" whose experimentation sets the fateful precedent of undermining the authority of established rules and laws. There is something in the "nature" of poets and musicians, then, that encourages or at least allows the flouting of established law and convention. Thus the exclusion of the poets and artists from the polis finds powerful support in the responsibility for the rise of theatrocracy attributed to them here.

But it is only in the *second* passage, or scene—since, as the Athenian himself notes ironically, his own arguments are themselves often quite theatrical, despite (or because of?) his aversion to theatrical spectacle—that the subversive force of theatrocracy reveals its true resource. This consists in the power to *move* and disrupt the consecrated and institutionalized boundaries that structure political space: those, for instance, that separate the sacred from the profane, the "altar" from the public. Theatricality demonstrates its subversive power when it forsakes the confines of the *theatron* and begins to wander: when, in short, it separates itself from *theater.* For in so doing it begins to escape control by the prevailing rules of representation, whether aesthetic, social, or political. Its vehicle is irreducibly plural and, even more, heterogeneous: not just "*a* choir" but rather "*a number* of choirs," which "turn up" in the most unexpected places, disorganizing official sacrifices, not so much through brute force as through the seductive fascination of their chants, "harrowing the feelings of their audience with their language, rhythms, and lugubrious strains" and thereby subverting the success of the sacrificial ceremony. Such wandering groups or choruses do not attempt to take the altar by storm, from without, as it were. They simply sidle up *next* to it, in "actual contact with it," brushing up against it without overrunning it; *touching* it and touching all those who cannot resist the insidious force of their "lugubrious strains." The power of such choruses is seductive, contagious, hypnotic. It breaks down the borders of propriety and restraint in others while itself remaining difficult to control or even to identify. What makes these "choirs" all the more wondrous is that they seem to be composed neither of simple amateurs nor of pure professionals. And yet, since the need to which they respond appears undeniable, the Athenian is led to make the following, exasperated suggestion:

> If there is really any need for our citizens to listen to such doleful strains on some day which stands accursed in the calendar, surely it would be more proper that a hired set of performers should be imported from abroad for the occasion to render them, like the hired minstrels who escort funerals with Carian music. The arrangement, I take it, would be equally in place in performances of the sort we are discussing. (800d–e)

If the "arrangement . . . would be equally in place in performances of the sort we are discussing," it is for the simple reason that the relation of employer to employee, the "hiring" of professional musicians, would impose upon the performers a relatively recognizable social role and respect for the rules. Salaried musicians can be expected to know their place, at least if they want to keep their salaries. Conversely, it is precisely the absence of such knowledge and discipline in theatrocracy that so alarms Plato. When theater rules, people forget their proper place. And places become so unstable that they can hardly become familiar, much less forgotten.

It is the stability of place and the durability of placing that theatrocracy profoundly disturbs. In this respect, its perverse effects are the culmination of Plato's worst fears concerning mimesis in general: "The mimetic poet sets up in each individual soul a vicious constitution by fashioning phantoms far removed from reality, and by currying favor with the senseless element that cannot distinguish the greater from the less, but *calls the same thing now one, now the other*" (*Republic*, 10.605b-c, my emphasis).

Imitation destroys the self-identity of the "same" and the fixity of values by implanting "in each individual soul" a propensity that leads it to confuse phantoms with reality and to "call the same thing now one, now the other." The exemplary space in which such a "vicious constitution" can unfold to the extreme is none other than the theater, in which mimesis comes, as it were, to be (dis)embodied in the audience: "And does not the fretful part of us present many and varied occasions for imitation, while the intelligent and temperate disposition, always remaining approximately the same, is easy neither to imitate nor to be understand when imitated, *especially by a nondescript mob assembled in the theater*" (604e, my emphasis).

Assembly in a theater is, for Plato, the sinister parody of the assemblage of citizens in the forum. In the theater, everyone tends to forget his or her proper place. And as already suggested, the fascinating power of theatrical mimesis cannot be explained simply by an appeal to "pleasure," not, at least, in any univocal sense of the term. As the words of Socrates just cited make clear, it is "the fretful part of us," rather than the "intelligent and temperate disposition," that presents the most "varied occasions for mimesis." The power of those errant choirs, we recall, was displayed in the irresistible appeal of their "lugubrious strains," which defied and defiled the official ceremonies of sacrifice. Theatrocracy establishes its rule by appealing to fear, care, and mourning as much as to simple "pleasure."

In the example of the vagrant choirs, the result was an audience moved to tears. But there is another aspect of mimesis gone wild that Plato, himself the consummate dramaturge, knew only too well: the power of laughter.

> There are jests which you would be ashamed to make yourself, and yet on the comic stage, or indeed in private, when you hear them, you are greatly amused by them and are not all disgusted at their unseemliness . . . there is a principle in human nature which is disposed to raise a laugh, and this which you once restrained by reason, because you were afraid of being thought a buffoon, is now let out again; and having stimulated the risible faculty at the theatre, you are betrayed unconsciously to yourself into playing the comic poet at home. (*Republic*, 10.606)

Laughter breaks out and breaks down the barriers of propriety, shifting the stage from theater to home, undermining the division of public and private space, disturbing domestic as well as civil tranquility. In the outbreak of laughter, articulate, reasonable discourse is progressively drowned out by the reiterative amplification of gesticulations that can, upon occasion, suggest a body out of control.

Precisely this link between theatricality and laughter distinguishes the reemergence of a certain theatrical paradigm in theory and criticism over the past two centuries. This reemergence passes by way of texts such as Kierkegaard's *Repetition*, Nietzsche's *The Birth of Tragedy*, Benjamin's *Origin of the German Mourning Play* and his essays on Brecht and Kafka, and reaches a certain culmination, perhaps, in the writings of Artaud, Genet, Deleuze, and Derrida. The list could obviously be extended. Here, however, I will limit myself to citing and summarily commenting upon several passages from a few of the authors mentioned, in order to indicate how they begin to rethink the relationship between the theatrical, the theoretical, and the media, as well as some of the political consequences such rethinking can have.

First, from Nietzsche's *The Birth of Tragedy*:

> At bottom the esthetic phenomenon is simple; one need only have the ability to see continually a living play and to live per-

petually *surrounded by hosts of spirits*, and one is a poet; one need only feel *the drive to alter oneself* [*sich selbst zu verwandeln*] and *to speak out of alien bodies and souls*, and one is a dramatist.

Dionysian excitation is capable of communicating to a whole multitude this artistic power of feeling oneself surrounded by such a host of spirits, with whom one knows oneself to be inwardly one. This process [*Prozeß*: also, trial] of the tragic chorus is the originary *dramatic* phenomenon: *seeing oneself altered right in front of oneself* [*sich selbst vor sich verwandelt zu sehen*] and now acting as though one had really *entered another body*, another character. This process, this trial marks the beginning of the unfolding of drama. . . . Here already there is an abandonment of the individual by entering into an alien nature. Moreover, this phenomenon arises as an epidemic: a whole throng feels itself enthralled in this way.[12]

Nietzsche's account of the tragic chorus as dramatic *Urphänomen* both repeats and transforms the Platonic nightmare vision of the wandering choirs. Contrary both to certain other statements of Nietzsche himself, in *The Birth of Tragedy* and elsewhere, and, even more, contrary to a certain reception of this text, the "dramatic phenomenon" described by Nietzsche never relinquishes its distinctively theatrical dimension, which is to say, it never simply results in a mystical, ecstatic union with "the Lord and Master, Dionysus."[13] The chorus, Nietzsche insists, does not cease to "look at" this God, even if what is visible is not a figure but a phenomenon caught in a *process* of *Verwandlung*: metamorphosis and trial at once, involving both change of place and change of identity. But the German word used here by Nietzsche, *Verwandlung*, goes further than this duality of meaning. The root of the word is *wandeln*, which comes from the verb for *turning*: *wenden*, in turn related to *winden*, to *wind*, in the sense of twist, coil, or twine. This accords with Nietzsche's allusion to the St. Vitus's Dance as a medieval manifestation of the Dionysian, for the movement implied in Nietzsche's account of the theatrical is more of a twisting and turning, a spasm or tick, than a continuous progression toward a goal. At the same time, throughout *The Birth of Tragedy* Nietzsche never ceases to insist on the inseparability of the Dionysian from the Apollonian, which is why *The Birth of Tragedy* is concerned ultimately more with theater than with religion or, rather, with theater as a *possible substitute for religion.* The "visionary" dimension of the *theatron* is conserved, and those who are in it are as little free to come and go as Plato's cave dwellers. But with Nietzsche the theatrical site loses what ever since Plato and Aristotle has been the predominant feature of all sites, including that of theater: a certain stability and, indeed, immobility. Instead of functioning as the unmovable container of bodies that are, in principle at least, movable—a principle presupposed even and especially by the Platonic cave, precisely in its negation[14]—the theatrical site itself splits and stretches, twists and *turns into* a space of alteration and oscillation, of *Verwandlung.* The twin principles of containment and constancy are thus dislodged: just as the site does not contain the body, the body is not *informed* by the soul. Rather, it is, in a literal sense, *beside itself.*

A significant consequence of this repositioning of place and body is that the relation of life and death is no longer construed according to a logic of simple opposition. When Nietzsche writes that the "individual" gives itself up to this movement of *Verwandlung* both by entering into alien bodies and souls and *at the same time* by *seeing* itself splitting apart in the process, he describes a recursive movement that does not come full circle. In the gap opened by such noncircular recursivity, the scope of life and death is altered. To be alive cannot be understood in terms of spatial identity: being "here" as opposed to being "there" or "gone," since the individual caught up in the movement of *Verwandlung* is no longer simply here, but here *and* there at once. This "at," however, splits the oneness of the once by rendering (and rending) it repeatable. What results is not just a plurality of individuals, each different and yet each self-contained, but rather the fracturing of the individual as such. In the elusive space-time of this irreducible "dividuality," unity cannot be restored through any sort of reassembled "collective" that would surmount the limitations and isolation of the individual.

The theatrical collective—for instance, a "cast" of "characters"—remains marked by a certain disunity: it is "cast" not in stone, as it were, but in "parts" that bear the trace of such *Verwandlung.*[15] This transforms the relation of the living to the dead by disrupting the place of each. The "lively play" to which Nietzsche refers in the passage just cited includes an observer "surrounded by a host of ghosts [*Geisterschar*]." The perspective from which this spectacle must be seen is thus not just that of an irreducible plurality, of a "host," but that of an irreducible spectrality. As a "host of spirits," individuals do not merely cease to exist: they persist, but as *dividuals*, divided between life and death, spectator and actor, strange and familiar, entering an alien body and soul on the one hand, while on the other remaining sufficiently detached to *see* themselves taking leave of their selves (rather than of their "senses"). The individual thus altered is here and there at once, and consequently can be neither exclusively here nor there, neither simply itself nor simply other. This impossible "situation" splits the site itself, rendering it something like a *ghost of itself*, lacking an authentic place or a proper body.

Such traits begin to indicate just how and why a certain theatricality could be compatible with the spread of contemporary, electronic media. As Marshall McLuhan has observed, "Nothing can be further from the spirit of the new technology than 'a place for everything and everything in its place.'" This phrase served as a motto for an influential book published in 1985 that bore the telling title *No Sense of Place*. In it, Joshua Meyrowitz sought to interpret "the impact of electronic media on social behavior" in terms of the changing sense of place. Since then, it has become more or less accepted to speak of the "de-localizing" effects of electronic media. But the notion of "de-localization" tells only part of the story and, taken in isolation, can be highly misleading. What is at stake in the changes being brought about by the spread of the new media, in particular by their electronic varieties, involves not just a "de-localization" of "*physical* settings: places, rooms, buildings and so forth," as Meyrowitz wrote in the preface to his book,[16] but rather a change in the structure and function of such settings, in their relation to the "physical," including bodies. The passages we have been reading, from Plato and Nietzsche, remind us of what is not any less decisive for being evident: namely, that there can be no movement of de-localization without an accompanying re-localization. However, the two need not be construed as being simply symmetrical. What results from the self-abandonment of the individual as described by Nietzsche is not simply another individual, in the sense of an *alter ego*, but a spectacle that offers itself to sight while at the same time eluding any purely perceptual grasp. This is why Nietzsche stresses the traversing of limits and frontiers rather than the emergence of a new figure, albeit an alien one: the individual sees itself "as though it had entered into a foreign body and character." This "as though," which recalls Kant's Third Critique, indicates the decisive shift that is taking place here: that from a notion of aesthetics as the realm of an irreducible "as if" to a notion of theatricality as its medium. A *medium*, however, is not a *realm*, because its distinctively spatial quality—its status "in between"—indicates that it can never be construed as self-contained or self-regulating. Rather, it is relational and situational, depending decisively on alien or extraneous instances that, in the case of theater, are generally identified with the spectators or audiences. This identification is by no means exhaustive, but it can be a first step in rethinking place as something other than a condition of identity. In *The Genealogy of Morals*, Nietzsche speculates that the Greeks invented the Gods to serve as spectators to their suffering, thereby endowing it with meaning.[17] Similarly, in *The Birth of Tragedy* Nietzsche's description of *Verwandlung* as the *Urphänomen* of all drama comes in the context of his insistence upon the chorus as the origin of Attic tragedy. But he explicitly distinguishes his conception of the chorus from that of Schelling, who holds it to be the "ideal spectator." Here his theory of theater, despite certain formulations, begins to part company with traditional aesthetics, both extending and transforming the Kantian third *Critique*. For the position of the other in the theater is no longer that of a simple spectator, but rather of a participant who is not a protagonist. The chorus participates as the decisive element in Nietzsche's conception of theater precisely in and through its alterity: it becomes other than itself, changing its place, irreducibly dispersed into a host of ghosts without hearth or home. This itinerant host defines the space of theater, theater as space or, rather, as irreducibly *problematic re-localization*. This ongoing and never conclusively settled setting of the scene distinguishes the theatrical play from the artistic work, at least insofar as the latter is considered to be sufficiently meaningful and self-contained to serve as the object of and support for a detached and comprehensive perception. The spectator, audience, or addressee is never an essential component of the classical work of art, considered to be constituted independently of its reception, circulation, interpretation. A *staging*, however, never adds up to a *work*, not even to the "setting to work of truth," as Heidegger defines the work of art.[18] The irreducibility of the addressee is the mark of this difference.

But the function of the other in theater cannot be understood as that of simply another subject or an alter ego. Theatrical staging is not just a work in action. Rather, it has a structure and dynamics that are radically different from those of the work, or of its associated category, *form*, at least as both have traditionally been conceived. Walter Benjamin seeks to highlight this difference, in his discussion of Brecht's Epic Theater, through the notion of *interruption*. Interruption, as Benjamin elaborates the term, involves the disruption of a temporal process or progression, associated with narrative-based drama, by spatial factors associated with theater as medium and, above all, with the stage. Benjamin begins the first version of his essay on Brecht by insisting on this very point:

> What is at stake in theater today can be more precisely defined in relation to the stage than to the drama. It concerns the filling-in of the orchestra pit. The abyss that separates the actors from the audience like the dead from the living, this abyss, which among all the elements of the stage most indelibly bears the traces of its sacred origins, has lost its function. The stage is still elevated but it no longer rises out of fathomless depths; it has become a podium. On this podium theatergoers must find their place [*sich einzurichten*].[19]

What begins with the ostensibly familiar gesture of defining theater in terms of what today would be called a "level playing field"—one in which the aesthetic sublimity of fiction is brought down to earth—reveals itself situated in the Nietzschean tradition: not that of Dionysian ecstasy as *unio mystica*, but that which confounds the living with the dead. The level playing field ostensibly established by the "filling in" of the orchestra pit does not simply place the living on the same level as the dead, but rather complicates their relationship, which can no longer be thought under the aegis of a logic of identity or of mutually exclusive oppositionality. To reduce the bottomless pit separating players from audience, stage from orchestra, was for Benjamin (if not for Brecht) to create not so much a "Living Theater" as what Tadeusz Kantor years later was to call a "Theater of the Dead."[20]

The primary interest of Benjamin's text, in our context, is that it begins to "flesh out" just how theatrical spectrality can be concretely construed. Benjamin's response to the question "What is Epic Theater?" has two parts, both "borrowed" from Brecht and yet both transformed in the process. First, there is gesture. Epic theater, Benjamin asserts, is above all gestural theater. But this determination is not sufficient. Epic theater is not just gestural: it is also citational. It renders gestures *citable*. This is not quite the same as "quotable," which is how it has been rendered in English. Even in English, however, to "cite" is not simply to "quote." This is all the more true in German, where even today the verb *zitieren* still carries with it etymological resonances from its Latin root, *citare*, to set in movement. In English, this resonance is buried in verbs such as "incite" and "excite." And yet setting-into-movement is only half the story here. In both German and English "to cite" has another meaning that is decisive for Benjamin. To cite means not simply to set something in movement, but also—as American drivers know only too well—to arrest movement by diverting it, as in the sense, of course, of receiving a traffic citation, a summons to appear before a tribunal in order to account for an excess of speed.

In short, for Benjamin the "stage" in respect to which epic theater, and theater in general today, must be situated, is determined as a site and as a sight, but also and above as a scene of citability. Why, however, this emphasis on citability and why, precisely, gesture?

Concerning the first part of this question, Benjamin's response brings together the two dimensions of citation, inciting and arresting, by retracing their common origin to the fact that "the basis of citation" in general is "interruption." Citation, which in English might suggest an appeal to authority, also involves disruption, detachment, dislocation, and relocation, all moves from which the violence of a legal order is never entirely absent; "citational index," on the one hand, and "traffic citation," on the other. Both are involved in Benjamin's notion of "citability of gesture" as a decisive aspect of epic theater. "Interruption," he reminds his readers, "is one of the fundamental procedures through which form is given."[21] In other words, if we have reason to regard "form" as the constitutive category of modern aesthetics, then Benjamin indicates here that the origin of the work of art, its very "formation," is based less on a model of creativity or construction—much less on one of expressivity—than on a process of *separation*, by which an intentional, teleological movement—call it a "plot"—is arrested, dislocated, and reconfigured. Reconfigured as what? As a gesture rendered citable. Benjamin's insistence on the notion of citability, as distinct from citation, heightens the sense of interruption, but as a rendering-possible rather than actual or real. The actuality of the stage, as a site of citable gestures, is defined with respect to a potentiality rather than a reality. Whatever is cited, is cited simultaneously as the possibility of its being re-cited, moved elsewhere, transformed. This is why the stage is a place where potentialities are tried out, rather than realities enacted or performed. When a gesture is deployed so as to be citable, it does not merely harken back to what has been: it appeals to possible future transformation and transposition. Citability means recalling the past as the possibility of a future that would be different from the present. To the extent that theater involves the citability of gesture, it cannot be assimilated to the aesthetic work. Construed from the perspective of aesthetics as the individual instantiation of a more general set of characteristics and principles collected under the concept of genre, the work is here no longer self-contained, but determined through interruption and fragmentation, and also by the possibility of becoming other than itself, being moved elsewhere. An intuition of this situation is perhaps reflected in the use, in certain languages, of words that suggest fragmentation to designate what in English is called "play," for instance, *pièce* or *Stück*. As a place of possibility and of experimentation, epic theater knows *pieces*—but not works.

Gesture, then, replaces the aesthetic concept of form in Benjamin's rethinking of theatricality. With the notion of form, however, it shares the attribute of being "fixed" and "delimited":

> Unlike human actions and undertakings, [gestures have] a definable beginning and a definable end. This strict, framelike enclosing of every element in a posture [*Haltung*] that as a whole is caught up in a living flux is one of the basic dialectical phenomena of gesture. From this an important conclusion can be drawn: gestures are obtained all the more someone engaged in an action [*eines Handelnden*] is interrupted. (p. 521)

A gesture, then, is a bodily movement that interrupts and suspends—the German word *Haltung* literally suggests a "holding" or "stopping"—the intentional-teleological-narrative progression toward a meaningful goal and thereby opens up the possibility of a different kind of space: that of an incommensurable singularity. It does this by replacing action with acting. Or, rather, it detaches the movement of acting from the conscious and goal-directed decision of *eines Handelnden*, someone acting. Acting is no longer reducible, if it ever was, to some *one*, for instance, to an actor or an agent as individual or as subject. Instead, it reveals itself to be a function of its *placement* or what

Benjamin, adopting and adapting a Marxist term from Brecht, calls its *Zustand*.

Normally translated and understood as "condition," often in a causal sense, the German word *Zustand* changes once it is defined as the site, not just of a gesture that is cited, but of one whose citation reveals its potentiality to be re-cited, its citability. Cited as citable, gesture is never simply present, but split between past and future, invoking the past to portend an unpredictable future. A form of repetition, citation reveals that it is not necessarily a return of the same. Or, rather, that the return of the same is itself not necessarily identical or unchanging—as with repetitive, ritualized habits that have become so automatic as to escape conscious control. Benjamin seems to have this sort of repetition in mind when he notes that what is essential in epic theater rests

> not on great decisions, which lie along the flight-lines of expectation [*Fluchtlinien der Erwartung*], but on the incommensurable, the singular. "It can happen that way, but it can also happen entirely differently [*ganz anders*]"—this is the basic attitude of anyone who writes for epic theater. He relates to the story the way that a ballet teacher relates to his pupil. His primary concern is to loosen her joints to the limits of the possible.[22]

The reference to ballet here recalls how closely the notion of gesture is bound up with, although not reducible to, that of the body. But this body is to be understood, not in the Aristotelian sense, as a vessel or container, but rather in terms of its articulations. The essence of gesture, as bodily movement, is to be sought neither in the head nor in the heart but rather in the *joints* that make such movement possible while also exposing it to interruption—for instance, as spasm or paralysis. To experience the body, not simply as a continuous medium or entity, but as the possibility of an imperfect, disjointed machine—this is what Benjamin seems to envisage in and through the notion of "citable gesture" or, as it might also be rendered, "gesture on the move."

Just this experience of the body as the interruption of organicity and as machine is intensified by the spread of electronic media. Such "media" can no longer be regarded as the passive element or condition of the realization of "works" or acts. Rather, media transform the very places "in" and through which they take place. This transformation affects not merely individual subjects and objects, things and events, but also traditional conceptions of place and body as (unmoved) container and (movable) contained, respectively. It is against this context of the transformation of place and body through electronic media that the renewed significance of theater and the theatrical is to be sought.

A major function of the theatrical in an age of electronic media is to articulate the ways in which sites—and sights, but also sounds and other "sensations"—remain linked, in however mediate a manner, to bodies, although not necessarily to *human* bodies, at least as traditionally understood. With the increasing problematization of the principle of containment as defining the mutual relation of place and body, the privilege of the human body, dominant in the Greco-Christian history of the West, can no longer be taken for granted. Despite a persistent and popular tendency today to equate "body" with "human body," electronic media and "popular culture" both underscore that "bodies" are not necessarily less bodily for being nonhuman. To speak of "the" body in the singular, whether gendered or not, almost inevitably means to privilege the human body over all other kinds: animal, plant, inorganic. By contrast, to invoke the citability of gesture as a determining mechanism of contemporary theatricality is to call attention to the body as an organic whole, something other than a vessel or container of the soul—as something other than what today is so often and so confidently designated as "embodiment" (today's secular successor to "incarnation").

The resurgence of theatricality as citable gesture calls into question the self-evidence of this "in" or "em-." In so doing, it brings into play one of the chief axioms of Western modernity: that of the immanence of the subject. What is involved can be illustrated by going back to one of the earliest discussions of "digitality," long before the age of binary computation. In his discussion of place and its relation to the body in book 4 of the *Physics*, Aristotle distinguishes the way place can be said to "contain" bodies from the way these "contain" their component parts or members:

> The next step we must take is to see in how many ways one thing is said to be *in* another. In one way, as a finger is in a hand, and generally a part in a whole. In another way, as a whole is in

its parts; for there is no whole over and above the parts. . . .
Again, as the affairs of Greece are in the King, and generally
events are in their primary motive agent. . . . And most properly
of all, as something is in a vessel, and generally in a place.[23]

What happens, however, when the vessel begins to move, when it
becomes a vehicle, and when its movement is not primarily locomotive, involving a change of place? What happens when the function
of the finger is no longer determined primarily through the fact that
it is located "in a hand" as "generally a part" is located "in a whole"?
What happens then to the "interior" of the hand and of the body? If
one observes carefully what distinguishes the gestures of Balinese
dancing and theater, for instance, from those of conventional Western
theater, including traditional ballet, one might speculate that the
movement of the extremities, and in particular of the fingers, plays a
decisive role precisely to the extent that such fingers can no longer be
said to be simply "in" the hand, but rather to *draw* the hand, and the
body to which it is attached, to its outermost limits and beyond,
toward a space that is both distant and near at the same time. It is
difficult to imagine a single King or God dominating or informing
such bodily movements, which seem to be determined, not by what
they try to hold or hold onto, but by their ability to let go, and in
letting go to establish a different kind of "contact" or relation. That
contact or relation might come close to what Benjamin referred to,
in German, as *Zustand*, normally translated as "condition" or "situation." I prefer to render it, here at least, as *stance*.[24] That involves what
the word in German literally says: a *standing toward* something else, a
gesturing elsewhere, pulling the body after it.

The possibility in the new media and their technologies for such
gesticulation and dismemberment fascinated Benjamin, just as their
"uncanny" and "automatic" aspects fascinated Freud, especially when
they involved a "severed hand."[25] If Aristotle regarded the relation
between hand and finger as that of whole to part, what Freud discovered to be profoundly "uncanny" was their separation, a condition of
all relation, including that of "the" body to "itself." What could be
more familiar than the fingers of a hand? But when those fingers are
no longer "in" the hand, what could be more uncanny?

In this context of uncanniness, "digitalization" reveals its curiously
ambivalent character. On the one hand, the "digit" suggests discrete-

ness: the clearly defined unit of the finger serving as model for the no less clearly defined and distinct numerical unit. On the other, however, the numerical unit does not relate to the combinations it constitutes as a part to a whole. It is a relational element in a combinatorial process. In computers, that relation is built upon binary opposition: 0's and 1's, closed and opened circuits, positive and negative, each only "meaningful" as the other of the other. This combination of otherness constitutes the medium of the new media, at least insofar as they are increasingly "digital." There is no inherent limit to the combinatorial sequences that constitute digitized code, no more than there is any intrinsic limit to the combination of letters, words, and their sequencing in discourse. This lack of *intrinsic* limitation, and hence delimitation, is what excludes the relation of part to whole from serving as a paradigm for code or discourse. But this also makes it increasingly difficult to *hold* the human body to be the exemplary occupant of the motionless vessel traditionally understood as "place."

However, as the figure "hold" in the previous sentence suggests, this "breaking" or perhaps better, *jarring* of the vessels, calling into question the paradigm of an organic whole containing its parts, has long been anticipated by the very functions that have served to valorize the different bodily organs. The hand, for instance, has been privileged as the organ of grasping and seizing, holding and controlling, perceiving and conceiving: in short, getting a handle on the world. In this, it relies upon "its" fingers doing its bidding. The fingers must be "held" to be subordinate to the intention "embodied" in the hand. The hand is thus the organ that "empowers" the body, which in turn is "held" to "embody" the soul, the spirit, or, more secularly if not securely, the personality. And yet the finger remains discrete, separate from the hand, not merely an integral part. If it is required for grasping, it can also engage in very different kinds of contact: that of touching, for instance, caressing, or pointing.[26] Pointing can be a means of anticipating the seizure and appropriation of what is being pointed at or out, but it can also involve a movement *away* from the familiarity and control of the grasping hand. In pointing, the finger can pull the body elsewhere, as in the Balinese dance-theater already mentioned. A finger can be recognized as a finger, even and especially when it is severed from the hand, from the body. It still remains discrete.

With the spread of "digitalization" something quite similar may be happening today to the sense of the body and to the notion of identity that it supports. The "digital" points away from its immediate manifestation, is "allegorical" in the sense given the term by Benjamin: it signifies something other than what it represents, situated elsewhere. Every "here and now" points toward a "there and then."[27] Visual, verbal, acoustic "qualities," the objects of "sense impressions," are produced by sequences of relations that have no intrinsic relation to anything other than the most rudimentary form of relationality itself: that of binary opposition. The most familiar manifestation of human identity, the individual body, which since the Reformation serves increasingly as the model for the isolation of the individual before God, comes to be regarded with suspicion and even fear. To be sure, such suspicion is massively channeled into directions designed to preserve established categories and perspectives, above all, the principle of containment. Fear and perhaps hope of a radical alternative is preempted by the question "What" can the body "contain"? Popular films from *The Body Snatchers* through *Alien* to the *Terminator(s)*, *Matrix* and beyond, all bear witness to the becoming-uncanny of what seems most familiar, the (not always human) body, as well as to its canny reappropriation as container of the (not always human) soul. It seems to matter less what it contains than *that* it contains something at all, albeit beings from outer space. To be sure, the actual depiction of such beings, which tend to assume the form either of amorphous organisms or of machines, suggests an experience of the body as the place where the clear-cut figure of the self-evidently human blurs. A body that is no longer clearly demarcated from its surroundings inevitably raises the question of its relation to place, which is no longer simply its exterior. Rather, this body can itself be a place, a stage or staging area for effects whose scope is not clearly predictable. The ensuing uncertainty is often reinscribed in a narrative that claims to be meaningful and self-contained, with an immediately intelligible beginning, middle, and end. The narrative form of the story finally reasserts the wholeness that this problematization of the body and place as containers tends to upset. Not its content but its ending as such that is "happy," insofar as it provides a coherent frame to which the "viewer" can cling in the hope of being only someone who merely "views."[28]

The commercial constraint of this narrative reassurance of the spectator has profound political ramifications. Ever since the eighteenth century, the "body politic" has provided an important paradigm in constructing the putative unity of a variegated and heterogeneous political entity, whether as "nation," "people," "class," or "community." A "democracy" is only conceivable insofar as the *demos*—the people—is presupposed. How can a people "rule" if it is not, in principle, unified and whole? And yet, the narratives that traditionally provided a framework for such unification have been undermined by the tendency of the televisual media to furnish discontinuous series of images rather than continuous sequences of scenes. The popularity of the sitcom and reality show suggests a desire of viewers to accede to the kind of continuity that the socioeconomic constraints of "globalized" capitalism tend to disrupt. The increased mobility of capital contrasts ever more sharply with the reduced options of those dependent on wage labor to survive. In a globalized society, wage labor has a hard time keeping up with "delocalization."

Concomitantly, the technological and institutional status of the "media" grows increasingly dependent upon the exigencies of short-term profit maximization.[29] The media tend to reproduce the instabilities for which they simultaneously offer palliatives, not just in the "content" of programming, but in its "frame": what is euphemistically but symptomatically designated as the "commercial break." The commercial break exploits the anxiety associated with far more drastic breaks to come. In announcing the "commercial break," the television speaker enjoins viewers to "stay with us," assuring them that "we'll be right back." "Staying with us" in this sense is the capitalist version of the other tendency of the media, whether old (language) or new: namely, "parting with." The television viewer is thus encouraged not to leave ("stay with us") and promised a speedy return of the same subject-matter. This incessantly broadcast appeal reveals something distinctive about contemporary theatrocracy. To have staying power, today's media audiences must answer "present" to the call of the media. They must respond or, as one says today in the era of total communication, "interact," however ambiguous such interaction inevitably is. The audience is, after all, the commodity that networks sell to their clients, the advertisers. And so it is decisive that the audience should indeed "stay with us," *during* no less than *after* the "break."

Such theatricality tends both to confirm and to undermine the rule of the audience. On the one hand, it confirms that the audience is an integral and determining part of the media as spectacle, constantly monitored by network producers and writers. On the other, the "interactivity" of the audience is largely defined by the "interval" framed by the commercial breaks. Those breaks themselves can never be called into question as structuring framework. Instead, the not so subliminal message is that to survive the coming "breaks" it may be prudent not to question their totalizing, framing function. It may be best to sit tight and "interact" in the ever shorter intervals granted between the breaks. For the break is what "saves": whether as "breaking news" or "news breaks." The Good News that television brings to its viewers is that they can survive the break—but only if they stay put.

"Give me a break!" (from the break)—this is the unsung plaint of theatrocracy today. The media respond by interrupting their programs to bring a special announcement. The more catastrophic the message, the better, so long as it fills the "break" that separates viewers of the broadcast media today and enables them to "survive" the spectacles they behold.

All of this is changing, of course, with the Internet, in which the function of the screen is no longer—or not yet?—as rigorously, and linearly, framed by the commercial break as in broadcast television.

To be situated before a television screen—even more, before a computer screen—is of course something very different from being situated in a theater before a stage. The orchestra pit has been replaced by the commercial break. And yet, this new situation is determined by a tension between anticipation and reflection, storytelling and interruption, that has a long history, reaching back to the emergence of theater itself. And yet insofar as all these situations are determined by a tension between anticipation and reflection, storytelling and interruption, they participate in a long history, which reaches back to the emergence of theater itself, as practice and as theory. In the following chapters we will discuss a few of these earliest articulations in order to explore how the medium of theater has, from its inception, responded to the enduring desire to *survive the break.*

2

Technics, Theatricality, Installation

Gestalt, Gestell, Geschick

AT THE CONCLUSION of his essay questioning— and in quest of—technics, Heidegger suggests that the problems involved point beyond the consecrated disciplinary discourses that have hitherto monopolized the field:

> Because the goings-on of technics [*das Wesende der Technik*] are not technical, essential meditation upon technics and decisive confrontation [*Auseinandersetzung*] can only happen in a realm that is, on the one hand, related to that essence and on the other fundamentally different from it.
>
> Such a realm is art. But only when artistic meditation for its part does not shut itself off from the constellation of truth that our *questioning* is after.
>
> In so questioning we bear witness to a state of emergency: because of technics itself [*lauter Technik*] we do not yet experience the goings-on of technics, because of aesthetics itself [*lauter Aesthetik*] we no longer experience the goings-on of art. Yet the more we question the goings-on of technics, the more enigmatic become the goings-on of art.[1]

In this conclusion, which does not merely name an enigma—that of "art"—but is itself enigmatic in its allusiveness, Heidegger asserts that, in order to reach a genuine understanding of what is at stake in modern technology, it is necessary to go beyond the concepts and discourse of "technology itself," of what he calls, in German, *lauter Technik*, the din of which tends to drown out rather than reveal what is really going on in and as technics. Just as the over-loud discourse of traditional aesthetics—*lauter Aesthetik*—obscures through its specious familiarity what might really be going on under the deceptively familiar name of "art."

In what follows, I will take Heidegger's suggestion as a point of departure in trying to discern more precisely certain aspects of the "enigma" or "secret" hidden by the ostensible clarity of aesthetics, in order then to move in a direction that Heidegger himself would surely never have followed but in which his questions nevertheless seem to point. I will suggest that the "affinity" of art and technics is perhaps nowhere more suggestively problematic than in the history of what is called "theater," of its "theory" as well as its "practice," and, above all, in the persistent difficulty in keeping the two apart. Against the backdrop of this convergence, certain distinctive effects of modern technics—especially in relation to what is called "media"—display and deploy their significance.

Let me begin, then, by recalling, resuming, and in the process simplifying the major arguments that lead Heidegger to conclude that the goings-on of technics must be examined from the perspective of an "art" that is "poetic," but not necessarily "aesthetic."

Both "poetics" and "technics" are initially, according to Heidegger, forms of *Entbergung*, usually translated as "revealing." This term is unsatisfactory for at least two reasons. First, it utterly effaces an essential dimension implied by the German word, which can also mean to "save," in the sense of to protect or secure.[2] For this reason, I have in previous writings preferred to render the word as "unsecuring" rather than as "revealing." Yet there is another reason not to overlook this less obvious, more connotative meaning of *bergen*. The notion of "securing" does not just add another meaning to that of "revealing": it implies a different structure of meaning, one that is irreducibly conflictual, requiring negotiation and compromise. Where there is "unsecuring," there must also be a threat, a danger. "Unsecuring" points to a conflict and, in turn, to a relation of forces that requires a response of some sort. But no single, unified response can, as such, resolve the conflict. What is decisive in Heidegger's use of this, as of other terms, is that such words are always the site of an unresolvable ambivalence. What is not necessarily obvious in the English word *revealing* is how the movement it designates is indissociably bound up with a counter-movement that doubles and splits it. Precisely this ambivalence allows Heidegger to assimilate *Entbergen* to his notion of truth, *alētheia*. Truth, as *alētheia* or *Entbergung*, marks the irreducibility of such ambivalence, whether with respect to thinking, being, or technics.

In order, therefore, to understand what is actually going on in Heidegger's account of technology, it is indispensable to take into account his emphatically ambivalent approach to truth. Although he discusses this notion in many places in his work, none is more relevant to his analysis of technics than "The Origin of the Work of Art," written in 1936, because, as already mentioned, Heidegger suggests that art—a certain notion of art—can provide the key to the goings-on of technics. In the earlier essay, which defined art as "the setting to work of truth," the ambivalent structure of truth as *alētheia* emerges with relative clarity:

> Truth is un-truth insofar as part of it derives from the realm of the not yet (un)revealed in the sense of secured concealment [*Verbergung*]. . . . Truth goes on [*west*] as truth in the counter-movement [*Gegeneinander*: literally, "against one another"] of lighting-clearing and concealing-securing. Truth is the originary strife [*Urstreit*] in which, always in its own way, the Open is striven for [*erstritten*], into which everything stands in [*hereinsteht*] and from which everything that discloses itself as [a] being [*Seiendes*] holds back [*sich zurückhält*] and withdraws.[3]

In its constitutive ambivalence, Heidegger's elaboration of truth as *alētheia* diverges radically from the traditional notion of truth as *adaequatio* or correspondence in its constitutive ambivalence. Whereas the notion of truth as adequation presupposes an underlying identity as *tertium comparationis*, *alētheia* insists upon an irreducible and generative *strife* as that which transforms the relationship from an essentially static one, presupposing a self-identical referent as its ground, to an unstable dynamic that participates in the relation it both engenders and undercuts. In place of the self-contained ground, the referent, there emerges a conflictual process in which something can "reveal" itself, step into the open only by at the same time withdrawing or obscuring that upon which it depends. Truth as *alētheia* must thus compose with a differentiation that is as inevitable as it is unstable and that is therefore highly contentious:

> Whenever and however this strife breaks out and occurs, the disputants, clearing and concealing [*Lichtung und Verbergung*], di-

verge. Thus the openness of disputed space is conquered [*erstritten*]. The openness of this opening, i.e. truth, can only be what it is, namely *this* openness, if and so long as it *installs* itself in its opening. Hence, there must always be a being in this opening, wherein openness takes its stand and its constancy. . . .

Truth happens only by opening a space of strife and play [*Streit- und Spielraum*] in which it installs itself [*sich einrichtet*]. Because truth is the countercurrent [*das Gegenwendige*] of clearing (*Lichtung*) and concealing [*Verbergung*], what is here called installation belongs to it. (OA, pp. 67–68)

In order for the general, but abstract movement of truth as *alētheia* to concretize itself—which means to *singularize* itself, to become *this* truth and not just truth in general—it must "install" itself, institute itself, set itself up (and down) in a particular place and in a particular manner: as *this particular being*. But what is so particular about installation is that it can not be understood in terms of the relation of part to whole. This, at least, is what its simultaneous "withdrawal"—in Heidegger's German, *Entzug*—seems to suggest, since all such emergence involves simultaneously a withdrawal,[4] every move a remove. The term that perhaps best designates the peculiar particularity of a part that is not just part of a whole is *singularity*. The singular is neither the particular nor the unique: rather, it is that which doesn't *fit in*, the *odd*, and as such, that which is never self-contained. We will return to this shortly.

For the moment, however, let us follow a bit further Heidegger's question of technics and its strange goings-on. Technics, he argues, should not be reduced to neutral instrumentality in the service of man. Rather, in communicating with truth as *alētheia*, it entails a mode of being that is prior even to knowledge and science, with which it is, however, associated from the Greeks on. This nonidentity of technics and knowledge is why the less idiomatic translation, "technics" is to be preferred to the more familiar "technology." For Heidegger, *Technik* is in many ways closer to *technique* than to technology, in the sense of a systematic organization and application of knowledge. Technics involves a practice, a way of being in the world that cannot be reduced to knowledge, however closely it is related to it.

Initially, as understood in ancient Greece, technics involved a process of revealing, of bringing forth that which on its own could not see the light (QT, p. 13). Modern technics, however, while still a mode of revealing and unsecuring, no longer consists primarily in a "bringing-forth" in the sense of *poiēsis*, but rather in a "driving out [*Herausfordern*]" (QT, p. 14) in the sense of extracting energy for subsequent storage. This extraction for storage in turn involves a redefinition of place and placing that is decisive in Heidegger's approach to this question. The following celebrated—or notorious—example well illustrates that redefinition:

> The hydroelectric plant is set in the current of the Rhine [*Rheinstrom*]. It sets up its water pressure, which then sets the turbines turning. This turning sets machines in motion whose thrust sets up electric current, for which the long-distance power station and its cable network have been ordered and set up. In the realm of the interlocking effects of this placing-on-order [*Bestellen*] of electrical energy, the Rhine current itself appears as something placed on order [*als etwas Bestelltes*]. (QT, p. 16)

Though phenomena of "nature" are generally held to contain their own principle of movement within themselves, the Rhine here is described as having become a mere occasion for the technical intervention of the hydroelectric plant. And this is not just any intervention: it is, Heidegger stresses, one that transforms place, *Stelle*, into the particular form of *placing* signified by the German verb *bestellen* and later by its nominative counterpart, *Bestand*. The word *bestellen*, the translator of this text, William Lovitt, notes, normally means "to order, command" (QT, p. 15 n.); he adds that it can also mean "to plough or till the earth," preparing it, setting it in order to be planted. What is crucial here is the subordination of the notion of place or placing, *Stelle* or *Stellen*, to a very particular kind of project, one that, according to Heidegger, increasingly characterizes modern thought and society: that of "regulating and securing" (QT, p. 16), which in turn implies, as its ultimate aim and criterion, the amassing of a *Bestand*, of a "standing reserve," as Lovitt translates. But *Bestand* is also the noun formed from *bestehen*, that which "stands" the test of time, as it were, by staying the same, being constant. Heidegger sums this up as follows:

> Everywhere [everything] is placed on order [*bestellt*], on constant standby [*auf der Stelle zur stelle ze stehen*], ready in place for the

further placing of orders [*für ein weiteres Bestellen*]. Whatever is thus placed on order has its own standing. We call it the *Bestand*, standing stock. This word here says more, and something more essential, than mere "reserve" [*Vorrat*]. . . . It designates nothing less than the manner in which everything approaches [*an-west*] that is affected by the [movement of] extracting-exacting revealing-unsecuring [*herausfordernden Entbergen*]. Whatever stands by, in the sense of standing-stock, no longer stands over against us as ob-ject [*Gegenstand*]. (QT, p. 17)

In short, the ascent of the *Bestand* is marked by the decline of the *Gegenstand*, the ob-ject. Modern technology is thus defined as the epoch of a certain subjectivity, which tolerates no separate objects but rather seeks to transform everything into the means of its own survival. "Regulation and securing" imply an organization of the world in which all being is turned into a means of *staying the same*, of *bestehen* as *Bestand*.

This defining tendency of modern technics culminates in what Heidegger calls, in German, the *Gestell*:

> *Gestell* is called the collecting of that setting and placing [*jenes Stellens*] that sets after humans, challenging them to reveal and unsecure the real in the manner of the placing of orders [*Bestellen*] as standing stock [*Bestand*]. *Gestell* is called the kind of revealing that prevails in the goings-on of modern technics but that itself is not at all technical. (QT, p. 20)

Gestell, which Lovitt translates as "enframing" and I have rendered as "emplacement," is not itself "technical" because what it defines is never simply identical with itself, self-same. Rather, it entails the effort to produce or secure self-containment, self-preservation, constancy, but under conditions that are irreducible to any univocal mode of being. Heidegger therefore introduces another term to indicate wherein the *Gestell*, and hence the goings-on of technics, can never be limited to the perpetuation of a *Bestand*. This term is, once again in German, *Geschick*, past participle of the verb *schicken*, which collects the modes of "sending" and thus constitutes "the essence of history as *Geschichte*." History, in this sense, involves not the fulfillment of a story or of a subject, but a process of sending and being sent. This means, quite simply, that everything that is, is what it is only by virtue of coming from somewhere else and of pointing elsewhere. Of course such a movement is anything but simple.

Normally, we would understand this movement, as we tend to do all movement, in the sense of *locomotion*: that is, as a change of place. Places are preassigned and stable, unmoved movers enabling movement to be construed as passage *from* one *to* the other. Movement thus construed presupposes a certain prior fixity of place. Already in *Being and Time*, however, Heidegger questions this model of locomotion as the sole paradigm of movement.[5] Instead of *Bewegung*, he calls for a rethinking of *Bewegtheit*, in the sense of *being moved*, or, if one takes care not to psychologize the word, of *e-motion*. A hint of this kind of being moved, in all of its conflictuality, can be seen in our oscillating translation of *Entbergung* as both "unsecuring" and "revealing." Such oscillation and uncertainty reflects the highly paradoxical redefinition of place going on in Heidegger's elaboration of the *Gestell*. On the one hand, modern technics relates places to a more general process of placing and replacing, of placing on order and reordering places. In this replacement, nothing is secure. All places become sites of "securing" and "controlling," and as such are made available and disposable. In this sense, the *Gestell* that for Heidegger defines the (ambivalent) essence of modern technics sets the stage for a highly contradictory and unstable attempt to establish stability. It entails the effort to secure positions by rendering places replaceable.

Even the most empirical, unreflected experience of the recent past furnishes ample evidence of the prescience of Heidegger's insights here: the obsession with "security," whether national, international, local, or personal, has not ceased to grow and dominate political discourse since the end of the Second World War.[6] And it has increasingly played itself out as a striving and struggle to make places disposable.

Nevertheless, it would be grossly inaccurate to suggest that Heidegger condemns purely and simply the goings-on of modern technics. Rather, he warns of the destructive consequences of allowing modern technology to become an end in itself. This would be tantamount to making "control and securing" (or, in current American military language, "command and control") the ultimate criterion by which world order is to be measured. To "command and control" means also to "search and destroy," which in turn means to locate and position: "global positioning" in the name of security. Such control and securing presupposes an ultimately self-present self or subject, to be maintained and preserved as it is. But insofar as it is also a *Geschick*, the *Gestell* of modern technics takes part in a movement that goes beyond the destructive complicity of total dislocation with total stability. That movement Heidegger seeks to articulate by retracing the usual use of the German noun *Wesen*, generally translated into English as "essence," to an earlier, more dynamic linguistic condition, that of *wesen* as verbal infinitive:

> It is from the verb *wesen* that the noun is derived. *Wesen* understood as a verb is the same as *währen* ["to last or endure"]. Already Socrates and Plato think the *Wesen* ["essence"] of something as the ongoing [*das Wesende*], in the sense of the *Währenden* ["enduring"]. But they think enduring as continuing [*Fortwährende*] (*aei on*). Enduring, however, they construe as that which maintains itself, staying the same [*das Bleibende*] in everything that occurs. This staying the same they in turn discover in appearing [*Aussehen*] (*eidos*, *idea*), for instance, in the idea "house."
>
> But it can never in any way be established that enduring is based solely in that which Plato [thinks] as the *idea*. . . . Instead of *Fortwähren*, "continuing," Goethe once used the word *Fortgewähren*, "granting further." (QT, p. 30)

It is striking how often Heidegger turns to the gerund as a way of moving the static noun toward the more dynamic verb. In so doing he accentuates the difference between a notion of "enduring" construed as staying the same, remaining oneself, as *fortwährend*, and a movement of granting through which other possibilities are given: *gewährend*.

Nowhere here does Heidegger actually specify just what such granting might consist in. But while never stating it as such, he nevertheless *says* it, or rather, *writes* it. And perhaps this is the only way that such granting can be adequately articulated, particularly if what it involves is more a matter of *how* than of *what*. In his *Introduction into Metaphysics*, Heidegger argues that the predominance of the copula, the *is*, in determining how the to-be has been thought in the West, is symptomatic of the way thinking has reduced being to the status of an entity or a property that can be predicated of an entity. Such privileging of the copula has in turn reflected the way in which time has been construed on the basis of the "now," understood as a self-contained moment of presence. As a historical alternative Heidegger refers to the Greek *enklysis*, the forerunner of our infinitive.[7] However, the German infinitive, when used as a noun, tends to overlap in English with the gerund. And in German Heidegger resorts to the gerund precisely when he seeks to reconcile the generality of the to-be with the singularity of its occurrence or event (*Ereignis*), as in the passage just quoted.[8] *Wesen*, he argues there, is misunderstood when capitalized as a noun. Instead, it must be understood above all as a verb, as an infinitive, *wesen*, and even more, as a gerund, *das Wesende*, which should therefore be translated, not as "what essences" (present indicative), but rather as something like "the ongoing," whereby the *tense* counts as much as—if not more than—the conceptual content of the word. In the same passage, Heidegger repeatedly uses the gerund to articulate the particular type of movement involved in granting, *das Gewährende* (or *Fortgewährende*), which he distinguishes from *das Bleibende*, literally, from "remaining—or staying—the same."

What is being articulated here is perhaps nothing other than the aporetical juncture of being (as *Sein*) with to-be (as *Seienden*): that is, what might be described as the *aporetical singularity of being*, which, Heidegger never tires of saying, is not to be understood as a general concept, a genre, under which beings are to be subsumed as species. Rather, what is involved is a process that is partially brought to a halt in singular beings, which in turn are never simply reducible to their present state. Two aspects of the gerund and the present participle allow them to articulate this notion of being. First, since they take place as a series of iterations, they are never simply in one place at one time. They can therefore be said to define a mode of *being present* that is never present *to itself*. In repeating that self, the present participle or gerund displaces it, dislocates it, shifts it away from wherever it has been, moves it *fort*, while at the same time fixing it *da*. This ambivalent presentation results in the second trait, which consists in the way the presence of the present participle is structurally split, *defined by simultaneity with its utterance or articulation*. This fold *creases* presence rather than simply increasing it.

Granting as sending, *Schicken*, and as destined, *Geschick*, would thus *con*-sist in the disjunctive reiterations of a series that never comes full-circle, the "con-" of the prefix literally marking out the irreducible *relation to*, or *being with* that Jean-Luc Nancy has suggested is the irreducible character trait of being as such. Another possible "translation" that would attempt to articulate this disjunctive quality of being would be that alluded to above as "parting *with*." But insofar as such being or parting with implies a constitutive relation to something else that can never be made fully available as a *Bestand*, as standing stock, "with" here signifies "without" as much or more than "within."[9] The "with" turns the self inside-out, exposing it to the other: separation as relation.

But to speak simply of such granting as the creasing or splitting of an interiority, exposing the irreducible relationality of all immanence, is to remain confined by a perspective still determined by the horizon of what it seeks to supplant: by the *Bestand* of the standing stock and, hence, by the subject. What Heidegger, not without a certain religious pathos, describes as the "saving power" (QT, p. 33) of the *Gestell* suggests an alternative to such subjectivity: not the individual self is saved, but rather possibilities of taking place that would no longer be those of a "subject." To discover how Heidegger construes those possibilities, we need only recall the key phrase in the passage cited earlier regarding *alētheia*: "The openness of this opening [*Offenen*], i.e. truth, can only be what it is, namely *this* openness, if and so long as it *installs* itself [*sich einrichtet*] in its opening [*in ihr Offenes*]" (OA, p. 67).

Truth does not simply exist in general: it must "install" itself "in its opening" as "*this* openness." The decisive question here is how such a singular process of installation—what Heidegger calls *sich einrichten*—the installation or institution of truth in and as the openness of a certain here and now—is to be construed. "The Origin of the Work of Art," from which this passage is taken, provides an initial response. Such installation in the open, understood as the singularization of being, takes place in and with the work of art or, rather, with a certain conception of the work of art. It is the work understood, not in the sense of classical aesthetics, as a harmonious resolution of contraries in a well-formed and meaningful whole, but rather in the more conflictual sense of a *Streit*- and *Spielraum*, an arena of strife, conflict, but also play. This place is singular, which means situated, localized, but not closed or complete. The work is structured by what Heidegger calls the *Riß*, the tear or break. It is a tear that does not simply pull apart but *in separating* also joins. (Heidegger plays here on a series of German words with the common root *Riß*: *Grundriß*, *Aufriß*, *Umriß*, and, above all, *zusammenreißen*, literally, "tearing together," though used in German as a synonym for "pulling oneself together," OA, p. 71.)

The work of art, then, appears as a singular space structured by a sundering, by a *Riß* that joins what it separates through *Fugen*, through joints and articulations. And yet Heidegger is not satisfied with this account. Some twenty-five years later, in 1960, he returns to this text, originally published in 1936, in order to add a series of notes and comments. One of these marks out the limits beyond which his initial discussion of the work, in his retrospective view, could not go:

> In referring to the self-installing of openness in the open, think-
> ing touches a region that cannot be explicated any further here.
> It should be noted only that, if the essence of the uncon-
> cealedness of [the singular] being [*des Seienden*] in any way be-
> longs to the to be itself (cf. *Being and Time*, §44), then the latter
> allows the play-room [*Spielraum*] of openness (the clearing of the
> there) to happen and introduces it as *such*, wherein each being
> [*Seiende*] emerges [*aufgeht*] in its way. (OA, p. 68)

How is the emergence of singular being to be construed? Each emerges "in its way," which presumably is not simply the way of the others. Such emergence is described here as that of a certain openness installing itself in the open. Through such "self-installation" the to be is put into play, but with reference to a certain space or place—the German word *Raum*, cognate to English *room*, designates both. Space converges with place as "room," in particular, as the "play-room" of "beings." The question thus shifts to this "play-room": how is it to be thought?

In "The Origin of the Work of Art," to which Heidegger returns, implicitly, at the end of his quest after technics, this room is still construed as that of a *work*. However riven, sundered, and conflictual, the notion of work still determines the horizon of the instantiation of being in this text. To be sure, it is no longer the work of classical aesthetics, a work that would be meaningfully self-contained; rather, it is a work repeatedly designated as a *Spielraum*, a play-room, but also—lest we be overtaken by the Schillerian overtones of this term—a stage of conflict and dispute. Heidegger accordingly conceives of the "work" as that which defines itself through the *Anstoß* (impulse) it provides (OA, p. 73): through its "manifold jolting" (*dieses vielfältige Stoßen,*" OA, p. 75), which *moves* the beholder, reader, or listener elsewhere.

The medium in which this jolting takes place is thus one of alteration, displacement, dislocation. But insofar as this space is defined by Heidegger as "the setting to work of truth," the specific manner in which truth sets itself (in)to (the) work as *this* truth, *this* work—the question of its *Einrichtung* as a *singular installation*, remains obscure.

In his 1960 addendum, Heidegger takes up this obscurity in two remarks. First, he notes that the question points toward the relation of language to poetry, which in turn involves "the interrelatedness [*Zusammengehörigkeit*] of the to be and saga [*Sage:* also, "saying"]" (OA, p. 100). Having suggested the direction in which the question of installation must be pursued, he then goes on, in a second and related remark, to underscore "the inescapable state of emergency" that afflicts both reader and author with regard to this text, and not just this text alone. The difficulty for the reader consists in the impossibility of relating the explicit propositions of the text to the "silent sources of that which has yet to be thought [*des zu-Denkenden*]," whereas the author remains constrained, "on the various steps of his way, to speak in whatever language is most favorable at the time" (OA, p. 101).

Although such an acknowledgment appears on the one hand to be a truism—every discourse depends to some extent on the language available "at the time of" its enunciation—the remark becomes less banal, although no less ominous, when related to the particular time of "The Origin of the Work of Art." In this context, the statement can be taken to refer specifically to Heidegger's conjuration in the 1936 essay of a "historical people" as providing the decisive framework within which the "setting to work of truth" must be construed. The essay does not discuss just how this notion of "historical people" is to be thought *ontologically*. But however much it undoubtedly speaks the "language . . . most favorable at the time" of its writing, *in the place it was written*, Heidegger's invocation of a "historical people" shows how little able he was, in "The Origin of the Work of Art," to draw practical consequences from the analysis of the copula and present indicative delivered one year previously, in 1935, in the lectures that were to form the basis for the *Introduction into Metaphysics*. His valorization of the "people" and its relation to the "earth," for instance, depends on the unquestioned ontological value of the present indicative and of its auxiliary, the past perfect, as the following passage clearly demonstrates:

> The poeticizing cast [*Entwurf*] of truth that sets itself to work as figure [*Gestalt*] is never executed out of the void and indeterminate. Rather, in the work truth is cast toward the coming preservers [*den kommenden Bewahrenden*], i.e. toward an historical humanity [*geschichtlichen Menschentum*]. . . . What is cast (in this way) is never arbitrarily attributed. The truly poeticizing project [*dichtenden Entwurf*] is the opening of that wherein "to-be-there-and-then" [*Dasein*] as historical is already cast. This is the earth and for a historical people its earth, the self-enclosing ground upon which it reposes *with everything that it*, still concealed from itself, *already is*. (OA, pp. 86–87)

The present participle and gerund are inscribed here three times: as "the *poeticizing* cast," as "the *coming* preservers," and as "the truly *poeticizing* project." With the partial exception of the second occurrence, however, they are subordinated in each instance to the telos of a noun ("project," "figure," "historical humanity") that is grounded in the fact that it "already *is*," which is to say, in the *parousia* of the present indicative, of the *now* that "is." The notion of "people" is thus the marker of a *specification* of being based on this temporality, and hence, as a generic species, a "historical humanity." "Humanity"—*Menschentum*—is a word that claims to establish utter continuity between the general and the specific, the genre and the species, a continuity that bares its imperial teeth, as it were, whenever it is extended, as here, to the determination of a particular "people."

Notwithstanding, what Heidegger cannot *think* or *say* in this text he nevertheless *inscribes* in it, precisely where he seeks to determine its limits and hence the task for thinking that derives from them. The task of thinking must be directed at the *zu-Denkenden*, using the gerund to define an obligation of the present toward the future (a temporal structure that, to be sure, is implied in all obligation). The task or obligation thus described, however, cannot be construed as the property of any *work*, however open or riven it may be. In the passages previously cited, which discussed the character of the work as open and openness, *Offene* and *Offenheit*, the present participle, gerund, or its derivatives—for instance, the verbal noun *Öffnung*, "opening," were nowhere to be found.

Can we conclude from this that the task of thinking what Heidegger refers to as the *installation of being* in and as the conflictual *Streit-* and *Spielraum* of beings exceeds the limits set out in "The Origin of the Work of Art," particularly where those limits are construed in terms of the work as *Gestalt?*[10] And that this excess leads necessarily from *Gestalt* to *Gestell* and beyond, to their *Geschick?* The directions in which such questions point suggest that the "salvation" of technics cannot be sought simply in the "work," as riven *Gestalt*, but that both work of art and technics must be thought differently, in terms of *destination*.

An Uneven Playing Field

In his 1936 essay, Heidegger already characterizes *technē* as that which "brings the on-going [*Anwesenden*, the present] as *one such* [als ein solches, note the indefinite/singular article] *out* of concealment *into* the unconcealment of its appearing [*seines Aussehens*]." In a text written the same year, but in a different place and for a very different audience, Walter Benjamin also addressed the singular movement of technics, approaching it, however, from what would appear, at first sight at least, to be an entirely unrelated perspective. In a lecture entitled "The Author as Producer," Benjamin described the "venerable chance and resource of theater as that of *exposing the present* [die Exponierung des Anwesenden]."[11] To be sure, the Heidegger of 1936 had already taken precautions to exclude any such theatrical misreading of his notion of technics and its relation to the *Spielraum* of the to be as openness and clearing (*Lichtung*). Such a proleptic measure was doubtless felt to be necessary by Heidegger, given the emphasis he had placed on the tendency of all truth to dissimulate its own dissimulation. Hence the need for the following disclaimer: "the open place in the midst of being(s) [*des Seienden*], the clearing, is never a rigid stage with constantly raised curtain, upon which the play of being(s) plays itself out" (OA, p. 58).

But what if the stage is not "rigid" and the curtain not constantly "raised"? Would a less "rigid stage" be more appropriate for thinking the process by which being, as Heidegger seeks to understand it, strives to install itself—*sich einzurichten*—as "this" being? It is striking, at any rate, that the same German word imposes itself upon Benjamin in a text written about the same time, which we discussed in the previous chapter. In this passage, Benjamin argues that in contemporary theater the stage is no longer separated from the audience by the "chasm" of the orchestra pit. Although the stage is still distinct from that of the audience, "still elevated," it functions more as a "podium" than as a sacred space. Benjamin concludes: "On this podium theatergoers must find their place [*sich einzurichten*]."[12]

The German verb used by Benjamin here is significantly difficult to render into English. *Sich einrichten* means to set oneself up in relation to an already existing, structured place into which one has just moved. It signifies to "take one's place" or "make oneself at home," both colloquial equivalents of the German phrase. And yet, in these idiomatic equivalences something disappears: the relation to a place where one has not been before—another place, an *elsewhere*—is decisive in determining the place of the self. The self is never therefore simply "at home" on a podium, or on a stage. For a stage is not a house, not even a House of Being.

Perhaps the stage can come to stand for a place in which one is always already placed, without ever being fully at home or definitively positioned. The place would then be the site of a *Gestell*, a "being-placed" or emplacement that is never simply *gestellt*, placed once and for all. But in German, *gestellt* also means "set up" in the sense of being posed, feigned, or contrived. This is also part of what happens on stage. However, as a "podium," a stage reveals additional qualities: above all, perhaps, it is a place of address. In being raised above the horizontal, it is positioned to appeal to others. This is true of stages in general, but to the extent that a stage is also a podium its relation to its addressees has become more emphatic. It becomes a site from which others are not just addressed, but enjoined. In the presence of a podium, spectators are expected to do more than just observe.

The relation of audience to podium is thus precisely not that of what today would be called a "level playing field": not just because, as already noted, the podium is elevated, but because the game being played confronts the living with the dead, if we take Benjamin's figure literally. What would it mean, however, to take it in this sense? Do the actors on the podium-stage announce what Heidegger calls the "coming preservers" or what Benjamin some ten years earlier had called "the mortification of works"?[13] A podium, on which political harangues as well as discussions can take place, appears here as a site where the living confront the dead. Whatever else Benjamin's notion of *Einrichtung* may entail, it refers to the relation of the living to the dead, of the present to the past—and hence also of both to the future.

In the context in which the notion of stage as podium is introduced, it would be natural to assume that Benjamin draws the term from Brecht's writing on Epic Theater. There are reasons to doubt this, however. The stage as podium occurs in a very different context, involving another writer with whom Benjamin was concerned at the time he was writing on Brecht. The podium turns up in a chapter from Kafka's unfinished first novel, formerly known as *Amerika* and in recent years retranslated, more accurately, as *The Man Who Disappeared*.[14] The title *Amerika* was the product of Kafka's friend and literary executor, Max Brod, but the notes in Kafka's journals show that he had a very different title in mind: *Der Verschollene*.[15] Someone who is *verschollen* has dropped not so much out of sight as out of earshot: *schellen* means to resound, resonate, reverberate. The *Verschollener* is one from whom nothing has been heard for a long time, and of whom every trace has been lost. This is the title that Kafka selected for his first novel. One chapter in this unfinished text figures prominently in Benjamin's essay on Kafka, to which I will now turn, in the hope of learning something more about the singular installation that appears to be missing, almost without a trace, from Heidegger's elaboration of the *Gestell*, but to which his interpretation of modern technics nevertheless persistently points.

Backdrop

Heidegger is of course hardly the first philosopher to regard theater with suspicion. Such an attitude is as old as the reduction of being to beings, of *Sein zum Seienden*, which Heidegger retraces at least as far back as Plato and Socrates. All the more reason, therefore, for him to have hesitated before endorsing the condemnation of the "stage" that is at the core of the philosophical mistrust of theatricality. To be sure, the Platonic rejection of theatricality has to do not with the "rigidity" of that stage, but with its mobility. But Heidegger, despite his strictures against a metaphysics that valorizes identity in terms of its ability to be *fortwährend* rather than *gewährend*, shares this traditional mistrust of theater, however "theatrical" his writing may be in its elaboration of *alētheia* as a revelation that dissimulates its own disguises.

Benjamin, who was not a philosopher nor even a "thinker" in the Heideggerian sense, does not share this mistrust.[16] To be sure, he is less concerned with "theater" in the traditional sense than with a *theatricality* that need not be limited to the stage. He finds it in Brecht's Epic Theater, but also—to the discomfort of Brecht—in the writings of Kafka.[17] His essay on Kafka was written in 1934, ten years after the writer's death, one year after the Nazis came to power, two years before "The Origin of the Work of Art." In the center of Benjamin's interpretation is an attempt to distinguish Kafka from the role of prophet and religious founder that early commentators had ascribed to him. Against this notion Benjamin brings forward two arguments. "Kafka was a parabolist, not a founder of religions" is the first (p. 424). His parables invite citation, recitation, and discussion, but *Lehre*—the lesson, doctrine, teaching, or moral of the story—"is not there; at most all we can say is that this or that alludes to it." In the absence of an established and authoritative set of values—whose historical emergence Benjamin had retraced in his study of the German mourning play as a reaction to the radical antinomianism of the Reformation— "organization" becomes an end in itself. Benjamin varies the famous phrase of Napoleon in his conversation with Goethe to read "organization is destiny," arguing that "the organization of life and of work in human community" (p. 420) gains in importance in proportion to the lack of a transcendent justification. Since this organization lacks legitimacy, however, it remains opaque, impenetrable, something to be surmised and alluded to, the object of parables rather than the basis of doctrine.[18] In Kafka's writings, Benjamin argues, the model of such an unavoidable but opaque organization of everyday life is not the tribunal or the castle but *theater*. A very special kind of theater, however: one that is difficult to characterize or situate. Benjamin cites and then comments upon a passage toward the end of *The Trial*:

> "K. turns suddenly to the two men in top hats, who pick him up, and asks: 'In what theater do you act?' 'Theater?' asked one of the men, looking to the other for help, the muscle in the corner of his mouth twitching. The other gestured like a mute struggling with a resistant organism." They do not answer the question but everything suggests that it has had its effect on them. (p. 423)

The ubiquity of the theatrical, if not of theater, is thus the result of the absence of clear-cut authority, structure, or meaning. But if it is thus fairly easy for *theatricality*, an abstraction, to crop up everywhere, it is all the more striking when something similar occurs with theater itself. This seems to occur with the "Natural Theater of Oklahoma," at least in Benjamin's reading of it:

> Kafka's world is a world-theater. In it man is from the start [*vom Haus aus*] on stage. And the crucial test is that everyone is placed [*eingestellt*] in the Natural Theater of Oklahoma. As to the criteria used in determining acceptance [*Aufnahme*], they are impossible to decipher. Aptitude for acting, which is what one might think of first, apparently plays absolutely no role at all. This can be expressed in another way: nothing is demanded of the applicants other than to play themselves. That they seriously could *be* what they assert they are is excluded from the realm of possibility. (pp. 422–23)

With the extension of the theater to the "world," the notion of "role" also assumes a different significance: traditional acting, Benjamin asserts, plays "absolutely no role" in determining the place, or role, to be assigned to the "applicants." They will be asked merely to "play themselves." But what they assert themselves to *be* is in principle "excluded from the realm of possibility." In short, what is possible has nothing to do with what the applicants initially *assert* that they *actually are* or would like to be. It has more to do with what they have been or what they *say* they have done (whether true or not). This imparts a thoroughly ambiguous quality to the process through which the Theater of Oklahoma filters its applicants, an ambiguity, as we will see, that is endemic both to theatricality in general and to this text in particular. Precisely this ambiguity prevents the novel from being finished. Kafka will break off work on it after he has written this chapter. He will write one more page of the chapter that was to follow and then stop, never to resume again. Such incompleteness is perhaps the novel's most revealing trait. It marks the interruption of the narrative drive toward closure and signals the emergence of a theatricality that excludes the kinds of meaningful conclusion often associated with works of art.[19] If, as Kafka's novel suggests, the theatrical suspension of narrative progression may well be involved in all *Einrichtung*, this could explain why Heidegger was unable to give a fuller account of it in "The Origin of the Work of Art."

It may even be possible to point toward exactly the area that eluded Heidegger or, rather, that he acknowledged, but only to reject. In an appendix to "The Origin of the Work of Art" written in 1960, Heidegger retrospectively warns against a possible misunderstanding of his use of the word *Einrichtung*:

> Once again we must avoid taking *einrichten*—"installing"—in the modern sense and understanding it according to the lecture on Technics, as "organizing" and as "finishing off" ["*organisieren und fertigmachen*"]. Rather "installing" thinks the "trait that draws [*Zug*] truth toward the work," . . . how truth, in the midst of being(s), itself being work-like, comes into being [*inmitten des Seienden, selber werkhaft seiend, seiend werde*]. (OA, p. 98)

Two points need to be clarified in this passage, at least. First, Heidegger rejects the equation of "installing" with "organizing"—but only by assimilating "organizing" to what he calls *fertigmachen*, "finishing off." In German the phrase *fertigmachen* has the colloquial meaning of "terminating" in the sense of "doing in" or "away with" a person or a thing. The notion of "organizing" is thus equated here, not just with closure or completion, but also with the more sinister sense of "finishing off." As we will see, "organization" has a similar connotation in Kafka. But in *The Man Who Disappeared* it remains just that: a connotation, one possibility among others to be meditated, not simply to be accepted or rejected. For Kafka, "organizing" can also signify "finishing off," but this remains one possibility among others. Indeed, it is perhaps just to keep this possibility in suspense *qua possibility* that the novel itself remained unfinished. The conclusion of *Der Verschollene* is itself *verschollen*, like an echo that has faded into inaudibility. The German word *verschollen* carries with it a sense of uncertainty: someone has not been heard from for a long time but *might* conceivably turn up again, unexpectedly. The person has "gone missing" without a trace. But precisely because of the lack of traces, the person's final destiny is still in doubt.

Second, installation is not "organization" because it is "drawn by truth toward the work." Installation is in a "work-like" way: *werkhaft seiend*. The "work" is the way installation installs itself, singularizes itself, a process that is linguistically marked by the passage from the generality of the gerund as (capitalized) noun (*Seienden*), to the singularity of the present participle as adjective (*seiend*): "daß die Wahrheit inmitten des Seienden, *selber werkhaft seiend, seiend werde.*" The pull of truth draws "installation" toward being that itself is "worklike." The relative determinacy and fixity of being a work, however, do not exhaust the possibilities implied by a present participle that can never be entirely delimited or defined. Hence, the present participle is associated, not with entities or beings, but with a *Zug*, a trait that pulls or draws the work *away* from wherever it has been.[20] Such a *Zug* retains its meaning of a *train* or a *way* while overdetermining it. A train is usually expected to move *between* set points of departure and arrival. A train that pulls away, however, moves inevitably toward an uncertain destination, like the train ostensibly taking the newly accepted applicants to Oklahoma. The departure of this train precipitously ends the chapter on the Theater of Oklahoma and ushers in the following one, which, however, soon breaks off with a shudder, the wind literally chilling the faces of the passengers as they watch the world outside fly by. Kafka could write only one page before stopping, suspending this voyage and leaving his theater members stranded, as it were, forever on their way: *unterwegs*, as Heidegger might say; or more aptly, with Derrida, *en train*. In short, the voyagers in the train will never arrive at their destination, but they will not remain immobilized either, as the chain or train leading from Kafka to Heidegger, Benjamin, Beckett, Derrida, and elsewhere suggests. If, in Heidegger's language, the train could be described as a figure of *Geschick*, Derrida's notion of *arrivant* once again seems even more apt. Given that it designates a movement that must be conceived as anterior to the distinction between "person" and "thing,"[21] it describes a movement that is discontinuously "present," rather than simply past. The train, precisely by virtue of the suspension of its progress, can develop a different type of movement, even if it will never "arrive" at its destination.

Instead of leading toward a conclusion or fulfillment, Kafka's theater is thus stranded in what appears to be an unbridgeable gap between intention and goal, the space of a *Zug*, a train ride going nowhere or at least never arriving.[22] Such voyages proliferate in Kafka's writings, and Benjamin was most attentive to them. One instance is the voyage to "The Next Village," the title of a text by Kafka that is brief enough to quote in its entirety:

My Grandfather used to say, "Life is astonishingly short. Now in my memory it seems so foreshortened that, for instance, I can barely grasp how a young person can decide to ride to the next village without fearing that—even apart from unfortunate accidents—the span of a normal, happily passing life will never suffice for such a trip."[23]

But the possibility that every voyage, however long or brief, can be cut short by the potential brevity of human life makes up only one side of the coin. Another, more seductive face finds expression in the short text "The Wish to Become an Indian":

If in spite of everything one could be an Indian, always ready, and on a racing horse, askance in the air, trembling again and again over the quivering earth [*immer wieder kurz erzitterte über dem zitternden Boden*], until one shed one's spurs, for there were no spurs, threw away the reins, for there were no reins, and scarcely saw the country in front as smoothly mowed heaths, with the horse's mane and head already gone.[24]

The suspension of the journey as a change of place, as locomotion, as goal directed and defined, allows for another kind of movement to deploy other, less linear, no longer couched in the present indicative or the past participle, but in the iterability of the present participle: the "trembling again and again" of the earth that announces its own disappearance. Even the ground under the hoof beats disappears as the horse races ahead.

As with Heidegger, then, the texts of Kafka describe a movement that exceeds every determinate being as presence, as something that is, and in its stead makes room for a movement that is more like a trembling than a change of place.[25] Another such instance, cited by Benjamin from Kafka's long fragment "The Building of the Great Wall of China," is also marked by the use of the gerund: "To hammer a table together with painstaking exactitude and skill and at the same time do nothing, yet not so that one could say, 'for him hammering is nothing,' but rather 'for him hammering is real hammering and at the same time nothing,' which would make the hammering even bolder, more determined, more real and, if you like, more insane."[26]

Cut off from its instrumental, productive purpose, "hammering" becomes "real hammering and at the same time nothing": "bolder," but also "more insane." When the elusive iterability of the present participle lays claim, as gerund, to a certain substantiality, it becomes insanely audacious because it asserts a "reality" that is both immediately present yet impossible to define or delimit. Benjamin compares such "madness" to two figures or motifs in Kafka's writings: first, to students who study without any visible purpose; second, to actors. Of the students, he notes: "Perhaps these studies are (worth) nothing. But if so, they are close to that nothing that is required for anything to be useful—namely, the Tao" (p. 435). In the actors, even more than the students, however, Benjamin finds the true practitioners of an activity that, cut off from its goal and meaning, touches on the unreal reality of the present participle. In English, precisely this "unreal reality" distinguishes "acting" from "action" or "act."[27] An "acting" president, for instance, is one who is only temporarily invested with the office he "holds": he is merely a replacement or a surrogate.[28]

What distinguishes "acting" from action? Without ever making this distinction explicitly, Benjamin suggests that it is dependence upon a *script*: "Actors have to be instantaneously ready for their cue. And they resemble the assiduous (artisans and students) in other ways as well. For them 'hammering is real hammering and simultaneously also nothing'—namely, when it is contained in their role. They study their parts, and if they were to forget a word or gesture, they would be bad actors" (p. 435).[29]

Kafka's writing, according to Benjamin, is "theatrical" above all in the sense of suspending, through what Benjamin calls *gesture*, the goal-directed movement of meaning and, with it, of meaningful action— for instance, the plot, which is generally associated with theater as well as with narrative. He therefore tends to equate "theater" with "gesture." And *gesture*, as he uses it, is excluded from the work of art as traditionally understood. Why? Because gesture involves suspending and opening the closure required to delineate the integrity of the work. What the *Riß* is for Heidegger, gesture is for Benjamin. But the consequences are different, as the following passage suggests:

When Max Brod says, "The world was unfathomable [*unabsehbar*] in what for him [Kafka] were its most important facts," the most unfathomable of all was surely gesture. Each one is a process, indeed, one can say, a drama in and of itself. The stage on which this drama plays itself out is the world theater, whose background represents the sky. This sky is only a backdrop, however; to search for its proper law would be equivalent to hanging the painted stage backdrop in an art gallery, framed. Behind every gesture Kafka—like El Greco—tears open the sky; but . . . it is the gesture that remains decisive, at the center of what is going on. (p. 419)[30]

What marks the theatricality of the gesture, as here described, apart from the traditional work of art is the status of the *frame*. The work of art, as understood by traditional aesthetics, is self-contained and meaningful, "framed" in a space designed to make it visible. Its frame and site are thereby taken for granted, allowing the beholder to ignore the singular position in which it is displayed. Such indifference to place is materialized in the museum or, more commercially, the art gallery, where by virtue of this indifference the work is predisposed to become an object of speculation. Kafka's world, by contrast, is theatrical insofar as it is "framed," not by a sky or heaven, but by a painted backdrop, which is to say, by an artifact that is part of the scene rather than just its delimiter. The "stage backdrop" is a function precisely of its relation to the stage and the audience. This *relativity of place* and of *placement* distinguishes the stage, as a theatrical site, from the Aristotelian tradition that construes place as an "unmoved mover," providing the stable condition of movable bodies.[31] The stage is never separable from *staging*. And this is why the theatricality of theater involves more than just acting.

Strangely enough, Benjamin seems to forget or overlook this in his discussion of the "Theater of Oklahoma." That is all the more surprising because, unlike Heidegger, he is, as we have seen, willing to acknowledge the importance of "organization" as "destiny." But in his discussion of the theater in *Der Verschollene*, this aspect is missing.

This is all the more reason, however, to turn to Kafka's text. As we will see, the transformation of the stage into a "podium" is the effect, not just of theater in general, but of a very special kind of theater: a theater that is also, and perhaps above all, an *organization*.

Theater as Destiny

The novel begins with a scene of arrival:

As seventeen-year-old Karl Rossmann—whom his parents had sent to America because he had been seduced by a maid, who had had a child by him—entered New York harbor on a ship moving at considerably reduced speed, he saw the Goddess of Liberty, whom he had been observing for quite some time, as though in suddenly intensified sunlight. Her arm with the sword seemed to jut upward in the fresh wind.

"So high," he said to himself and, without thinking really about leaving, he was pushed up against the railing by the ever-swelling crowd of porters passing him by [*an ihm vorüberzogen*].

A young man, with whom he had made slight acquaintance during the journey, said in passing, "Don't you want to leave?" "Sure, I'm done [*Ich bin doch fertig*]," replied Karl, smiling.[32]

Karl's coming to America is hardly the result of a spontaneous decision: seduced by the maid, sent away by his parents, pushed off the boat by the crowd of porters and passengers, he is, in German, *fertig*, literally, "finished"; idiomatically, ready for anything. But if he is "done," Karl also hesitates to leave the ship, perhaps in part because of the hectic tempo of the new world into which he is arriving. It is a place of sudden, surprising changes. Unobtrusive details cast a strange light on the scene. The boat carrying Karl is described as moving "at considerably reduced speed" as it enters the harbor, almost as though it, too, hesitates to reach its final destination. And the Statue of Liberty, which here becomes a "Goddess," does not simply light the way with a torch. Rather, she holds up a more equivocal implement, a sword, which "seem[s] to jut upward" in the wind. Instead of showing the way, this armed Goddess is bathed in what *appears* as a "sudden" burst of sunlight. Even the sun does not shine constantly in this harbor. Small wonder that Karl hesitates to leave the ship. What awaits him is not just promise and light, but the spectacle of a sword jutting into the sky, equivocal in its significance: freedom, justice, vengeance? A Last Judgment?

This last idea returns in the chapter that is of particular interest here, which begins:

At a street-corner Karl saw a poster that read as follows: "The Oklahoma Theater is recruiting personnel today at the Clayton Racetrack from 6 A.M. until midnight! The great Oklahoma Theater is calling you! If you miss this chance, you miss out forever! If you think of your future, you're one of us! Everyone is welcome! If you want to be an artist, join us! Our theater can use everyone—everyone in his place! If you decide to join us, we congratulate you here and now! But hurry up and don't miss the midnight deadline! At twelve o'clock sharp everything closes for good! Accursed be all, who do not have faith! Off to Clayton!' (p. 271)

The great Theater of Oklahoma may be a World Theater—in fact as his friend, Fanny, will inform him, Karl soon learns that "it's the biggest theater in the world," even though she herself has yet to see it and in the meanwhile must trust "some of my colleagues, who were already in Oklahoma" and who "say that it is almost without limit" (p. 276). But limitless or not, this theater, as Karl is to find out, is not just a stage, a theater, a company of actors, but above all, a *company* tout court, a business, and a big one at that. The Theater of Oklahoma is a global enterprise, at the very least. As already noted, it is curious that Benjamin, who in contrast to Heidegger is generally not averse to considering the socio-economic aspects of institutions and installations, and who acknowledges that for Kafka "organization is destiny," nevertheless ignores or passes over in silence this aspect of the theater, so evident in the text. To be sure, the Theater of Oklahoma is no ordinary business. It appears to overlap with other social institutions, above all church and family, because it promises that in it everyone can and will find his place. And it threatens that those who do not heed its call will be "cursed" forever.

At the same time, since this theater is *also* a business enterprise, its promises (if not its threats) are regarded with suspicion and skepticism by those who read the poster. Karl, after recounting the text of the poster, goes on to interpret the lack of enthusiasm it elicits:

> A good many people stood in front of the poster, but it did not seem to meet with much approval. There were so many posters, no one believed posters any more. And this particular poster was even more implausible than posters usually tend to be. Above all, it had one great defect: there was not a word in it about payment. Had it been even in the slightest worth mentioning, the poster would certainly have included it; it wouldn't have forgotten the most tempting thing of all. No one cared about becoming an artist, but everyone wanted to be paid for his work. (p. 271)

One is reminded of certain official political discourses today that exalt full employment, but forget to mention the conditions under which such employment is to be had. Although Karl does not dwell on this point, the fact that the poster makes no mention of payment casts a shadow over everything that is to come, opening its evangelical promises to endless doubt.

The poster can ignore "the most tempting thing of all"—salary—because it has something even more tempting, indeed irresistible, to offer:

> For Karl, however, the poster contained, in spite of everything, a great temptation. "Everyone is welcome," it stated. Everyone, meaning also Karl. Everything he had done before would be forgotten, no one would reproach him for it. . . . He asked for nothing more. He wanted finally to find how to begin a decent career and perhaps here it was. Even if all the great promises on the poster turned out to be a lie, even if the great Oklahoma Theater turned out to be a traveling circus, it was ready to hire people and that was sufficient! Karl didn't read the poster a second time, but only the part that announced, "Everyone is welcome!" (p. 272)

Far from home, family, and the country of his birth, lost in the immensity and cruelty of "America," Karl yearns for a place that will take him in and let him stay, a kind of second home. What he finds, however, is the Theater of Oklahoma.

What sort of a theater is it? We will never really find out, not even whether it is a theater at all. We will never learn whether it can keep its promises; none of that will be settled in this text. Like so many of Kafka's other figures, Karl Rossmann will remain on the fringes of this "theater." On the fringe he will, however, encounter certain aspects of theater and of theatricality that are often omitted from more explicit treatments, even from texts, such as Benjamin's, which are concerned with the distinctive transformation of theater in the current age, including its technical and institutional alterations.

Before we get to this strange theater—if we ever really arrive there—it may be helpful to underscore the ways in which the Theater of Oklahoma anticipates Heidegger's analysis of technics as *Gestell*, *Geschick*, and installation. This theater appeals to those who have no "position," who are unemployed, which in German can also be designated as being "placeless," *stellungslos* (p. 283). Such persons are thus *Stellungssuchende*, a word that occurs several times in the chapter (pp. 274, 287). This theater, as an organization and, more specifically, as an *Unternehmen*, a business enterprise, is in the business, among other things, of offering "places," "posts," "positions"—*Stellenangebote*, which even today is the title of the "job offers" found in classified ads of German-language newspapers. As an enterprise, this theater is in the business of recruiting personnel. Unlike today's enterprises, except perhaps in certain sectors, this one seems unlimited in its ability to hire, place, and position. Karl remains understandably skeptical as he mulls over whether or not to spend a major part of his dwindling cash reserves to buy a ticket to Clayton: "According to the poster the number of people to be recruited [*die Zahl der Aufzunehmenden*] was unlimited, but this is how all such job offers [*Stellenangebote*] were always formulated. Karl realized that he either had to renounce the position on the spot [*auf die Stelle*] or take the trip" (p. 272).

Here and throughout the chapter, we encounter yet another characteristic of Heidegger's account of technics: the demand for instantaneous and ubiquitous availability, *Bestellbarkeit*. Candidates for the Theater of Oklahoma must be on constant call, long before pagers and mobile phones provided the technology to reconcile total availability with total mobility. In order to qualify for a position in the Theater of Oklahoma, readiness is all: one must be ready, here and now, *auf die Stelle*, to drop everything and respond to the call. One may have doubts, but there can be no hesitation to *believe*. Otherwise, one will not merely miss out: one will be cursed and damned for all eternity.

For there will be no second chance. The irreversibility of time and the brevity of human life, which make every voyage, even one to the next village, such an unlikely undertaking, exacerbate the hope of ever finding a safe haven where one can *stay* and survive as one and the same (*Fortwähren*). "Accursed be all who do not have faith!" fulminates the poster, which otherwise holds out the hope of a glowing future: Be saved or be damned. Damned are the unbelievers, those who do not have faith, do not give and take credit, for they will miss out, once and for all, and find no place, no job, no post. This rhetoric of intimidation and seduction resounds today in the murmured "messages" of all commercial media: "Stay with us, we'll be right back . . .

after the break." "If you think of your future, you're one of us!" proclaims the poster, implying that if you don't think of your future, your future will nevertheless think of you.

Thus, even though "nobody believed posters any more," Karl nevertheless risks his dwindling savings on a subway ticket to Clayton. What greets him upon his arrival, as he reemerges out of the depths, is, first of all, a deafening din: the wild cacophony of "many trumpets" blown without any regard for one another, "ruthlessly," *rücksichtslos*.[33] Strangely, however, "this did not bother Karl, rather it confirmed that the Theater of Oklahoma was a major enterprise" (p. 272). But noise is not all he encounters as he comes up out of the subway station. What strikes his eyes is precisely what Benjamin, in his essay on Epic Theater, will designate as the distinguishing feature of contemporary theater: the stage as *podium*: "In front of the entrance to the racetrack, a long, low podium had been constructed, on which hundreds of women, dressed up as angels in white sheets with large wings on their backs, blew on long, golden, gleaming trumpets" (p. 272).

For Benjamin, the redefinition of the stage as podium marks the desacralization of theater, which had traditionally separated stage from audience by an unbridgeable abyss, the orchestra pit. The elimination, "filling in," or leveling out of this "abyss" signifies, according to Benjamin, that actors and audience are no longer "separated" the way the "dead" had been opposed to the "living." Although the stage as podium signifies that this opposition is no longer absolute, it still does not amount to a "level playing field." What it does suggest is the situation of the German baroque *Trauerspiel*, where, Benjamin had argued some ten years earlier, the exclusion of transcendence leaves the dead no alternative but to wander the earth as ghosts—or as allegories.[34] Indeed, what Karl confronts on that "long, low podium" is an allegorical representation, albeit in a parodic mode, of the Last Judgment: hundreds of women, clad as angels, blowing for all they are worth into golden, gleaming trumpets. What they are announcing, however, is not so much the end of time as the Coming of the Theater of Oklahoma as universal placement office: in Heideggerian terms, as the organization of modern technology, *Gestell* as *Geschick*, emplacement as destiny.

Just what sort of a placement is announced in and as this "theater"? The following description of the angels supplies a detail that is missing from Benjamin's account but that provides a possible response to this question:

> [The angels] were, however, not directly on the podium; rather, each stood on a pedestal [*Postament*] that could not be seen, since the long, undulating sheets of the angels' costumes concealed it completely. Because the pedestals were very high, probably around two meters, the women's figures appeared gigantic. Only their small heads disturbed slightly the impression of size, and their loose hair was too short and almost ridiculous, hanging down between the large wings and on the sides. In order to avoid uniformity, the pedestals were of different sizes, so that some women were very low, not much above life-size, next to whom others rose to such heights that the slightest breeze risked blowing them over. And now all of these women blew their horns. (p. 273)

My translation has, if anything, fewer double entendres than the German original. The parodic allegory of the Last Judgment resembles an obscene vaudeville in which innocence and corruption are impossible to separate. Everything seems to demonstrate what was previously described as the ambivalence of Heidegger's notion of *Entbergung*, an unconcealing that dissimulates its own dissimulation. The higher the figures are positioned, the greater the risk of falling: this distinguishes theatrical placement from the more pragmatic search for security, constancy, and self-fulfillment that implicitly dominates the discourse of contemporary technics and explicitly that of contemporary politics. Generally excluded from mainstream discourses of technics and politics, ambivalence returns in the fascination of the "media" with the rise and fall of public figures, contemporary analogue to the Boethian "wheel of fortune."

Although Benjamin makes no explicit mention of this particular scene, he does call attention, implicitly and as though in passing, to a related motif in his double reference to the paintings of El Greco, in which enlargement of the body and elevation of its position together with a shrinking of the head, as though to suggest the disproportion between worldly positioning and the capacity to control its effects. Above all, there is the constant danger of losing one's balance at the slightest gust of wind. Or as Fanny, one of the trumpeting angels, who turns out to be an old friend of Karl, will respond when he asks if he can play her trumpet: "Certainly . . . but don't spoil the Chorus or I'll be fired." No specified wages, but also no job security in the Theater of Oklahoma.

In short, the combination of technics and economics produces a theater that responds to the challenge of modern technics by assigning everyone a place while at the same time making it unmistakably clear that this place is replaceable, movable, transformable, detachable: a place one must be ready to assume *or change* at any and every moment, in the most radical sense of *Bestellbarkeit*. The place thus offered promises constancy, *Bestand*, only to those who arrange themselves with—and not just, within—the great placement agency that is the Theater of Oklahoma. What this agency shares with theater is a certain mutability and transience: it places, but temporarily, conditionally. The great Theater of Oklahoma is a placement agency for temporary workers.[35]

Like every modern organization, this theater has its own admissions procedures—in German, *Aufnahmeverfahren*. If one is to be assigned a proper place, that place must first be determined, as the personnel director explains to Karl: "As our poster states, we can use everyone. But naturally we have to know what profession he previously exercised, in order to be able to place the person properly, where his knowledge can best be put to use" (p. 279).

The question of installation, crucial both for Heidegger and for Benjamin, here exceeds the analyses of each: those of Heidegger, because the organization will determine just how the *Einrichtung* will take place; those of Benjamin, because *Einrichtung* applies, not just to the stage as podium, but also to the organizational constraints upon which it depends. Why and how this is so is demonstrated by Karl's very first contact with this theater.

The podium is a construct: one that is temporary, that can and will soon be dismantled and moved elsewhere. In short, the space of the theater, the stage in particular, is not fixed and unmoving but as movable as though it were a body. The "angels" are not simply placed upon this movable, transportable podium, they are elevated above it by being perched on precarious stands: *Postamente*; once again, a Germanified Latin gerund—the stand is itself something *being posed*. On such stands, the angels are posted, but also exposed to the "slightest gust of wind" (p. 273). The precariousness of their perch, itself posed on the podium-stage, can be read as a theatrical staging of Heidegger's *Bestand*. The instability of these "one-day stands" on stage is, however, partially concealed by the angels' flowing costumes, in which they are "completely enclosed or veiled [*hüllten es vollständig um*]."

Such veiling and enclosing contrasts sharply with the protective function often associated with place, especially with regard to the bodies that occupy it. Here, by contrast, the angels' bodies are not secured by their *Umhüllung*: that only hides the *appearance* of vulnerability. This sense of vulnerability is emphasized by the perspectival foreshortening of the angels' heads, as well as by the description of their hair, which "was too short and almost ridiculous, hanging down between the large wings and on the sides" (p. 273). The smallness of the heads is thus complemented by the hanging down of the hair, emphasizing the disorderly and fragile positioning of these feminine "angels."

Such disorder is thus associated with their femininity. In the Christian tradition, at least, angels are supposed to be unaffected by gender. The angels in the Theater of Oklahoma, however, recall a bowdlerized burlesque show. This becomes clear as soon as Karl, in the name of all, actually installs himself on the stage. Initially this is not at all his intention. He starts out merely to get information on what the prospective recruits—the *Aufzunehmenden* (p. 272) and all the *Stellungssuchenden* (p. 274)—should do next. In order to get such information, however, he has to cross the podium. As he walks across the stage, he suddenly hears his name:

> "Karl," called an angel. Karl looked up and out of joyful surprise began to laugh; it was Fanny. "Fanny," he called and greeted her by raising his hand. "Come up here," called Fanny. "You're not going to walk right past me." And she jerked her garments apart, exposing the pedestal and a narrow stairway leading upwards. "Is it okay to go up?" Karl asked. "Who's going to stop us from just shaking hands," cried Fanny and looked around with anger, to see if someone was not about to arrive with just such a ban. But Karl was already climbing the stairs. "Slower," cried Fanny, "the pedestal will topple over and take us along with it." (p. 274)

Once he has arrived at the top, Fanny greets him by exclaiming, "Just look at the job I've got." Her job is to blow as hard as possible into the trumpet while trying to avoid being blown over by the slightest gust of wind. Fanny's angelic costume conceals not just the pedestal on which she is precariously perched but also a narrow stairway leading up to it. Her costume veils both the situation of her body and the access to it. The body of this angel recalls the fetish, which a decade later Freud will describe as tied into a double knot: on the one hand, seemingly complete, rising above the threats of sexual difference to self-identity, and on the other rendered all the more vulnerable by virtue of its very elevation.[36] Like the fetish, Fanny raises her skirt just a bit to reveal, not a proper part of her anatomy (foot) or even of her clothing (shoe), but a *stairway* leading not just *to* her, but *into* her. Yet all there is to go into is a show, a spectacle, a theatrical presentation. Or worse, a publicity stunt. At any rate, nothing substantial, nothing corporeal that can be seen as such. At the heart of the theater, again as with the fetish, lurks the secret, invisible, but, perhaps even more, inaudible. *Verschollen.* In this acoustical respect the theatrical angel parts company with the fetish, in its traditional visual manifestation, at least.

The Theater of Oklahoma appeals to the ear as much if not more than to the eye. But it makes this appeal not by speech, song, or even music but by *noise*, a blaring of horns that is all the more powerful for being situated at the limit of music. The trumpets of the angels suggest the apocalypse that the Theater of Oklahoma both conjures up and promises to avert. This is not without bearing on the question of installation. The din may die down long enough for Karl to converse briefly with Fanny, but this respite does not last very long. That is perhaps why Karl never tries to set himself up on the podium. The podium presents itself to him from the very beginning as a passageway to be traversed rather than as a place to be occupied. Indeed, it soon becomes clear that this podium, as stage, stands between the applicants and their admission: to be admitted to this theater one must *cross* the podium, but not linger on it. If Benjamin suggests that the hallmark of theater qua podium is the obligation of installing oneself on it, then in Clayton this can happen only by treating the podium and every-thing on it as a passageway. The podium is here, in Kafka's text, al-ready a forerunner—and descendant—of the Parisian passages that will fascinate Benjamin as the emblematic space of the nineteenth century.

But Karl is far from Paris, and the podium is situated in front of a racetrack, not a labyrinth of streets. The calculated disorder of the city is here replaced by an enigmatic series of procedures, rites of selection and admission that recall nothing so much as traditional military recruiting and channeling. All that is missing from the military scenario is the proper battle and its vehicle, the "enemy." Where is the enemy in a world where all are to be admitted, and by implication there are only to be victors, no defeated? Theater, like the military, has a place for everyone, perhaps even for the enemy. That alone distinguishes the *troupe* from the *troop* (both condensed in the German word used to describe the group to which Fanny belongs: *Truppe*).

The military aspect of the organization is strengthened by the terms used to designate its elements. When Fanny tells Karl that her time with him is up ("I have to blow again"), she urges him to "try in any case to get a position [*einen Posten*] with this troupe [*bei dieser Truppe*]" (p. 276). Later we will learn that the group to which she belongs is "the 10th Recruiting Troupe [*Werbetruppe*: also, advertising team] of the Theater of Oklahoma" (p. 283). The troupe has its own *Führer* as well as its own "personnel director [*Personalchef*]" and so shares the organizational characteristics both of a business enterprise and of a military unit. The German term used in the text, *Werbetruppe*, can designate both: recruitment in both the military and commercial senses of the term, as well as that of advertising, *Werbung*, and, more traditionally, erotic entreaty, "courtship." All of these converge in the *Werbetruppe* that recruits for the Theater of Oklahoma, which, as we have seen, is, not just a theater as commonly understood, but an organization that is both an employment agency and a business enterprise. Precisely what sort of business it is in, what sort of theater it performs, will never be clarified. This is not the most important aspect for Karl. Rather, what appears to count above all is its ability, as organization, to withstand the passage of time. Thus when Karl expresses his regret upon learning that Fanny and her *Werbetruppe* have already "left for the next point on [their] itinerary," he is quickly consoled: "'You'll see her again in Oklahoma,' said the servant, 'but now come with me, you're the last one left.' He led Karl along the rear of the podium, on which the angels had stood before, but where now there were only the empty pedestals" (pp. 286–87).

All that is left of the angels and their show are "only the empty pedestals." The podium remains deserted, no longer a site of representation or performance but an empty space, to be traversed on one's way elsewhere. To where? The image of the empty pedestals is not reassuring. It suggests another "site" that accepts everyone or almost everyone: the cemetery. Or a stage, where performers relate to the audience as do the "dead to the living." The question remains, however, just how one "installs" oneself in, on, or in view of such a site. The difficulty of providing a response to this question that would be *narratable*, at least in terms of a traditional novel leading to a conclusion, is perhaps why Kafka was unable to "finish" this novel. Or, perhaps, why he decided to finish it by leaving it unfinished.

What we are left with, as far as this single chapter is concerned, is a loosely connected series of scenes that tell an inconclusive story of Karl seeking entry into the enigmatic world of the Theater of Oklahoma. In conclusion I will discuss two scenes that are particularly revealing of the ambiguous recruitment procedures of the Oklahoma Theater.

These consist in a series of interviews through which the organization gathers information about the candidate's previous training, with a view to placing him in a position corresponding to his experience. In one of these interviews, Karl is asked to present his "legitimation papers." When he admits that he has none, a dispute develops between the supervisor, the *Kanzleileiter*, and the secretary (literally, the scribe, *der Schreiber*) charged with recording all information and taking minutes. Karl aggravates the suspicion of the supervisor by providing an obviously false (generic) name: "Negro." When the supervisor is reluctant to approve Karl, his secretary, ostensibly a subordinate, with a movement of his hand, suddenly and surprisingly brings matters to a head: "The supervisor [*Leiter*, also "head"] turned with open mouth to the secretary, who, however, with a conclusive sweep [*abschließende Bewegung*] of his hand, said 'hired' and immediately recorded the decision in the registry" (pp. 281, 210).

Benjamin, we recall, placed "gesture" at the core of Kafka's writing and attributed to it a theatrical significance. This resided in its power to make interruption a positive mode of articulation. The effect of such interruption, however, is never self-contained. It retains its relation to what it is not, just as an interruption only defines itself with respect to what it interrupts, never entirely on its own terms. All of this is powerfully condensed in the gesture the clerk makes with his hand and his resulting proclamation of Karl's "acceptance" into the organization. Here, then, in this organization the hand rather than the head is decisive, but it is a hand that interrupts and suspends an intention, thus calling attention to the movement, the procedure, the ritual, rather than the meaning.

At the same time, in thus defying expectation this interruptive gesture fulfills one of the oldest demands placed on theater, which receives its initial and canonical formulation in Aristotle's insistence, in the *Poetics*, that tragic plots be "complex" rather than "simple" and, above all, be organized around a *peripeteia*: a sudden and unexpected turn of events. The clerk's gesture accompanies just such a *peripeteia*. It is, of course, comic or farcical rather than tragic. And this is so to the extent that it does not satisfy the second demand Aristotle adjudged indispensable to the success of a good tragedy plot: that of *anagnōrisis*, recognition. Here, the only "recognition" that follows the scribe's act is one of puzzlement: Karl, and with him the reader, can at best recognize the insufficiency of their expectation and of the cognition that informs it. In an enigmatic way, the Theater of Oklahoma depends more on the hand than the head, on the scribe than on the boss, on recording than on deciding. But this awareness does not add up to new knowledge, not in the positive sense, at least.

As already indicated, it is in gesture that Benjamin sees the hallmark of Kafka's writing. It is a movement whose theatricality consists in the shattering of existing frameworks, while not necessarily putting anything stable in their place. Thus, although the clerk's gesture and announcement are described as *abschließend*—definitive, conclusive—they tend to open questions rather than to close them. Most obviously, how or why is it possible for a scribe to take a decision that a department head hesitates to make? All that the reader can conclude is that in this strange theater authority and power are not always to be found where one might expect. The question, "Who or what decides?" remains unanswered in the Theater of Oklahoma. Is it the head or the hand? Both or neither? And what is the role of the organization itself in determining the "final say"? Especially when that organization is also a theater? Who has the final say in a theater? The actors? Director? Producer? Audience? Patron? Censor? Someone else? Or could it possibly be the destiny of the organization—organization as destiny—that *no one* has the final say, no single figure, at least? Could this be what distinguishes, not just organizations, but *theater as destiny*: that there is no final say, no last word, perhaps because all words and saying are "final"? But "final" in what sense, from what point of view?

To answer such questions with any degree of plausibility would require what Aristotle, once again, demanded of the ideal tragedy and its audience: to survey and take in the work as a *whole*, once and for all. This seems unattainable for the vast Theater of Oklahoma. Surely it is not insignificant that this theater recruits at a *racetrack*. This site, Fanny tells Karl, has been chosen because of its spaciousness. In addition to being vast, a racetrack is also a site of speed, competition, sudden surprises, and even shocks. Even if no horse races are being run, it still recalls risk and chance, winners and losers, hope and despair. Something specific, however, takes place, in this place, when it becomes a place of selection and recruitment, involving humans as well as animals—humans, perhaps, *as animals*. As a place of selection, the Clayton Racetrack foreshadows other stadiums—from Paris in 1942 to Santiago de Chile in 1973 to Kabul in 2000—whose shadow will cast a pall over much of the twentieth century and in all likelihood over the twenty-first as well.[37]

Such posthumous history is by no means simply external to the ostensibly harmless details that mark Karl's experiences at the Clayton Racetrack. Following his successful, if strange, admission, for instance, he is on his way to meet the leader of the whole "recruitment troop" when suddenly "behind him a machine began to creak and hum [*schnarren*]. He turned around and saw an apparatus on which the names of the victors in the race were made public, but where now the following inscription flashed high above: 'Salesman Kalla with spouse and child.' Here, then, the names of those admitted were transmitted to their [respective] departments" (p. 283).

The "publication [*Veröffentlichung*]" of the names of the successful candidates on the screen high above the racetrack, where the names of the victorious horses would normally be displayed, is intended, not for the successful candidates or their colleagues, but rather for the *Kanzleien*, the departments, who are thus directly informed of the personnel decisions that have been taken. This kind of communication characterizes the organization both as a *theater* and as a *medium*. It is an unorthodox theater, to be sure, since it neither tells an intelligible story nor itself easily fits into one. It is also unorthodox in apparently defying Aristotle's assertion that a "tragedy" can exist without characters (*ēthē*), but never without action (*praxeōs*). In this theater, at least, there is very little action as such, at most the confused reaction of the various applicants to the process of selection. Of course, it is not a tragic theater, although nothing is less certain than that it has a happy ending. What does seem more certain is the constant and characteristic derailing of dialogue and intention. The following scene, in which Karl is briefly welcomed by the troupe leader and then even more quickly dispatched, indicates the kind of "communication" that takes place in the Theater of Oklahoma:

> Karl bowed as a sign of leaving, and wanted to say goodbye to the other man, but the latter was already walking back and forth, as though he were completely done with his work, his face directed upward, toward the platform. While Karl descended, next to the stairs the inscription flashed across the board, "Negro, technical worker." Since everything seemed to be proceeding correctly, Karl would not even have minded so much if his real name had been displayed on the board. Everything was very well organized, because at the foot of the stairs, Karl was met by a servant who put an armband around his arm. When Karl lifted his arm to see what was on the band, it was, quite rightly, "technical worker." (p. 286)

Although Karl, somewhat reassured, begins to regret not having used his real name, it is too late. Instead, he receives an armband designating the role to which he is assigned: "technical worker." His real, proper name doesn't appear to matter so much as this second, generic name, which will define the place—or role—he is to assume in the organization. In this perfectly organized theater, only one thing is lacking: time. There is no time to thank or say goodbye to his benefactors. As he tries to say a word of thanks, the director is "already walking back and forth," already elsewhere, "his face directed upward, toward the platform," looking away from Karl. Karl, who has lost his "real" name and much of his history, has acquired a new one, but it is generic and functional in character. Karl is to be constantly available, as a "technical worker," constantly on order, *bestellbar*.

What Karl thus seeks but never will find in this theater is what Benjamin, in another context, defines as the *aura* of the *reciprocated glance*. Theater as organization is marked by the lack of any such reciprocity. As we have seen, this makes it virtually impossible to say goodbye. There is literally no time left, for separation has already taken place. Joining the theater involves leaving one's previous life behind. And this takes place even before one can take notice of it, quicker than the speediest racehorse. Karl tries to say goodbye and finds himself "hanging," as it were.

All those searching for a position, the *Stellensuchende*, seek desperately to reassure themselves by searching for a glimmer of recognition or acknowledgment in the eyes of those in charge. But those others never look back, only up and away. This is described unforgettably toward the end of the chapter, when Karl belatedly joins the great banquet held to welcome the new members of the theater:

> Everyone was buoyant and excited, and at the very moment when Karl, the last to arrive, took his place unnoticed, several persons stood up with raised glasses. One made a toast to the leader of the Tenth Recruiting Troupe, whom he called "father of the job-seekers [*Vater der Stellungsuchenden*]." Someone pointed out that he could be seen from where they were, and indeed not very far away two men could be glimpsed in the judge's box. Suddenly all glasses were raised in their direction and Karl too grasped the glass in front of him, but however loudly they cried and however much they sought to call attention to themselves, nothing indicated that the men in the judges' box had seen the ovation or even tried to. The leader leaned back in a corner while the other man stood next to him, chin in hand. (pp. 287–88)

The search for the "father of the job-seekers" remains without conclusive result, not because no one is found, but because those who are do not respond and, moreover, are *positioned* so as to make such response impossible: the leader, *leaning* in a corner, his assistant, *chin in hand*. Neither the one nor the other seems to have the force to support himself, to stand up on his own, without props. Stage props? At any rate, these reclining figures, with their literal dependence upon place, take the place of upright arbiters and judges, if not of leaders as such.

The response to this disappointing lack of response or even acknowledgment confronts us with a situation that will be familiar to many:

> A little disappointed, they all sat down again, now and then someone would turn to look at the stewards' stand, but soon they were quite preoccupied by the plentiful meal . . . and anyone who didn't care to participate in the general conversation

could look at pictures of the theater in Oklahoma, which had been piled up at one end of the table, from where they were supposed to be passed from hand to hand. But no very great attention was paid to the pictures, and so it happened that Karl, at the end of the row, got to see only one of them. To judge by this one picture, though, they must all have been very well worth seeing. This picture showed the Loge of the President of the United States. At first sight, one might think it wasn't a loge at all, but the stage, so far did the curved balustrades jut out into empty space. The balustrades were made entirely of gold. In between little pillars that might have been cut out by the minutest scissors, there was a row of portraits of former presidents. . . . The loge was brightly lit from all sides and from above; white and yet somehow mild light laid bare the front of the loge, whereas its recesses, deepening pleats of red velvet falling full length and swagged by cords, were a darkly glimmering void. It was hardly possible to imagine human beings in this box, so sumptuously self-sufficient did it look. Karl didn't forget to eat, but he looked often at the picture, too, having put it next to his plate. (215)

Karl at the banquet table with a picture of the President's Loge placed alongside his plate—what better image of a certain type of consumption? The dinner guests do not receive a reciprocated glance instead, pictures of the theater are made available to them. These pictures do not show the theater as such, only parts of it: for instance, the President's Loge. The picture does not depict the president either, any more than it does the theater, rather, "a row of portraits of former presidents," hang on its walls, "in between little pillars that might have been cut out by the minutest scissors." The presidential picture-portraits are thus framed explicitly by "pillars" and implicitly by a certain type of "cut-out," which appears like the work of "the minutest scissors." The "former presidents" are, therefore, most emphatically *cut out* of the theater, which does not seem to require them to be present. The Presidential Loge appears in the picture to be so sumptuously self-contained as to no longer need a president to fill it. The "loge" no longer has any contents except itself: its ability to contain. It is pure organization, pure theater, pure place. It is a vessel that contains nothing except itself or, rather, the nothing that *is* itself: its "recesses, deepening pleats of red velvet" and its "darkly glimmering void." In its emptiness it is strangely full, in its darkness "glimmering." Difficult not to recall that a President's Loge was also the site of the first assassination of an American president: could it be such a memory that "darkly glimmers" from the "void" of this loge?[38]

But this "so sumptuously self-sufficient" box is actually more than a box, in the theatrical sense. Its "pleats of red velvet" recall the curtains of a stage. What they display, however, cannot be assimilated to any sort of "plot." Nothing happens: no event, no action, only "a row of portraits of former presidents" framed by "little pillars." This row of portraits suggests not heroes but ornaments, delimiters of a place that celebrates the absence of all those former presidents, and its resulting independence from anything human. The picture of the President's Loge is a visual declaration of the independence of place from the bodies it was traditionally held to contain. The Theater of Oklahoma stages itself here as the emancipation of place from body through the medium of visual representation. What is ultimately represented is not just a gallery of portraits, portraying the absence of the sovereign figures whose faces they depict, but concomitantly the creased and riven space that has come to supplant them: the space of the spectator as consumer, a "box" or *étui*, as Benjamin would have written, in which the commodity is uncannily—*unheimlich*—at home.

This picture of the Theater of Oklahoma is not without its effects: "Karl didn't forget to eat, but he often looked at the picture, too, having put it next to his plate." Like the morning newspaper at the breakfast table or the nightly news at dinner, what it says is less important than that it is *there*, to dissimulate the void.

• • •

The Consolation of Philosophy is thus replaced by the Consolation of Media, which because of its disposition of space and place is necessarily also a theater. It is a theater that performs the staging of images, framing the void of time through a string of portraits of former presidents. No one portrait counts, but the series as such, for only as a series does it *take place*. Theater has migrated from person to place, from individual to office, from politics to podiums, pedestals, and pillars. Why theater? Because, in the convergence of organization and business, "theater" remains the ambivalent guardian of the *power to place as the power to displace.* Theater places everything and everyone "on call," makes everything *bestellbar,* while undermining the hope of ever staying in place, of a *Bestand.*

Although only Karl is privy to it, the picture of the Presidential Loge in the Theater of Oklahoma thus enshrines what the "place-seekers" experience and cannot accept: the absence of acknowledgment. The image of that absence is enshrined as the Presidential Loge, in which it is the loge itself that *presides.* It presides as image, as hope, and as theater. Only a certain theatricality can provide the place-seekers with what they so desperately crave. Thus, upon learning that he will not get the position with Fanny's troupe that he had hoped for, Karl finds consolation in "repeating, again and again, that the kind of work counted far less than the possibility of being able to find any place at all where one could stay continuously" (p. 286).

In German, the consolation is expressed even more tentatively, by means of the present participle: "Es kam nicht so sehr auf die Art der Arbeit an, als vielmehr darauf sich überhaupt irgendwo *dauernd* festzuhalten." This is what draws him and the others to the Theater of Oklahoma and to this the organization seems to respond. But its response remains equivocal, and the candidates are therefore constantly seeking to reassure themselves. As one of Karl's fellow job-seekers remarks: "It seems to be a good business, even if it's not easy to find one's way around in the beginning. But that's the way it is everywhere" (p. 282). The German here retains a dimension that is lost in English, for it speaks not of "finding one's way around" the "business" but rather of "finding one's way *into* it":[39] "Allerdings kann man sich nicht gleich *in alles einfinden,* so ist es aber überall." But how does one find one's way into a theater whose epitome is the sumptuous "self-sufficiency" of the Presidential Loge? Can one hold onto a picture of a spectator's box, even if it is that of a president? Especially that of a chief executive who was assassinated by one of the actors he was supposed merely to behold?

We begin to see how the hectic hesitation with which the novel began, the slowing down of the ship upon entering New York harbor, was already a harbinger of things to come: of unpredictable and menacing bursts of sunlight illuminating the "jutting" sword held by the Goddess. We begin to understand why Karl is always arriving too late, never on time. Even and especially at the Clayton Racetrack, where the servant assigned to lead him to the banquet has to hurry him up in no uncertain terms:

> "Come along more quickly, it really took very long for you to be accepted. They must have had their doubts, no?" "I don't know," said Karl, astonished, since he didn't think so. Some fellow human being was already ready, even in the most limpid of situations, to create concern. But faced with the friendly spectacle of the great stadium stands, where they now arrived, Karl soon forgot the servant's remarks. (p. 287)

But Karl is not permitted to forget those remarks for long. Although he remains unperturbed by the lack of response to the attempted toast, he is unsettled by the manner in which the banquet is abruptly brought to a close by the personnel director. "Karl had strayed away from his place [at the banquet table] far too long, [and] was just about to go back to it, when the head of Personnel" suddenly appears to announce that

> "the train that is going to take you to Oklahoma is leaving in five minutes. It is a long journey, but you'll see that everything has been taken care of. Here I want to introduce the gentleman who will be in charge of your transportation, to whom you owe full obedience." A short, thin man climbed up on the bench on which the personnel director was standing, took barely time to make a fleeting bow, then began immediately to indicate, with nervously extended hands, how everyone should gather, get organized, and then get moving. At first no one followed him, for the person who had already given a speech pounded on the table and began a word of thanks despite everything. Karl became very anxious—because they had just been told that the train was about to leave. . . . The speech was paid for by having to run to the station in a military jog [*Laufschritt*]. That wasn't very hard, because—as Karl noticed only now—no one carried any baggage. (p. 290)

In the time since Kafka wrote this text, stadiums, racetracks, and precipitous transports by train, leaving barely time to pack one's luggage, have assumed a sinister significance that was hardly obvious in 1916. The horrific events of the Second World War and its aftermath give this unfinished text a resonance of which its author could presumably never have dreamed. That, however, it should have been a theater—the Theater of Oklahoma—that provides the site and incitement for such a horrifically prophetic depiction should give us cause to pause and reflect.

It is a theater in which, as Benjamin notes, "the applicants are asked to do nothing other than play themselves."[40] Nothing could seem more innocuous. But as the Theater of Oklahoma suggests, perhaps nothing is more difficult, or more dangerous.

3

Scene and Screen: Electronic Media and Theatricality

Synopsis

W H A T I S the place or role of "theatricality" in an age increasingly dominated by electronic media? What is the place of "theater"? Or, since there is more than one kind, of "theaters"? What is the relation between such "theaters," which seem to name something concrete, and "theatricality," which need not take place in theaters, at least as commonly understood?

Perhaps most of all, what is the place of "place," the role of "role," which is to say, of the terms to which we have resorted in order to ask these initial questions? What is the relation between the two terms *theater* and *theatricality*, which frame our questioning and which we have begun by using as though they were synonymous, which they clearly are not? Whatever else it is, a "theater" is a place, but not only or necessarily one in which plays are performed before audiences. The definition provided by a contemporary dictionary begins with ancient Greek drama and ends with nuclear weapons:

> **the.ater** *or* **the.atre** *n* [ME *theatre*, fr. MF, fr. L *theatrum*, fr. Gk *theatron*, fr. *theasthai* to view, fr. *thea* act of seeing; akin to Gk *thauma* miracle] (14c) **1 a:** an outdoor structure for dramatic performances or spectacles in ancient Greece and Rome **b:** a building for dramatic performances **c:** a building or area for showing motion pictures **2:** a place or sphere of enactment of usu. significant events or action (the ~ of public life) **3 a:** a place rising by steps or gradations (a woody ~ of stateliest view—John Milton) **b:** a room often with rising tiers of seats for assemblies (as for lectures or surgical demonstrations) **4 a:** dramatic literature: PLAYS **b:** dramatic representation as an art or profession:

DRAMA **5 a:** dramatic or theatrical quality or effectiveness **b:** SPECTACLE 1a   **c:** entertainment in the form of a dramatic or diverting situation or series of events (their public feud made for good ～) **6:** THEATER OF OPERATIONS theater *adj* (1977): of, relating to, or appropriate for use in a theater of operations (～ nuclear weapons)

What are the traits that seem to mark the use of the word, according at least to this definition? First, it entails a *place* in which *events* take place. Second, although these events are generally defined as either "dramatic performances or spectacles," they can also be of a quite different nature: "significant events or actions . . . of public life," for instance, medical demonstrations, lectures, or, more alarmingly, military events, such as those involving "nuclear weapons." Certainly the spectacle of atomic explosions, recorded on and disseminated by photography, film, and then television, has burned itself into the popular imagination ever since the first atomic bombs devastated Hiroshima and Nagasaki in 1945. Does this suffice to render such a spectacle a good example of a "theatrical" event, much less of a theater?

One widespread and very ancient premise that we find at work in this dictionary definition—a premise we have already begun to question—is the identification of "spectacle" with the "theatrical." "Theaters of military operations" need not be so blatantly spectacular or so obviously destructive. But the dictionary confusion or confounding of theater with spectacle is surely as significant as it is symptomatic: the allusion to "nuclear weapons" brings to the fore one of the striking and distinguishing factors affecting the notion of "theater" and "theatricality" today, namely, the preponderance of energy over matter, of force over bodies, of power over place. The allusion to "nuclear weapons" as an exemplary manifestation of a "theater of operations" indicates that the "operations" involved do not simply "take place": what distinguishes them is their power to quite literally *volatilize* or *pulverize* places, reducing the bodies that occupy them to dust or vapor. That such an operation could be cited as an illustration of the use of "theater" is possible only from a perspective that emerged historically with the introduction of the airborne film camera in the First World War, followed by various forms of remote audiovisual monitoring. Such a perspective is presupposed by the "mushroom cloud" that has since come to be the emblem of nuclear explosion as spectacle.

In any event, this banal and yet dubiously symptomatic dictionary example suggests how complex and contradictory the relation between "theater" and "media" has become. "Media" is a collective noun often used in the singular, but I will employ it as a plural noun in order to recall its heterogeneous composition. There are a variety of quite different "media": broadcast media (radio, television), recording modes (digital and analog), recording supports (photography, film, video, audio), Internet (i.e., computer as medium), and so forth. Almost all of these very different types of "media," despite their obvious and less obvious distinctions, depend upon electricity as their energy source, whether in order to record, to store, or to transmit. One of the traits that distinguishes electricity as a source of energy, at least insofar as it pertains to the electronic media, is its tendency, by virtue of its velocity, to transform traditional experiences of space and time, of distance and proximity, and hence of bodies, which in great part are defined through their spatio-temporal mode of being situated. What would seem to be specific to theater, by contrast, and presumably also to theatricality at least, as both are traditionally construed, is their dependence upon the "Euclidean" experience of space-time that the electronic media tend to relativize if not to abolish: above all, recourse to the opposition between presence and absence as well as to that of proximity and distance in the situating of bodies, especially *living* bodies.[1]

But the situation is, as usual, considerably more complicated. It requires us to return to the founding text of systematical thinking of theater in the "West": Aristotle's *Poetics*. In this text—reconstituted long after the fact, apparently from notes, and hence anything but simply complete or finished—Aristotle defends theater against the Platonic critique both by devalorizing its material environment, the specifically scenic *medium* of theater—everything having to do with spectacle, with *opsis*—and subordinating it to *muthos*, "plot." Plot has as its object the "imitation not of men, but of a life [*biou*], of an action [*praxeos*]." Through the structure of what Aristotle calls "complex" or "intricate" plots, merely contingent *opsis* is transformed into the condition of *synopsis*, the act of taking in the spectacle "with a single view." In order, however, to be susceptible to such synoptic viewing, tragedy must possess an inner structural unity that mere appearances do not have. Just how Aristotle conceives the condition of that unity is elucidated by his interpreter and editor Gerald Else, who describes *muthos* as "a single course of action laid on by a particular will to achieve a particular goal. The reversal of a focused, unitary intention, in which the whole life of a man may be concentrated, is at the very heart of tragedy as Aristotle conceives it."[2]

Else thereby touches on one of the most striking and curious points in Aristotle's text: the way it links *praxis* to *bios*, "action" to "life." Whether the life and action referred to are understood as those of an "individual," as Else argues, or in a more general way, the association of the two seems designed to bring out their unifying function. Such unity also defines the key function of "reversal," *peripeteia*, which, as described by Aristotle, does not simply disrupt the action, but ultimately prepares the way for the recognition of its underlying unity. Such recognition (*anagnōrisis*) may come to us a shock, but its shock value only reinforces the unity of action and of life that it reveals. A mainstay of Aristotle's *Poetics* is the thesis that the convergence of *peripeteia* and *anagnōrisis* invests tragedy with meaningful unity and thereby elevates it from the otherwise contingent medium of theatrical spectacle—*opsis*. This thesis thereby defines tragedy as an essentially *dramatic* genre, and at the same time as the supreme poetic form.

Aristotle thus construes the medium—and this will become the traditional conception of "media" as such—as a means to an end. *Medium* equals *means*, instrument, element, a necessary but not sufficient ingredient of poetry. At the outset of the *Poetics*, in its second chapter, Aristotle attempts quickly to dispatch questions of media by dividing them into categories drawn from the senses, essentially visual and auditory, sight and hearing. Shapes and colors are attributed to the former; rhythm, speech, and melody, to the latter. He then goes on to inveigh against those who confuse the media with the specific use to which they are put (thus anticipating the critique of "formalism" that has been so popular ever since). He illustrates this confusion by pointing to critics who confound the poetry of Homer with the scientific writing of Empedocles simply because both are formulated in verse.

Similarly, any aspect of the scenic medium is considered by Aristotle to be a means subordinate to the ends to which it is used. In the best case, the medium will efface itself and thus be defined by the quality of being *diaphanous*, or transparent. This is precisely the quality he attributes to media in general. In his treatise *On the Soul* (books 2 and 3), Aristotle discusses the function of the medium in terms of sense perception, above all, visual perception. His discussion makes it clear that he construes the medium primarily as a spatial interval between two points, generally an emitter and a receiver, or correlatively, a manifestation and its reception. The medium is what bridges the distance between the two, between origin and end, departure and arrival, and thereby allows an indirect contact, a transmission or communication, to take place. In so doing it cannot be held to be completely passive or neutral, but rather functions as a facilitator, joining through separation, as does a bridge.

Applied to theater, or, as Aristotle conceives it, to drama, the scenic medium allows mimesis quite literally to *take place*, but only to the extent that it fades into pure transparency. In tragedy it is the plot, the *muthos*, that transforms theatrical *opsis* into meaningful *synopsis*. The scenic medium thus becomes the transparent space that allows the plot to emerge.

Thus any discussion of the relation of "theater" to "the media" must begin by distinguishing different traditions of interpreting theater itself as medium. In the "West," the tradition that begins with Aristotle's *Poetics* is surely the most powerful, in the sense of being the most influential, not just in terms of theory, but also with respect to practice.[3] But, as we shall see, neither is it the only possible interpretation nor is the text itself entirely consistent.

With Aristotle, then, begins a tradition that systematically and prescriptively equates medium with means, and in so doing defines through *synopsis* the scenic medium of theater as a means of perception, of vision, and of understanding. It does so by conceiving theater on the model of tragedy or, more precisely, on the basis of its interpretation of tragedy, namely, as the enactment of dramatic conflicts ultimately resolved through a unified and self-contained plot. The "living presence" of actors and audience is taken into account, of course, but only as a necessary means toward the end of representing the unity of an "action" and, through it, of a "life."

Having thus summarized the prevailing argument of Aristotle's treatise concerning the relation of tragedy to theater, we must immediately add that the text is more complex than this résumé would suggest. Although the conception of theater as medium just described predominates in the *explicit* arguments of the *Poetics*, in at least one place the questions of place and medium appear to resist instrumentalization in a curious and significant way. Early in the lectures (§5), Aristotle discusses the origins of tragedy and comedy and relates how different cities have tried to lay claim to their paternity:

> They [the Dorians] use the names "comedy" and "drama" as evidence; for they say that *they* call their outlying villages *kōmai* while the Athenians call theirs *dēmoi*, the assumption being that the participants in comedy were called *kōmōidoi* not from their being revelers but because they wandered from one village to another, being degraded and excluded from the city—and that they call "doing" and "acting" *dran* while the Athenians designate it by *prattein*. (48a35–45)[4]

"The allegations of the 'Dorians,'" Else notes, "are neither true nor to the point. "Comedy is from *kōmos*, revel, an Attic word, not from *kōmē*, village" (p. 85). Philologically, Else is presumably correct. But apart from his palpable annoyance at having to bother with this passage at all, since it is "neither true nor to the point," Else does not stop to consider just what the point might be, or whether a point might not be of interest even if it is not "true" in the sense of being etymologically accurate. Alternatively, I would like to suggest that Aristotle's text here touches on a number of issues that stand in very significant relation to theatricality. Within the context of an etymological speculation designed to establish the right of a particular city-state to be regarded as the "father" of theater, the association of "comedy" with a certain extraterritoriality, with exile and with wandering, both echoes and anticipates one of the hallmarks of the history of theater, again in the West: its problematic relation to property, to politics and to established, consecrated places and institutions, both private and public, political and domestic. Before Aristotle, Plato had already condemned theatrical mimesis on similar grounds,[5] and his judgment was to be echoed throughout the centuries that followed, often justifying bans on theater as such.

Of course, none of this is made explicit in the fragmentary text of Aristotle that has been handed down under the title *Poetics*. But the problem is coextensive with the birth of tragedy and, above all, with the particular tragedy that Aristotle and many others take to be the epitome of the genre: Sophocles' *Oedipus Tyrannos*. What does it mean to be the native of a city-state, as opposed to being a stranger? What of Oedipus, who considers himself a foreigner in the city he rules before discovering himself to be a native? The situation of Oedipus suggests that, far from confirming the totalizing and unifying conception of theater advanced in the *Poetics*, Sophocles' play may be read as its theatrical dismantling. This opens up a different understanding of or approach to theater, in which the distinctively scenic medium is no longer merely a means to an end, but, rather, is the spatio-temporal condition of what Benjamin, writing almost three millennia later, was to call "the exposing of the present [*die Exponierung des Anwesenden*]." Benjamin employs this expression in several essays, one of which is of particular interest in our context, since it has to do with defining the specificity of theater with respect to the "new media," which at the time, for Benjamin, were above all film and radio. In what follows, then, I will first indicate briefly how Oedipus can be read as a problematization of theatrical space qua medium, and then go on to discuss Benjamin's attempt to interpret that space with respect to the new media.

More than One: *Oedipus Tyrannos*

Everything relating to theater as medium, to the scene and the spectacle, to *opsis*, exists, insofar as Aristotle is concerned, only to serve the *synopsis*. The machinery of representation is thus useful only to the extent that it is able to efface itself, to become transparent, revealing a more direct view of the thing itself—which is to say, of the unity of an action and a life—than is possible in other forms of mimesis, especially epic. In tragedy, he emphasizes, no mediating narrative intervention is required, since the mimesis is enacted directly by living persons, "here and now," on stage. The scenic medium of theater thus allows a certain "here and now" to take place and ostensibly to become transparent, revealing the more fundamental immediacy of *a* life, if not of life *itself*.

The question that emerges from this Aristotelian approach to theater is: what sort of "here and now" is presented on stage? Is it one that can efface itself in a diaphany that allows (a) life itself to appear, in its inherent and meaningful unity? Aristotle's response, as we have seen, is that the "shock of recognition"—shock and surprise followed or accompanied by recognition—involves (which is to say, either produces or entails) a "purgation" by which extraneous elements are removed or "purged"—the famous *katharsis*. However one interprets this term, whether traditionally, as relating to the sentiments of the audience, or, as Else suggests, as concerning the tragic act itself, it seems undeniable that its function is to confirm the transformation of *opsis* into *synopsis*, of medium into means, and of the events represented on stage into the complete and meaningful sequence of a unified action and life.

Now, it is striking that all of these elements are explicitly inscribed in *Oedipus Tyrannos*, but as elements of Oedipus' predicament, of the tragic *hamartia* rather than of its solution. Perhaps the most striking way to demonstrate this is by juxtaposing the following, extremely theatrical passage from Oedipus' opening speech to the terrible words that the seer Tiresias will address to him. Here is Oedipus, speaking to the citizens of Thebes, who have gathered anxiously before the Royal Palace:

> I have not thought it fit to rely on my messengers
> But am here to learn for myself—I, Oedipus,
> Whose name is known afar.[6]

And now, Tiresias's parting words:

> I will go . . . when I have said my all. Thus to your face
> Fearful of nothing you can do to me:
> The man for whom you have ordered hue and cry,
> The killer of Laius—that man is *here*;
> Passing for an alien, a sojourner among us;
> But, as presently shall appear, a Theban born. (p. 38)

Both of these discourses have the same "referent," of course, but in each case with a totally different significance. Even more importantly, perhaps, each defines a very distinct approach to the "here and now," and with it, to the question of presence in general and theatrical presence in particular. Oedipus, in "presenting himself" not just to the citizens of Thebes, to the Chorus, but also to the audience of the play, does so in a thoroughly "Aristotelian" manner: which to say, in one which seeks to do away with the mediations of the medium, with all "messengers," in order "to learn for myself." That self, Oedipus believes he can assert, is transparent in his person: he has come "here," presenting himself before the Thebans, in order to hear their distress directly and see what he can do to alleviate it.

Oedipus can ostensibly be all the more confident in so presenting himself since his very presence, as King of Thebes, seems to testify to his ability to resolve enigmas. If his "name" is "known afar," conquering distance, it is because he was able to respond to the riddle of the Sphinx, thus liberating Thebes and becoming its new ruler. The present is thus understood by Oedipus to be an identical repetition of the past: what once was will come again, and the renown of his name is proof of this. The "here and now" is transparent because it seems to be an identical repetition of the "there and then," the present a repetition of the past, the future a potential repetition of the present. Repetition, here, is understood in the sense of the recurrence of the identical, not as its alteration or transformation.

This conception of time, of present, past, and future, fills Oedipus with confidence in his ability to restore the transparency that has been lost: "I will start afresh, and bring everything into the light" (p. 29). Once it has thus been brought to light, the problem will be resolved by "purification," which is to say, by eliminating the noxious element, the *miasma*, from the body politic and thus restoring health to the city.[7]

It is thus Oedipus who quite literally *presents himself* as the embodiment of the conception of theater, later to be schematized by Aristotle as a presentation, an enactment capable of bringing about pure transparency. This in turn presupposes a certain conception of place, of what it means to be "here and now," for instance, as distinct from "there and then." The terrible parting words of Tiresias repeat this conception, but in repeating also dismantle it. The person you are seeking out "there," Tiresias tells Oedipus, is in fact right "here," "here and now." But that person is not here as you believe things are here, which is to say, accessible to a synoptic vision. "Have you eyes, . . . And cannot see what company you keep?" (p. 37). The very notion of what it means to see and, hence, to see in a theater, to see and hear a play, for instance, is also implicitly called into question by Tiresias, and by the play. For Oedipus, as for Aristotle, the medium of theater, the *theatron*, is both desirable and unproblematic because it is a medium that ultimately effaces itself, becoming diaphanous. This is why he can reject Creon's offer to go inside the palace to discuss the words of the oracle with the grandiloquent admonition: "Speak before all. Their plight concerns me now more than my life" (p. 28).

"[I] am here to learn for myself," Oedipus begins by announcing. But his conception of learning presupposes the very logic of identity and of opposition that his situation undercuts: that to be "here and now" is not to be "there and then"; that to "learn for myself" is incompatible with learning "from others"; that being a foreigner and being native born must be as mutually exclusive as being oneself and being a stranger. The mainstay of that logic, however, is the argument that one cannot be both one and many. He clings to this as he is deluged by the very "messengers" he had thought to exclude, confiding to Jocasta a last hope:

> *Oedipus.* That is my only hope; to await the shepherd.
> *Jocasta.* And why? What help do you expect from him?
> *Oedipus.* This: if we find his story fits with yours,
>   I am absolved.
> *Jocasta.* In what particular point?
> What did I say?
> *Oedipus.* You said he spoke of *robbers*—
>   That *robbers* killed him. If he still says *robbers*,
>   It was not I; one is not more than one. (p. 49)

"One is not more than one": and yet is this not precisely what the tragedy of Oedipus both confirms and denies? Oedipus is the stranger, come from afar, and the native-born Theban. He is both the avenger of Laius and his murderer, or, in the words of Tiresias

> . . . brother . . . and father at once, to the children he cherishes;
>   son
> And husband, to the woman who bore him; father-killer,
> And father/supplanter.
> Go in, and think on this.
> When you can prove me wrong, then call me blind. (p. 38)

Oedipus, who comes to see for himself, not through the eyes of others, who comes to banish the dark and bring light, who hopes to save Thebes from the plague as he saved it from the Sphinx—Oedipus, as Hölderlin puts it, again in his remarkable "Remarks," "entirely forgets himself, because he is entirely in the moment," equating the present with the past and the past with the future. He thus comes to stand for a notion of presence that is as simple as it is untenable: the specious simplicity of the present indicative, the *is*. All of Oedipus' fame, and his intelligence, rests on his having been able to answer the riddle of the Sphinx by providing a response in the form of a predication and a name: "man." This is also how he responds to the predicament in which he finds himself: to rid Thebes of the plague, he seeks to find a culprit who can be banished. To explain the words of Tiresias, he again seeks to identify a conspirator, Creon. The other exists only as a possibility of identification, of judging, predicating, naming, and thus knowing. In Oedipus, according to Hölderlin, knowledge "has broken through its limits [*seine Schranke durchrissen hat*]" and stands for a moment, "intoxicated." Indeed, one can argue that the redefinition and reimposition of precisely those limits constitutes the major dramatic moment in the play, the "caesura," which, in Hölderlin's reformulation of the Aristotelian reversal, interrupts and suspends the forward thrust of the "action," but not necessarily in the sense of *anagnōrisis* Aristotle had foreseen. This moment can be situated quite precisely. In response to Tiresias, who has just told him that "the killer you are seeking is yourself" (p. 36), Oedipus taunts the seer, asking him where he was when the Sphinx tormented Thebes, and then threatening him with "sharp punishment." This threat elicits from Tiresias a response that begins as follows:

> King though you are, one right—
> To answer—makes us equal; and I claim it.
> It is not you, but Loxias, whom I serve;
> Nor am I bound to Creon's patronage. (p. 37)

With these words, Tiresias begins his final, devastating prophecy, predicting suffering and scorn, blindness and exile for the tortured king. But his words also indicate a very different sort of thinking and of speaking from that which Oedipus has hitherto practiced. It is a thinking that has not "forgotten itself in the moment," which is to say, in the present, not the thinking of a speaker who believes himself to be in control because transparent to himself, just as language seems transparent to him. Rather, what Tiresias insists on is that, despite their differences in status and power, before language both the seer and the king are equal, for both enjoy—and are subject to—the "right of response." Tiresias, who cannot see with his eyes, is free from the *hubris* of a certain conception of sight, which thinks or believes that one can "see for oneself," without the aid of others, without the intervention of "messengers" or of "media." It is the *hubris*, in short, of a certain belief in the diaphany and docility of language. "I see your words, sir, tending / To no good end" (p. 34), Tiresias tells Oedipus at the beginning of their confrontation. The seer also insists that he "never should have come." And yet he has no choice but to come, not simply because the king has summoned him, but because he must respond to the call of the other, no matter what the cost: "when wisdom brings no profit, / To be wise is to suffer" (p. 34).

The difference between Tiresias and Oedipus, then, could be summed up as follows: each is playing a part that has long been pre-scribed, recorded, already like a role in a play even before "the play" in which they appear was actually written. But whereas Oedipus thinks he is the self-made ruler, sovereign, the *tyrannos* over Thebes and over language, Tiresias knows that he takes his cues from *another*, that he serves "not you, but Loxias" (p. 37).

This "wisdom" concerning the right and indeed the responsibility to respond, to take one's cue from the call of another who will never simply be present, opens the way to a different conception and, in-deed, practice of theater, in which the *medium* reemerges as of decisive significance. That reemergence is marked by the importance of the *response*: Tiresias's response to Oedipus, his insistence on the obliga-tion of responding, but also the response of the Chorus to the con-frontation between the two. It is a response that begins in the discursive mode of the *tyrannos* but moves gradually toward that of the seer:

> From the Delphian rock the heavenly voice denounces
> The shedder of blood, the doer of deeds unnamed.
> Who is the man?
> . . .
> Out from the snowy dawn on high Parnassus
> The order flashed, to hunt a man from his hiding.
> And where is he?
> . . .
> Terrible things indeed has the prophet spoken.
> We cannot believe, we cannot deny; all's dark.
> We fear, but we cannot see, what is before us. (p. 39)

The Chorus begins by asking questions of identity and, related, of place: "Who is the man?" And "Where is he?" To be identified, the culprit must be located. But if the perpetrator is both here and now, right in front of us, and yet in the place of the ruler, then the space and time involved are no longer the transparent conditions of identification but rather elements of a more ambiguous, more ambivalent dynamics: "We cannot believe, we cannot deny. . . . We fear, but we cannot see, what is before us." What is "before" the Chorus is the split and shifting scene, or scenario, of a play that enacts, not simply the unity or totality of an "action" or a "life," but also their irreducible disunity, in which "one" is always "more than one"—more and less, at once.

This is, perhaps, why the end of the play is not, here at least, the end of a life. Rather, it is the beginning of the end of a family, a lineage, perhaps of a city-state. It involves the self-mutilation of a body, and a move into exile. Oedipus, like the comic players in the etymological debate quoted by Aristotle, is banned from the city and begins to wander. It is against this background of an end that is more like an interruption than a conclusion that the concluding Chorus should be set:

> Sons and daughters of Thebes, behold: this was Oedipus,
> Greatest of men; he held the key to the deepest mysteries;
> Was envied by all his fellowmen for his great prosperity;
> Behold, what a full tide of misfortune swept over his head
> Then learn that mortal man must always look to [episkopounta]
>   the final day,
> And call no one happy before he has crossed life's border [terma
>   tou biou] free from pain. (ll. 1524–30)

This anticipated ending of life, terma tou biou, is most definitely not the end of the tragedy, the end of the play. And yet precisely because the end of the play cannot meaningfully coincide with the end of the story, nor this with the end of a life, precisely in this noncoincidence of "ending" and "meaning," a certain theater is involved. It is a theater marked by interruptions or, to once again recall the formula of Benjamin, by the "exposing of the present." The present is ex-posed in being placed before "us," before our eyes, but in a way that can never simply be seen, because it is never fully there. Rather, such presence is overdetermined by being situated in a space that is limited and yet never fully closed or defined. It must be seen, heard, commented upon, and responded to, yet without being entirely comprehended in any of those responses. The limits thus placed on comprehension determine the relation of theater to the "new media."

Groupings

This relation can be approached via a short text of Benjamin entitled simply "Theater and Radio." It has, however, an important subtitle: "On the Reciprocal Control of Their Pedagogical Work." Benjamin's opening remarks on the relationship between these two media sound quite familiar today, and yet also quite remote. He begins by noting that, despite the harmony suggested by his title (presumably by the "and"), the relation between the two media seems actually to be more competitive than collaborative, with radio clearly expanding its activities and theater just as clearly caught in an ever-growing crisis. Nevertheless, Benjamin insists on the possibility of their collaborating on "cooperative projects [*Gemeinschaftsarbeit*]," albeit strictly of a "pedagogical" nature. At this point his remarks touch on one of the most important distinctions and problems affecting any discussion of media today: its relation to the public and private—in particular, economic—spheres. Radio, at the time Benjamin was writing and in Europe until the last few decades, was exclusively owned and operated by the state. However much it served the interests of the ruling group, it still was considered a public service. In the last decades, this has radically changed, not just in Europe but globally, as the American model of privately owned media for profit has imposed itself everywhere.

No single historical development is of greater importance than this shift of the broadcast "media" from the realm of "public service" to that of private enterprise. Any discussion of the global impact of the media that does not begin and end with an interpretation of this fact, however variegated its effects may be in different areas and at different times, will not be able to do justice to the complexity of the phenomenon. As Adorno reminds his readers at the beginning of his essay "Prologue to Television": "The social, technical, artistic aspects of television cannot be treated in isolation from one another."[8] Benjamin does not, to be sure, dwell on this point specifically in his short essay. But it is clear from his discussion of contemporary developments in

Weimar Germany that he presupposes this aspect of radio. Benjamin thus mentions the various plays of Brecht that have been broadcast by the Southwest German Radio, as well as other educational programming, in the framework of *Schulfunk*: radio school. In this sense, the comparison between theater and radio is based on very specific and ostensibly very distant conditions. Curiously, however, if one substitutes "television," specifically "cable television," for radio, one discovers today, in Europe at least, a somewhat similar phenomenon beginning to emerge. In order to fill the possibilities of programming opened by cable and satellite transmission, the—now largely corporately funded—providers of television programs are forced to appeal to programming that under previous broadcast conditions, through the "Hertzian" airwaves, with their limited transmission space, would have been both impossible and unnecessary. One of the results of this programming deficit has been the creation of a number of channels entirely devoted to theater and/or music, including music theater, opera, and dance. Thus, some seventy years after Benjamin wrote his essay, once again theater and the media find themselves in uneasy collaboration, although this time the medium concerned is private cable television rather than public radio.

Benjamin's point of departure, then, may not be as entirely out of date as it might have seemed just a few years ago. The arguments he elicits from it, in any case, are certainly no. They can be framed around a single word, a German word that I have already cited several times in connection with theater, but that is anything but easy to render in English. That word is *Exponierung*, which it would be convenient to translate simply as "exposure," although that, as we shall shortly see, doesn't quite fit the bill. Here are the two arguments. First, concerning radio:

> With respect to theater, radio involves [*stellt . . . dar*] a technology that is not only newer but also more advanced, more audacious [*exponiertere*]. Unlike theater, it does not have a classical age to fall back on. The masses it grips are incomparably larger; finally, and above all, the material elements upon which its apparatus is based and the intellectual ones on which its productions are built are both most intimately connected with the interests of listeners.[9]

The term *exponiert* has to do with being "exposed," but in a variety of senses: here, the term suggests risk, taking chances, uncertainties—all of which relate to the points Benjamin mentions: the absence of a "classical" tradition to fall back on, the size and therefore heterogeneity of the audience and hence of its "interests." If the contemporary media have obviously never lost track of the size of their audience—since, in the perspective of private enterprise, precisely this size measures the value of the commodity the media have to "sell" to their advertisers, and hence, the value of the "media" themselves— what those media have only recently been compelled to acknowledge, in seeking to fill the programming slots made available by satellite and digital transmission, is the potential heterogeneity of that audience.

It remains to be seen to what extent the notion of *Exponiertheit* that Benjamin applied to radio in the twenties can be said to pertain to the media today, whether radio, television, or, more interestingly perhaps, the transformation of these two institutions currently taking place under the impact of the Internet. I will return to these questions in a moment. First let me continue retracing Benjamin's arguments, which, as we have already begun to see, will allow us to pose, if not to ex-pose, a number of significant questions concerning the relation of the media to theater today.

Having established the clear-cut superiority of radio over theater in terms of the degree of "exposure" of the respective technologies concerned, Benjamin proceeds by asking two questions: "And what does theater, by contrast, have to throw into the balance? The employment of living beings[10]—and nothing but. Perhaps the situation of theater in crisis can be unfolded most decisively from the following question: What does the employment of a living person in it tell us?" (pp. 584/774).

Benjamin once again brings us back to the Aristotelian *bios*: not, however, as the frame of the action imitated in the plot, but as the means through which that mimesis takes place. Benjamin thus poses, or exposes, the "living means" as a decisive constituent of the theatrical medium. Characteristically, his exposition is two-fold, reflecting what he calls a "regressive" and a "progressive" approach to theater: "The former in no way sees itself obliged to take notice of the crisis. For it, the harmony of the whole is and remains undiminished, and man its representative. It sees him at the height of his power, as Lord of Creation, as personality (even if he be the lowliest wage-laborer). His frame is today's cultural sphere, and over it he holds sway in the name of the 'human'" (pp. 584/774).

No matter what specific content it assumes, such triumphant theater "always realizes itself as 'symbol,' 'totality,' and *Gesamtkunstwerk*." It is a theater of education and cultivation (*Bildung*) as much as of entertainment and diversion (*Zerstreuung*), for, however opposed they may seem, they are "really only complementary manifestations." However, Benjamin concludes, no matter how grandiose the means that such theater may have at its disposal, it is no match for what radio, film—and, we can add today, television—have to offer. In the light of contemporary Hollywood films, however, Benjamin's evaluation must be modified: the hundreds of millions of dollars spent in the production and marketing of films today is in no way rendered obsolete by the technologies of the media, since the two have become increasingly complementary if not, indeed, from an economic standpoint symbiotic. The *Gesamtkunstwerk* is now realized not simply at the level of the "work" but—and in this, it is once again quite theatrical—at the level of its "execution," which includes its distribution and reception as well as its performance and display, and thus also its transformation from one medium to another, from film to video to CD to t-shirt, moving from one geographical "zone" to another, all under the auspices of a coordinated marketing operation of global proportions.

At the center of this convergence of theater and media we find precisely the figure that Benjamin described, one that we also encounter at the beginning of *Oedipus*: that of "man" as self-made, as *tyrannos*, in command of others as he seems to be of himself. The "crisis" is there, but only as an obstacle to be surmounted, a riddle to be resolved through the magic name *man*. This privileged notion of "man," of the "human," links Oedipus to the onto-theological subject, the "personality" that dominates much of modern Western theater. It confirms the continuity of creation that Oedipus presupposes in passing precipitously from his all too general interpretation of the oracle's words to an all too particular, all too personal search for a foreign culprit who can be banished.

It is precisely such a continuum, with its humanistic and onto-theological presuppositions, that the alternative conception of theater, the "progressive" conception that Benjamin now goes on to elaborate, calls into question. Such a theater, he emphasizes, relates differently to the techniques of the new media, radio and film. Instead of simply *competing* with them—or, given the necessary modifications we have introduced, of *completing* them—Brecht's Epic Theater, which serves Benjamin as the model of a progressive theater, adopts and adapts the techniques of "montage" elaborated in film and radio—not from the perspective of simply outdoing competing media by creating ever-greater works, but in order to demonstrate, as directly as possible, the untenable character of such totalizing perspectives. The key word here, which Benjamin will develop in his essay "What Is Epic Theater?," is *interruption*. The distinctive, defining trait of Epic Theater, he asserts, resides in the way "it brings the plot in its sequence to a standstill and thereby forces the listener to take a position with respect to that sequence, forces the actor to take a position with respect to his role" (pp. 584/775).

To fully understand the implications of Benjamin's concept of "interruption" as applied to theater, it helps to recall where his terms come from. Benjamin describes the disposition of Epic Theater in adapting the techniques of the new media for its own ends as "sober" or "prosaic"—in German, *nüchtern*—a word that, more than any other, articulates "the tendency of [Hölderlin's] late" works.[11] This term and tendency is tied to a notion that is the forerunner of Benjamin's use of interruption: the Hölderlinian notion of "caesura," which Benjamin discusses in his early essay on Hölderlin's poetry. Why "sobriety" in connection with "caesura"? Because the "caesura" marks a decisive interruption and limitation of exaltation and sublimity, in particular, of what Hölderlin, in his "Remarks," calls the "tragic transport":

> The tragic transport is, namely, authentically empty, and the most unfettered. Through it, the rhythmic succession of representations, wherein the transport presents itself, that which in prosody is called the caesura, the pure word, the counter-rhythmic interruption, becomes necessary in order, namely, to counter the surging alternation of representations at its height, so that what then appears is no longer the alternation of representations but representation itself [*die Vorstellung selbst*].[12]

Here Hölderlin is thinking specifically of the confrontation between Oedipus and Tiresias, in which the forward thrust of Oedipus' desire to find an external culprit is brought to a halt by the response of the seer. According to Hölderlin, the effect of this cut or caesura is, not just to suspend the rush to judgment, the "alternation of representations," but to allow "representation itself [*die Vorstellung selbst*]," which Hölderlin also calls "the pure word," to emerge. What is this "pure word," this process of *speaking*, as distinguished from actualized speech, the process of *representing* (*Vorstellung*) rather than the alternation of concrete representations? In German, *Vorstellung*—literally, "placing-before"—signifies not just "idea" or mental "representation," but also theatrical performance. And it is precisely this, the production of the theatrical process in its distinctive mediality—*Vorstellung* as *representing before* rather than simply as *representation*—that Benjamin associates with the "interruption" practiced by Brechtian theater. When it is suspended, identity comes up short, and it does so through "gesture." Gesture interrupts action, which, as a movement of meaning, constituted for Aristotle the primary object of tragic representation. By interrupting this movement of fulfillment—and action almost always connotes fulfillment—gesture allows the representing to emerge as a process of setting-before.

Benjamin borrows this distinctively theatrical process of setting-before, of *Vor-stellen*, from Hölderlin and Brecht, yet he transforms it, as the following passage indicates: "To the dramatic *Gesamtkunstwerk* [total work of art] Epic Theater opposes the dramatic laboratory. It returns in a new way to the great and venerable resource of theater—exposing the present [*die Exponierung des Anwesenden*]. At the core of its experiments [*Versuche*] stands man in our crisis" (pp. 584/775).

There is a shift here, but also a surprise. The shift takes place in redefining the theatrical performance as a "placing before" (*Vor-stellung*), that is also an *Exponierung*, "exposing." The surprise is the reintroduction of the notion of "man." Was not "man" at the heart of the "reactionary" conception of theater from which Benjamin is distinguishing "Epic Theater"?

But is it the same "man"? Benjamin goes on to assert that this "man in our crisis" is also the man that is excluded, "eliminated from radio and film." What sort of human being is this? It is a human being that is defined, first of all, as having been "sidelined [*kaltgestellt*]" by the prevailing media apparatus, to which it appears as little more than a "fifth wheel." Epic Theater, however, far from attempting a nostalgic recovery of this relegated human being, submits it to a series of tests and examinations. It is this process that constitutes the return of theater to its sources: the exposing of the present, and not simply of "the audience," those that are "present" for the performance. What is exposed by Epic Theater, and by theater generally, is the claim of humanity to be present to itself, in the guise of the autonomous individual.

That is why, when Benjamin proceeds to indicate how this reintroduction of "man in our crisis" is to function in Epic Theater, and presumably also in the new media, a certain repetition of the most "mechanical sort turns out to be essential: "What results is this: events can be changed, not at their high-points, not through virtue and decision, but only in their strictly habitual course, through reason and practice (*Übung*). Out of the most minute elements of behavior patterns (*Verhaltensweisen*), to construct what Aristotelian dramaturgy called "acting" (*handeln*)—this is the sense of Epic Theater" (pp. 584/ 775).

Epic Theater thus exposes the "living" by stripping it of its heroic claims to sovereignty, claims that confound the divine with the human and that find their secular and dissimulated embodiment in the cult of "personality." This "cult," as Benjamin well understood, is by no means limited to Stalinism but is inculcated ever more globally by the media and the uses to which they are put in determinate social contexts. In this context, Benjamin's explicit allusion to "Aristotelian dramaturgy" is precise and revealing. Aristotle, we recall, sought to separate the unity of an action, and even of a "life," from the unity of character, even going so far as to assert that the tragic plot could consist of "actions without character but not character without action." Benjamin revives this antipsychological approach of Aristotelian dramaturgy in attacking what might be called the "heroic" conception of action. At the same time, however, he changes the very notion of "action" and its relation to "life." The nature of that change is already indicated in his use of the gerundive, *Handeln*, "acting," rather than the more static noun *Handlung*, "action" or "plot." By appealing to the present participle, Benjamin indicates that the "acting" which constitutes the true medium of theater is incompatible with the self-contained unity suggested by the present indicative. On the stage, no action is ever fully self-present. As acting, such "action" is ex-posed in and through the iterations of a present participle that can never be totalized. Such acting is less like heroic action than the "strictly habitual course" of instinctively performed repetitions that constitute conventional "behavior patterns" or, rather, ways of behaving, *Verhaltensweisen*. But "acting," by redoubling such patterns, does not merely limit itself to repeating them *identically*: rather, in repeat*ing* them, it exposes them, which is to say, *almost immobilizes them*, in the "trembling contours" of singular *gestures*, gestures that, as Benjamin writes in "What Is Epic Theater?," can themselves *be cited*.

In short, what emerges is a reiterative singularity that is no longer simply taken for granted as the transparent medium of identification, of recognition, but that becomes identifiable and recognizable only through the "trembling" of an irreducible alterity. This alterity is irreducible for two reasons. First, because it has been extrapolated and isolated from the ostensible continuity of a quasi-instinctive, habitual pattern, and second, because in this isolation and extrapolation it reveals itself to be transferable, movable, transformable—synonyms for what Benjamin designates as "citable." This is why the "contours" of such a "gesture" must be described as "trembling": their location is always the result of a *tension* that is both in- and ex-tensive, affecting both internal composition and external situation. Both are what they are, but at the same time both are radically alterable, could be entirely different. Because these possibilities can never be reduced to or measured in terms of any single set of realizations, the medium of this theater is more akin to a "laboratory" than to a "work," at least in the sense of a *Gesamtkunstwerk*, a notion that marks the consummation of an aesthetic tradition that has always sought to subordinate the medium to its instantiation, precisely qua *work*. The work in this sense is held to instantiate the genre, and thus in this tradition the general always takes precedence over the singular. The interruptive gesture calls this precedence into question, even as it questions the notion of performance and of performativity, at least as teleological processes of fulfillment.

Benjamin concludes with a final remark that once again demonstrates the uncanny prescience of his approach to media. It has to do with the element that ties the medium of theater to the new media and that is perhaps characteristic of all media, as distinct from the genres of aesthetics. This element is situated in the aftermath of performance. From the viewpoint of traditional aesthetics, a work is considered to be self-contained and the effects it produces the result of its internal structure. Theater has from the very beginning been suspect because of its tendency to subordinate the work qua instantiation (of a genre) to the *effects* through which it constitutes itself, as it were, post facto. Significantly, the remark with which Benjamin concludes his brief text "Radio and Theater" has to do with the audience. In it, he sums up the relation of Epic Theater to conventional theater: "In this way Epic Theater distinguishes itself from the theater of convention: it replaces education [*Bildung*] with schooling [*Schulung*], distraction [*Zerstreuung*] by grouping [*Gruppierung*][. . . .]The education (of knowledge) is replaced by the schooling or training (of judgment)" (pp. 585/775–76).

This remark is particularly prescient for two reasons. First, because it demonstrates that the medium, whether theater, radio, television, or all of these, now unified and transformed through the Internet, produces its audience rather than simply reproducing the latter's expectations. Therefore the analysis of a medium can never be limited to strictly internal relations within a work, a play, understood as the exemplification or instantiation of an equally self-contained system or set of rules. Rather, what distinguishes medium from work is precisely the complex interaction between production and reception, caught up in a movement that might be described as "circulation," but only if we understand that such circulation never returns to its point of departure, never comes full circle.

This is why all attempts to justify a medium in terms of a given audience forget, overlook, or obscure the fact that the medium also contributes to the definition of that audience. It never does so in a vacuum, however, but always in the context of other media and "conventions." To be sure, those "conventions" are never arbitrary or natural, because they are never self-identical or self-contained. Rather, they are the product of a process of iteration that endows them with a relative fixity but also leaves them open to change.

The second point that demonstrates Benjamin's prescience with respect to the new media is suggested by the term he employs to describe the distinctive kind of synthesis or collection they produce. That term is, quite simply, *grouping*. Starting in his earliest writing, "On the Program of the Coming Philosophy," Benjamin calls for a concept to replace that of "synthesis," a concept that could do justice to the alterity upon which all such "bringing together" depends and which it never simply eliminates or integrates.[13] His use of the word *grouping* signals one such attempt. It suggests that the media, radio or theater, can bring together "addressees" or "receivers" in structures that are neither monolithic nor eternal and, above all, are never simply the expression of natural or intrinsic characteristics—such as race, gender, or ethnicity—but that are always determined by historically changeable situations, by "media" and "conventions," by "conventions" that are media and by media that are structured "conventionally." Such "groupings"—and not simply "groups"—are, Benjamin suggests held together by what he calls "interest." Social, economic, and political interest, to be sure. But in the context he develops, the notion of "interest" has also to be taken as literally as possible. *Groupings* held together by *interest* are those whose "being" is situated in a space *between*: *inter-esse*. That space is like a "stage" or a "scene," but temporally it also resembles a "scenario." It is constituted by its relations to what it is not, to determinate possibilities that are never actualized or present as such. This is why it is more appropriate to speak of *groupings* than of *groups*, in the fixed and familiar sense of "interest groups." These *groupings* of interest never finish getting their act together, taking their cue—like an actor playing a role, a *part* that will never be whole—from events that come from elsewhere.

The emergence of such "groupings of interest" is powerfully promoted by the "new media," but it is by no means exclusive to them. It is rooted in a process that is endemic to "media" as such or, rather, to "media" as distinct from "works." What is "new" is only—but this is hardly insignificant—that the new, electronic media have made manifest what was always at work in the "work" itself: namely, its mediality, just as alterity has always been "at work" in the constitution of identity. As Jacques Derrida has observed:

> Private space [*le chez-soi*] has always been structured by the other, both by the host and by the menace of expropriation. It has been constituted only in the shadow of this menace. Nevertheless, we are witness today to a new expropriation, a deterritorialization, a delocalization, a disassociation of the political and the local, of the national, of the national-state and the local, that is so radical that the response, or rather the reaction, is to wish to be "at home [*chez moi*]," finally at home, with my family [*avec les miens*], with those closest to me [*auprès de mes proches*].[14]

In short, what is new today is an exacerbation of a conflict that is very old:

> At every instant television introduces into my home [*dans le chez moi*] the elsewhere, the global. I am more isolated, more

privatized than ever before, with my home being visited by a permanent intrusion, desired by me, of the other, of the foreigner, the far-off, of another language. I desire it and at the same time I close myself off with this alien, wishing to isolate myself with him and without him, wishing to be at home. The recourse to one's own space [*au chez soi*], the return toward the *chez-soi* is all the more powerful, naturally, the more potent and violent the technological expropriation, its delocalization is.

Moreover it is not accurate to speak even of a *response* here, as though it were a question of a secondary reactivity that arrived to compensate, to react belatedly as it were—no, it is the same movement. It is part of the constitution of the proper and derives from the law of ex-appropriation of which I have spoken previously: no appropriation without the possibility of expropriation, without the confirmation of this possibility.[15]

What Derrida describes here as characteristic of the new media entails not so much a response to a provocation as a quasi-simultaneous movement of ambivalence, splitting the same, *chez soi*, in order to delimit it. Derrida's generic term for this is *iterability*, the irreducible *possibility* of indefinite repetition as alteration, as a reproduction that constitutes what it repeats *différance*, both difference and deferral, both altered and alterable.

The challenge, of course, is to understand both how such iterability could be the structural condition of identity-formation and at the same time provide the basis of all historical specification, especially with respect to today's "tele-technologies" and the "media" they entail.

Here the writings of Benjamin can be of great use. Benjamin's identification, in the wake of Hölderlin, of the structuring effects of *interruption*, whether as tragic "caesura," theatrical *peripeteia*, or cinematic "montage," suggest that the "cut" does not simply destroy: in segmenting, it becomes a formative factor. But the "forms" that it parts with thereby "tremble" like an image projected upon a screen. And only a vision very different from that of King Oedipus will ever be able to see it.[16]

4

Antigone's 'Nomos'

From the Rule of Law to the Law of the Rule

T R U E   T O its Protestant heritage, American society has never taken the existence of the "group" for granted. Its emphasis upon the individual as the basic unit of experience, whether religious, social, political, or ethical, has always cast the "rule of law" in an ambiguous light. On the one hand, as Tocqueville already noted, issues and controversies that in Europe would be decided by political instances tend in America to be resolved by judicial institutions.[1] This inclination to "legalize" politics implies an elevation of established, positive law over the more conflictual process of law making, which is based on shifting relations of forces.

On the other hand, however—and herein perhaps lies the ambiguity of law in the American tradition—the historical emphasis on the "individual" and the local, as distinct from the European tradition of centralized states, stands in a certain tension to the rule of law, which always implies a dominance of the general over the particular. The law is constructed for general purposes, which are then "applied" to particular "cases." From the perspective of the rule of law, the "individual" is only a "case": an instantiation of the general. Hence, the cult of the "outlaw," the criminal, and, more recently, of the Mafia: all are seen as antilegal, antistate, anticentralist agents and institutions, representing the individual and the local against the anonymous powers of the State, Big Business, and "the Law" in general. Conversely, recent rejection of international law in favor of the politics of preventive warfare, preemptive strikes, and imprisonment and trial without due process, testify to the sentiment that legal procedures are inappropriate, ineffective, and perhaps in the end counterproductive when it comes to securing the "homeland."

At the same time, this move from the rule of law to the rule of rule poses the question of the *ruler*, which is to say, of the powers and prerogatives of the state. This is all the more obvious in the contemporary American situation, where a government whose ideology traditionally would place it on the side of "the individual" sees itself constrained to increase the police and military powers of the state, ostensibly to protect the rights of its individual citizens.

Of course, the problematic relationship between state, individual, and family is by no means limited to the United States. It is one of the hallmarks of the history of the "West." Nothing less is suggested by the continued and indeed growing popularity of the first of Sophocles' Theban tragedies: *Antigone*. This play, which in so many ways seems so close to us, also keeps a certain distance—one that may well be the source of its continuing power.

For a contemporary reader it is perhaps not entirely obvious that the "action" of the play, *Antigone*, as with all of Sophocles' Theban plays, has "begun" long before the curtain rises. To read *Antigone*, whether as text or as theater, is to be confronted with the signifying chain of a mythic prehistory that is never present *as such*, but that exercises a decisive influence upon everything that happens, whether on stage or in the text. Throughout, the play implicitly stages this dependency of the explicit upon the implicit, from Antigone's opening speech, which echoes—or, rather, since *Antigone* is generally considered to have been written before *Oedipus Tyrannos*—anticipates[2] the context in which the "action" unfolds:

> Ismene, my sister, true child of my own mother [*autodelphon*],[3]
> do you know any evil out of all the evils bequeathed by Oedipus
> that Zeus will not fulfill for the two of us in our lifetime? There
> is nothing—no pain, no ruin, no shame, nor dishonor—that I
> have not seen in your sufferings and mine. And now what is this
> new edict [*kērugma*] that they say the general has just decreed to
> all the city? Do you know anything? Have you heard? Or does
> it escape you that evils from our enemies are on the march
> against our friends? (ll. 1–10)

Two sisters, not merely of the "same blood" as it is sometimes rendered, but more literally "of the same womb" or "mother"—or also "of the same brother [adelphon]," which, although not idiomatic, is difficult to ignore given that the "edict" Antigone has just discovered concerns their dead brother, Polyneices—meet in front of the palace where their father, Oedipus, once ruled and where he, at the beginning of Oedipus Tyrannos, will have made his initial appearance, both before (in the chronology of the plot, the muthos) and after (in the chronology of the writing) this scene: two sisters meeting to bear the brunt of their heritage. Everything that happens in Antigone, as in Oedipus Tyrannos and Oedipus at Colonus, takes place in the shadow of a myth that it in turn displaces and transforms. If tragedy in general can be described as the staging of myth, the myth that is staged here and elsewhere in Sophocles' Theban plays is organized around the question of a family and its relation to the polis.[4] The family, of course, is that of Labdacus, grandson of Cadmus, founder of Thebes. The son of Labdacus, who in turn was king of Thebes, was Laius. Different versions of the myth have survived, and no one of them is clearly established as authoritative in the plays of Sophocles. The closest the play comes is the account of the family curse given by Jocasta to Oedipus: "An oracle came to Laius once—I will not say from Phoebus himself, but from his ministers—saying that he would suffer his doom at the hands of the child to be born to him and me" (ll. 711–15).

"I will not say from Phoebus himself . . ." The source of the curse is thus indirect, "his ministers" and not the god himself. Certainly Jocasta seeks to assuage Oedipus by questioning the authority of the legend, but from the perspective of the drama its origin has to remain unclear, problematic. The question that emerges here is not where the curse ultimately came from—whether from god or from man—but rather what such a curse signifies. It is with this question that Oedipus grapples until his end, and it returns to haunt Antigone, the play and the figure. However obscure and conflicting the diverse versions of the myth, the question must be addressed. According to most of them, Laius was first forbidden by Apollo to have children, whether in punishment for a crime, as one version attests,[5] or for some other reason. What Sophocles deploys are the effects, not the cause: a legacy of "pain, sorrow, suffering, and dishonor" (l. 4).

What is striking, then, is that "causes" are ignored or left obscure, and in so doing, effects emphasized. What might these signify? First and foremost, the end of a (royal) family. Laius' progeny will have no descendants. The father dies at the hands of his son, and his son's sons, bearers of his name, perish by their own hands. In short, the family of the Labdacides is condemned, whatever the "reason" for this condemnation may have been.

To ignore causes—or, rather, to refuse to equate them with "reasons"—and to stage only effects, as does Sophocles, places readers and audiences before another sort of question: How can such "effects without causes" continue to fascinate and challenge audiences over two and a half millennia and in particular today? Correlatively: could such fascination have to do precisely with the *absence* of identifiable causes? Any response to these questions must begin, and perhaps end, with the destinies of Oedipus and Antigone. But destinies are never isolated: they entail networks that consist of relations and never simply of "individuals." The destiny of both Oedipus and Antigone is inseparable from a curse visited upon their family. This is, however, not because of anything that either of them, or perhaps even their antecedents, has done or, rather, done *knowingly*. That is why, in the texts of Sophocles at least, the question of guilt seems irrelevant. Or, if not irrelevant, detached from its familiar and consecrated link to conscious intention, and hence to moral responsibility, as generally understood.

Instead, we must look for the meaning of their fate in the structure of the family and the events that befall it. Long before Jean Bollack, this insight guided Hegel's interpretation of the play in *The Phenomenology of Spirit*, where Antigone is mentioned only once, but where the tragedy that bears her name ushers in the first unmediated appearance of *Geist*, the "spirit" manifesting itself in and as "the ethical world." As the essential manifestation of the dialectic, however, spirit appears only in disappearing, thus rendering any summary or paraphrase of its manifestations extremely difficult (indeed, in principle impossible). This is perhaps why discussions of Hegel's text are often so reductive. In his arguments, Hegel never "takes sides," since the dialectical movement entails precisely the dynamization of alternative "sides" as static polarities. Instead, they are revealed as always already having been "moments or disappearing quantities."[6] To identify the Hegelian interpretation of *Antigone* with the position of Creon, for instance, privileging the authority of the state over that of the family, is to ignore the dialectical structure of the Hegelian text. What is essential in Hegel's interpretation of *Antigone* is the emphasis it places upon a certain *immediacy* of spirit—of a spirit that, it should be remembered, is constituted by and as *mediation*. In short, "the ethical order" in which Hegel inscribes Antigone is that of the *initial* manifestation of spirit *as such*, which is to say, as "the ethical spirit of the people insofar as it is *immediate truth*; the individual, that is a world" (p. 460). Discussions of this Hegelian approach often miss the fact that *all* the figures that people this "world," Creon no less than Antigone, are equally implicated in its limitations and therefore share its destiny—which, following the dialectical sequence of the *Phenomenology*, is to dissolve and transform itself into what seems its diametrical opposite and contradiction, which Hegel calls the "state of law [*Rechtszustand*]." The ambiguous, ambivalent relation of ethics to law, already mentioned, in particular with respect to the American tradition, is thus inscribed in its general form in the Hegelian dialectic. What Tocqueville notes of the relation of Americans to Descartes (at the beginning of the second volume of *Democracy in America*),[7] applies in a different way, but no less, to their relation to Hegel: The American tradition remains Hegelian even if most Americans have never even heard of, much less read Hegel because, by virtue of its individualist bias, American political "culture" is situated precisely at the dialectical juncture of the "ethical world" and the "state of law."

What is common to both of these poles and determines their relation to one another as one of mutual but symmetrical negativity can be described as a certain *hypostasis* of the *individual*. This hypostasis also frames the relation of "family" to "state" as it is staged in *Antigone*. And it also, in a certain sense, makes those two institutions "moments"—or, to use another vocabulary, *signifiers*—of something else. That something else has to do with the determination of identity in terms of *individuality*: not individuality as such, but individuality mediated and reflected in its constitutive negativity, which is to say, individuality as "spirit."

This notion of the individual underlies the two institutions that are commonly associated with the "Hegelian" reading of *Antigone*, understood as a conflict between allegiance to the family, embodied in Antigone, and allegiance to the state, represented by Creon. If one reflects on the destiny of the house of Labdacus, we see that both elements are involved from the start: the fate of a family and the fate of a *polis*, Thebes, that has been founded and then governed by the heads of that family. In short, family and state overlap here, and this makes the destiny of Laius distinctive and significant. The curse that afflicts him, for whatever reason, also has political implications. But to interpret them, the significance of the family must first be addressed, since that is the institution that is immediately put into question—and into play—by the destiny of Laius.

Hegel frames his consideration of the family by posing the question of the relation between the individual and the general. The family gives institutional expression to the way in which the finite singularity of its individual members is negated and overcome—but also "supplemented [*ergänzt*]" through the generality of generation, through "blood relationship": "Blood-relationship therefore supplements the abstract natural process by adding to it the process of consciousness, by interrupting the work of nature and by snatching the blood relations from destruction, or better, because destruction—its becoming pure being—is necessary, it takes upon itself [*über sich nimmt*] the act of destruction" (p. 471).

The "taking over" of this "act of destruction" occurs for Hegel in two ways. First is through the organization of burial rites that enable the family to take charge of an individual who is both consummated and at the same time relegated to pure passivity by death: "The family protects the dead from the dishonoring action of unconscious desires and abstract beings, sets its own in [their] place [*an die Stelle*] and weds the relative to the bosom of the earth as to an elemental and immutable individuality; it thereby makes him the member of a community [*Gemeinwesen*]" (p. 472).

The second moment or aspect is already anticipated in the nuptial language used to describe the function of burial rites: the dead materiality of the departed relative is "wedded" to the earth, thus engendering something new: no longer the isolated individual, trapped in mortality, but the "member of a community"—literally, of a "common being," a *Gemeinwesen*—a word large enough to encompass the collective being of the earth understood as a biosystem undergoing continual transformation. Degeneration of an individual entity is thus transformed and transfigured into regeneration of a collective entity. This is, according to Hegel, "divine law" as distinguished from "human law." Divine law thus remains tied to the individual as individual, and its "power," which is considerable, derives from what Hegel designates "the *abstractly* pure *Universal*, the *elemental* Individual" (p. 472). To this abstract and elemental universal, Hegel opposes the effective and actual universality of "human law," anchored in the "whole people [*das ganze Volk*]," which implies in a "people" that is the realization of the ethical whole. The family itself accedes to this whole through generation, which is to say, first of all through children, who leave behind the family in its finitude, embodied in the ephemeral status of aging parents. With their aging parents left behind, the youthful children are now able to come into their own by participating in the more enduring political institutions of the "people."

At this point, where the Hegelian dialectic confronts the question of gender in respect to family and state, it is necessary to interrupt this impossible summary so as not to lose touch with the question of the curse visited upon Laius. We will return shortly to the issue of gender difference as it relates both to the Hegelian dialectic and to *Antigone*. The characteristic of the family that emerges in this account, however, suggests what is at stake in the history of the house of Labdacus. The prophecy that the father will be slain by his son, who will then replace him both as ruler and as husband, is tantamount to condemning the family of the Labdacus to extinction, according to the laws of patrilineal descendence. In Hegelian terms, the "ethical"—*sittlichen*—character of this family is compromised, inasmuch as this character is defined precisely by the ability to rise "above" the contingency of mere empirical finitude and to attain an initial, immediate level of universality by surviving *spiritually* in, through, and as its descendants. But the family of the Labdacus will not survive, and this transforms its relation to the "individual," or what Hegel also calls the *singular: der Einzelne*. If the fate of this particular family, from such a distant time, has fascinated throughout the ages and continues to fascinate even today—perhaps especially today—it is probably because the same hopes continue to be invested in the "family" that Hegel described and that Sophocles staged: the hopes that through it the singular may somehow survive.

To be sure, the "singular" here must not be conflated with the "individual," not, at least, if we take those terms at their face-value. The "individual" is, literally, that which is in-divisible and undivided. From the perspective of the Hegelian dialectic, however, which is moved by mediation and negativity, nothing can be held to be intrinsically indivisible. Everything is what it is only by virtue of its relation to what it is not: in Hegelian parlance, by being "mediated" through "determinate"—and *determining*—"negation." The determinate negation of the "individual" renders the latter eminently *divisible*, and this divisibility distinguishes the individual from the *singular, dem Einzelnen*. The singular is never self-contained. It is constituted by its relation to others from whom it is separated. Such separation, however, is not tantamount to isolation. Rather, it constitutes a mode of being *solitary: ver-einzelt*, singular.

If such singularity—rather than individuality—is what the family is about, then this would explain: first, why its constitutive relations should be marked as much by *separation* as by *joining*; and second, why the family draws its raison d'être from the desire of the singular to *survive*. As the institution organizing the possibility of such survival, the family is a site where the "written" positive laws of man confront the "unwritten" precepts of what is more and other than human: the divine. The oracle's prophecy condemning the family of Laius to self-destruction through nonprocreation thus *sets the scene* for a drama involving, not just the institution of the family, but the other collective institution that also seeks to guarantee a certain survival beyond the limits of the singular: the state. With this in mind, we can now turn to the specific configuration deployed in Sophocles' *Antigone*.

Go Figure: Antigone Calculates

By juxtaposing two speeches, we can best gauge what is at stake in the conflict that opposes Antigone to Creon. The first is Antigone's description of Creon's *kerygma*, the "proclamation" announced by the herald viva voce, which must therefore be repeated by Antigone to Ismene in order to be "heard":

> *Antigone*. Have you heard? Or does it escape you that evils from our enemies are on the march against our friends?
> *Ismene*. To me no word of our friends, Antigone, either bringing joy or bringing pain has come since we two were robbed of our two brothers. . . .
> *Antigone*. I knew it well, so I was trying to bring you outside the courtyard gates to this end, that you alone might hear.
> *Ismene*. Hear what? It is clear that you are brooding on some dark news.

Antigone. Why not? Has not Creon destined our brothers, the
one to honored burial, the other to unburied shame?
Eteocles, they say, with due observance of right and custom,
he has laid in the earth for his honor among the dead below.
As for the poor corpse of Polyneices, however, they say that
an edict has been published to the townsmen that no one
shall bury him or mourn him, but instead leave him unwept,
unentombed, for the birds a pleasing store as they look to
satisfy their hunger. Such, it is said, is the edict that the good
Creon has laid down for you and for me—yes, for me
[*k'amoi, legō gar k'ame*]. (ll. 9–33)

From the very start, Antigone challenges the authority of her un-
cle's proclamation, and she does so by introducing the notion of singularity. The law, human law, must always aim at the general; but for
Antigone this *kerygma* is just that, a pronouncement, moreover, one
aimed at particular persons: "for you and for me—yes, for me." The
addressee of this pronouncement is not the general public, not all the
inhabitants of Athens, but, rather, singular beings. These beings—
"you and me"—are defined, not by their individual personalities, nor
even by their membership in the *polis*, but by their family *position*.
For Antigone, then, the conflict is not, as is often supposed, between
"human law" and "divine law"; rather, it arises from a pronouncement, a *kerygma*, whose claim to have the force of law is illegitimate,
because from the very start it is directed primarily at singular beings
determined through their positions within a family.

But this is no ordinary family. As has already been noted, the house
of Labdacus is the family that founded and rules Thebes. This convergence of family and *polis* has been underscored by the arrival of Oedipus, who, ostensibly a foreigner, continues the rule of the Labdacus
clan while preparing its end. This is the irony of Oedipus as *tyrannos*:
that is, as one who acquires power rather than inheriting it, for his
destiny demonstrates how politically unviable inheritance can be.
Creon, brother of Jocasta, is also a *tyrannos*, since he is not a member
of the Labdacus clan. His authority is even more fragile than that of
Oedipus. He accedes to power practically by default, as next of kin,
but his kinship is not a "blood relationship." If the blood relationship
of Oedipus proves his undoing, then the lack of such a relationship
in Creon seems hardly an effective alternative. The lack of a firm

legitimation of his sovereignty constrains him to begin his rule by attempting to lay out the general principles upon which it will be based:

> My fellow citizens! . . . I now possess all the power and the throne according to my kinship with the dead. Now, it is impossible to know fully any man's character, will, or judgment, until he has been proved by the test of rule and law-giving. For if anyone who directs the entire city does not cling to the best and wisest plans, but because of some fear keeps his lips locked, then, in my judgment, he is and has long been the most cowardly traitor. And if any man thinks a friend more important than his fatherland, that man, I say, is of no account. Zeus, god who sees all things always, be my witness—I would not be silent if I saw ruin, instead of safety, marching upon the citizens. Nor would I ever make a man who is hostile to my country a friend to myself, because I know this, that our country is the ship that bears us safe, and that only when we sail her on a straight course can we make true friends. Such are the rules by which I strengthen this city. Akin to these is the edict which I have now published to the citizenry concerning the sons of Oedipus (ll. 175–94)

Creon's inaugural speech thus begins by invoking the general good of the *polis*, which calls for no less general laws in order to subordinate all particular considerations, institutions, and relations: above all, that of "friendship." The *ship* of state has two functions.[8] First, it provides a vessel capable of *containing* the various elements that make up a *polis* and, by so containing them, imparts a certain unity and duration to them. Second, once again as a *vessel*, it navigates the obstacles that time places in the path of any entity seeking to maintain its identity essentially unchanged. The "state of law" is the expression of these two "moments," inasmuch as it brings together containment and continuity by prescribing the application of general principles to particular and varying temporal instances. The death of Polyneices is one such instance, and Creon's entire rule will depend, and ultimately founder, on his attempt to bring this singular event fully under the authority of the "laws" of the state. As the metaphor of the vessel indicates, the attempt to establish the legitimacy of political power depends on the notion of safeguarding a self-contained *place*, that of the *polis*, here *Thebes*. The project of imposing this rule and justifying it defines that place as a kind of courtroom, a tribunal, but also as a theater, both as a spectacle for the Gods ("Zeus, god who sees all things always, be my witness")[9] and as a sight that humans will not quickly forget: "leave him unburied and a sight of shame, with his body there for birds and dogs to eat" (ll. 206–7).

Without the "ship of state" to protect and contain them, there can be neither friendship nor family: this is Creon's justification for his treatment of Polyneices. At the same time, it is a challenge to the family, insofar as the latter aims, as Hegel would have it, to save the solitary individual from precisely the degeneration to which Creon condemns the corpse of Polyneices: the disintegration and scattering of passive organic matter.

As we have seen, from her very first words Antigone challenges the authority of Creon, the "general [*stratēgos*]," to wage war against the dead or, rather, to rule over their memory by controlling those who wish to mourn them. This challenge resonates in Hegel's discussion. Far from simply opposing "family" to "state," Hegel emphasizes that, with respect to the "ethical world," the state is not simply the state. It articulates itself through an institution that does not merely "oppose" the family but also mirrors it. The word Hegel employs to distinguish this particular form of the state—which is not at all equivalent to the State in general—will be familiar to most English-speaking North Americans, for whom the political concept of the "state" retains a foreign resonance. The word Hegel uses to designate the political organization of the "ethical world" is *Regierung*; in English, *government*. The passage in which he describes what this institution entails takes up certain images used by the Chorus in its initial ode ("Shaft of the sun, fairest light of all that have dawned on Thebes of the seven gates"; ll. 100–101): "The commonwealth [*Gemeinwesen*], the uppermost law, whose validity is clear as sunlight [*an der Sonne geltenden Gesetz*], has its effective vitality in the *government*, in which it finds its individuality [*als worin es Individuum ist*]. Government is the self-reflected real and effective spirit, the simple *self* of the entire ethical substance" (p. 473).

Qua "government," the state is structured as the very "individual" to which it opposes itself—while remaining on the same level, as it were, informed by the same notion of self-identity: namely, that of simple self-sameness. This is why the state as "government" is no more stable than the family: both seek to sustain a notion of "individuality" as simple self-identity, a notion that denies mediation, negativity, alterity. The expedient by which the state as government attempts to preserve this spirit of "simplicity [*Einfachheit*]," according to Hegel, is quite simply that of periodic wars, which enable it "to injure and confuse" the centrifugal striving toward "independence [*Selbständigkeit*]" of its component individuals and isolated institutions. In so doing, however, "government" reinstates and confirms the power of "divine law" by elevating *death* to the negative principle of its internal cohesion—for death is the enabling limit of the individual.

Thus for Hegel the state qua government cannot simply escape "divine law" or the claims of the "family." But the resistance of Antigone to Creon's proclamation goes further, as she defiantly announces to him:

> *Creon.* You, you with your face bent to the ground, do you
> admit, or deny that you did this?
> *Antigone.* I declare it and make no denial.
> *Creon.* . . . (*To Antigone.*) You, however, tell me—not at length,
> but briefly—did you know that an edict had forbidden this?
> *Antigone.* I knew it. How could I not? It was public.
> *Creon.* And even so you dared overstep that law [huperbainein
> nomous]?
> *Antigone.* Yes, since it was not Zeus who announced to me that
> edict, and since not of that kind are the laws [*nomous*] which
> Justice [*Dikē*] who dwells with the gods below established
> among men. Nor did I think that your decrees were of such
> force, that a mortal could override the unwritten and
> unfailing statutes given us by the gods. For their life is not of
> today or yesterday, but for all time, and no man knows when
> they were first put forth. (ll. 446–59; translation modified)

As Lacan puts it in his seminar, *The Ethics of Psychoanalysis*, what Antigone invokes to challenge the authority of Creon is neither positive law nor even law as such, but rather "the conditions of legality," conditions that are very different from law or right. Hence, the invocation of Dikē, goddess of the underworld and of justice. Why should "justice," as distinct from right and law, be associated with the underworld? Perhaps because the conditions of legality, as distinct from positive law and right, converge with the significance of mortality in the *singular experience* that marks "our" separation from the "departed" and our separability from ourselves. "Justice" stands in an aporetical relation to the law by virtue of the nonuniversalizable and incommensurable dimension of singularity, as Derrida argues in his discussion of Benjamin's "Critique of Violence" and in his commentary on Kafka's "Before the Law."[10] To be effective, a law must be enforced. To be enforced, however, it must be able to "subsume" the individual to which it is applied as "a case" under its generality. As mortal, however, the singular resists such subsumption, even and especially under the political, under the state of law or of right. Yet the singular only "is," only articulates itself in, through, and as this *resistance*: it has no self-same, self-standing, independent existence. It is not the "individual," in the sense of being at the center of the "ethical world," including both the family and the "state" qua government. This is why family and government go hand in hand even while opposing and rivaling one another. They share a common horizon: the notion of the simple identity of the individual, of identity *as* individual, self-contained and self-sustaining. The only difference is whether that identity is determined through the "private" institution of the "family" (nuclear or extended) or through the "public" institution of the state qua government—or, for that matter, through "the people," "the race," the "ethnos," all understood equally as homogeneous, self-contained entities requiring the definite article. All such "cases" presuppose the "rule of law," the "state of right"—the *Rechtszustand*—insofar as they define the "particular" as a part of the whole, subsumed from the start under the general, under the all-in-common, the *All-ge-meine*. Against this all-embracing notion, the blasphemous cry of Antigone resounds and resists, even if Hölderlin alone was audacious enough to try to preserve this aspect of it in his translation: "*My Zeus* did not report this to me [*ou gar ti moi Zeus*]."[11]

What relation to the gods, to Zeus, to Dikē, does Antigone presuppose? One should be careful not to assume it is a "personal" relation, one of an "individual" appropriating the gods. Antigone rejects that kind of relationship, the one implied but also dissimulated in Creon's appeal to the general good and his invocation of the ship of state. Creon, spokesman of the "government," seeks to subordinate the heterogeneous—the relation to the gods—to the undivided individuality of the state. It is this that Antigone challenges. The position on which she "camps," as Lacan puts it,[12] is precisely not that of the isolated individual but rather of a certain familial relationship that implies and includes *separation*. This, paradoxically, is the significance of her allegiance to her brother. Hegel sees this, in his discussion of the relation between sister and brother, although he seeks to inflect its implications in the direction of a dialectical interpretation of the family:

> The brother, however, is for the sister above all the restful, self-same being [*das ruhige gleiche Wesen überhaupt*]; her recognition in him is pure and unadulterated by natural relations; the indifference of singularity and the ethical contingency of the same is therefore not present in this relation; rather, the moment of the recognizing and recognized singular Self [*einzelnen Selbst*][13] can here assert its prerogative [*darf hier sein Recht behaupten*], because it is tied to the balance of a relation based on blood that is also free of desire. The loss of the brother is therefore irreplaceable for the sister and her duty toward him therefore the highest.
>
> At the same time this relation is the limit at which the self-contained family dissolves and goes beyond itself. (p. 477)

The dialectical dissolution of the family, as Hegel describes it in this passage, has as its frame "above all the restful, self-same being," which he identifies with that of the brother for the sister, entailing the equilibrium of a blood relation that is unperturbed by sensual desire. Given, however, that Hegel's text implicitly but unmistakably refers to *Antigone*, nothing could be further from Sophocles' text. For the domestic equilibrium or repose of the Labdacides is constantly disrupted by desire. Indeed, the downfall of this family is inseparable from uncontrollable desire: that of the father followed by those of his sons. But the significance of such desires cannot be measured in terms of the individuals who are driven by them. The drive originates elsewhere, and its significance therefore surpasses those whom it moves. The oracle condemns the family of Laius to reproduce not its life but its death and thus to demonstrate its finitude. In so doing, this family raises, rather than resolves, the question of singularity—not, however, in the way described by Hegel: a singularity that could be considered to be "restful [*ruhig*]" because self-contained. Antigone's relation to her dead brothers, like her relation to the gods, presupposes separation and even loss. Derrida elaborates this aspect in *Glas*, emphasizing that the opposition at work in *Antigone*, insofar as the play entails the "ethical world" described by Hegel, cannot be understood simply as between "singularity and universality" but rather as between their respective "laws": "More precisely, the two terms of the opposition are not the singular and universal but the *law* of singularity and the *law* of universality. The opposition is determined between those forms of generality that are laws (*Gesetz der Einzelheit, Gesetz der Allgemein-heit*), since it operates within the ethical realm that is the rule of law."[14]

But the "law of singularity" is not one law among others: it is a law that calls into question the status and stability of the legal, since it articulates itself through difference and discrepancy rather than through identity. If this singular "law" entails negation, it is not that of a totalizing dialectic as *Aufhebung*—elevation, effacement, and com-prehension—but rather one involving refusal and resistance. "*My* Zeus did not tell me that," Antigone responds to Creon, thereby confronting the ruler's claim to represent the whole with an appeal to the gods as irreducibly singular. Whereas Creon's proclamation claims to speak in the name of all, Antigone speaks only in her own name, and not just of her *relation* to Zeus, but of "*my* Zeus." But the "my" of Antigone is not the possessive pronoun of an autonomous individual. Rather, it is that of someone whose "address" to the gods cannot be defined exclusively in terms of her appurtenance to a political entity. Instead, she will describe her position in terms of a singularity that is doubly determined: first, by her relation to her family; and second, by her situation as a mortal. Although these two aspects cannot be sepa-rated, neither do they simply coincide. This inseparable nonconver-gence marks her discourse, in particular its use of the personal pronouns "I," "me," and "my." Her determination to challenge Creon appears all the more powerful and drastic because she claims to speak neither in the name of all, nor even in the name of a truth that could be known beyond all doubt. Antigone's truth, if there is one, remains conjectural, not apodictic. In another English translation, this is how she confronts Creon:

> That order did not come from God. Justice, Dikē,
> Who dwells with the gods below, knows no such law.
> I did not think your edicts strong enough
> To overrule the unwritten unalterable laws
> Of God and heaven, you being only a man.
> [Those laws] are not of yesterday or today, but everlasting,
> Though where they came from, none of us can tell. (ll.
>   450–56)[15]

Creon's edicts make no distinction between the living and the dead. In so doing, he is consistent, for if, as he declares at the outset, "our country is our life," then the needs of society would seem to include all aspects of life, including the fate of the dead. Antigone challenges this total, if not totalitarian claim:

> *Antigone.* . . . There is nothing shameful in respecting your own flesh and blood.
>
> *Creon.* Was not he your brother, too, who died in the opposite cause?
>
> *Antigone.* A brother by the same mother and the same father.
>
> *Creon.* Why, then, do you pay a service that is disrespectful to him?
>
> *Antigone.* The dead man will not support you in that.
>
> *Creon.* Yes, he will, if you honor him equally with the wicked one.
>
> *Antigone.* It was his brother, not his slave, who died.
>
> *Creon.* But he died ravaging this land, while he fell in its defense.
>
> *Antigone.* Hades craves these rites, nevertheless.
>
> *Creon.* But the good man craves a portion not equal to the evil's.
>
> *Antigone.* Who knows but that these actions are pure to those below?
>
> *Creon.* You do not love someone you have hated, not even after death.
>
> *Antigone.* It is not my nature to join in hate, but in love.
>
> *Creon.* Then, go down to hell and love them if you must. While I live, no woman will rule me. [*emou de zōntos ouk arxei gunē*]. (ll. 513–24)

Creon, who rules by edict (*kerygma*), condemns Antigone in order to avoid what he designates woman's "rule" (*arxei gunē*): no woman shall come "first [*arxei*]," which is to say, before the man. Today his reasoning would be labeled "sexist," and with good reason. But like all sexism, his is founded on a logic of commensurability which is ultimately a logic of identity, one that confounds politics and moralism: "But the good man craves a portion not equal to the evil's," he argues. There is good and there is evil, as there is man and woman, I and you, self and other: they are opposed, and in their opposition fully complicit, because commensurable. Good comes before evil, deserves *more* than evil, just as man comes before woman, self before other, hate before love. And what is Antigone's counterargument? In the exchange with Creon, it ultimately seems to rest upon "love": "It is not my nature to join in hate, but in love." Nothing could be more familiar to a Christian tradition of philology. The only problem is that Antigone does not leave it at that. After Creon has departed, shortly before she is led away to be buried alive, Antigone interrupts her lament to give a response to this question, in a passage that has bothered readers at least since Goethe told Eckermann he hoped that one day a philologist would come along to show that the speech was inauthentic, an interpolation that could then be purged from the text. In the middle of her passionate protest, Antigone suddenly stops short— and begins to *calculate*:

> Now, Polyneices, it is for tending your corpse that I win such reward as this. And yet I honored you rightly, as the wise understand. Never, if I had been a mother of children, or if a husband had been rotting after death, would I have taken that burden upon myself in violation of the citizens' will. For the sake of what law, you ask, do I say that? A husband lost, another might have been found, and if bereft of a child, there could be a second from some other man. *But when father and mother are hidden in Hades, no brother could ever bloom for me again. Such was the law whereby I held you first in honor.* (ll. 907–12, my emphasis)

This kind of cold, formal reasoning, Goethe argues, simply does not fit the grand passion of Antigone's situation, or her character. But it also doesn't fit the characterization of Hegel, namely, that the mode of thinking appropriate to Antigone is that of *Ahnung*, of "premonition."[16] Antigone does not anticipate anything here, she simply calculates the bottom line. It is true that the "law" she invokes to explain and justify her resistance *seems* to confirm and conform to Hegel's portrayal of the role of the woman in "the ethical household": "in the house of ethics, it is not *this* husband, *this* child, but rather *a husband, children as such*—not the sensation, but the universal on which the woman's relationships are founded" (p. 476).

Yet there is a subtle but decisive difference between Hegel's version of the ethical household and Antigone's argument that Hegel, characteristically, does not take into account. Antigone does not justify her action in universal, moral terms. It is not because she has lost a "brother as such" that she does what she does, but rather because she

137

has lost a brother in a situation that renders him irreplaceable. Her emphasis on irreplaceability acknowledges a singularity that resists the logic of commensurability invoked by Creon. When father and mother are gone, the loss of a brother "by the same mother and the same father" is irreplaceable. It is not family obligation *as such* but, through the family, *the experience of irreplaceable singularity* that commands Antigone's action. This obligation to the singularity, and not the *individuality* of Polyneices—his personal qualities, merits, or demerits—constitutes Antigone's *nomos* and compels her to act as she does.

It would thus be precipitous to translate the Greek word she invokes, *nomos*, as "law"—even if this is the usual translation, adopted by Jebb as well. "Law" suggests "legislator," but, as Antigone reminds Creon, the *nomoi* that guide her actions have no legislator: "For their life is not of today or yesterday, but for all time, and no man knows when they were first put forth." She invokes Dikē and the gods only to underscore a certain alterity: their life is not of today or yesterday, but for all time, whereas the lives of those to whom the *nomoi* are addressed are limited and finite. It is the respect of such limits that Antigone's *nomos* enjoins.

Antigone's *nomos* thus recovers some of the sense of the verb to which it is related, *nemein*, "to distribute." Far from designating something that is homogeneous and monolithic, its unknowable origin and timeless "life" underscore the heterogeneity and alterity of the human life they challenge and command. Such heterogeneity marks the *archē* that Creon fears and seeks to dismiss as "woman's rule." It is the irreducible heterogeneity of this *archē* that emerges out of the calculations of Antigone, calculations that readers from Aristotle to Jebb have sought to dismiss or disqualify.[17]

The principle of Antigone's defiance, then, is the obligation to commemorate the incalculable incommensurability of the singular, encountered in its most radical form: the loss of what for Hegel would be the simple immediacy of a "this-there," the *Diesda* of an irreplaceable brother. "Woman's law," however, does not respond to the absence or presence of a "this there": it commemorates its passing and thereby reinscribes it in a medium marked by temporal irreversibility. This medium, however, does not mediate in the sense of the Hegelian determinate negation. It does not generate but, rather, degenerates. This is not the least of the ironies that torments Antigone: that she will go to the grave without progeny, without having generated a generation to succeed her, her brothers, and her father.

Antigone's *nomos* prescribes mourning as the commemoration of that which in passing leaves traces. Its legitimacy, if it has any, is thus very different from the generality of Creon's "law," which he identifies with his "edicts"—different from, but also prior to, since the traces it commemorates are also the condition of the generality required for any law to be "applicable" to particular "cases." The *nomos* to which Antigone appeals precedes the application of law, but also remains after it has been applied. It entails the excess of such application, just as Antigone is excessive in her "stubborn" resistance. Antigone "camps" on her impossible position and principles, and her stubborn tenacity reveals the fragility and dependence of any position, including her own.

This suggests that every "application" of a general law to a particular case is bound to remain problematic, for such generality never simply contains the universal in itself. It always depends on the singular position(s) it occupies—in this "case," that of Antigone as daughter and sister. What Goethe, Jebb, and generations of readers before and after found shocking and disturbing, the sober "calculation" of exchangeability that informs Antigone's argument, is precisely what is required of the incommensurability of the "singular." Only by comparison and substitution can the incommensurable be determined, but such determination always remains incomplete, an object of mourning and commemoration rather than of cognition and/or prescription. This is what Antigone's prosaic calculation, her inauthentic "principle," makes explicit.

But her inauthenticity here is not limited to the content of her words. It also affects their form, and in so doing indicates how this tragedy is always *also* concerned with its own textuality and with its own theatricality. Antigone speaks here not simply in "her own" words or voice, or even in those of her "author," Sophocles. Antigone's speech is not original with her, with him: it is a citation. Her argument re-cites an episode in which Herodotus (*Histories*, III, 19) describes the situation of a woman whose entire family had been condemned to death by Darius. Responding to her supplications, Darius gives her the option of choosing one member of the family to be spared. She chooses her brother and justifies this choice to Darius by means of the argument employed by Antigone. Antigone, like an actor in a play, repeats a role that has already been inscribed elsewhere. But this repetition is not simply a return of the same. It becomes the medium through which a certain difference, indeed incommensurability, is articulated. In Herodotus, the family of Intaphernes is condemned to death for external, contingent reasons. Antigone, by contrast, is condemned not simply because of her act, the immediate cause, but because of the destiny of her family, a destiny that can best be understood in terms of its effects, not in terms of its cause. The curse imposed upon Laius exposes the enabling limitations of the family. The family can no more transcend human finitude than can the state. It can only serve as a medium for mourning as the commemoration of singularity: of what is left. Far from taking the Hegelian form of *Erinnerung*, interiorization, as its model, such commemoration appears more like *exposure*, and in this it resembles a certain theatricality. But exposure does not mean simply rendering visible: it can also mean concealment, just as Antigone seeks to cover the body of Polyneices with dust, or as Oedipus goes off to die in a secret place, invisible to all except the ruler who has befriended him.

The emergence of such exposure as the medium in which visibility and invisibility can coexist and even overlap also distinguishes the theatrical scene. Such a scene is the site of a spectacle that cannot simply be seen or heard, but that must be read: deciphered, interpreted, translated. The tragedy of the Labdacus, of which Antigone is a part, reveals the family to be the ever-problematic framework of a scenic *medium*. Between *muthos* and *logos*, the scene is that medium informed by Antigone's *nomos*.

5

The Place of Death: 'Oedipus at Colonus'

A s i s well known, Sophocles' Theban Plays were composed neither as a trilogy nor in narrative sequence: *Antigone* was written first, probably around 442–441 B.C.; *Oedipus Tyrannos* some twenty years later; and *Oedipus at Colonus* shortly before Sophocles' death in 406. Yet despite the divergence of biographical chronology from mythical-narrative coherence, the relations between the three plays are more significant than the epithet *Theban* might suggest. Although there is no unity of time and place in the composition of the three plays, the place-name of the city, *Thebes*, stands for a commonality of concerns that is more than just thematic. At the same time, there is a finality to the last-written play that belies or, rather, *complicates* its intermediary position in the chronological progression of the story of the decline and fall of the house of the Labdacus, founders of Thebes.

Oedipus has come to Colonus—Sophocles' birthplace—to die. And yet, before dying, he will present his death as a "gift" (l. 577) to his hosts. How does death come to be a gift? Here, at least, by being *staged* in a very singular manner, namely, as a *secret*. Only Theseus, ruler of Athens (which includes Colonus, its "brazen threshold," l. 57), who has welcomed and protected Oedipus, is to "know" the secret, but in a way that will enable it to survive and protect its guardian, Athens, from the perils of time and the destruction of war. By keeping the secret—keeping it secret—and by transmitting it to his "chosen heir," Theseus will enable Athens to thrive.

Oedipus comes to Colonus, then, not just to die there but to bestow upon the city the gift of his death. In order for this death to be a *gift*, however—which is to say, to have the power of being transmitted through its effects—it must be kept secret. Not the fact *that* it has taken place, but rather the particular *place* it takes. This place must remain unseen, invisible, unknown to all save one: Theseus alone, as

King of Athens and Colonus, is permitted by Oedipus to witness his *passing*, and thus his final resting place. Only so, Oedipus claims, can the gift of his death protect Athens, not just against the ravages of time, but specifically against the "Dragon's brood"—which is to say, those who, like Oedipus himself, are said to have sprung from the dragon's teeth sown by Cadmus, founder of Thebes.

This secret brings with it a no less enigmatic question: How or why should the secret of Oedipus' final resting-place—which is to say, the place of his death—have the power to protect a city, Athens, better than any military or political alliance ever could? What, in other words, allows Oedipus to make the following promise:

> O son of Aegeus, I will unfold that which shall be a treasure for this thy city, such as age can never mar. Anon, unaided, and with no hand to guide me, I will show the way to the place [*khōron*] where I must die. But that place reveal thou never unto mortal man—tell not where it is hidden, nor in what region it lies; that so it may ever make for thee a defence, better than many shields, better than the succouring spear of neighbors.
>
> But, for mysteries which speech may not profane, thou shalt mark them for thyself, when thou comest to that place alone; since neither to any of this people can I utter them, nor to mine own children, dear though they are. No, guard them thou alone; and when thou art coming to the end of life, disclose them to thy heir alone; let him teach his heir; and so henceforth.
>
> And thus shalt thou hold this city unscathed from the side of the Dragon's brood. (ll. 1518–32)[1]

What is it about keeping the place of his death secret that can lead Oedipus to make such claims? What is it about this secret that can continue to exercise a power of fascination when the particular historical circumstances, which may or may not have motivated Sophocles to write these lines, have long since lost their relevance? If there is an affirmative answer to this question—one which can be articulated without "profaning" the "dread mysteries"—must it not be sought in the relation between death and place, between the secret and the *polis*, between sight and sound, stage and spectacle? Between a certain *theatricality* and its ability to *touch*? These are some of the suspicions and questions that will be addressed in the following pages.

But in what way? What is involved in "addressing" a question and, in particular, the kinds of questions just described? Is "addressing" a question the same as "answering" it? Are the questions raised by the secret of Oedipus' death, by the way in which that secret is *staged*, questions that can be *answered* the way Oedipus himself solved the riddle of the Sphinx and thereby became the *tyrannos* as which we first encounter him? Or do Sophocles' Theban plays in general, and *Oedipus Tyrannos* in particular, show that "answering" a question is only one way of responding to it? Oedipus solves the riddle of the Sphinx, but his response only prepares the way for other questions, questions that cannot be answered by a simple name because they do not entail a simple object. This is what Oedipus has to learn the hard way, beginning with his meeting with Tiresias: he must learn that what he is asking about involves, not a determinate object "out there," but rather his own over-determined position, which is never simply reducible to a sum of identifiable events. In this sense "myth" is at work in these plays, but in a manner fundamentally different from the meaning of the word as used by Aristotle in his *Poetics*. In Sophocles' Theban plays, by contrast, "myth" designates a network of reference that has no simple beginning or end, and that therefore cannot be taken in at a single view or a single sitting. A certain number of "facts" are of course revealed in the course of *Oedipus Tyrannos*, but they never add up to a single, self-contained, meaningful story. Precisely the "end" of Oedipus—his death—is left ambiguous by its "mythical" transmission (and "myth" here is as much a question of "transmission" as it is of "narrative," in the sense of the telling of a finished story). Certain variants have Oedipus dying in Thebes, others in exile.[2] Significantly, although *Oedipus at Colonus* clearly inscribes itself in the latter tradition, it repeatedly has Oedipus commenting upon his status as an exile, first in his confrontation with Creon:

> In the old days—when, distempered by my self-wrought woes, I yearned to be cast out of the land—thy will went not with mine to grant the boon. But when my fierce grief had spent its force, and the seclusion of the house was sweet, then wast thou for thrusting me from the house and from the land—nor had this kinship any dearness for thee then. (ll. 765–71)

And later, in the even more bitter meeting with his son Polyneices:

> villain, who when thou hadst the scepter and the throne which now thy brother hat in Thebes, dravest me, thine own father,

143

into exile, and madest me citiless, and madest me to wear this
garb which now thou weepest to behold, when thou hast come
unto the same stress of misery as I. The time for tears is past: no,
I must bear this burden while I live ever thinking of thee as of a
murderer. (ll. 1355–62)

Contrary to what one might expect, the rewriting and redefining
of the ambiguous mythic tradition here, far from imposing a timeless
scheme, introduces the significance of temporality, albeit in a different
sense from that presupposed by Oedipus in his solving of the riddle of
the Sphinx. This riddle, as it is generally reported, can be "solved"
only by comprehending the multiplicity and alterations imposed by
time as properties of a single, self-contained, nameable subject:
"man." The sense of time, however, that is deployed in *Oedipus Tyrannos* and that is explicitly addressed in *Oedipus at Colonus* cannot be
"contained" or "comprehended" by a single name, concept, or story:
hence the need, not just for a "secret," but for a "keeping-secret."
Only the "keeping" of the secret confronts the challenge of "time"
as it is staged in this play, which is to say, as a medium of change
exceeding all comprehension and containment.

Thus in the passages quoted Oedipus justifies his fury against Creon
and Polyneices by referring, not to some eternal, timeless transgression, but rather to something far more practical and temporal. When
I needed exile, Oedipus bitterly tells his son and brother-in-law, it
was denied me; when I needed repose, I was banished. This tends to
de-heroicize Oedipus by demonstrating his subjection to a medium—
time—that can never be appropriated by a subject as the element of
its self-realization.

Yet such efforts at appropriation are never entirely abandoned, ei-
ther. What ensues is a tension that surfaces in an exchange between
Oedipus and Ismene, who has come to bring him the latest news from
Thebes:

> *Oedipus.* What are they? [the oracles] What hath been
>   prophesied, my child?
> *Ismene.* That thou shalt yet be desired, alive and dead, by the
>   men of that land, for their welfare's sake.
> *Oedipus.* And who could have good of such an one as I?
> *Ismene.* Their power [*kratē*], 'tis said, comes to be in thy hand.

Oedipus. When I am naught, in that hour, then, I am a man [*anēr*]? (ll. 388–93)

Oedipus' ironic conclusion about what it takes to become "man" recalls his response to the Sphinx. *Anēr* is not simply the same as *anthrōpos*, human. First of all, it is gendered, and thus no longer refers to a creature that speaks "with a single voice." Second, the Greek word *anēr* connotes a temporal reference—"a man in the prime of life" state Liddell and Scott[3]—and is thus defined with respect to the very *temporal change* that Oedipus' response to the Sphinx sought to subsume. The riddle, as legend has it, described a single creature that apparently possessed incompatible attributes: biped, triped, and quadruped, all at once. What Oedipus had to surmount, in order to figure out the riddle, was the expectation that what it described was a static, self-identical creature, as distinct from one that changes with the passage of time. The question of unity or continuity in change is thus concentrated in the attribution to the creature of a "single voice." All of this remains implicit in Sophocles' plays, and yet is permanently presupposed by everything they stage. The question that emerges from that staging is how a voice can remain "one" while "at the same time" being "more than one." It is a question that Oedipus himself foregrounds when he explains to Theseus that time leaves nothing unchanged and that this is precisely the problem both men and polities have to confront:

> Kind son of Aegeus, to the gods alone comes never old age or death, but all else is confounded by all-mastering time. Earth's strength decays, and the strength of the body; faith dies, distrust is born; and the same spirit is never steadfast among friends, or betwixt city and city; for, be it soon or be it late, men find sweet turn to bitter, and then once more to love. (ll. 608–15)

Whereas Oedipus was able to resolve the riddle of the Sphinx by invoking a notion of time that could be subsumed under the ostensibly self-identical and generic name *man*, the conception of time he here deploys no longer would permit such an unequivocal response. Far from imposing continuity and constancy upon temporal change, the notion of "man" has no particular privilege in the account just cited. Time as here deployed imposes nonidentity and disunity, not just upon "man," but upon all the powers of the "earth," including those of the "body." "Man" no longer provides a generic solution to the riddle of time. But the response of human beings to what is more of a quandary than a riddle *is* distinctive. The second Chorus of *Antigone* had already summed up this situation: "Yea, he hath resource for all; without resource he meets nothing that must come: only against Death shall he call for aid in vain" (ll. 359–60).[4]

Man bends all to his sway, with the notable exception of mortality. And the implication, both in *Antigone*—where this Chorus must be read as an implicit rejoinder to Creon's classically political "state of the union" address—and here, in *Oedipus at Colonus*, is that political organization must be measured against this insurmountable and defining limit of human existence. As distinct from the riddle of the Sphinx, the destiny that has led Oedipus to Colonus allows no simple or straightforward "resolution."

Oedipus has come to Colonus in order *to find the place of his death.* This is almost the only assertion about this play that can be advanced unequivocally. Hence, the aptness of the title. The hero it names is no longer defined in terms of a political attribute or property, for instance, as a *tyrannos*, but rather in terms of a location. Or rather, given the events that take place, or fail to take place: in terms of a dislocation.

Oedipus describes himself as "cityless [*apolin*]" (l. 1357). Although this is first of all a description of his immediate situation, it also applies to his life more generally. Oedipus, whose birth was already a transgression, has never really had a city, a family, a *place* of his own. And so, unlike Odysseus, he has no "home" to return to. His "exile" is therefore not an exceptional situation that he has encountered: it was there from birth, indeed, from before birth. If his situation is to be taken as in any way exemplary of the larger problem of human finitude and of its political implications, it is related to this "innate" lack of a native place. Oedipus is always defined with respect to a place and to places that are neither natural nor native to him. This allows him to exemplify one of the traits traditionally associated with place itself, for instance by Hegel, who emphasizes the indifference of place as such to that which it contains and thus also to itself insofar as it is determined by its content.[5] The place that Oedipus is looking for will thus, in a certain sense, be both profoundly his and at the same time also profoundly indifferent to his being-there, its negation rather than its accomplishment. The place where Oedipus is most at home is the place where he finally ceases to be.

In its paradoxical relation to its content and definition, every place as such is a place of death. A place only "is" in referring to somewhere else, to "another place."[6] This self-referential separation from itself makes any place, as place, intrinsically transmissible. But what it transmits is its own secret *alibi*, the "secret" of its separation from itself.

Oedipus appeals to this power of place; he *mobilizes* it, sets it into motion, through his promised gift to Theseus. Only by mobilizing the secret transmissibility of place, of a movement that "stays the same," stays "in one place" even while splitting that place and imparting it elsewhere—only such a mobility and mobilization can hope to withstand the deleterious effects of time, as Oedipus describes them to Theseus:

> And if now all is sunshine between Thebes and thee, yet time, in his untold course, gives birth to days and nights untold, wherein for a small cause they shall sunder with the spear that plighted concord of today; when my slumbering and buried corpse, cold in death, shall one day drink their warm blood, if Zeus is still Zeus, and Phoebus, the son of Zeus, speaks true.
>
> But, since I would not break silence touching mysteries, suffer me to cease where I began. (ll. 617–25)

The vampirelike act of his corpse described by Oedipus here appears to refer to the defeat inflicted upon the Thebans by the Athenians at Colonus, in 410 or 407. More generally, the political "message" he will transmit to Theseus toward the end of the play seems related to the sense of crisis that prevailed around the time the play was written, beginning with the defeat of the Athenian expeditionary force in Sicily in 413, and culminating with the occupation of the city by the Spartans, one year after Sophocles' death, in 404.[7]

And yet, if such historical references can help to explain why the portrayal of Oedipus as a *sōter*, a savior, might have appealed to an Athenian public increasingly pessimistic in its struggle with Sparta and thus deeply concerned about its immediate future, they do not address the more specific question of how Oedipus can attribute such political power to the keeping-secret of his burial place.[8] The interpretation of the play must hinge on this question, however, since here the problem of finitude and singularity develops a significance that goes beyond the immediate scope of individual existence and becomes political.

How does a "secret" become political? Oedipus himself warns against a too facile attempt at interpretation: "But, for mysteries which speech may not profane, thou shalt mark them for thyself, when thou comest to that place alone" (ll. 1525–26). A singularity is involved in the secret that does not lend itself to a certain type of communication, through universalizing discourse. Theseus will have to follow Oedipus to the place of his death in order to receive the secret he is to keep and then transmit, in a "whisper," to his chosen successor. It was doubtless in response to this admonition that Karl Reinhardt concluded his interpretation of the play by warning against any attempt to resolve such a secret into discursive transparency:

> Oedipus' tomb and the mystery that attaches to it will preserve Athens from the hubris and from the decline of so many cities. The devastation of the city by the "descendants of the dragon," if it takes place, would be a result of the city's "excess." But how can the mystery possess such a power? And what must its nature be for it to be effective in this way? Let us not succumb to the temptation of wanting to analyze the Mystery: If its meaning is to be accessible to us, it must be in the light of the poem as a whole, not on the basis of this or that external detail. Whatever the secret may be, it in any case implies that one possess knowledge of Oedipus, of his violence in suffering, of his curses as of his blessings, and also of his integration into the ritual.[9]

Reinhardt's warning only displaces the question: How, after all that Oedipus has undergone, can one simply appeal to a "knowledge," either of "the poem as a whole" or of Oedipus"? Is it not the very status of any such "whole," whether that of the "poem" or of a life, that this play irrevocably calls into question?

To approach a secret—which, as Benjamin emphasizes, must be sharply distinguished from a puzzle or riddle—is not to equate it with a "fragment," that could, together with other such pieces, fit together to form an intelligible whole. Rather, it is to confront the complicity of *distance* with a "veil" that can never simply be raised: "The riddle [or puzzle: *das Rätsel*] is a fragment, which, together with another fragment that matches it, makes up a whole. The secret [or mystery: *das Geheimnis*] has always been associated with the image of the veil, which is an ancient accomplice of distance. Distance appears veiled."[10]

The place where this complicity of distance with the veil is perhaps most powerfully—which is to say, paradoxically—revealed is the theater, in which the curtain is raised but never simply disappears, and whose ancient resource, as discussed in the previous chapter, Benjamin describes as "the exposing of the present [*die Exponierung des Anwesenden*]." Oedipus, we should recall, undergoes such *exposure* as an infant and remains marked by its effects in his body, his name, and his destiny. A homeless exile, he is utterly exposed to and dependent upon foreigners, and this situation determines the way in which his passing will be staged. Whether Benjamin, in writing of such *Exponierung*, had Oedipus or any other of the expelled and exposed ancient heroes, such as Moses, in mind, will have to remain an open question. What is unquestionable, in any case, is that Benjamin's determination of the *podium* as the stage of such "exposing" finds a correspondence in the initial scene of this play—one that is all the more uncanny because of its historical distance.

Benjamin characterizes *contemporary* theater as being more determined by the "stage" than by the "drama." This stage, which, as Benjamin conceives it, no longer constitutes a radical separation of (profane) audience from (sacred) actors, he describes as a "podium." If, as Benjamin insists, contemporary theater can best be approached from the vantage point of the stage rather than that of the drama, and if he characterizes that stage as a "podium," already at the beginnings of Western theater a kind of podium is present. This is how a contemporary critic describes Oedipus' initial encounter with a group of aged "inspectors" who have come from Colonus to inspect the sacred grove where Oedipus initially sat himself down:

> The stage soon ceases to be a place on which Oedipus acts autonomously and becomes instead a place on which the chorus deploys him. . . . The chorus bids Oedipus to stop and not to move his foot outside "this platform of living rock" (192). "Platform," the standard term for the raised place where a speaker stood in a public assembly or in a law court, may be here a metaphor for the raised stage on which Oedipus and Antigone are seen or it may even be a theatrical term.[11]

This occurs shortly after Oedipus has been discovered by the Chorus, at which point, Edmunds notes, "the stage becomes a stage in relation to the orchestra" (p. 50). The "platform" [here, "bēmatos"], is Benjamin's "podium": the place where one "steps" onto

149

and places one's "feet," not in order to go anywhere, in the sense of moving from one place to another, but rather to "move" others, to set them into motion, to mobilize. Through the peculiar history of his "feet" and the "steps" they have taken, Oedipus has always been involved in a singular relation to *movement*: first, by having his feet pierced and marked for life; second, by committing the fated and fateful deed of killing his father at a triple crossroads, where ways come together, but where all ways are blocked, in a kind of impasse, to be opened only by an act of violence; third and finally, in his answer to the Sphinx's riddle, which also refers to feet and which he is able to "resolve" only by finding a way to comprehend the different feet and their differing movements within the scope of a single name and concept, namely, man.

Lowell Edmunds, to whose perceptive analysis of *Oedipus at Colonus* as a play that stages its own theatricality I have already referred, points out that Oedipus, when confronted by the Chorus in this scene, owns up to his presence in the forbidden holy shrine with the following words: " 'This is that one,' he says, and he adds, 'I.' The whole sentence is: 'This is that one—I.' " The phrase, he observes in a footnote, anticipates the phrasing Aristotle will use in section 3 of the *Poetics* as a "formula for mimesis": "This is that."[12] As I have already tried to show,[13] Aristotle's use of the phrase subordinates it to a conceptual logic of predication: "This individual is a so-and-so," as Else renders it.[14] This scene, however, demonstrates a difference between Aristotle's subsumptive logic of demonstration and the theatrical function of Oedipus' words. Oedipus first takes the position of the Chorus, when he describes himself to the others as "This is that one." Then, however, he proceeds to relativize that position by adding: "I." Oedipus' words condense, in a single if divided phrase, the division constitutive of all theatricality and of its spatiality: a division that at first sight seems to be *between* the "they" and the "I," then goes on to reveal itself as dividing each of those two instances from itself. Thus Oedipus at first portrays himself from the viewpoint of those who are inspecting, or spying upon him, but also looking at him, as an audience. But at whom are they looking, and just who is this "they"? The latter is split between Chorus and audience, and that split could be extended to the audience "itself." On the other side, the "I" of Oedipus remains an I that is split between "one and more than one," between what it "is," what it has been, and what it will be. And it is this split, as we will see, that will constitute the "secret" and its power to be both more and less than itself, in becoming the object of a transmission, of a tradition, and indeed, of a way of relating to others—what I have elsewhere called "parting-with"—that could found a new sort of polity. Insofar as he is destined to exemplify the potential power of such "parting-with," Oedipus is raised above those who seek only to identify him, to put him in his place and thereby to secure their own places.

What is that place? For Oedipus it can only be a place of death. But what is *a* place—or *the* place—of death? It is in the light, however obscure, of such a question that the specific localization of place comes into focus or, rather, into play. It comes into play because in being specified, the topographical significance extends far beyond the limits of the particular historical situation described. Commentators have long insisted, understandably, on the importance accorded throughout this play to local determinations.[15] Indeed, Edmunds sees the play as, in part at least, an "apology" for Colonus, which had come into disrepute with the majority of Athenians as the site of the "assembly at which the 400 came to power" in 411 B.C.[16] For a period of about four years, the 400 imposed an oligarchic regime upon the city of Athens, before they themselves were deposed and democracy restored. In this situation, the very positive portrayal of Theseus and the insistence upon the close ties binding Colonus to Athens must, according to Edmunds, be judged to reflect an "apologetic" intention on the part of the author, while also explaining at least some of the considerable inscription of local detail in the description of the sites.

However, once those very limited historical conditions have passed, such details can continue to signify powerfully only to the extent that their significance transcends the circumstances in which they originated. Only thus can Oedipus' last day be anything but a huge bore on the stage. It is certainly not heroic and, with the possible exception of the two confrontations with Creon and Polyneices, not very dramatic, either. Even if the situation were designed as an apology for Colonus, and perhaps for the oligarchs, even at the time, and all the more so since, such an apology could only have been effective to the extent that it could draw upon forces and desires that far transcend such limited historical interests.

What, then, could such details signify other than the attempt to rehabilitate the locality of Colonus from the onus of its association with the restoration of oligarchy? The text provides a number of clues. From his very first words, Oedipus, who of course cannot see where he is or what is around him, asks Antigone insistently, and with some impatience, to describe and identify the particular *place* they have reached. Edmunds points out that at first Oedipus asks about the *topos* or *khōros* he has reached. When he learns that he is in a sacred grove dedicated to the Eumenides, he recognizes that he has arrived at the spot prophesied by Apollo, who foretold that "when I came to a last region [*khōron*] . . . I would find a seat [*hedran*] of the dread goddesses."[17] Hereafter Oedipus will use the word *khōra* constantly (fourteen times), instead of the words *topos* and *khōros*. Against these generic terms for place, *khōra* suggests both "a last place" and a "region" pertaining to a larger territory, a city. This relationship to another place is thus at least double. On the one hand, it refers the outlying district of Colonus to the city—the *polis*, Athens—of which it is a part. On the other hand, as a "last place," *khōra* refers to another place, the underworld, of which the Eumenides are the (often furious) guardians. There is, however, another word that sums up this double function of *khōra*: the Greek word used by the very "stranger" Oedipus interrogates about his whereabouts: the word is *hodos*, and it is commonly translated as "threshold":

> *Oedipus.* What then is the place that we have entered?
> *Stranger.* All that I know, thou shalt learn from my mouth. This whole place is sacred; awful Poseidon holds it, and therein is the fire-fraught god, the Titan Prometheus; but as for the spot whereon thou treadest, 'tis called the Brazen Threshold of this land, the stay of Athens; and the neighboring fields claim yon knight Colonus for their primal lord, and all the people bear his name in common for their own. (ll. 52–60)

The place that Oedipus has entered, the grove of the Eumenides, is overdetermined by its relation to two other terms: the "brazen threshold" and the "stay of Athens," as well as to one other, here not explicitly mentioned, "threshold." This is how R. C. Jebb glosses their relationship:

> Somewhere near the grove of the Eumenides, but not within the stage-scene, was a spot called "the threshold" of Hades—a steeply-descending rift or cavern in the rock, at the mouth of

which some brazen steps had been made. . . . From this *spot*, the immediately adjacent *region* (including the grove) was known as "*the brazen threshold.*" . . . Linked by mystic sanctities with the Powers of the Underworld, this region of the "brazen threshold" is called . . . the *stay* of Athens: a phrase in which the idea of physical basis is joined to that of religious safeguard.[18]

If the "brazen threshold" where Oedipus finds himself is called "the *stay* of Athens," that is by virtue of its relation to the unmentioned threshold marking the border separating (and joining) the living and the dead. The Greek words for "brazen threshold"—*khalkopous hodos*—already contain part of *Oedipous*' not so proper name: *pous*. The region that he entered, and that he transgresses, is part of his name and his destiny: one that involves the "feet" taking "steps," even and especially those that lead into forbidden regions. Not for nothing did the riddle of the Sphinx raise the question of *walking* and its relation to the one who walks. Oedipus' destiny thus leads him to thresholds that can neither be avoided nor simply traversed.

This destiny, however, cannot be discussed strictly in terms of a purely individual *history*: it must be seen in the context of the *myth* that Sophocles inherits, but also transforms. To recapitulate an argument made in the preceding chapter, with respect to *Oedipus Tyrannos*: The curse that strikes Laius and his descendants forces them, and above all, Oedipus, to confront the dilemma of finitude without the usual compensations of family or politics. Neither familial nor political collective can, for Oedipus and his children, provide a "solution" to the quandary of mortality. The house of Labdacus will perish, and the polity founded by it will fall into disrepair. Such a fate can in no way, as Oedipus never tires of reminding his listeners, be justified from the moral viewpoint of retribution:

> Tell me, now—if, by voice of oracle, some divine doom was coming on my sire, that he should die by a son's hand, how couldst thou justly reproach me therewith, who was then unborn—whom no sire had yet begotten, no mother's womb conceived? And if, when born to woe—as I was born—I met my sire in strife, and slew him, all ignorant what I was doing, and to whom—how couldst thou justly blame the unknowing deed? (pp. 969–75)[19]

Without the consolation of survival through familial succession—survival of the paternal name—the name *Oedipus* is thus called upon to signify the enigma of mortality stripped of its usual social supports.

However, the exemplarity of Oedipus resides not only in the way he is forced to confront the enigma of singularity without recourse to family or city. Rather, what is unexpected is the manner in which this confrontation with singularity shows itself to be eminently *theatrical*. The "topography" that plays such a manifest role in this play is a *scenic* topography. Oedipus acknowledges himself to be an "I" only with respect to the eyes of others, exemplified in the Chorus, knowing all the while that its perception of him can never fully accord with his own sense of self. The divergence of or distance between these two perspectives, which, however, remain inseparable from one another, marks the sites of this play as irreducibly *theatrical*: as stage, "platform," or podium—a place to set one's feet, a place to be seen, and yet not necessarily understood. A place that *moves*, but that is never simply a springboard for a change of place. In this sense, the *khōra* where Oedipus finds himself is both "last place" and "threshold," always gesturing somewhere else and yet at the same time a place beyond which one cannot go.

The problem is that this "threshold" does not *lead anywhere*, if by "anywhere" is meant another place that could be reached by a movement away from the "threshold," a place that could be located, situated, given firm borders and a univocal determination. In this sense, the threshold, which is the site of a *passing*, is at the same time also a dead end.[20] As such, it adds a new dimension or chapter to the riddle Oedipus believed he had answered in his response to the Sphinx. This time, Oedipus sets (mutilated) foot in a place whose name ("bronze-footed") suggests that its "feet" are as enduring as Oedipus' are time-bound. But how do such bronze feet move? Are they slower or quicker than those of the one-, two-, and three-footed creature in the Sphinx's riddle? Or is their movement of a radically different sort?

A "threshold" is not simply another species of living creature, if indeed it is a creature at all. A "threshold" that is "bronze-footed" would imply, not a movement *between* places, from place to place, but a movement *of place*. Can places move?

As Oedipus approaches his end, he, at any rate, begins to move differently. He no longer asks to be led by Antigone, but instead follows the "light" he cannot see but nevertheless *feels*: "O light, no light to me, mine once thou wast, I ween—but now my body feels thee for the last time!'' (ll. 1549–50).

Oedipus "touches [*haptetai*]" the light that he cannot see with his body (*demas*) or, rather, he is touched by it—he feels the light touching his body and follows it toward the night of Hades. "Touch," which replaces "sight" for Oedipus, here becomes what it always has been: a way of experiencing separation through contact. Through touch, the "veil" that Benjamin associated with the "secret" is staged—not, however, without paradox, since in theater touch is generally excluded. Oedipus touches (and is touched by) what he cannot see, while the audience sees what it cannot touch. As he approaches the end, however, Oedipus suddenly refuses to be touched: "My children, follow me—thus—for I now have in strange wise been made your guide, as ye were your sire's. Only—touch me not—nay, suffer me unaided to find out that sacred tomb where 'tis my portion to be buried in this land" (ll. 1542–46). One must renounce a certain kind of touching and being touched in order to approach a separation that is beyond distance and that hence cannot be overcome by an embrace or a caress.[21]

Oedipus thus begins to move, on his own, with his own swollen feet, moving toward the spot where "brazen feet" tread—and thus he moves off the stage, out of sight. But not without a parting word left to resonate behind him: "Blessed be thou and this land [*khōra*], and thy lieges; and when your days are blest, think on me being-dead [*memnēsthe mou thanontos*], for your welfare evermore [*eutukheis aei*]" (ll. 1554–55, translation modified).

What, exactly, is Oedipus asking here, in return for his benediction? His words anticipate the parting words of another former king to his child: "Adieu, adieu, adieu, remember me!"[22] What King Hamlet is asking of his son may be far from clear, but its object is relatively well defined: Do not leave unavenged the murder of a father, the betrayal of a husband, the usurpation of a king. By contrast, the admonition of Oedipus is far less transparent. It is not for his sake that he asks not to be forgotten, but for those who do not forget: for his children, for Theseus, for Athens. Just how such mindfulness could benefit Theseus and Athens is left unsaid. But a clue can perhaps be glimpsed in Oedipus' formulation. Previously we have discussed the close connection of the present participle to the ambivalent temporality of theatrical staging. Here, however, just before he leaves the stage,

Oedipus' last words—in direct discourse—invoke, not the present participle, for he is speaking of a time in which he will no longer be present, but the aorist. To this future, the simultaneity of enunciated and enunciation that characterizes the present participle will no longer apply. The supplication to be *mindful* of someone who is no longer alive suggests, however, that a different kind of relationship is possible. Wherever there is a "participle," there is a relationship between the participating parts. To understand the kind of relationship, and temporality, that Oedipus' words suggest, a remark of the classicist, Leo Meyer, is helpful. Discussing the general nature of the aorist participle, he argues that it first of all shares the characteristics of participles in general, "which is to say, to designate an act with which no sentence can as yet be considered to be complete." Having thus described the trait common to all participles, he goes on to distinguish aorist from present participle in terms of their respective articulation of time: "Unlike the present participle, which entails duration, [the aorist participle] designates something in respect to which the temporal duration that it involves is either irrelevant or considered to have lasted only a very short time."[23] To retain the form of the participle—*being dead* as distinct from "the dead," as Jebb translates it—is to suggest a state of (non)being that with respect to the living subject is no longer simultaneous, but with respect to those Oedipus implores to be "mindful," will be.

Such remembering begins shortly thereafter with the appearance of the messenger, who recounts Oedipus' death. His story reveals what is perhaps the ultimate and aporetic function and appeal of all narrative: that of recounting the "end" and giving it "meaning." What the messenger recounts is never the end as such—Oedipus' death—but only its approach and effects. By contrast to the passion of Christ, the death of Oedipus is deliberately shrouded in darkness and never represented or recounted "as such." The most the messenger can recount is the effect that this death had on the one person who witnessed it, Theseus:

> But when we had gone apart, after no long time we looked back; and Oedipus we saw nowhere any more, but the king alone, holding his hand before his face to screen his eyes, as if some dread sight had been seen, and such as none might endure to behold. (ll. 1648–52)

All the messenger could witness, when he turned around and back again, was yet another witness, Theseus, shielding his eyes. Oedipus is described neither as dying nor as disappearing, but as abruptly gone. Between his being *there* and his being *gone* there is no continuity, no smooth transition, but a gap, a gash, a cut, as when de Gaulle's motorcade passes by in Godard's *Breathless*: First there is the motorcycle escort in front of the limousine, then the cut, and finally the motorcycle escort bringing up the rear. Oedipus' death never takes place as a visible, visualizable, or determinable event. Yet something has happened or, perhaps more precisely, something *is going on*, even if just what and where it is going can only be gauged through the tension between anticipation and its aftereffects.

What is there, then, "not to forget"? Antigone responds: "And at the last a sight and a loss that baffle thought are ours to tell. . . . We can but conjecture" (ll. 1676–79). Lowell Edmunds glosses this remark: "Her words attest to the unnarratability of the event that, in the context of the messenger's speech, signified also the extra-theatricality of the event."[24] If the messenger's narrative attempts to palliate and supplement the limits of the stage, its own limitations return us to a power of theatricality that is specific neither to theatrical representation as such, nor to narrative: the power of *putting the other on the spot*. Whether as audience or spectator, listener or reader, the addressee is called upon to *bear witness* to a turn of events that *as such* can never be seen. This and only this constitutes theatricality as medium (as distinct from genre). A *spot* that entails a *turn* of events can also be called a "threshold." Its brazen steps trace a path that can be neither avoided nor traversed.

But without becoming an object of knowledge, it can be remembered. And this memory can be handed down from generation to generation—like a place that is both well known and also unknown. A place that is both inaccessible and unavoidable.

Not the memory of his *person* but of this inaccessible and secret *place* will, according to Oedipus, protect the *polis* against its enemies better than all shields, armor, and allies could ever do. The security of the "homeland" will thus depend upon its willingness to live in the shadow of an uncanny place it will never be able to call "home."

Although what is narrated is not shown on the stage, the "cut" that it *depicts*—this word is to be understood as literally as possible—stands in for the abrupt *turn* of events—turn of *the event*—that constitutes theatricality as medium. Whether as the nonconvergence of the "that one, I," or as the "threshold" at whose limit theatrical events take place, the messenger's tale points to a happening that divides the place it "takes" while "moving" it somewhere else. This division or cut defines the place of death as one that, however concealed it may be, remains potentially, if grimly, theatrical. And vice versa. Theater, as a medium that cannot be contained in a story, involves a space that always tends to be a place of death. Or rather, a place where life brushes up against *being* dead. Whenever any thing or event takes place theatrically, it tends to be split between a *glance* that mistakes and an *agent* that dissimulates.

It is in the chiaroscuro of this strange "cut" that the "gift" promised by Oedipus to Theseus and to Athens must be read. Oedipus' parting admonition, "Do not forget me being dead," plunges Antigone into despair. How can she remember him properly without being able to mourn at his grave? But what if "not forgetting" were not quite the same as *remembering*, but rather a form of *letting go* as a way of *staying with*, in the sense of "never forgetting to forget" that Paul de Man read out of (or into) Hegel.[25] *Not forgetting*, as distinct from simply remembering, would entail the paradoxical connotation concealed behind the ostensible familiarity of the expression *parting with*. To part *with* requires a nonsacrificial *giving up* as a way of *relating to*. Oedipus does not sacrifice himself, and yet he asks that his *being dead* not be forgotten. Not to forget Oedipus "being dead" would, however, involve, not simply recalling an image or an event that has taken place, but rather repeating a cut that divides, and in dividing articulates—a cut that, in parting, im–parts. As a singular event, such a cut would be situated in a determinate place. By virtue of that same singularity, its place would never be representable as such but only in its effects, in the traces it leaves behind. Like a secret, it endures only so long as it is "kept." "Not forgetting Oedipus being dead" would thus entail the keeping (of a) secret of a place, but of one that, like *khōra* and as *hodos*, is constitutively split, divided, separate from itself, and thus whose being, like that of everything singular, only "is" in *being transmitted*, moved elsewhere. This is the *medium* that in *imparting*, *parts with*. It is always associated with a singular place and a singular person, but it is never identifiable with either of them as their property or attribute: they only serve as caretakers, watching over it and handing it on.

What passes thus from hand to hand is more like a swollen foot than a clenched fist. Oedipus' place of death is singularly inaccessible.

It is inaccessible as a result of what happens, and does not happen, there. Death will have taken place, while at the same time never visibly happening. Like the place itself, it is always on the move, although never simply going anywhere.

Oedipus claims that such a gift can protect Athens better than shields, armies, and allies. Protect against what? Against the ravages of time? Against the effort to translate singularity into a question of homeland security? In any case, the singular is never simply a question of the home or the nation, as Antigone (will have) reminded Creon, who will have forgotten how *not* to forget the place of death.

6

Storming the Work:
Allegory and Theatricality in Benjamin's
'Origin of the German Mourning Play'

IN HIS STUDY of German baroque theater, *Origin of the German Mourning Play*, Walter Benjamin emphasizes the ostensibly unbridgeable distance that separates the German *Trauerspiel* from Greek "tragedy." The latter, he argues, relying primarily upon the work of Franz Rosenzweig and of his friend Florens Christian Rang, articulates the revolt of the "self" against a mythical-polytheistic order whose language it could and would no longer speak. Benjamin thus implicitly defines Greek tragedy as a configuration of silence, consisting not only in the refusal to accept and speak a pagan language but also in a mute prophecy of the coming of a new and different kind of god. The German baroque *Trauerspiel*, by contrast, emerges at the other end of the historical spectrum announced by (this notion of) Greek tragedy, at a paradoxical historical configuration, characterized, on the one hand, by the hegemony of Christianity in Europe and, on the other, by the threatened implosion of this hegemonic force through the challenge of the Reformation and the devastating wars of religion that followed. The Treuga Dei[1] that marked the end of these wars and at the same time accompanied the rise of the modern European political system of nation-states also saw the emergence of a theatrical medium called upon to respond to anxieties that the traditional Christian eschatological narrative had sought to assuage. The following chapter seeks to stage the story of this emergence and of its implications for the cultural significance of a certain theatricality.

In the summer of 1924, as he was completing work on his study of German baroque theater, Benjamin met and fell in love with Asja Lacis, a Latvian woman actively involved in the Russian Revolution and a committed Marxist. In her memoirs, written decades later, she recalls the following incident:

He was deeply immersed in his book on *The Origin of the German Mourning Play*. When he explained to me that it concerned an analysis of seventeenth-century German baroque tragedy, that the literature was known only to a few specialists, that the tragedies were never performed—I replied with a grimace, "Why concern oneself with dead literature?" He was silent for a while, then said: "First of all, I am introducing a new terminology into aesthetics and literary studies. Regarding more recent drama, the concepts "tragedy" and *Trauerspiel* [mourning play] are used indiscriminately, as mere words. I demonstrate the fundamental difference between tragedy and *Trauerspiel*. The baroque dramas express desperation and contempt for the world—they are literally "sad," mournful plays [*traurige Spiele*]. By contrast, the attitude of the authentic Greek tragedians is unbending in its opposition to the world and to destiny. This difference in attitude and bearing is important. It must be kept in mind and leads ultimately to a distinction between the genres of tragedy and *Trauerspiel*. Baroque drama is in fact the origin of the melancholy plays that are widespread in German literature of the eighteenth and nineteenth centuries."

Secondly, he added, his investigation was not merely academic but directly related to current problems of contemporary literature. He emphasized explicitly that in his work he designated the baroque drama's search for a formal language as an analogous manifestation to expressionism. This, he said, is why [he] treated the artistic problematic of allegory, emblems, and ritual so extensively. Previously, aestheticians tended to downgrade allegory as a second-rate artistic technique. He wanted to prove that allegory was an artistically valuable device, even more, that it was a particular form of artistic perception.

At the time, I was not satisfied with his responses. . . . Back then, in Capri, I did not really grasp the connection between allegory and modern poetics. Retrospectively I now understand how incisively Walter Benjamin had penetrated modern problems of form.[2]

But Benjamin had done more than Lacis was willing to acknowledge, even retrospectively, and perhaps even more than he himself was aware of. At the heart of his study, as Benjamin indicates in his response to Lacis, is an effort to rethink and indeed to "rehabilitate" allegory as a mode not just of articulation but also of "artistic perception." The perception involved, however, is not merely artistic, at least in the traditional sense. This is why the key to an understanding of this text lies not only in an examination of the question of allegory, nor even in the distinction between the "genres" of tragedy and *Trauerspiel* to which Benjamin alludes in his response to Lacis, but rather in the relation between the two: between the significance of the *Trauerspiel*, on the one hand, and that of *allegory*, on the other. Such reflection reveals that the *Trauerspiel* is as little a traditional aesthetic *genre* as allegory a device of rhetorical or aesthetical style.[3] Allegory, as Benjamin approaches it, consists above all in a distinctive *mode* of *signification*. In this, it continues Benjamin's initial Habilitation project, which he had been forced to abandon when he discovered that a young German philosopher named Martin Heidegger had beaten him to the punch by publishing a book on the same medieval scholastic treatise that Benjamin had intended to interpret, *De modis significandi*, which at the time was ascribed to Duns Scotus but which has since been reattributed to Thomas of Erfurt. Although he reacted very negatively to Heidegger's study, he finally decided that it would be more prudent to choose another dissertation topic, which turned out to be German baroque theater.[4] The notion of allegory that emerged as this theater's distinctive mode of articulation shows, however, that Benjamin's shift in theme and period by no means meant that he had abandoned his earlier interest in language, only that he had shifted the terrain of investigation from that of a philosophy grappling with religiously motivated problems of signification to that of a theater reacting to a religious crisis of epochal proportion.[5]

To be sure, Benjamin's concern with history has often been noted; indeed, he himself, in the highly speculative "epistemo-critical prologue" to his book, designates the method he follows as "historical-philosophical." But however much his notion of *Geschichtsphilosophie* diverges from what one might expect, and however sharply he himself demarcated it from what might generally be considered to be empirical history, the last is by no means unimportant to the way in which Benjamin approaches the relationship between allegory and theater, to which his interpretation of modernity will remain indebted.[6]

Benjamin's historical references—although they are intended to be something other than just chronological or empirical—play a decisive role in the link he goes on to establish between theater and allegory. His historical concerns are foreshadowed in a remark that he makes in a letter to his close friend Florens Christian Rang, whom he regarded as the ideal reader of his study and whose writings on Greek tragedy were an important source for his demarcation of tragedy from *Trauerspiel*. Writing to Rang in 1923, he asks his friend for help:

> At this point in my work I am confronted by two problems, concerning which anything you might have to say would be extremely important. . . . The first concerns the Protestantism of the seventeenth century. My question is, what is responsible for the fact that it was precisely the Protestant writers (the Schlesian dramatists were Protestants and emphatically so) who developed ideas that were extremely medieval in character: drastic notion of death, atmosphere [of] the dance of death, conception of history as a great tragedy. . . . My suspicion is that the answer must be sought in the then-prevailing condition of Protestantism, but I have no access to this. The second [problem] concerns the theory of tragedy. (*GS*, 1.3:890)

The importance of these two questions for Benjamin's study can hardly be overestimated. His interest in the theory of Attic tragedy was, above all, to demonstrate how radically distinct it was from the seventeenth-century *Trauerspiel*, which he considered to be a response to a historically specific crisis in Christian eschatology. He therefore sought to establish a radical discontinuity separating the Greek epoch from the Christian one, including their respective theaters. Nevertheless, his two questions about Protestantism and tragedy turn out to be inseparable, for they hinge on a problem that informs Benjamin's entire approach to the German baroque—and through it, to modernity in general: that of the *individual* and its relation to theater. The two "historical" references around which that axis will be elaborated are both made explicit in the letter to Rang: on the one hand, Greek myth; on the other, the Protestant Reformation.

Another of Benjamin's letters indicates that Rang replied to both questions, although his remarks on the subject of Protestantism have unfortunately been lost. To the second question Rang responded, first with a short discussion "Agon and Theater," and then, in another letter, with a longer gloss elaborating his initial remarks. Rang interprets Greek tragedy as an elaboration of the notion of *agon* ("competition"), which prefigures later Christian elements. At the center of his agonistic conception of tragedy is the significance of mortality: the *agon*, he writes, derives from the ritual sacrifice to the dead (*Totenopfer*).[7] In the agonistic dimension of tragedy, Rang discerns a shift in the Greek attitude toward death. His thinking here is inscribed in a long and suspect tradition that sought to trace the roots of modern Germany back to ancient Greek culture, out of which the "Aryan" tradition of "Germanic" culture was said to evolve.[8] Rang articulates the continuity in this relationship by means of an ambiguity in the German word *Opfer*, which has two distinct if related meanings: "victim" and "sacrifice." According to Rang, the shift articulated in Greek tragedy involves a change in which the significance of the dead for the living is no longer construed in terms of passive victimization but rather in those of "loving" sacrifice. Rang saw the "agonistic" struggle of tragedy, epitomized in the dramas of Aeschylus, as manifest in the "protagonist's" refusal to submit passively to the fatality of death and with it to a polytheistic order for which mortality was the determining difference between humans and gods. Although we lack the letter in which Rang responded to Benjamin's question about the relation of Protestantism to medieval motifs, his agonistic interpretation of Greek tragedy can already be seen as preparing the way for the experience of Protestantism that Benjamin will foreground in his study. For the means by which the tragic hero "breaks through" and "out" of the vicious circle of the established mythical order is a certain *faith*: "*Agon* comes from mortal sacrifice [*Totenopfer*]. The one to be sacrificed can escape if he is quick enough. Ever since, pale anxiety before the dead, who demand the survivor as sacrificial victim, was overcome by the faith that lovingly blesses the dead. Or rather: not just the dead, but rather an even more sublime dead [*ein höherer Toter noch*]."[9] In this "faith" that death, pure and simple, will not have the last word but will acquire a "higher" significance, the tragic hero already prefigures the Protestant challenge that Benjamin will place at the center of his interpretation of the *Trauerspiel* and that will find doctrinal expression in Luther's notion of *sola fides*, of "faith alone" as the path to salvation.

The triumph of faith over works is thus anticipated in Rang's account of the tragic hero's struggle to replace the pagan gods with "a higher Savior-God." Such a struggle, he asserts, assumes a number of different if interrelated aspects. First, it takes place in and as the flight

of the hero, literally his racing—his *Lauf*—across the stage, a movement that, Rang writes, "cuts the amphitheater in two and sets the
spatial border of the scene [*skene*]." In short, the flight of the hero
from pursuing, avenging gods and furies is simultaneously a search for
a savior, but one that leads, not to a new, liturgical ritual, but to a
theatrical practice that constitutes its space precisely by *dividing* it.
Theatrical space—the stage—in this sense is *dividual* par excellence.[10]
Its division, however, no longer separates gods from humans, Rang
continues, but rather the gods among themselves or, better, the existing pagan gods from the god to come. This coming "Savior-God"
will entail a very different relation of humans to the divine. The dividing line separating humans from gods will be redrawn in a manner
not unlike that which splits the stage. It will no longer separate two
fully heterogeneous spheres, the sacred from the profane, but rather
will establish a certain continuity between the two. God will become
mortal, so that through his self-sacrifice man can become immortal.

This is not made entirely explicit by Rang, but his argument goes
clearly in that direction, as is indicated by the second set of figures he
employs to characterize the flight of the tragic protagonist. It takes up
the link, long recognized, between tragedy and tribunal, drama and
trial, moving *das Gericht* ("the court") toward *das jüngste Gericht*, the
Last Judgment. Tragedy as trial, he writes, looks toward a day when
finally "the community"—*das Gemeinde*—will emerge as the highest
court of appeal, with the power to "recognize and authorize the sacrifice [*das Opfer*], death, but at the same time to decree victory both to
man and to God."[11]

The affirmation by Rang of a "victory" of "the community,"
however, elicits further questions from Benjamin: "From your final
sentence I take it that the conclusion of tragedy is still far removed
from any certain sense of the victory of the Man-Savior-Principle and
that there, too, a sort of *non liquet* remains as the undertone" (*GS*,
1.3:892). Benjamin, in short, is less certain than is Rang about the
victory of the community over death, even less about the definitive-
ness of the Last Judgment with respect to the pagan gods. In his response Rang seems to agree with Benjamin, but with a characteristic
displacement:

> This is absolutely my opinion. The particular tragic solution
> [*Lösung*] found is salvation, to be sure, but it remains a problem-

atic one, postulated in prayer but not realized . . . Or—to speak
in the figure of the agonistic race—: the Savior-God that is attained ends one act but is not the final station of the fleeing soul;
it provides a destiny of grace in a particular case, but no assurance, no total rest, no Gospel. (GS, 1.3:892–93)

In short, Rang argues that Greek tragedy is an agonistic anticipation of the Protestant community of believers, united by faith rather
than by works. Moreover, for Rang the fact that tragedy is a *prefiguration* of such a community rather than the community itself makes it
theatrical. Only through such a space can resistance to the established
mythical-astral order deploy itself as prophecy:

> *Tragedy is the break with astrology* and thus the escape from a des-
> tiny based on the orbits of the stars. . . . You know that . . . the
> form of the sacred edifices in the cultural sphere of astrological
> religion (which covered all of Europe) is that of Uranus: in some
> sense an image of the cosmos. Of a destiny that is closed. Now,
> in addition to the Circus, which is nothing but the architectural
> fixation of the movement around the master's grave . . . and
> which already acknowledges a redemption [*Erlösung*] within the
> orbit of astrology and of destiny—[in addition to the circus] it is
> the hemispherical theatrical construction that offers a way *out* of
> this circle. (GS, 1.3:893)

Precisely this capacity of theater to offer a possible *way out* of the
dilemmas resulting from a failing religious and cosmic order will guide
Benjamin in his approach to the German *Trauerspiel* and to modernity
in general. Theater, it should be remembered, is here defined as a
space that is riven, spatially and temporally, and that therefore can
offer a possible escape from the circular orbit of a closed but discred-
ited cosmos.

Thus for Benjamin as for Rang, theater constitutes the response of
an uncertain *spatiality* to questions of life and of death, involving the
relation of the human to the divine, but also that of knowledge and
faith. Benjamin and Rang diverge in their respective evaluations of
the "problematic" character of theatrical salvation or "redemption
[*Erlösung*]." The *non-liquet* that Rang saw as the most powerful argument for the power of faith, will, for Benjamin, tend to contaminate
"faith" itself, thus foregrounding, in the most problematic way imag-

inable, its relation to "knowledge." This problematic relationship of faith to knowledge will play itself out in, and even more *as* the German baroque *Trauerspiel*, which, as Benjamin interprets it, is as irreducibly theatrical as it is allegorical.

· · ·

Rang is not the only inspiration for Benjamin's theory of tragedy. The other major source, as Benjamin himself indicates, is Franz Rosenzweig, above all his major work, *The Star of Redemption*. As the title indicates, Rosenzweig, like Rang, reads tragedy from the perspective of redemption, in German, *Erlösung*. What Rosenzweig adds to the theories put forward by Rang in his letters to Benjamin underscores the *defiance* of the individual hero. Whereas for Rang the tragic protagonist is defined above all by his anxious if ecstatic attempt to escape the closed circle of an unredeemed nature, for Rosenzweig the tragic hero does not merely flee: he or she *resists* by rejecting the language of an order s/he no longer accepts. Benjamin adopts this conception of the tragic hero without feeling obliged to support it with any sustained discussion of individual tragedies. What interests him, it appears, is the speculative theory of tragedy built on the categorical refusal of the tragic hero to speak. This refusal is interpreted dialectically following Rosenzweig, who was, of course, an eminent reader of Hegel. According to this dialectic, the refusal of the tragic hero to speak implicitly announces the coming of a new language and a new community. By refusing to speak, the tragic hero demonstrates the dialectics of the self:

> For the characteristic sign of the Self, the seal of its grandeur as of its weakness, is its silence. The tragic hero has only one language that corresponds to it: silence. Thus it is from the very beginning. Precisely for this reason it was necessary for the tragic to create the art form of the drama: in order to depict that silence. [. . .] By refusing to speak, the hero burns the bridges that tie him to God and the world, lifting himself above the sphere of a personality that demarcates and individualizes itself against others by speaking, and [conversely] entering the frigid solitude of the self. The Self knows nothing outside of itself, it is absolutely solitary. (*GS*, 1.1:287)

Benjamin combines Rosenzweig's conception with Rang's to interpret the silent self-sacrifice of the tragic hero as the portent of a new world to come. Tragedy thus becomes a "preliminary step of prophecy," linguistic through and through. In refusing to speak the established language of pagan polytheism, the tragic hero silently but performatively prophesies the coming of a radically different community and world order.

Benjamin's syncretic blending of Rang and Rosenzweig thus casts Greek tragedy in the role of the pagan refusal of paganism, which becomes a dialectical prefiguration and prophecy of the monotheistic era that was to follow. To call this era Judeo-Christian, however—something Benjamin never does and probably never would have dreamed of doing—would be to beg the point. Precisely the conflicts and discontinuities *within* the ensuing monotheistic era make up the not so hidden agenda of the German baroque *Trauerspiel* as Benjamin interprets it, and more generally of Western modernity as such. Benjamin construes both the baroque *Trauerspiel* and the modern period that followed as responses to the problematic situation of an isolated self and its difficult relation to the community its silence is said to announce. Because of the difficulties of this relationship, promise and prophecy can easily assume the proportions of a nightmare. It is this nightmare that Benjamin associates with the emergence of the Reformation in Europe and with the responses it elicits. The German *Trauerspiel*, and implicitly western modernity itself, must be understood in terms of these responses.

To understand the response, however, it is first necessary to recall the situation in which it arises. This situation, as Benjamin portrays it, has two salient features. The first he describes as the attainment of a position of unquestioned hegemony by European Christendom: "Of all the profoundly divided and ambivalent periods in European history, the Baroque was the only one that fell in a period of undisturbed rule of Christendom" (GS, 1.1:258).

This meant, by contrast to the middle ages, for instance—whose relationship to the baroque had been the initial object of Benjamin's question addressed to Rang—that no purely *external* enemy could be held responsible for unresolved problems and unfulfilled prophecies. These problems and crises, which came to a head *within* the history of European Christianity in the sixteenth century, are linked to the emergence of the Reformation. This is how Benjamin describes that link:

> The great German baroque dramatists were Lutherans. Whereas
> in the decades of Counter-Reformation restoration Catholicism

permeated worldly life with the accumulated power of its discipline, Lutherism had always assumed an antinomian position
with respect to everyday life.[12] The rigorously moralistic conduct of civil life that it preached stood in direct opposition to its
rejection of "good works." By denying these any spiritual or
miraculous effect, by rendering the soul dependent upon the
grace of faith alone, and by making political and worldly affairs
the testing grounds of a life destined to display civic virtues but
with only an indirect relation to religious matters, it inculcated
in the people a strict sense of duty and obedience, but in its
leaders a disposition to melancholy. Already in Luther, whose
last years were filled with a mounting sense of oppression, *a
sharp reaction developed against the storming of the work.* To be sure,
"faith" still helped him survive this challenge, but it could not
prevent life from becoming shallow. . . . An element of Germanic paganism and a sinister belief in the submission to fate
expressed itself in this overcharged reaction, which in the end
dismissed not just the redemptive qualities of good works, but
these works as such. Human actions were deprived of all value.
Something new arose: an empty world. (*GS*, 1.1:317, my italics)

The decisive elements in this description are the "storming of the
work," on the one hand, and the "sharp reaction," tinged with melancholy, that sets in almost immediately, with Luther himself. To understand the nature of the reaction, one must first realize that, as
Benjamin argues, this "storm against the works" is directed not
merely against "good works" and their redemptive capacity, but
against *all* "works as such." Their significance is subordinated to an
act of "faith" that is no longer felt to be mediated or assured by super-
individual institutions such as the Church, with its rites, sacraments,
and dispensations, but rather to result from the relatively isolated encounter of the individual with God via the mediation of Scripture.
This redemptive if problematic power is in turn transferred to "the
book" in general. Though the relationship of the Gutenberg era to
the Protestant Reformation is well known, the perspective through
which Benjamin approaches it reveals a dimension that has been less
widely recognized and discussed. In the somber light of a world emptied of meaning by the devalorization of works and actions, the book
becomes "an Arcanum against attacks of melancholy." Its significance

resides in its ostensible capacity to "house and cover [*das Behauste und Gedeckte*]" (*GS*, 1.1:320) the inhabitants of an "empty world" devoid of meaningful works. In other words, the value of the book to the baroque consists in its protective volume as much if not more than in its meaning. But—and this is decisive for Benjamin's argument—the book is no panacea either, since the evacuation of meaning from human actions as well as their products, affects books no less than the world in which they exist. "Immersion" in either "led all too easily into the abyss" (*GS*, 1.1:320). Benjamin summarizes the result as follows: "If the secularizing [*Verweltlichung*] of the Counter-Reformation gained force in both religious confessions [Catholic as well as Protestant], religious inclinations still did not lose their weight: it was only that the century refused them a religious resolution, in order to impose or demand a worldly one in its place" (*GS*, 1.1:258).

One decisive aspect of the Counter-Reformation's "worldly response" to the radical antinomianism of the Protestant Reformation is the spread of melancholy, which is associated with the distinctively allegorical theater of the German baroque *Trauerspiel*. It is an ambivalent response, insofar as it recognizes from the start that what it has to offer cannot meet the need and desire for a Last Judgment. Yet in Benjamin's reading it emerges as a paradigm for the modern response to a crisis to which it is inextricably—*originally*—bound.

The radical antinomianism that comes to the fore in the Protestant Reformation places human being and society in a situation that is as intolerable as it is insoluble: it exalts the situation of the individual while subjecting that individual to an uncertain destiny, alone before God, unable to influence the future by action, dependent upon a faith whose status remains fundamentally opaque. To this challenge, what Benjamin calls the "Counter-Reformation"—a term that is only apparently familiar, since he causes it to veer away from its usual meaning—seeks to respond, not simply in the name of Catholicism but in that of all organized religion and perhaps all organization as such. This is the situation of the German baroque and it will mark Europe in the centuries to follow.

The Reformation, with its attack on good works, brings forth a paradoxical situation: On the one hand, it stresses the immanence of faith within each individual. On the other hand, it renders problematic the relation of such individualized immanence to anything outside of itself—above all, to divine transcendence. Before the Reformation, the legitimacy of the Catholic Church, an institution that defines itself in part through its claim to universal validity, offered a guarantee of an orderly, transparent relationship of immanence to transcendence through the sacraments and rites that it organizes and defines as "good works." However, when this connection between the world of mortal human beings and the immortal world of the gods is severed, a situation emerges that is quite literally *unworkable* (my term, not Benjamin's). Such unworkability plays itself out in the conception of politics, history, and art. In each of these realms, effective action, as defined by the production of meaningful works, becomes increasingly problematic. In the political realm, the rise of the authority of the secular state with respect to the power of the Curia endows princes with a power that tends toward the absolute. But such absolute power reveals its limitations, since it is no longer able to claim a transcendent justification, and hence the power to endow collective life with a meaning that could comprehend and surpass individual mortality. The sovereign is thus *primus inter pares*, but still subject to the guilt and corruption held to pervade an essentially unredeemed and guilty creation, consisting of mortal, perishable, and largely unsalvageable individuals. This view of an essentially flawed, guilty, and corrupted creation carries over, naturally, to the works and institutions intended to organize and authorize life in the created world.

All of this marks with particular radicality, but also particular brutality, the historical situation of the German baroque, which, by contrast to that of Spain and England, is unable to sustain the kind of politically centralized nation-state that might counterbalance the antinomian thrust unleashed by the Reformation:

> Whereas the Middle Ages portrayed the vulnerability of world events and the transience of all creatures as stations on the way to salvation, the German mourning play buries itself entirely in the disconsolate character of worldly existence. . . . The move away from eschatology characterizes spiritual plays in all of Europe; nevertheless, the frantic flight into an unredeemed nature is specifically German. (*GS*, 1.1:260)

This "frantic flight into an unredeemed nature" is itself, however, anything but purely natural. And here the distinctive dimension of Benjamin's staging of the German baroque emerges. If the Reformation, as he analyzes it, poses a profound crisis to *all* institutions, above all political and religious ones, at the same time it opens the way for a very traditional institution to assume a radically new role. That institution was the theater. And the role it was to assume is that of restaging history and politics, not as transparent representations of unquestionable realities, but as *allegories*. Why theater, and why allegory?

The answer to both questions is the same. Theater emerges as the paradigmatic worldly institution in a world where *meaning*—which, in the Christian framework at least, is structured as a completed and self-contained narrative, with beginning, middle, and end—is subverted by the deprecation of *works*. A work can be understood as an activity or product that is localized, determined spatially and temporally, and invested with a certain narrative meaning as the result of an intention of which it is the effect. First there is the intention, then there is the execution, finally there is the work as result and fulfillment of the two previous phases. A rite, in this sense, can also be a work. A mass takes place at a certain prescribed place and time, authorized by the institution of the Church and invested with a meaning that places the mortal body of the individual in symbolic communion with the immortal body of Christ through consumption of the wafer. The Church provides the intermediary framework that enables the mortal body of the individual to commune with the immortal spirit of Christ. It implements this communion by providing it with a repeatable, predictable, localizable time and place, a consecrated site, as well as with a significance that transcends such localization.

The Reformation challenged the validity of such institutionalized communion. One major response to this antinomian challenge was the development of another approach to the question of localization, one that foregrounded the constitutive role of the individual as opposed to that of the conventional and consecrated sacrament. Since, however, the situation of an individual is determined primarily by its "here and now," such situatedness must be invested with significance if it is to be preserved from inevitable change and neutralization. In such a movement of signification alone can the mortal individual find possible consolation for the unredeemed limitations of pure immanence or secularization. "Secularization" for Benjamin involves, therefore, "the conversion of originarily temporal data into a spatial inauthenticity and simultaneity" (GS, 1.1:260). The "originarily temporal data," defined by their position within an eschatological narrative articulating a movement toward grace and salvation, are thus "spatialized" and "secularized," but in an inauthentic spatiality defined by a "simultaneity" that marks disunion and divergence more than simple self-identity. Such inauthentic simultaneity is thus the sole chance available to an individual otherwise condemned to perish by virtue of its unredeemable authenticity.

Since "history," under the antinomian impact of the Reformation, comes to be understood as the rush of an unredeemed "nature" or "immanence" toward an end emptied of significance, or at least rendered totally opaque, the only hope available to the baroque is to attempt to stem this forward tide by creating a space that, by virtue of its very inauthenticity, might slow if not abolish the irresistible pull toward a catastrophic terminus. This inauthentic locale is construed as a theatrical stage, a showplace, a *Schauplatz*: "It is not the antithesis of history and nature that has the last word for the baroque, but rather the limitless secularization of the historical in and as the Creation. The hopeless course of world events is not contrasted with eternity, but with the restoration of a paradisiacal timelessness. History wanders onto the stage" (*GS*, 1.1:271).

This stage is, however, literally a "showplace," a *Schauplatz*. By contrast to Greek tragedy, for instance, it is a place delimited and constituted *essentially* by those who witness it as audience and as spectators, as onlookers. Here the contrast with tragedy, which, as we have seen, Benjamin considers a historically distinct phenomenon by virtue of its association with the singular situation of ancient Greece, takes on a significance that remains implicit in his book. Whereas tragedy is said to challenge "myth" with the silent prophecy of a future in which human being is elevated above the limitations of mortality—Rang's prefiguration of the Gospels, Rosenzweig's silent prophecy—the German baroque *Trauerspiel* can be read as a kind of epochal "return of the repressed" in which the tidings are no longer good, no longer guaranteed by the institutional authority of a universal Church. Such a "return" does not, of course, involve a simple regression to the status quo ante, to a pre-Christian state of pagan polytheism. Rather, what "returns" does so *within* the parameters of the Christianity it splits: that is, contests but also defends. The form this ambivalent split assumes cannot, therefore, be directly religious. Instead, it is itself double: *theatrical* and *allegorical*. In this "return," the ambiguity of

pagan polytheism is repeated but also transformed by allegorical theater. Again, why allegorical? Because allegory is the traditional means
of investing a manifestation with a signification that it cannot possibly
have in terms of a purely immanent, self-contained structure. It
thereby brings the signifying potential traditionally associated with a
generalized transcendence to bear upon the claims of a localizable and
individualizable secular immanence.

If allegory marks the more or less forced convergence of phenomenon and meaning, it does not achieve their fusion or unification. Such
convergence remains, therefore, *disjunctive*. This disjunction defines
the specifically *theatrical* medium of the German baroque *Trauerspiel* as
irreducibly *allegorical*. The localized space of the theatrical stage may
be that of a world theater, but the world of this theater remains inau-
thentically historical, insofar as "history" is understood either as *Heilsgeschichte*, eschatology, or as its secularized counterpart. Both are
conceived in terms of *fulfillment*: whether of a divine plan of salvation
or a human one of development. What Benjamin, by contrast, designates throughout this text as "natural history" refers to a movement
of perdition rather than progress, a "fallen" creation that is doomed
to finitude and mortality without any perspective of a meaning that
would transcend such limitation. It is, therefore, a story not of grace
but of guilt, not of freedom but of destiny. The German baroque
mourning play seeks to respond to such "natural history" by bringing
it on stage and exposing it to the view of those caught up in it. In so
doing, the hope seems to be that, qua allegory, such staging will either
contain the temporal push toward oblivion or at least slow it down by
displaying it.

By virtue of such staging, allegorical theater—theater as allegory,
and allegory as theater—never definitively takes place. Not just because whatever it displays could, qua allegory, mean something other
than what it appears to be, but because the space of the stage, which
it inhabits, is no more definite or stable. There are no steadfast walls
of a National Theater to define its status or space, but only an audience, which is as mutable and inconstant as the "natural history" deployed on stage. Indeed, the stage itself is always on the move. History
may "wander" onto the stage, but the stage itself wanders: it is quite
literally, in German at least, a *Wanderbühne*, a "wandering theater,"
just as the political institution upon which it depends and which it
mirrors, the "court," is movable, with the seasons. To be sure, this

does not differentiate the German "courts" from those in France, Spain, and England. The German courts and their theaters, however, unlike their Spanish, English, or French counterparts, have neither a unified nation-state nor a national religion to fall back on. This is why the antinomianism Benjamin attributes to Luther and the early Reformation assumes such decisive importance for the German baroque mourning play, as distinct from the theater of the more unified European nations. Such unity, Benjamin seems to imply, is a condition for the production of artistically great "works," such as the dramas of Calderon and Shakespeare, to which he constantly refers, although primarily, as with Greek tragedy, invoking them as a contrasting background against which to highlight the fragmentary nature of the German *Trauerspiel*, which, he insists, is constitutionally unable to produce great aesthetic works. But such aesthetic inferiority is also the means by which German baroque theater, taken not as individual works but as an ensemble of fragments, is able to reveal aspects of the dilemma of the age far better than any theatrical masterwork ever could. One of the things it reveals—and it is not the least significant—is that the theatrical *medium*, as opposed to the artistic *genre,* does not instantiate itself in individual, self-contained, and meaningful *works*, but rather in plays that never come together to form a self-contained whole, remaining true to their name: plays, fragments, pieces (in German, *Stücke*; in French, *pièces*).

This irreducibly fragmentary character predestines the theatrical medium—which is to say, theater *as medium*—to emerge increasingly as a paradigm for the modern situation. What, then, is the nature of this theatrical medium? Perhaps its most salient character is its replacement of character or, rather, of the hero, by "natural history," which is to say, a notion of history derived from the Christian promise of individual redemption, but also cut off from its fulfillment. Severed from its symbolic connection with transcendence by the subordination of good works to individual faith, the Christian history of salvation—*Heilsgeschichte*—turns into its opposite, *Unheilsgeschichte*, a story of unremitting decline and fall. Against this notion of history as catastrophe, as *Unheil*, the staging of history as *Trauerspiel* seeks to seal off all openings to a transcendence feared as a threat of perdition rather than desired as a path to salvation. Returning to the question he had posed to Rang concerning the relation of medieval to baroque theater, Benjamin places the problem in the following historical context:

Christianity or Europe [reference to Novalis' famous essay of that name] is divided into a series of European Christendoms, whose historical actions no longer claim to be situated within the trajectory of a process of salvation. The affinity of the *Trauerspiel* to the Mystery Plays is called into question through the inescapable despair that seems to have the last word in secularized Christian drama. . . . It is the tension of an eschatological question . . . without a religious solution, which was denied by the century. . . . All these attempts remained confined to a strict immanence and without any prospect of opening onto the beyond of the Mystery Plays. (*GS*, 1.1:258–59)

In short, what you see in the *Trauerspiel* is all you are going to get: all and nothing. What is performed on the stage is all there is: it has no further intrinsic, symbolic significance, except perhaps that of confirming the lack of symbolic significance, the lack of a transition leading from the secularized stage of the Counter-Reformation to a world beyond. But at the same time what you see is not what you get, since the significance of what you see depends upon things not seen and not shown. This lack of symbolic immanence opens the theatrical site to a potentially endless, if by no means simply arbitrary, series of possible allegorical interpretations, which in turn call into question the stage itself. The direction in which this questioning of the stage moves is suggested by the following comparison between the *Trauerspiel* and Greek tragedy: "Whereas the spectator of tragedy was solicited and legitimated by the drama, the *Trauerspiel* must be understood from the standpoint of the viewer. The latter experiences how, as on the stage, an interior space of feeling devoid of any connection to the cosmos, situations are placed before him" (*GS*, 1.1:299).

To be "placed before" means not to be made transparent, but rather to be made enigmatically proximate to what remains irreducibly elusive. The external stage is as cut off from the rest of the world as the spectator's inner world of feelings is from the cosmos. Nothing could be further from the relation of the spectator to a tragedy. This relation, according to Benjamin, was essentially unambiguous because tragedy could still be considered a work, an entity that is self-identical and meaningful, and as such one that is capable of determining unequivocally its relation to its audience. However, in a world in which works no longer have such unambiguous value, the *Trauerspiel* must depend more upon the response and situation of its audience. It presents them with an image of their own lack of connectedness or, rather, of the radical incommensurability between their inner feelings, the realm of "faith," and the external, phenomenal world in which they live. The divided theater is the spatial expression of this discrepancy or, as Benjamin puts it, this "relationless inner space." And yet, given that the space *outside* the theater, that of "natural history," is *also* experienced as one of guilt and perdition, it is only by upping the ante and asserting its precarious artificiality and *inauthenticity* that theater can possibly survive. This explains the baroque tendency to extremes, to exaggerations, and, above all, to "ostentation": "Its images are arranged in order to be seen," from the perspective of the spectator. The sight of these images is intended to compensate for the emptying of the world. But they remain allegorical "masks," and hence the world they "reanimate" is a world of the living dead, of ghosts and ghouls, rather than of the resurrected.

What is displayed on stage remains deeply enigmatic, ambiguous, allegorical. Allegory results precisely from the aporetic insistence upon an immanence that refuses to relate to anything outside of itself. Threatened by pure tautology, such refusal paradoxically winds up signifying anything and nothing, in danger of both exploding and imploding. Benjamin describes this as the "antinomies of allegory," in which

> Every person, every thing, every relationship can signify an arbitrary other. This possibility announces to the profane world an annihilating yet just verdict. For that world is designated as one in which details are not so important. And yet, for anyone familiar with the allegorical explication of texts, it is also unmistakable that such properties of meaning, precisely through their ability to point elsewhere, acquire a power that makes them appear incommensurable with profane things and raises them to a higher level, indeed, can even sanctify them. (GS, 1.1:350–51)

Allegory can thus be understood as the return of a mythological ambiguity within the monotheistic tradition that was supposed to supplant it definitively. Paradoxically, this return is ushered in by the radical individualism emphasized by the Reformation. It entails the return of a certain theatricality, which is now no longer subordinate to the eschatological narrative of redemption otherwise known as "history." When history is said to "wander in and onto the stage" as allegory, it brings with it a drastic change in the status of the tragic "action," of the "plot," which ever since Aristotle had increasingly framed and dominated performance, defined as "drama" rather than as "theater." With the restaging of natural history as allegorical theater, however, the movement on-stage is no longer framed by a linear and goal-directed concatenation of events, by a meaningful and unified plot constituting the play as a self-contained "work." Rather, narrative recounting, storytelling, is revealed to be what it always has been: part and parcel of a staging that is not necessarily informed or comprehended by a closed storyline.

In Benjamin's account of the German baroque *Trauerspiel*, the consequences of this shift become manifest in the figure and function of the "intriguer" or "plotter." That figure emerges out of the crisis of secular authority marked by the rise and fall of the political sovereign, emblem of a history that has fallen back into an unredeemed nature. The sovereign's inability to rule, followed sooner or later by his demise, exposes the unbridgeable "antitheses between the power of the ruler and his capacity to exercise it effectively" (between *Herrschermacht und Herrschvermögen* (*GS*, 1.1:250). Out of this crisis the figure of the intriguer emerges, the plotter and courtier who aids and gradually supplants the ruler who cannot rule. Through this replacement, the position of the hero or the protagonist loses its dominance. But the plot also changes its position and function. With the "plotter," the "plot" reveals itself to be part of the scenario rather than its informing frame. The "plotter," like the allegorical scholar, whose knowledge is just as cut off from its object as the plot is from a totalizing goal, manipulates links and connections simply for the pleasure of doing so, not in the hope of accomplishing anything, least of all leaving behind a great work. In this irremediably fallen creation, "power" changes its meaning: it is no longer transitive, the power to do or accomplish anything, but rather a mode of being that arranges and combines, manifesting itself in *virtuosity* rather than control.[13] Although Benjamin doesn't cite him, it is hard not to think of Loge in Wagner's Tetralogy, that somber tale of the decline and fall of the Germanic gods. Loge is a facilitator, exacerbator, seducer, but never one who acts to acquire power for himself, in his own interest. Indeed, apart from exploiting the contradictions of the gods themselves, Loge appears to have no proper interest. This is probably why he has no role to play in the second half of the *Ring*, which, as a *Gesamtkunstwerk*, still has a conclusion to present, a *Twilight of the Gods*. For the intriguer, by contrast, the exercise of power as the manipulation of others must be its own reward. In the absence of the Work, virtuosity is all that is left. Anyone who thinks otherwise might well ponder the fate of Wotan, his family, and the nation that followed in their footsteps.

Benjamin, for his part, compares the plotter-courtier-scholar to a more theatrical figure, that of the choreographer or ballet master, who trains and tortures his (feminine) pupils to make them learn and master their bodies, not as organic unities, but as articulations of joints and of *membra disjecta*, ready to be placed in space rather than deployed as a whole. One is reminded here, although once again Benjamin himself makes no mention of it, of the near-dictatorial role exercised by many of the most innovative theatrical directors of the past one hundred years: from Artaud to Kantor, from Peter Stein to Pina Bausch. Indeed, the theatrical "director" seems a mirror image of the political dictator: this, too, is characteristic of the despotism that rules, precariously, the baroque world and, in more veiled forms, its modern successors, politically as well as theatrically.

Once again, such despotism, less "Oriental" than "Western," is itself a desperate reaction to a no-win game. The theatrical medium does not so much seek salvation as ward off impending catastrophe through its spatio-temporal, that is, localized suspension on stage. Such a desperate project is therefore predicated upon inevitable and considerable *violence*. The inauthentic spatialization of the theatrical medium must be violent—or, as Artaud calls it, "cruel"—insofar as it is rooted in an irreducible *violation*: the violation of whatever convention has consecrated as natural, organic, and self-contained. In addition to his references to the despotic practices of the ballet master, choreographer, political tyrant, and intriguer-courtier, the violence of this violation described by Benjamin announces the coming collaboration and convergence of the "new" media with their more traditional predecessors, purged of their traditional aestheticism: the convergence of photography and painting, of cinema and theater, of digitization and analogical representation, of text and "hypertext." From the moment when, in the spirit of the Reformation, all works are declared to be intrinsically empty, which is to say, powerless to assuage the anxiety of mortality without being informed by something interior and invisible called "faith," the world of appearances, which is the medium not only of works but of acts and hence of "subjects," the world to which Western modernity aspires, can no longer be taken for granted. The light that illuminates it no longer comes from within, no longer illuminates the space it renders visible, is no longer a *lumens naturale*. It comes from elsewhere, an elsewhere that bears no intrinsic relation or affinity to that which it illuminates. Like a *spotlight*—a recurrent figure in Benjamin's descriptions of the baroque—it casts a harsh glare, violating everything it thereby renders visible. This kind of light alters, perhaps forever, the status of the image:

> The image in the field of allegorical intuition is fragment, rune. Its symbolic beauty dissolves once the light of divine erudition falls upon it. The false semblance of totality goes out. For the *Eidos* is extinguished, the similitude dissolves, the cosmos within dries up. In the parched rebus that remains, there resides an insight that is still accessible to the delving if confused scholar. Unfreedom, incompleteness, brokenness of the sensuously beautiful *phusis* was denied to classical art and aesthetics for es-sential reasons. Just this, however, is what baroque allegory, hid-den behind its insane ornateness, brings to the fore. A fundamental premonition [*Ahnung*] of the problematic of art . . . emerges as the recoil of [art's] self-celebration in the Renais-sance. (*GS*, 1.1:352)

To have retraced the genealogy of this "fundamental premonition of a problematic of art" remains, perhaps, the most important result of Benjamin's study. His notion of an allegorical theater, and of an allegorical theatricality exceeding the dimensions of theater in the nar-row sense, can help to reinscribe the problematic status of the work of art, and of *works* in general, in a concept of history that does greater justice to the aporias of singularity that even—and especially—today continue to mark the ongoing struggle of reformative and counter-reformative tendencies that also goes under the name of modernity.

7

"Ibi et ubique":
The Incontinent Plot ('Hamlet')

Sworn to Secrecy

W A L T E R   B E N J A M I N ' S discussion of the way the German baroque mourning play seeks to "reanimate" *theatrically* a world whose faith in the narrative of Christian redemption has been badly shaken reminds us of how central the question of life and death have always been to the theatrical medium—and to its repression. That medium has always assumed an equivocal position with respect to life and the living. On the one hand, it has claimed a certain superiority over other mimetic forms of representation precisely insofar as it involves living persons—living "means," as Benjamin called it. On the other, the very mimetic function of the stage undercuts the claim to reproduce and perhaps redeem the living, a claim that in recent years has been adopted by television ("live programming"). But in the new media, no less than in the old, this emphasis on *life* only serves to underscore the ghostly nature of the screen as well as the stage: what it brings to life is not simply resurrected, but also embalmed.

It is not the least merit of the writings of Jacques Derrida to have explored, in the most varied configurations, the complicity of spectrality with theatricality. Nowhere is this motif more pronounced than in *Specters of Marx*. Readers of this text will doubtless remember the insistent and recurrent references to *Hamlet* as an exemplary instance of the singular relation of "spectrality" to theatricality. Derrida emphasizes repeatedly that spectrality distinguishes itself from spirituality by being inextricably linked to visibility, physicality, and *localizability*. Such traits distinguish the materiality of ghosts from the ideality of spirits in the sense of the Hegelian, philosophical *Geist*.

In a word, according to Derrida, what distinguishes the *ghost* from the *Geist*, the specter from the spirit, not just in *Hamlet* but generally, is its relation to the phenomenal world. A ghost is obliged to appear, which means to appear *somewhere*, in a particular place. A ghost, in short, must *take place*. But it takes place in a way that differentiates it both from ideal spirits and from material beings. It is tied to a particular locale, and yet not to any single one. In short, a ghost, as distinct from a *Geist*, *haunts*. What it haunts is, first and foremost, *places*: houses, of course, but other kinds of places as well. Although the etymology of *haunt* is uncertain, it seems related to the idea of *habit* and thus to the notions of *recurrence* and *repetition*. To haunt and to have a haunt is to be compelled to return to the same place again and again, whether one wants to or not. Such involuntary recurrence also links spectral haunting to the uncanny: the haunted place is both familiar and yet, in its familiarity, irreducibly strange. Both ghost and haunt are *possessed*, without there being an identifiable possessor.

But if a ghost is compelled to appear and to return to the same place, that is also because it requires a particular audience. The audience is never entirely arbitrary, but rather stands in a significant relationship to the ghost, even if it is unaware of that relationship. For all of these reasons the haunts of ghosts inevitably have a theatrical quality. Nowhere is this quality more in evidence than in Act I of *Hamlet*.

• • •

Already in their initial encounter with the ghost, before Hamlet has yet appeared on the scene, Marcellus and Horatio react in a significant and symptomatic fashion: they seek to call it to account, engage it in dialogue, and, above all, to bring it to a standstill:

> *Horatio.*
> . . . Stay, and speak. Stop it, Marcellus.
> *Marcellus.*
> Shall I strike at it with my partisan?
> *Horatio.*
> Do, if it will not stand.
> *Bernardo.*   'Tis here.
> *Horatio.*   'Tis here.
> *Marcellus.*
> 'Tis gone. (1.1.139–44)

The ghost appears, but it is difficult to pin down, since, as Horatio anticipates, "it will not stand."

This "instability" of the ghost returns later in the first act and takes on an added significance. That occurs after Hamlet has spoken to, and above all *listened to*, the ghost and the story it has to tell. Hamlet's initial response to this story is to take an oath of revenge. But that oath in turn requires another one, this time on the part of all those who have seen the ghost: Horatio and Marcellus in particular. They must be sworn to secrecy about what they have seen and heard, lest Hamlet's oath of revenge prove impossible to keep. Hamlet thus enjoins his companions to swear not to speak about what they have witnessed. As Hamlet sets about organizing the oath, the ghost is no longer anywhere to be seen:

Hamlet.
  Give me one poor request.
Horatio.
  What is't, my lord? We will.
Hamlet.
  Never make known what you have seen to-night.
Both.
  My lord, we will not.
Hamlet.   Nay, but swear't.
Horatio.   In faith,
  My lord, not I.
Marcellus.   Nor I, my lord, in faith.
Hamlet.
        Upon my sword.
Marcellus.   We have sworn, my lord, already.
Hamlet.
  Indeed, upon my sword, indeed.

Note Hamlet's insistence upon all the external trappings of a formal oath: it is not enough for Marcellus to protest, "We have sworn, my lord, already," not enough that he has already agreed, verbally, to Hamlet's injunction "never make known what you have seen to-night." Although Hamlet, like Horatio, has studied at Wittenberg, the Protestant mistrust of sacramental ritual seems to extend to the "faith" that for Luther is supposed to supplant it. "Faith alone," *sola fides*, is for Hamlet no more reliable a criterion than "good works." He therefore insists, much to Horatio's surprise and discomfort, that his companions repeat the oath they have sworn *in faith*, this time *in deed*: "Indeed, upon my sword, indeed." The repetition of "indeed" serves more to unsettle its emphasis than to accentuate it. Neither "deeds" (good works) nor "faith" seem to be sufficient to allay Hamlet's concern, and, as we shall soon see, with good reason. Immediately after Hamlet's nearly obsessive insistence on swearing in deed, by his sword, something unexpected happens, which will call into question both deed and faith as the basis of a given pledge:

> *Ghost cries under the stage.*
> Ghost. Swear.
> Hamlet.
>   Ha, ha, boy, say'st thou so? Art thou there, truepenny?
>   Come on. You hear this fellow in the cellarage.
>   Consent to swear.
> Horatio.   Propose the oath, my lord. (1.5.149–52)

What the ghost says is doubly uncanny: not just because it is invisible, but because it echoes Hamlet's own voice, his injunction to swear, while making that all but impossible to accomplish. The ghost's echo thus illustrates the *antiperformative effect* of a certain iterability: by repeating the command to "swear," it renders the execution of that command impossible.[1] The utterance is both eminently theatrical, bringing into play—in the play—all of its theatrical elements, and eminently antiperformative: it renders impossible the performance of an act and the continuation of the plot.

The ghost is placed, not just out of sight, "under the stage," below the deepest of plots, but in a place upon which, literally, the scene is founded, and with it the action that takes place. That this place suddenly reveals itself to be the haunt of a ghost allows his voice, echoing the words of the others, to interrupt and impede the action they intend. The visible plot is suspended by a divisible voice, emanating from an invisible plot below and before all possible plots or plotting.

This interruption provokes a sudden and unexpected shift in Hamlet's tone: Hamlet recognizes the voice as that of the ghost, but responds to it with a desperate frivolity and familiarity bordering on disrespect: "Ha, ha, boy. . . . Art thou there, truepenny?" It is as if the ghost of King Hamlet, demanding that his son avenge his murder, then prevents him from beginning to act, not by doing anything, but merely by dividing and turning his voice and intention back upon

themselves. It is a reflection that dissolves the subject by foregrounding its theatrical iterability: that is, its divisibility.

This situation does not merely hold for the "act" (1.5.84) that the
ghost enjoins Hamlet to accomplish: it applies even more directly to
the ghost's parting words: "Adieu, adieu, adieu. Remember me." But
how can Hamlet "remember" a ghost who leaves him no room to
forget? "Room" here must be understood literally. In order to swear
his companions to secrecy, Hamlet must first find a *place* where the
speech act can be accomplished. But the attempt to find this place, to
find a "plot" where the plot can take place, is frustrated by the very
instance that gets the plot going in the first place: the ghost, invisible
but audible "under the stage."

A tension thus emerges between *plot as story* and *plot as stage*: between the demands of theater as the *presentation* of "plot" and the
spatio-temporal *medium* of that presentation. In order for the plot to
be presented theatrically, it must take place onstage. But everything
that takes place onstage relates, constitutively, to what has taken and
will take place offstage, which is to say, on *other stages*.[2] Every speech
onstage is already an echo and repetition of a "part" inscribed elsewhere, which must be remembered in order to be spoken, yet which
exists only in being spoken. The iterable *divisibility* of "representing"
thus contaminates the *visibility* of the represented. The intended *act*—
here, the oath—is derailed by the fact that it is always already the
product of *acting*.[3]

Thus just as the plot is about to get under way, the voice of the
ghost, echoing that of the hero, interrupts the expected progression
of the dramatic action by revealing its dependence upon a localization
that can only be called *aporetic*. Hamlet is quick to characterize the
new situation, although not so quick to recognize its novel implications:

> *Hamlet.*
> Hic et ubique? Then we'll shift our ground.
> Come hither, gentlemen,
> And lay your hands again upon my sword.
> Swear by my sword
> Never to speak of this that you have heard. (1.5.155–59)

"Hic et ubique" is as succinct a characterization of the divisible space
of a spectral theatricality as is possible, but "shifting our ground" is

hardly going to be an effective response. Not just "time" is "out of joint," but "space" as well: the space of the stage is split between "hic et ubique," here and everywhere.[4] The ghost has to be *somewhere*, but it does not have to be in one place at a time. The very fact that the ghost has *returned* from the dead to haunt the living indicates that it has no stable place. This is what it has in common with the figures on the stage, living or dead, animate or inanimate. Those figures are never just on the stage, but always somewhere else as well.[5] This double or split way of being is not so much represented as enacted by the recurrence of the ghost or, rather, of its voice, which here emerges, against all expectation, as the quintessentially theatrical organ. Despite the emphasis on visibility as a defining trait of theater, the divisibility of the stage can often be displayed better by the voice, for it is easier for a voice to be simultaneously here and elsewhere. No movement can therefore be quick enough to escape the ghostly echo of that voice:

> *Ghost.* [*beneath*] Swear by his sword.
> *Hamlet.*
> Well said, old mole! Cannst work i' th'earth so fast?
> A worthy pioner! Once more remove, good friends.
> (1.5.161–62)

Once again, Hamlet—Prince Hamlet—responds to the echoing voice of his father's ghost with a mixture of familiarity, exasperation, and determination. The specter repeats the words of his son, who responds by repeating his injunction to his companions. But by this point his "good friends" are much too shaken to "remove" themselves as Hamlet demands. Instead, Horatio can only express his dismay: "O day and night, but this is wondrous strange." It is ironic that precisely astonishment over the strangeness of the scene should provoke Hamlet to respond with what in the meanwhile has become one of those all too familiar formulas that tend to be obstacles rather than incitements to the reading of this play. Perhaps a reminder of the *context* in which this celebrated response is inscribed can help overcome the anesthetizing effect of its over-familiarity:

> *Horatio.*
> O day and night, but this is wondrous strange.
> *Hamlet.*
> And therefore as a stranger give it welcome.

There are more things in heaven and earth, Horatio,
Then are dreamt of in your philosophy.
But come. (1.5.164–66)

What escapes the imagination of Horatio's "philosophy"—and not just Horatio's—are things that are "wondrous strange," that do not fit in with existing schemes or familiar knowledge. Does Hamlet envisage *another kind* of philosophy or something *other than* philosophy when he urges Horatio to extend a welcome to what is "wondrous strange"? In any case, he does not simply welcome the ghostly voice, echoing his own, and he still clings to his project of keeping the secret to himself. And so, again and again, he insists that his friends "but come," shift their ground and follow him to another place where they can finally take the oath of secrecy.

Follow him where? To a place that is not "out of joint"? There is no place where an oath can be sworn because there is no place that is not divided in advance by its dependence upon *other* places, which in turn can never be located once and for all. For this reason, every *place* is always part and parcel of a *medium*, although never simply in the sense of an interval or transition *between* two fixed points or poles. The medium is what happens when places are haunted by an uncanny divisibility. Medium is the ghost of place: its haunt.[6]

This line of thought brings out a new aspect of Hamlet's all too famous complaint, with which he acknowledges the impossibility of ever accomplishing the oath of secrecy:

Hamlet.
The time is out of joint. O cursed spite
That ever I was born to set it right!
Nay, come, let's go together. (1.5.187–89)

If not just "the time" but also its localization as "place" is equally "out of joint," it will not be easy ever to "set it right," for there will be no right place where the time can be set straight. Hamlet's response is to invoke the traditional manner of dealing with this dilemma: that of *plotting action*:

Hamlet.   Let us go in together,
And still your fingers on your lips, I pray. (1.5.185–86)

Hamlet can only "pray" that his plot will allow him to find a place where he can escape the divisible disjointedness of time and place, of which the murder of his father, the king, is more a symptom than a cause. Some sort of action, or reaction, is required. But in a time and space that is divided and out of joint, there is no room for decisive *action*—only for *acting*. Yet the results of that acting will never add up to a coherent and meaningful story, a *muthos* capable of framing and containing the mediality that makes it possible and impossible at once.

"Come, let us go (in) together." This injunction—half resignation, half defiance—with which Hamlet reacts to the double bind of his spectral situation, marks the impossible transition from the theatricality of the first five scenes of Act 1 to the plot as such. To "come" is to "go," to exit the scene and enter the expected action. But in the end coming and going will turn out to be not successive alternatives but rather inseparable aspects of the same theatrical movement, one exemplified in the strange ability of the Berlin comic actor Beckmann to "come going," as Kierkegaard's narrator Constantin Constantius puts it in *Repetition*, a text to be discussed in the following chapter. This can perhaps help to explain why Hamlet's movements are so marked by hesitation: it is difficult to get anything done if coming and going can no longer be clearly kept apart.

In any case, if theatrical movement, determined by the divided space of the stage, *ibi et ubique*, always tends toward such coming while going (not simply coming *and* going, much less coming *or* going), then it will never be reducible to a "performance" in the sense of the accomplishing of an *action* or an *intention*. The English language differentiates, before and beyond any specialized knowledge, *acting* from *action:* the former mimics the latter, but is constitutively incapable of consummating or completing itself. It has more to do with responding to the unpredictable than with accomplishing an intention. This is also why theater takes place in "plays" rather than in "works," a concept that, in the aesthetic tradition of great art at least, always implies the *instantiation* of a genre: tragedy or comedy, for example. As the instantiation of genre, the "work of art" is generally understood to be structurally independent of the conditions of its taking place. In this respect, it can be deemed to exemplify the aspiration to transcend finitude. To maintain this aspiration with respect to theater, the stage, as materialization of the medium, must be considered to be nothing more than the neutral condition under which plot can be presented through action. As generic work, theatrical presentation is thus elevated above the restrictive limitations of its *localizability*, which for living beings is inseparable from *mortality*. Every self-contained "story" tends *as such* to be a story of salvation, every *Geschichte*, a *Heilsgeschichte*; every ending is a happy one for the viewer, listener, or reader who "survives" it.

The resurgence of the divisible space of theater complicates this kind of story, this kind of "plot," since life and death can no longer simply be opposed to one another as mutually exclusive. In the spectral space of theatricality, the two are revealed to be inseparable, as in the coming-as-going of the ghost. The "plot" does not disappear, but its role changes. It is no longer the plotting of action, but the plotting of acting, which is also the staging of the plot.

The Seat of Memory

As we have seen, Hamlet's futile attempt to have his friends swear an oath of secrecy follows upon the pledge he has made in response to the ghost's injunction to "remember me." Hamlet repeats these parting words of the ghost and in so doing makes them his own and the substance of his oath:

Hamlet.   Now to my word:
It is "Adieu, adieu. Remember me."
I have sworn it. (1.5.110–12)

Hamlet's oath echoes verbatim the ghost's entreaty not to be forgotten. These words come not simply from within but from without, echoing words spoken by another. But who or what is this other that asks to be remembered, and avenged? The question returns later as Hamlet questions the reliability of the story the ghost has related, the story of a murder with multiple faces: regicide, fratricide, murder of a father and of a husband. In the words of the ghost himself:

Thus was I sleeping by a brother's hand
Of life, of crown, of queen at once dispatched. (1.5.74–75)

One need not accept the particular historical interpretations of Carl Schmitt, and of Dover Wilson before him, to see a more general relationship here to what Schmitt describes as the "religious civil war [*konfessionellen Bürgerkrieg*]" that pitted European Christendom against itself in the seventeenth century, with an outcome that has marked Western modernity ever since:

The hundred-year civil war between Catholics and Protestants could only be overcome by dethroning the theologians, given that their doctrine of tyrannicide and just war fanned the flames of civil war ever anew. In place of the medieval feudal order of estates, there emerged a public tranquility, security, and order, whose establishment and maintenance became the legitimating task of the new institution, the *state*. . . . Sovereign states and politics stand in opposition to the medieval forms and methods of clerical and feudal rule.[7]

According to Schmitt, this genesis of the modern state and of modern politics as a response to the Christian "civil war" determines their development and structure. The result of an "internal" struggle or "war," both state and politics are inseparably bound to conflict: politics through its constitutive relationship to the enemy (elaborated by Schmitt in his *Concept of the Political*, published in 1932); and the state through the no less constitutive relationship of its sovereignty to that which escapes the rule of law: to the "state of exception" (articulated in Schmitt's *Political Theology*, (1922). Such conflicts thus cannot be resolved definitively, but only responded to case by case, insofar as both state and politics are assigned a task that, from a Christian perspective, at least, cannot be accomplished with worldly means alone, since it ultimately involves the question of *grace*: which is to say, the relation of finite beings to their "end," that is, to mortality. As a result, compromises have to be struck, of which the most familiar and perhaps most important for modern politics has been the translation of "grace" into "security" and its derivatives, "law and order"—a move that addresses the question of mortality mainly by displacing it.

From Schmitt's account of the emergence of modern politics, one of his most astute readers, Walter Benjamin, drew conclusions that sharply diverge from those envisaged by Schmitt himself. In his 1925 study, *The Origin of the German Mourning Play*, Benjamin traces how the German baroque period responded to the profound crisis associated with the Reformation; not directly in political means, but through a very distinct kind of theater. The *Trauer* staged by this theater is not just melancholic, nor does it simply mourn, as the following brief but incisive passage makes clear: "Sadness and Mourning is the sensibility [*Gesinnung*] in which feeling reanimates the emptied world by masking it [*maskenhaft neubelebt*], in order to draw an enigmatic satisfaction from its appearance. . . . The theory of *Trauer* . . . can, accordingly, be unrolled only through the description of the world that arises [*sich auftut*] in response to the melancholic glance."[8]

The world that emerges in response to the melancholic glance is "reanimated" through the "masks" it now wears: since nothing in this world can be deemed to be transparent any longer, the very opacity of the "emptied world" becomes the condition of its masked resurrection. But that resurrection remains a mask, tied to the theater. What otherwise will be known as "secularization" becomes, in Benjamin's account, something more like *allegorical theatricalization*. Such allegorical theatricalization cannot simply overcome time and mortality, but it can temporarily arrest, interrupt, or suspend their progress. Hence the tendency of baroque theater toward ostentation, since the only saving grace it can envisage is the demonstration of its own theatricality.

Such theatricality, however, implies the inversion of the traditional Aristotelian demand that tragedy represent a unified action in a no less unified plot. Instead of placing the emphasis on the *plot*, allegorical theater foregrounds the *play*. Hamlet, of course, is no exception, as recurrent plays on the meanings of "plot," "play," and "action" indicate. Language and theater cease to be mere instruments for the representation of action through plot and instead take on a more immediate, more opaque and ambiguous significance. The tendency of the plot to unravel, often noted in *Hamlet*, reflects a characteristic that distinguishes the German baroque drama from its Spanish counterpart: "the deficient development of the plot" that, Benjamin observes, constitutes the essential "insufficiency of the German mourning play." Benjamin observes of the *Trauerspiel*: "Only the plot [*die Intrige*] would have been capable of leading the scenic organization to that allegorical totality which, in the image of the apotheosis, begins something radically different from the sequence of images and which as such ushers mourning both in and out at once" (*GS*, 1.1:409).

Only the plot, in short, would have the power to point beyond the temporal-diachronic sequence of scenes and images toward a transcendent solution of the problems with which the mourning play grapples. Such a solution, however, remains inaccessible to the German mourning play, which, again unlike its Spanish counterpart, remains bound to the immanence of the theatrical: "However, the transfigured apotheosis that we encounter in Calderon is not to be attained with the *banal resources of the theater*. It emerges necessarily from a meaningful constellation of the whole" (*GS*, 1.1:408; my italics). Benjamin's reading of the German baroque mourning play is thus "framed" on the one side by Calderon, and on the other by Shakespeare's *Hamlet*.

Hamlet, the play and the figure, thus plays a small but important role on the fringe of Benjamin's study. Like Calderon's plays, Shakespeare's *Hamlet* is presented as the unattainable antipode of the German mourning play, but with a significant difference. The Spanish mourning plays, as Benjamin describes them, go beyond "the banal resource of the theater" by developing a plot leading to a transcendent apotheosis. Like religion itself, Calderon's theater goes beyond mere theater. The same is not quite true of *Hamlet*. Here too, according to Benjamin, a religious solution appears to be within reach: *Hamlet*, writes Benjamin, is unique in "striking Christian sparks" from the profoundly un-Christian world of melancholy. But it does this, not by simply transcending that world, but by allowing it to confront itself: "Only in a life of this princely kind does melancholy resolve itself precisely by encountering itself [*Nur in einem Leben von der Art dieses fürstlichen löst Melancholie, indem sie sich begegnet, sich ein*]" (*GS*, 1.1.335). I quote the German here to emphasize Benjamin's insistence on the reflexive moment of the play: melancholy "resolves itself . . . by encountering itself [*lost indem sie sich begegnet, sich ein*]." How is this reflexive return of melancholy to and upon itself achieved? Precisely through a positioning that is inseparable from a certain kind of *melancholically reflective spectator*:

> The secret of his person is shut up [*beschlossen*] in the theatrical but therefore also measured way he traverses all the stations of this intentional space [of melancholy] just as the secret of his destiny is shut up in a happening that is entirely homogeneous to this [melancholic] sight [*Blick*]. *Hamlet* alone is for the mourning play a spectator by and of the grace[s] of God; what can satisfy him, however, is not what they play for him, but only his own destiny. (*GS*, 1.1.335)[9]

If the mourning play for Benjamin is distinguished from tragedy precisely by the role it assigns to the audience, which assumes the role of plaintiff in an interminable trial of the Creation, then *Hamlet* appears as the quintessence and culmination of the *Trauerspiel*, insofar as he is able to stage his "destiny" as a spectacle that is homogeneous with his vision as *spectator*. Divine Grace, which after Luther is no longer accessible to "good works" and human action, thus appears to become accessible to a spectator who is also a director and a player—an actor—not just contemplating his own destiny as the object of his melancholy but *staging it as spectacle*. In this staging, the spectacle as such appears to be the saving grace, since it allows the spectator to recover his "destiny," but only qua spectacle.

Benjamin's insight here is suggestive, even if all of its complexities can hardly be discussed here. *Hamlet*, he implies, alone among mourning plays, resolves the problem of mourning, not just by making it into a theatrical spectacle, but by replacing the role of the *hero* with that of *spectator, actor, and director, all in one*. As has often been observed, Hamlet does not act in the purposive, effective way commanded by the ghost of his father: rather, he acts as an actor, while observing as spectator and staging as *director*. He does not so much accomplish his mission as stage it. He plays with and for Polonius, Ophelia, Claudius, and his mother; he uses the traveling players to stage his "mousetrap" and, together with Horatio, to observe its effects. He thus plays with everyone, with the exceptions of the ghost and Horatio. Horatio will ultimately serve as witness of the play that Hamlet stages and that significantly (for Benjamin's argument, at least) bears his name. Horatio will thus need at the end, and after the end, to bear witness to what has just been staged, so that it too may be remembered.

For it is not just the ghost of King Hamlet who wishes to be remembered:

> *Hamlet.*
> O God, Horatio, what a wounded name,
> Things standing thus unknown, shall live behind me!
> If thou didst ever hold me in thy heart,
> Absent thee from felicity awhile,
> And in this harsh world draw thy breath in pain,
> To tell my story. (5.2.33–38)

Following the Reformation's attack on "good works," memory takes on a new function, that of consoling a world in which action is no longer the unquestionable pathway to grace.

But there are different ways in which stories can be told and "wounded names" remembered. The most familiar, no doubt, and most consoling is that already described by Aristotle in his *Poetics*, the *muthos* of a *praxis* that was supposed to constitute the ultimate object of tragic mimesis. This *muthos* was to consist in a beginning, middle, and end, the latter being understood as that which was to make of everything previous a meaningful and intelligible whole. In such a story, the end is understood not just as cessation but as conclusion, one that completes the sequence rather than simply interrupting it. The "middle," in consequence, is "that which naturally follows on something else and something else on it."[10] The remembrance of such a story thus subordinates the medium to a bridge linking a beginning to a conclusion in a "natural" and "necessary" manner, which is to say, in the unity of a meaningful whole.

But the very tragedies that Aristotle cites as examples of the tragic *muthos* often call into question the subordination of medium to plot and the ideal of memory that informs it. Already the final chorus of Sophocles' *Oedipus Tyrannos* warns the audience to

> learn that mortal man must always look to his ending,
> And none can be called happy until that day when he carries
> His happiness down to the grave in peace.[11]

Such knowledge, to be sure, can never be self-knowledge, as Ophelia, in her "madness," fully recognizes: "Lord, we know what we are, but know not what we may be. God be at your table" (4.5.43–44) This renders the traditional demand of a story to be integral and whole applicable only to others, never to oneself. It places the listener or spectator in a fundamentally asymmetrical position with respect to the spectacle—precisely not the "homogeneity" that Benjamin attributes to Hamlet, as "spectator of and by the grace(s) of God."

Such asymmetry both calls for and is put into play by a theatricality that stages a different way of remembering and being remembered, one that in turn implies another way of *staging stories*. Staged stories do not define their "middle" as a natural, necessary, and totalizing transition from a beginning to an end, but rather recognize that beginnings and ends are always the *media* of other stories. Staged stories therefore never simply begin *in medias res*, since their *res* is already itself a *medium*. Staged stories are thus always stories "of" the medium *in* and *about* which they take place. The kind of listening and memory to which they appeal do not seek to recover a self-contained meaning or resurrect the dead. Rather, such memory knows itself to be inseparable from forgetting rather than its simple opposite; it does not strive to neutralize or surmount time in a transcendence of the self. As the

Player-King reminds his Queen, who protests that she will remain true to him beyond death:

> I do believe you think what now you speak,
> But what we do determine oft we break.
> Purpose is but the slave to memory,
> Of violent birth, but poor validity.
>
> . . .
>
> Most necessary 'tis that we forget
> To pay ourselves what to ourselves is debt. (3.2.168–76)

No one, of course, experiences the difficulties of paying back the debts of memory, whether to himself or to others, more acutely than Hamlet, and not only when he tries to carry out his pledge to the ghost. Those debts result not just from practical problems, but from the inseparable linkage of memory to forgetting. In his response to the ghost, Hamlet demonstrates that he is aware of this link and of its ramifications, which involve not just his character and the plot or plots in which he is engaged, but also his immediate *situation*, that of an actor on the stage. On the stage itself, such awareness can only take the form of an *interruption* that breaks the fictional continuity of a self-contained plot by referring it to its theatrical and medial conditions of possibility. Despite appearances, this reference is not just a practical or empirical one, since the medial conditions of representation to which it refers bear directly upon the issues represented. This, then, is how Hamlet begins his response to the ghost's story, admonition, and departure:

> *Hamlet.*
> O all you host of heaven! O earth! What else?
> And shall I couple hell? O, fie! Hold, hold, my heart,
> And you, my sinews, grow not instant old,
> But bear me stiffly up. (1.5.92–95)

To promise, as Nietzsche elaborates at the beginning of the *Genealogy of Morals*, implies the ability to overcome time and space as media of separation, alteration, and forgetting. Fully aware of this, Hamlet implores his "heart" to "hold, hold" and his "sinews [to] grow not instant old." Indeed, nothing less is required if he is to fulfill the Ghost's wish to be remembered and avenged. But immediately after thus sounding the reaches of earth, heaven, and hell, Hamlet's tone suddenly changes, as though it were overtaken by the language of another, which was beginning to get out of hand:

> Remember thee?
> Ay, thou poor ghost, while memory holds a seat
> In this distracted globe. (1.5.95–97)

From heaven and earth and hell, Hamlet's thoughts jump suddenly to a "globe" that is not just a synonym for the earth, or even for the head, anatomical seat of memory, but also the name of the theater in which *Hamlet* (the play) was written to be performed. This theatrical allusion could be considered as merely a facetious or narcissistic jibe, at the expense of the drama, were it not for the adjective that precedes and modifies the noun: the *globe* referred to, whatever else it may mean or be, is also *distracted*, literally and etymologically "torn asunder," as split in its meaning and being as is the stage and theatrical space in general. In this "distracted globe" "memory" may "hold *a* seat," but it is only *one* and only for a limited time. How long memory can hold that seat will depend on the general distraction in and of the theater. This, perhaps, is why Hamlet immediately declares his intention of emptying that theater, and its globe, of everything that might distract his memory:

> Remember thee?
> Yea, from the table of my memory
> I'll wipe away all trivial fond records,
> All saws of books, all forms, all pressures past
> That youth and observation copied there,
> And thy commandment all alone shall live
> Within the book and volume of my brain,
> Unmixed with baser matter. (1.5.95–104)

Memory, as Hamlet would have it, at least, should rule the roost in a "globe" purged of "all saws of books" and other "baser matter"—a globe that can thus become its undisturbed site: "thy commandment all alone shall live within the book and volume of my brain."

That such single-mindedness could turn out to be entirely compatible with global distractedness is, of course, one of the lessons that Hamlet will soon begin to learn. For nothing is more futile, whether in theater or in politics, than trying to purify the "globe"—in all of its senses—by turning it into the site of a coherent plot. "Remember me" are the ghost's parting words to Hamlet. But what does it mean to remember a ghost? To remember this ghost, at least, is to remember the story he tells and to draw consequences and conclusions from it. But what happens to such a story when it is emphatically "staged"? What happens to a *staged plot*?

The word *plot* returns in various contexts in this play. One of the most suggestive occurs toward the end, when Hamlet sees Fortinbras leading his army off to conquer Poland. Hamlet is overcome by shame:

> to my shame I see
> The imminent death of twenty thousand men
> That for a fantasy and trick of fame
> Go to their graves like beds, *fight for a plot*
> . . .
> Which is not tomb enough and continent
> To hide the slain? (4.4.59–65; my italics)

The *plot* of *Hamlet* does not try to "hide the slain." It does not seek to become the "continent" that would contain and comprehend theatrical spectrality. Perhaps that is also why it continues to fascinate until today: it does not try to give meaning to death, but rather to exhibit its effects. Such a plot can be described as *incontinent* since, by refusing to *contain* or *comprehend* the conflicts in which it consists, it inevitably, as in *Hamlet*, displays a certain disorderly excess.

Toward the end of the play, Hamlet, in a conversation with his friend Horatio, refers to this other kind of plot as involving a memory that does not seek to transcend time but only to *respond* to it:

Hamlet.
    So much for this, sir; now shall you see the other.
    You do remember all the circumstance?
Horatio.
    Remember it, my lord!
Hamlet.
    Sir, in my heart there was a kind of fighting
    That would not let me sleep. Methought I lay
    Worse than the mutines in the bilboes. Rashly,
    And praised be rashness for it—let us know,
    Our indiscretion sometime serves us well

When our deep plots do pall; and that should learn us
There's a divinity that shapes our ends,
Rough-hew them how we will—(5.2.2–10)

The memory that Hamlet here recalls is one of rashness and of indiscretion, which "sometime serve us well / When our deep plots do pall." The plot, or plots, of *Hamlet*—for there are obviously more than one—are of this kind. When plotting and scheming "pall" (fail, falter, fade, and die), then "rashness" is all. As Kierkegaard will write and Derrida will echo, spectrally and uncannily, "the moment of decision is a moment of madness." Even and especially when it involves the murder of a king. This holds for the *act* of murder as it does for the *act* of revenge: neither act, qua *action*, will ever be "tomb enough and continent / To hide the slain" or give death meaning. This issue, or lack of issue, this *aporia*, is what the play displays at its *end*, in the multiple corpses that lie strewn across the stage.

> *Horatio.*   Give order that these bodies
> High on a stage be placed to the view,
> And let me speak to th' yet unknowing world
> How these things came about. So shall you hear
> Of carnal, bloody, and unnatural acts,
> Of accidental judgments, casual slaughters,
> Of deaths put on by cunning and forced cause,
> And, in this upshot, purposes mistook
> Fall'n on th'inventors' heads. All this can I
> Truly deliver. (5.2.366–74)

Responding to Hamlet's wish, Horatio still dreams of a coherent and meaningful plot, one that will enable him to tell the story of "how these things came about." But the play has already shown its audience not just "how" these things "came about" but, no less importantly, *where*: namely, on a *stage*. In the end, this *staged plot* consists of "purposes mistook / Fall'n on th'inventors' heads," taking place in a "distracted globe" where memory and forgetting jostle for position. What remains are corpses strewn about the stage, which are now to be elevated, "placed to the view" "high on a stage." But however high they are to be placed, the stage on which they will be exhibited remains just *another stage of the stage* before the curtain closes upon it. However visible they may be, the staged exhibition of corpses will never add up to the single, all-embracing plot of which Aristotle and the tradition indebted to him continue even today to dream. On the contrary, the elevation of those corpses upon the stage reveals what has been known all along but perhaps not fully been recognized: that the theatrical stage remains a temporal stage, which comes only in going, and which, in departing, leaves room for what is to come.

8

Kierkegaard's *Posse*

T H E A T E R   A N D   *theory* share a common etymology and, as we have seen, a vexed history. At issue is the interpretation of *thea*, looking, of its site, *theatron*, of the onlooker or spectator, *theoros*, and, finally, of the spectacle itself. Ever since Plato and Aristotle, philosophy has sought to reduce the importance of the scenic, medial dimension by comprehending it primarily as *tragedy*.[1] The year 1843, in which Kierkegaard's essay *Repetition* was published, marks a decisive turning point in this history. It is as though a certain blockage of "traditional" philosophical paradigms—which Kierkegaard above all identified with the thought of Hegel—necessitated a rethinking of the relationship of theater not just to theory, but to a notion of *movement* that the hallowed philosophical opposition of theory and practice could no longer adequately articulate. The first paragraph of *Gjentagelsen*[2] sets the scene:

> When the Eleatics denied motion, Diogenes, as everyone knows, stepped up [*optraadte*] as an opponent. He really stepped up, because he didn't say a word but merely paced back and forth a few times, thereby assuming that he had sufficiently refuted them. When I was occupied for some time . . . with the question of repetition—whether or not it is possible, what importance it has, whether something gains or loses in being repeated—I suddenly had the thought: You can, after all, take a trip to Berlin; you have been there once before, and now you can prove to yourself whether a repetition is possible and what importance it has. At home I had been practically immobilized by this question. Say what you will, this question will play a very important role in modern philosophy, for *repetition* is a crucial expression for what "recollection" was to the Greeks. Just as

they thought that all knowing is a recollecting, modern philosophy will teach that all life is a repetition. . . . Repetition and
recollection are the same movement, except in opposite directions, for what is recollected has been, is repeated backward,
whereas genuine repetition is recollected forward. Repetition,
therefore, if it is possible, makes a person happy, whereas recollection makes him unhappy—assuming, of course, that he gives
himself time to live and does not promptly at birth find an excuse to sneak out of life again, for example, [under the pretext]
that he has forgotten something. (p. 131)[3]

This text stands almost alone in the nineteenth century for the
prescience with which it announces a new kind of philosophy. Only
Nietzsche, some forty years later, will have similar foresight in the
opening pages of *Beyond Good and Evil*, which predict the coming of
a "new species of philosophers," no longer bound to the oppositional
logic of traditional metaphysics, "philosophers of the dangerous 'perhaps.' "[4] But the opening gambit in *Gjentagelsen* does not merely pro-
claim the need for a new philosophy of "repetition" to supplant and
replace that of "recollection," which has prevailed since the Greeks.
By contrast to Nietzsche, Kierkegaard formulates this challenge in a
style that is fundamentally alien to philosophical discourse, not so
much because of the prominent role of first-person "narrative"—
which is to be found, for instance, in such inaugural texts as Descartes'
Meditations—but rather because of the abrupt shifting from one discursive mode to another: from third-person to first-person narrative,
from autobiographical anecdote to historical reflection, from seriousness to the jocular, which is unusual if not unique in writing usually
considered to be "philosophical." And yet what is perhaps most unusual is the use of a "pseudonymic" narrator-author. This confuses
the question of authorship and of authority. Who, after all, is really
speaking here? "Constantin Constantius"? What, then, about
"Kierkegaard"? This sort of confusion is generally associated with
texts considered to be "literary." It is precisely what philosophy, ever
since its inception with Plato, has unequivocally condemned: "When
the poet speaks in the person of another . . . he assimilates his style to
that of the person who, as he informs you, is going to speak. . . . And
this assimilation of himself to another, either by the use of voice or
gesture, is the imitation of the person whose character he assumes. . . .

In this case, the narrative of the poet may be said to proceed by way of imitation." Since, however, "one man can only do one thing well, and not many," what is practiced in poetry has to be avoided by those who would serve as "guardians" of the *polis*.[5] In *Repetition*, the disjointedness of the discourse introduces an uncertainty that is augmented by the ambiguous status of its "subject," Constantin Constantius. Let us look more closely at how this disjointedness works in the passage just quoted.

The passage begins with a philosophical anecdote from Diogenes Laertius' *Lives of Eminent Philosophers*.[6] In this anecdote, Diogenes demonstrates the existence of movement against the views of the Eleatics, Parmenides and Zeno, not by what he *says* but by what he *does*, namely, putting his own body into movement: "He literally did step up . . . paced back and forth a few times, thereby assuming that he had sufficiently refuted them." A strange way of introducing a book upon "repetition." And yet repetition is already very much at work in this initial citation, in a number of different ways—not just because it is a citation, and hence a form of repetition, nor because the citation is contained in a narrative *recounting* of an alleged event, nor even because the name of the figure narrated, Diogenes of Sinope, echoes or anticipates the name of the author of the text from which the anecdote is taken, Diogenes Laertius. All of these are important, nontrivial instances of repetition, and yet another instance is perhaps even more significant. Diogenes' demonstration itself is as illustrative of a certain repetition as it is of movement. In "stepping up" he makes a theatrical entry upon the scene: the verb *optraede* also designates the entry or appearance of actors on the stage. Here, he "really [*virkelig*]" "steps up," which is to say, makes his entry upon the stage, upon which he then "merely paced back and forth a few times." Not only did Diogenes not say anything, did not offer any sort of philosophical argument—he did not even *go* anywhere. He "merely paced" to and fro, marking time, as it were. We are not told what sort of effect this *optraeden* had on his opponents or on any of the other spectators. As readers of the anecdote, we are left to ourselves to decide. And the decision is not made any easier by what follows the anecdote: namely, without any transition, the jump to a first-person, autobiographical narrative: "When I was occupied for some time, at least on occasion, with the question of repetition . . . I suddenly had the thought: You can, after all, take a trip to Berlin; you have been there once before, and now you can prove to yourself whether a repetition is possible and what importance it has. At home I had been practically immobilized by this question."

Only at the end of this passage does a possible connection between the anecdote about Diogenes' *optraeden* and the autobiographical story that follows begin to emerge. Diogenes demonstrates a certain kind of (repetitive) movement by "really" stepping up and "merely" pacing back and forth. The narrator-author, "Constantin Constantius," remembers that he had been "practically immobilized" by the question of "whether a repetition is possible and what importance it has." A strange question to be "immobilized" by, one might think, and yet it is precisely this strangeness that Kierkegaard's text will go on to deploy and render plausible, on the condition that the reader never cease asking the question of *who* is speaking or, rather, *writing*, and *from where*.

This is no simple task, however, for "Constantin Constantius" is not easy to situate. It is easier to say what and where he *is not* than what or where he *is*. Above all, he is *not* Søren Kierkegaard, if by that name we mean the empirical "author" of this and other texts. He is also not simply a "fictional character," even though he has no existence apart from the text, and even though he does indeed "report" a kind of story. But his "report" does not disappear into the story or fade into transparency. And the reader who expects it to serve as a mere instrument by which that story, or message, is conveyed is bound to come away from this text very disappointed. Rather, "Constantin Constantius" will expose himself in this text in a manner not unlike that of Diogenes, "really" stepping up to engage in a variety of "repetitions" that, however, by no means provide a simple and straightforward answer to the question he is asking.

This begins, as it were, with his "name." More "allegorical" than "proper," more generic than individual, this name already *is* an instance of repetition. But not just any repetition. In repeating itself, it names a certain "constancy": a "standing-with" in the sense of "standing-firm." The distinctive repetition deployed in the name *Constantin Constantius* suggests something or someone that stays the same, despite the movement of time as the medium of change, alteration, passage. The passage of a life, for instance: "Just as they [the Greeks] taught that all knowing is a recollecting, modern philosophy will teach that all life is a repetition."

The interest of philosophy has thus moved from "knowledge" to "life" and in so doing has shifted its emphasis from "recollection" to "repetition." Not that the latter simply does away with the former. Rather, it *redirects* it from the past toward the future: "Repetition and recollection are the same movement, except in opposite directions, for what is recollected has been, is repeated backward, whereas genuine repetition is recollected forward."

Repetition, according to Constantin Constantius, is thus concerned with life rather than knowledge and with the future rather than the past. The consequences that Constantin draws from this are, however, anything but self-evident: "Repetition, therefore, if it is possible, makes a person happy, whereas recollection makes him unhappy—assuming, of course, that he gives himself time to live and does not promptly at birth find an excuse to sneak out of life again, for example, [under the pretext] that he has forgotten something."

This conclusion is anything but self-evident, for at least two reasons. First, it is not at all clear why "repetition" should make "a person happy, whereas recollection" should make him unhappy—unless, that is, one remembers "Constantin's" name and takes it literally: to *recall* something is to acknowledge that it *is no longer*, except in the recollection of it.[7] Recollection thus confirms a certain loss, a certain passing of the past, and hence a certain *inconstancy*. What is recollected no longer "stands with" us or with itself, no longer "stands firm" against the flow of time except as a memory, which confirms its passing. If, however, repetition is construed as recollection projected "forward," into the future, it ostensibly holds out the possibility of *recovering* that which, were it to remain simply past, would be irretrievably gone. Such recovery of the past "makes a person happy," especially if his name is *Constantin Constantius*, for it reaffirms the possibility of a certain *constancy*, that is, of *staying the same* in and in spite of the passage of time. Mere "recollection," by contrast, will make one unhappy, given one rather important assumption: "Assuming, of course, that he gives himself time to live and does not promptly at birth find an excuse to sneak out of life again, for example [under the pretext] that he has forgotten something."

There is, then, one condition under which "recollection" may not make one unhappy, and although it may sound at first quite bizarre, after a while it begins to resonate in a surprisingly familiar manner. The person who has to "find an excuse to sneak out of life again," because "he has forgotten something," does not "give himself time to live"—or to die. The only "thing" that he could have forgotten, in this context, would be the inseparability of living and dying, of arriving and departing, forgetting and forgoing—in short, the passage of time. And it is this *passage* that "sneaking out of life" brings to a (premature) end. Thus, the refusal to "forget" actually "sneaks out of" the very "life" it seems to want to remember. In seeking not to forget, the possibility of living itself is lost.

Although this joke, if it is one, turns out to be at the expense of Constantin Constantius, its uncanny familiarity suggests that the joke may not be on him alone. The meta-slogan of American TV advertising enjoins its viewers to "stay with us" during (and in spite of) the "commercial break," promising that "we'll be right back," the same and perhaps better than before. Why and how the same and better? Because the "break" turns out to mark the advent of salvation itself, if one follows the "message," which insists that the more you spend, the more you save and *are saved*. The commercial break is a repeatable *kairos* that opens up the possibility of salvation in a way not so very different from that described by Constantin, except that it collapses what for him is an alternative into a synthesis. The incessantly repeated call to consume is anticipated in Constantin's "definition" of repetition as recollection willed forward, which has the ability to make people "happy" rather than "sad," inasmuch as it holds out the promise of overcoming the passage of time. "Stay with us" thus really means "don't disappear in the break!" Be constant! Stay put!

The difficulty of this task, however, constitutes precisely the problem that "immobilized" Constantin Constantius "in the first place" and drove him to attempt his radical experiment with repetition. The problem was linked, as he later recounts it, to his search for "complete satisfaction":

> At one time I was very close to complete satisfaction. I got up feeling unusually well one morning. My sense of well-being increased incomparably until noon; at precisely one o'clock, I was at the peak and had a presentiment of the dizzy maximum found on no gauge of well being, not even on a poetic thermometer. My body had lost its terrestrial gravity . . . my walk was a floating . . . my being was transparent . . . I had a presentiment of every impression before it arrived and awakened within

me. All existence seemed to have fallen in love with me, and everything quivered in fatal rapport with my being. Everything was prescient in me and everything was enigmatically transfigured . . . when suddenly something began to irritate one of my eyes, whether it was an eyelash, a speck of something, a bit of dust, I do not know, but this I do know—that in the same instant I was plunged into the abyss of despair, something everyone will understand who has been as high . . . as I was. . . . Since that time I have abandoned every hope of ever feeling satisfied absolutely.

It was then that time after time I turned to and became excited about the idea of repetition, and there I once again became the victim of my zeal for principles; for I am completely convinced that if I had not gone abroad with the idea of assuring myself of it, I would have amused myself immensely with the very same thing. (pp. 173–74)

In short, Constantin's decision to return to Berlin, to see if "repetition is possible" is taken to decide, once and for all and *in principle*, whether or not the kind of blissful moment he describes, in which temporal, bodily existence is transcended by a being in which "everything [is] prescient," can be *maintained, repeated*—that is, *recovered*—in more than just memory. This was the question that had "practically immobilized" him "at home" and that led him to attempt his fateful "experiment."

For Constantin, at least, that experiment ends in catastrophe. He returns to Berlin, goes back to the pension where he had lived as a student, finds it more or less unchanged, does many of the same things he did before, but, in the end, discovers that "the only repetition was the impossibility of repetition" (p. 170). Or, as he puts it shortly thereafter: "It seemed as if all my great talk, which I now would not repeat at any price, were only a dream from which I awoke to have life unremittingly and treacherously *retake* everything it had given without providing a *repetition*" (p. 172).

In short, Constantin "awakes" to a nightmare. But to understand precisely why, it is helpful to remember that "the good Danish word" (p. 149) generally translated as "repetition," namely *Gjentagelsen,* actually involves a somewhat different semantic field. As the English translators of this text recall in a note, Constantin's formulation plays on the literality of the Danish word, whose two components, *gjen* and *tagelsen*, mean "again" and "take" respectively. In this literal sense, "repetition" is true to its word: it "takes again" in the sense of "taking back" everything it has been given. This, however, is not at all the kind of *taking back* that Constantin Constantius had hoped to find and that alone would have granted him happiness. There is repetition, but from the viewpoint of his desire it is an impossible repetition, for it is one that *takes again*, rather than *gives back*. Again and again.

The tension in this "impossible repetition" plays itself out in one of the two story-lines that make up the first part of this text. (I leave discussion of the second part, which contains the celebrated discussion of the Book of Job, for another essay.) After he has elaborated his introductory thesis that "Recollection's love is the only happy love" (p. 133)—a thesis taken from another text of Kierkegaard—Constantin remarks that its author "is at times somewhat deceitful, not in the sense that he says one thing and means another but in the sense that he pushes the thought to extremes, so that if it is not grasped with the same energy, it reveals itself in the next instant as something else" (p. 133). To "grasp" such a thought "with the same energy" can only be to "repeat" it by pushing it once again to the extreme, where, however, it will "reveal itself . . . as something else."[8] The two story-lines, that of Constantin and that of the young man, which in a certain sense add up to a single story, push the thought of repetition and recollection to such extremes.

First, there is the story of "the young man," which makes its appearance center-stage as abruptly as had Diogenes. This is a text full of abrupt *coups de théâtre*. Although I cannot give this "story" that isn't one the reading it demands, it may suffice to recall its main drift: "About one year ago," Constantin writes, he "became very much aware of a young man (with whom I had already often been in contact), because his handsome appearance, the soulful expression of his eyes, had an almost alluring effect upon me" (p. 133). Constantin is anything but a detached observer, and the young man soon confides in him "that he had fallen in love." Of all the long descriptions Constantin gives of this love, I will limit myself to the following quote, which also marks a high point in their relationship:

> His gait, his movement, his gestures—all were eloquent, and he
> himself glowed with love. Just as a grape at the peak of its per-

fection becomes transparent and clear, the juice trickling from its delicate veins, just as the peel of a fruit breaks when the fruit is fully ripe, just so love broke forth almost visibly in his form. I could not resist stealing an almost enamored glance at him now and then, for a young man like that is just as enchanting to the eye as a young girl. (p. 135)

Constantin confesses that he is "almost enamored" with the person at—or from—whom he "steals" a glance. But of this passion, as with so much else in this strange story, *nothing* concrete will emerge— nothing that could be measured in terms of what is often called "real people." And not without good reason: nothing is less certain than that the bearer of the name *Constantin Constantius* is anything like a "real person," any more than is the anonymous "young man," of whom Constantin will later acknowledge that "it seemed to me as if I were that young man myself" (p. 172). This confession comes immediately before his bitter admission, already quoted, that "life takes" without giving back, and that therefore there "is" no true "repetition" (p. 172).

Of course, the usual solution to this problem is speciously simple: it is merely to interpret both Constantin and the anonymous young man as "parts" of "Kierkegaard" himself, the real author who, just before writing this text, had broken off his engagement to Regina Olsen. But, as Howard and Edna Hong note in the introduction to their translation, although *Repetition* must be considered to be one of "the most closely personal" writings of Kierkegaard, his personal autobiography can never suffice to provide an interpretive framework for this text, for reasons that Kierkegaard himself later, in *Two Ages* (1846), formulated with extreme precision: "Anyone who experiences anything primitively also experiences in ideality the possibilities of the same thing and the possibility of the opposite. These possibilities are his legitimate literary property. His own personal actuality, however, is not. His speaking and his producing are, in fact, born of silence" (p. ix).

The text of *Gjentagelsen*, perhaps more than many others, must be read against the grain, or from the edges of what it explicitly states, and this is nowhere more necessary than in respect to the relationship to "the young man" and his "confidant," Constantin Constantius. Anyone who reads this "story" with the expectation of discovering exciting or palpitating events, will go away sorely disappointed. But anyone who reads it as a kind of philosophical or moral parable will hardly be any more satisfied. For in the strictest of senses, what happens in this ostensible love story is *actually nothing*. In this respect—that of its invisible climax—the story recalls both the death of Oedipus and the *Breathless* passage of de Gaulle's motorcade, discussed in the previous chapter. True, the cut here is not nearly as dramatic as in Sophocles or Godard, but it is all the more insidious given its place in Constantin's story of the young man's love. The "young man" confesses his love for the "young girl" to Constantin, whom he chooses as his "confidant" precisely so that "he could talk aloud to himself." But the essence of that love is like the bursting of the grape: no sooner has "love broke[n] forth almost visibly in his form," than it disappears. In a passage already quoted in Chapter 4, but which merits repetition in this discussion of *Repetition*, Constantin describes this curiously anticlimactic moment:

> He was deeply and fervently in love, that was clear, and yet a few days later he was able to recollect his love. He was essentially through with the entire relationship. In beginning it, he took such a tremendous step that he leaped over life. If the girl dies tomorrow, it will make no essential difference; he will throw himself down again, his eyes will fill with tears again, he will repeat the poet's words again. . . . For a long time nothing has affected me so powerfully as this scene. (p. 136)

The anticlimactic aftermath of the young man's love is laced through with repetition. It repeats the opening scene in two ways. First, by falling in love, the young man "leaped over life," somewhat the way the one who refuses to give himself time to live "sneaks out of life" because he has "forgotten something." The young man leaps over life and falls out of love almost as quickly as he fell into it, precisely in order to be able to remember them. Were the girl to die, "it would make no difference," since for him she is already gone, past, lost and thus made an object of nostalgic recollection. Reciting the poet's words, "pacing up and down" as had Diogenes, the young man demonstrates that there may be movement, but it does not necessarily go anywhere or change anything.

Constantin acknowledges that he is "powerfully" affected by "this scene," but it is a scene that is never seen, that remains invisible. Like the scene from *Breathless*, it never really—"actually"—takes place. In its place, there is a void or a cut: "He was deeply and fervently in love, that was clear, and yet a few days later he was able to recollect his love." How the young man moves from the one situation of being in love, to the situation of being able to recollect it, is never shown, never described. There is no transition, only a leap: "he leaped over life." And although this still seems to conform to a certain temporal sequence, in fact it was *there* from the very beginning: "In the very first moment he became an old man in regard to the entire relationship" (p. 136). The "young man" acts like "an old man" from the start, and in so doing, demonstrates his propensity for "recollection": "But so much is certain: if anyone can join in conversation about recollection's love, he can. Recollection has the great advantage that it begins with loss; the reason it is safe and secure is that it has nothing to lose" (p. 136).

Recollection has "nothing to lose" because it has already given up. This loss, however, is unacceptable to Constantin Constantius and to the modernity he represents. In the past, "recollection" could accept "loss" in the name of knowledge. For an age that is no longer informed strictly by knowledge, however, but by "life," such a loss has become intolerable, because the "life" it lives is largely that of the solitary individual. From that point of view, no "knowledge" can compensate for the individual's unsurpassable limit, death. Hence Constantin's desire to "will repetition." The "young man" does not understand this: "My young friend did not understand repetition; he did not believe in it and did not powerfully will it. . . . If the young man had believed in repetition, what great things might have come from him" (pp. 145–46).

Repetition as Constantin here describes it is an object of *faith* and of *will*: either one believes in it, and wills it, or one does not. The young man does not, although he, like everyone else, practices it, for instance, in repeating verses from the poet Poul Møller: "He repeated the same verse that evening when we parted. It will never be possible for me to forget that verse; indeed, I can more easily obliterate the recollection of his disappearance than the memory of that moment" (p. 146). Originally, Kierkegaard (or Constantin) wrote "death" instead of "disappearance," for in the initial version of the text the young man shoots himself. But, whether "death" or "disappearance," Constantin reacts to this "parting" by recollecting *repetition*, just as his notion of repetition will repeat recollection, only projected into the future. In both cases, Constantin's belief in repetition is inseparable from the hope of "taking back" what has been lost in the "parting." Constantin's hope is through repetition, *as* repetition, to be able to "take back" and thus to *stand fast*. His return to Berlin will definitively shatter this hope. But in the process another kind of repetition, of *Gjentagelsen*, will have begun to emerge: repetition as the medium of *difference* rather than as the means of *staying the same*. And that medium will reveal itself as being irreducibly *theatrical*. Constantin formulates the general principle involved quite clearly: "The dialectic of repetition is easy, for that which is repeated has been—otherwise it could not be repeated—but the very fact that it has been makes the repetition into something new. When the Greeks said that all knowing is recollecting, they said that all existence, which is, has been; when one says that life is a repetition, one says: actuality, which has been, now comes into existence" (p. 149).

This general formulation leaves open the question of *how* that "which has been" once again "*now* comes into existence" as repetition. To explore the question of "how-now," Constantin Constantius embarks upon his "investigative journey," his "experimental" voyage to Berlin. From the very start his voyage is an experiment in repetition, one that will surely strike the contemporary reader as quite familiar. Constantin, to be sure, does not travel by air, but by coach. And yet his experience is not so very different from what one undergoes in today's "coach" class:

> When I arrived in Hamburg I had lost not only my mind but my legs as well. During those thirty-six hours, we six people sitting inside the carriage were so worked together into one body that I got a notion of what happened to the Wise Men of Gotham, who after having sat together a long time could not recognize their own legs. Hoping at least to remain a limb on a lesser body, I chose a seat in the forward compartment. That was a change. Everything, however, repeated itself. (p. 151)

One of the things that repeats itself is Constantin's wondering whether he "will ever be human again," which is to say, whether or not he will be "able to disengage" himself "in the singleness of isolation, or if you will carry a memory of your being a limb on a larger body" (p. 151). The answer will come a bit later, and in an unexpected way, but it is worth remarking that the question of repetition here seems inseparable from a complex transformation in which forced and prolonged contact with other bodies transforms one's own into a "limb on a larger body" that, despite or because of this reintegration, still experiences the "singleness of isolation" that for Constantin is inseparable from being "human." Integration and isolation are thus by no means mutually exclusive in the bodily experience of repetition.

Upon finally arriving in Berlin, Constantin returns to his "old lodgings" in Gendarme Square, "the most beautiful in Berlin," surrounded by two churches and a theater, the *Schauspielhaus*. The theater turns out to be not just outside, but inside his rented lodging as well:

> Sitting in a chair by the window, one looks out on the great square, sees the shadows of passersby hurrying along the walls; everything is transformed into a stage set [*scenisk Decoration*]. A dreaming [*drømmende*] reality glimmers in the background of the soul. One feels a desire to toss on a cape, to steal softly along the wall with a searching gaze, aware of every sound. . . . The cloudless arch of heaven has a sad and pensively dreaming [*tankedrømmende*] look, as if the end of the world had already come and heaven, unperturbed, were occupied with itself. . . . But here, alas, again no repetition was possible. (pp. 151–52)

Although Constantin Constantius finds no repetition here, it is going on all the time, in the most theatrical of ways. Not the least of these is marked by the frequent use of the present participle, theatrical tense par excellence, to designate the strange goings-on of this "stage set": Constantin "*sitting* by the window," watching the shadows "*hurrying* along the walls" in a "reality" that seems to be "*dreaming*," and finally the moonlit heaven itself "dreamingly" sunk in thought. This scene, which in its own way recalls both the Platonic cave[9] and, as we will see in a moment, Descartes' shadow-play, epitomizes the dilemma that Constantin will encounter: repetition exists, but only in its most literal version, that of "taking again" without "giving back." The image that results, which will haunt him throughout this text, is not just one of the "end of the world," but of an end that has *come and gone*, an end that therefore repeats itself without end, in the endless "occupation" of "heaven" with "itself." In that occupation there is no need or place for anyone else: it is the image of a pure and perfect narcissism, but at the same time of the absolute absence of everything human. All that is left is the All: Heaven, repeating itself, for heaven's sake. "Rien que le tout," in the words of Clov, in Beckett's *Endgame*. Clov, who is looking out of the window at the earth, asks Hamm what he would like him to recount:

> *Clov.* Any particular sector you fancy? Or merely the whole thing?
> *Hamm.* Whole thing.
> . . .
> *Hamm.* I was never there.
> *Clov.* Lucky for you. (*He looks out of window.*)
> *Hamm.* Absent, always. It all happened without me. I don't know what's happened.[10]

Constantin, by contrast, "knows" what has happened, but cannot accept it. He finds that his "landlord, the druggist, *er hatte sich verändert*" [he had changed (himself)] (p. 152) and therefore he disqualifies him from the kind of repetition he is looking for. To change is not to stay the same, not to recover what has been lost, to rediscover oneself. Rather, it is to envisage a self that is not one, but also not simply another. In the scene under discussion, Constantin describes himself, but as the "*man*" who is both someone and no one.[11] This experience of being "man," and yet neither one nor another, both and neither, is bound up with the desire to "toss on a cape and steal softly along the wall." But "one does not do this" and instead only "sees a rejuvenated self doing it" (p. 152). In short, one becomes specularly reflective, observing oneself doing in fantasy what "one" cannot do in reality. This ambiguous situation of the spectator also haunts the scene from Descartes already mentioned:

> But meanwhile I am surprised at how prone to errors my mind might be. . . . For we say that we see the way itself if it be there, and not that we judge from the color or the figure that it is there. From whence I would immediately conclude that there the way is cognized by the vision of the eye, not by the inspection of the mind alone—if perhaps I had not now looked out the window at human beings going by in the street, whom themselves I also say, as a matter of the usage of language, that I see. . . . But what do I see besides hats and clothes under which automata might be concealed? Yet I judge that there are human beings there.[12]

Descartes, who is primarily concerned here with examining the conditions under which true knowledge is possible, exemplifies his worst-case theory through the confusion of humans with machines, with "automata." But for Constantin, concerned primarily with living life rather than acquiring knowledge, the nightmare is different. It is a vision in which the difference between humans and machines is not that decisive, for both are absent after the end of the world has come . . . and gone. What is left is the dissociation of reflexivity from human consciousness: it is heaven that is dreamingly pensive. But such *tankedrømmend*, far from proving the existence of a *cogito*, demonstrates its potential absence. *Something* may be going on, but it need not be the result of an I. The thinking *thing* here takes leave of the thinking *I*. Constantin repeatedly discovers this leave-taking to be the essence of repetition. It is not just a piece of wax that changes, but the thinking of it as well. What most fascinates and horrifies Constantin about this change is that it seems self-inflicted. "'*Er hatte sich verändert*,' in the pregnant sense in which the German understands this phrase and, so far as I know, 'to change oneself' [*at forandre sig*] is similarly used in some of Copenhagen's streets" (p. 152).

What has changed from Descartes to Constantin is that "change" and alteration have emerged as functions of the "self," and this transforms the status of thinking itself. For Descartes this status was compatible with the present participle, which defined its stability:

> *I* am, *I* exist, it is certain. But for how long? So long as I am cogitating, of course. It could perhaps also happen that if I would cease all cogitation I as a whole would at once cease to be. I am now admitting nothing except what is necessarily true. I am, then, precisely only a *cogitating* thing [*res cogitans*], . . . truly *existing* [*vere existens*]. . . . I said, *thinking* [*Dixi, cogitans*]. (pp. 104–5, my italics)

The temporal tense that defines the medium of such "thought" is not the present indicative, not the famous *cogito*, but the *present participle*. I am or exist *only as long "as I am cogitating."* The actuality of the "I think" depends upon the present participle, which is the tense that defines itself through repetition.

From Descartes to Constantin, the scene repeats itself but also changes. Memory and repetition, implicit in the Cartesian scene, are now explicit, although often in ways that Constantin himself is not willing or able to acknowledge:

> When I came home the first evening and had lit the candles, I thought: Alas! Alas! Alas! Is this the repetition? I became completely out of tune, or, if you please, precisely in tune with the day, for fate had strangely contrived it so that I arrived in Berlin on the *allgemeine Buß und Bettag* [Universal Day of Penance and Prayer]. Berlin was prostrate. To be sure, they did not throw ashes in one another's eyes with the words: *Memento o homo! Quod cinis es et in cinerem revertaris* [Remember, O Man, that dust thou art and to dust thou shalt return]. But all the same, the whole city lay in one cloud of dust. (pp. 152–53)

Although Constantin is quick to dismiss this fateful coincidence— "This discovery had no connection with 'repetition' "—there is every reason not to take him at his word. If repetition has, as he asserts, the function of making people "happy," it is by virtue of overcoming the "loss" that recognition, for instance, confirms. Repetition, as Constantin seeks it, is supposed to *bring back* what time has taken away. It is no wonder, then, that he seeks to separate this notion of repetition from the *memento mori* associated with the German *Buß und Bettag*.

His efforts in this direction, however, once again wind up repeating those of Descartes. Like Descartes, who withdrew from active life in order to devote himself fully and without distraction to his search for an Archimedean point that would "be firm and immovable," from which "the entire earth" might be "moved from its place" (p. 99), Constantin also seeks to establish himself "cosily and comfortably in his quarters" so as to have "a fixed point like this from which [to] rush out, a safe hiding place to which [to] retreat" (p. 153). Such a "fixed point" must be distinguished from what it had begun, the night before, to resemble: namely, a certain *theater*. In this kind of theater, there are no "fixed points," not even for the audience: "Everything is transformed into a stage set." Constantin must therefore leave this domestic theater behind him if he is to find the repetition he is looking for. Or, rather, he must try to put the stage-set back in its proper place: in the theater, where it belongs. Yet he will discover a theater in which there are no proper places and where nothing stays put for long:

Berlin has three theaters. The opera and ballet performances in the opera house are supposed to be *großartig* [magnificent]; performances in the theater are supposed to be instructive and refining, not only for entertainment. I do not know. But I do know that Berlin has a theater called the Königstädter Theater. Professional travelers visit this theater seldom. . . . When . . . I read in the newspaper that *Der Talisman* would be performed at that theater, I was in a good mood at once. The recollection of it awakened in my soul and stood before me as alive as though it were the first time. (p. 154)

It is in the hopes of rediscovering and, indeed, resurrecting a life that has disappeared that Constantin returns to the Königstädter Theater. But before he is forced to recount what awaits him, he reflects on what he calls "the magic of the theater," a magic that works most powerfully on the "young":

There is probably no young person with any imagination who has not at some time been enthralled by the magic of the theater and wished to be swept along into that artificial actuality in order, like a double, to see and hear himself and to split himself up into every possible variation of himself, but in such a way that every variation is still himself. . . . In such a self-vision of the imagination, the individual is not an actual shape but a shadow. More correctly, the actual shape is invisibly present and therefore not satisfied to cast only one shadow. The individual has a variety of shadows, all of which resemble him and which momentarily have equal status with being himself. (p. 154)

As Constantin describes it, the "magic of theater" consists in provoking what he calls "the passion of possibility." This passion is useful, according to Constantin, when it comes at the right time and place, while one is young. If it does not keep to its place, it can have "tragic or comic" results. Constantin compares its course to the wind plunging down from the mountains, first with a hideous "shriek, almost startling to itself," then modulating successively into a "hollow roar," a "moan," a "sigh," and finally "a gay, lyrical waltz . . . whose melody it renders unaltered day after day" (p. 155). Repetition here entails a process of domestication, taming the wild struggles of "the individual's possibility" by its actual self. Unlike the "mere passing of the wind," the theatrical passion of the individual "does not want only to be heard" but also "to be visible at the same time." By shaping—*gestaltend* (p. 155)—the individual attempts to endure without being trapped in an actuality that permits no alternatives, no possibilities of change. The *Gestalt* or *shape* it assumes is that of an "audible shadow." Such an audible shadow, however, calls for an appropriate environment:

> Then, in order not to gain an impression of his actual self, the hidden individual needs an environment as superficial and transient as the shapes, as the frothing foam of words that sound without resonance.
>
> The stage is that kind of setting, and therefore it is particularly suitable for the *Schattenspiel* [shadow play] of the hidden individual. (p. 156)

Through all this shadow play, the "hidden individual" still ultimately seeks "to recognize itself" (p. 156). This leads Constantin to distinguish between the individual's "predilection for theatrical *performing*" and what he describes as a "call to *scenic* art [*scenisk Kunst*]"; between, in short, *performativity* and *theatricality*. The former is bound up with the desire for self-recognition, whereas the latter is less concerned with the self than with "a capacity for detail" or, more literally translated, "a *disposition* for the *singular* [*Disposition til det Enkelte*]." This disposition, Constantin continues, returns in later life to determine a no less singular relationship to theater, namely, one that is "comically productive [*comisk productiv*]." This desire to descend into the street, onto the stage, is the same one that grips Constantin from his window perch in the pension. It is the desire no longer simply to look, to remain a spectator, in a fixed position. At the same time, it is a desire that knows and accepts its own impossibility. It does not go out into the moonlit street or descend onto the stage, but merely watches its "rejuvenated self" doing this in imagination. But this means that it returns to the role of spectator, precisely imagining itself as an active participant or protagonist. This could be called "comic productivity," were it not for the fact that comedy, as an aesthetic genre, is still too general and too perfect: "Since tragedy, comedy, and light comedy fail to please him precisely because of their perfection, he turns to farce [*Posse*]" (p. 158).

The translation of *Posse* as "farce" is unsatisfying insofar as it reduces the theatrical connotation of the word. *Possen* were burlesque, popular plays, which enjoyed great popularity in Vienna and Berlin during the 1840s. Perhaps the greatest author of such *Possen*, also an actor and director, was Johann Nestroy, whose play *The Talisman* Constantin returns to see.[13] In his notes to this text, Kierkegaard describes the *Posse* as the "extreme point of the humorous" (p. 326). An "extreme" marks the spot where something turns into something else. The *Posse* thus relates to the legitimate dramatical genre of comedy as the "exception" relates to the "universal." In his "Concluding Letter" to the reader, Constantin Constantius describes the relation of the universal to the exception as "a wrestling match in which the universal breaks with the exception, wrestles with it in conflict and strengthens it through this wrestling. . . . If one really wants to study the universal, one only need look around for a legitimate exception. . . . The exception thinks the universal with intense passion" (p. 161).[14]

The *Posse* distinguishes itself from aesthetic genres, whether theatrical or other, by the absence of a self-contained "work." It produces plays, pieces, *Stücke*, which can never be understood as instantiations of a general rule. Instead, they are what Constantin calls "accidental concretions," a term we will come to in a moment. Traces of this "accident" can be read in the etymology of the word itself. *Posse* derives from the French *bosse*, a dent, hump, or disfiguration, usually resulting from a violent blow or shock. Used in the plural, *Possen* also designates nonsensical, absurd, grotesque behavior, "practical jokes," buffoonery—in any event, a highly *theatricalized* mode of behavior directed at others. But on whom or on what is this sort of joke? If we recall, as Kierkegaard does in another place, that *posse* is also the Latin verb for "to be able," and that it therefore can be contrasted with *esse*, "being,"[15] the joke could just turn out to be on being itself, on being, that is, understood in the sense of a self-contained noun rather than a gerund, for instance.

From this perspective, *Posse* would entail a *possibility* that would not merely trace a mode of, or transition toward, a self-contained reality, but would have to be dealt with on its own terms. One of these terms is "accidental concretion" (p. 163), which repeats and transforms—perhaps *deforms*—Hegel's conceptualization of art as "the sensuously concrete form" of the universal.[16] *Posse* is precisely *not* art, however, inasmuch as it does not concretize the universal by instantiating it in sensuous particulars and thereby attaining a kind of self-contained "perfection." For the same reason, however, it is also not simply "performance," if by performance is meant the actualization or realization of an intention, because both work and performance relegate the spectator to the status of a more or less passive observer. *Posse*, by contrast, appeals to the audience's desire to be "comically productive," to participate *as singular beings* in a theatrical spectacle that can no longer be defined either as an object of sensuous perception or as a work.[17] The audience of the *Posse*, which is generally drawn from "the lower levels of society" (p. 159), is "not at all conscious of [itself] as audience but wants to be down there on the street or wherever the scene happens to be" (p. 159). This relationship to and dependence on the audience, in all of its heterogeneity, distinguishes the *Posse* from every *generic* conception of theater, and above all from *comedy* as well as tragedy. Compared to these, the *Posse* is imperfect and incomplete. But this is also its *chance*, because in its very incompleteness it has the capacity to elicit "an indescribable effect," which depends as much upon "the observer's mood" or situation as upon "plot," "character," or any other of the thematic contents represented on stage. By contrast, the *Posse* is never "contained"—and has, strictly speaking, no "contents." Instead, it is open to the advent of "accident," since the "mood" or situation of its audience is never entirely predictable, much less a "necessary" function of the universal. This distinguishes the audience of the *Posse* from a "proper" theatrical audience:

> A proper theater public generally has a certain limited earnestness; it wishes to be . . . ennobled and educated in the theater. . . . It wishes, as soon as it has read the poster, to be able to know in advance what is going to happen that evening. Such unanimity cannot be found at a farce, for the same farce can produce very different impressions, and, strangely enough, it may so happen that the one time it made the least impression it was performed best. (pp. 159–60)

Once again we discover that the efficacy of the *Posse* may have nothing to do with the quality of its *performance*. It involves repetition, but not necessarily repetition of the same, for "the same farce can produce very different impressions." The singularity of the *Posse* thus depends in great part upon that of its audience, which is never "unanimous." There is, to be sure, a kind of "actualization" on the stage, but that "actuality" never seeks to coincide entirely with its representational (thematic) content—for instance, a "fine character portrayal" (p. 160). Instead, what happens on stage cannot be isolated from what goes on off it, namely, in an audience that does "not come with a firm and fixed mood" but maintains itself in a "state in which not a single mood is present but a possibility of all" (p. 161).

Those in the audience, we recall, want to be "comically productive"; they would like to "descend" from the galleries to the stage. "But since this is out of the question, they behave like children who only get permission to look out of the window at the commotion on the street" (p. 159). The audience is condemned to watch—to be spectators of a spectacle. Nevertheless, this childlike audience does far more than simply "look" or even listen: it laughs. And its laughter involves it in a movement that epitomizes the way in which repetition, taken seriously, alters the very notion of movement itself. Laughter is a movement that disrupts the stasis of the body, destabilizes its situation, but not in order to change it for another place. Laughter is a repetitive movement of the body that, like Diogenes and the young man, is going nowhere and yet changing everything. Laughter goes to extremes, and as such it cannot always be subordinated to conscious volition: its onset requires a certain uncertainty, a certain lack of knowledge or relaxation of control. A certain disposition to assume the risks of such lack of knowledge and control is what distinguishes the audience of the *Posse* from more respectable theatergoers:

> Thus a person cannot rely on his neighbor and the man across the street and statements in the newspaper to determine whether he has enjoyed himself or not. The individual has to decide that matter for himself. . . . Seeing a *Posse* can produce the most unpredictable mood, and therefore a person can never be sure whether he has conducted himself in the theater as a worthy member of society who has laughed and cried at the appropriate places. (p. 160)

In short, the spectator of the *Posse* has no "universals" to fall back upon: neither those of "society" nor his own. He cannot rely upon the critics, the media, or his companions to determine his response:

> No effect in farce is brought about by irony; everything is naïveté. Therefore the spectator must be self-active wholly in his

singularity [*ganske som Enkelt vaere selvvirksom*]. . . . The amusement consists largely in the way the spectator relates to the *Posse*, something he himself must risk, whereas he seeks in vain to the left or right or in the newspapers for a guarantee that he actually has enjoyed himself. (p. 160)

This naïveté can obtain "for the cultured person" as well as those from the lower classes; indeed, for the former the *Posse* will "have a very singular meaning," deriving from "the copiousness of the abstract and then again by the interjection of a tangible actuality" (p. 161).[18] Among the many instances given of how this "accidental concretion" of the "abstract" and the actual takes place on the stage, probably the most memorable is the description of Beckmann, one of the stars of the Königstädter Theater. Beckmann is as notable for what he does *not do* as for what he *does*: "Beckmann . . . does not distinguish himself by character portrayal but by ebullience of mood. He is not great in the artistically commensurable, but is admirable in the singularly incommensurable. He does not need the support of interaction, scenery, and staging; precisely because he is in an ebullient mood, he himself carries everything along [*han Alt selv med*]" (p. 163).

The sense of the Danish phrase, which ends with the preposition, *med*, "with," is difficult to render in English: Beckmann brings everything *with*. With what? With "himself," to be sure. But nothing is less "sure" than that *selv*. For in what does that "self" consist? In the description that follows, it becomes clear that it is neither character nor any other portrayal. What distinguishes Beckmann as a master practitioner of the *Posse* is not his ability to represent character—or anything else, for that matter. It consists, rather, in his very singular way of *moving* onto and on the stage, a talent rarely found outside of the *Posse*, in legitimate theater:

> In an art theater proper, one rarely sees an actor who can really walk and stand. As a matter of fact, I have seen only one, but what B. is able to do, I have not seen before. He is not only able to walk, but he is able to *come walking* [*komme gaaende*]. To come walking is something utterly different [*ganske Andet*], and by means of this genius he also improvises the whole scenic setting [*Omgivelse*]. (p. 163)

If this essay on repetition revolves around the question of movement, beginning with the scene of Diogenes pacing back and forth, then the account of Beckmann's singular and genial way of moving about the stage discloses a new dimension of repetition. Constantin insists on the difference between actors who know how to "walk"—of which there are already not many—and the unique case of Beckmann, who doesn't just know how to "walk," but who knows how to "come walking" onto the stage. The most obvious difference between "walking" and to "*come* walking" is that the former takes the site for granted and simply moves around *on* it, whereas the latter raises the question of its delimitation and of its limits by *coming* from elsewhere, making its entry, its *optraeden,* from an "utterly different" place, perhaps. When an actor "*comes* walking," his coming brings with it—*med*—the question of *where* he is coming *from,* and hence implicitly raises the question of the relation of the stage to its setting or surroundings. These "surroundings"—*Omgivelse* in Danish, translated above as the "setting"—are never just the property of the stage, never merely a space contained *within* its borders, but also and above all that which *surrounds* the stage without containing it fully: in short, the "theater." Thus, the theatrical stage always relates to an *elsewhere,* which is never simply another *place* or an entirely indeterminate *space.* Neither space nor place, it is between the two, and that intermediary position makes it as temporal as it is spatial. This ambiguity is retained in the English word *stage,* which translates the "good Danish word" *Stadier,* used by Kierkegaard in the title of one of his most famous writings, *Stages on Life's Way.* It is because the "stage" is also a temporal "stage," although not simply in the sense of a transitional movement, that Beckmann's "coming" is so "utterly different," so *ganske Andet*: it comes from an utterly different space and time from that we are used to, and it moves in a very different way.

When Beckmann *comes,* it is not just *walking.* The Danish phrase translated in this manner actually says something else as well: it tells us that Beckmann *comes going, komme gaaende.* In Danish as in German the verb *gaaen (gehen)* means both "to walk" and "to go," in the sense of "to leave." The excellent German translation of this text, by Emanuel Hirsch, translates the Danish phrase into German as *gegangen kommen,*[19] literally, "gone coming." But Beckmann is not simply "gone"—he is very much *there,* on stage, although his *actual* being-there, on the stage, involves "leaving" as much as "coming." His "coming" is also his "going," not in the sense of simple presence or absence, but in the curious and singular mix that we already have encountered in Aristotle's designation of actors as *prattontes*, literally, as "actings" (anticipating the terms and tense of the Scholastic theory of signs and signification, *signans* and *significandi*, and of its structuralist reprise, Saussure's *signifiant*). Beckmann's "coming" to the stage is, from its very advent, an *event*, since in "arriving" he is simultaneously "going" somewhere else: arriving and departing in the discontinuous iterations of the present participle, whose "presence," as already discussed, is defined by its problematic co-presence with its articulation. Constantin describes the results as follows:

> He is able not only to portray a *wandering* apprentice [*vandrende Haandvaerksbursch*]; he is also able to come going like one and in such a way that one experiences everything, surveys the *smiling* hamlet from the dusty highway, hears its quiet noise, sees the footpath that goes down by the village pond when one turns off there by the blacksmith's—where one sees B. *come going* [*komme gaaende*] with his little bundle on his back, his stick in his hand, carefree and untroubled. (p. 164, my italics)

What is striking about this scene is how absent humans are from it: the "hamlet" may be "smiling," but its inhabitants are nowhere to be seen. Instead, there are only *traces*: the dusty highway, the quiet noise, the footpath leading down to the village pond, the turn-off at the blacksmith's. Only the figure of the wandering apprentice himself seems an exception. If we read on, we discover just how exceptional that figure is: "This workman is no character sketch; for that he is too rapidly traced in his masterly contours. He is an incognito in whom the demon of lunatic comedy dwells, who is always ready to break out and carry away everything in utter abandonment" (p. 164). Just as Beckmann "comes walking," his figure—the *wandering apprentice*—comes going, abandoning itself in a movement that moves from song to dance and beyond: "In this respect, B.'s dance is incomparable. He has sung his couplet, and now the dance begins. What B. ventures here is neck-breaking. . . . He is now completely beside himself. The sheer lunacy of his laughter can no longer be contained either in figures or in lines" (p. 164).

The figure coming almost immediately makes way, first for the traces of the smiling hamlet, then for a dance that soon takes leave of all representation. One would be tempted to say that the figure is replaced by the dancer and the dancer by the dance, but the "neck-breaking" movements place every figure and every dance "beside" itself. All that is left is "the sheer lunacy of laughter," a laughter that "can no longer be contained either in figures or in lines." Figuration explodes into disfiguration, and the iterative movement of corporeal self-abandonment soon spreads, contagiously, from Beckmann to the audience, from the stage to the galleries, where Constantin's description now shifts.

Constantin is, of course, himself a part of this audience. He thus recounts how he at first takes his "place in the first balcony," where "relatively few sit" and where one is relatively unhampered "by the exaltation of an art that makes people jam a theater to see a play as if it were a matter of salvation" (p. 165). It may well turn out to be nothing less for Constantin, but if so, that will depend less upon what he *sees*, that is, the spectacle, than upon what he *hears*:

> So you are sitting alone in your box, and the theater is empty. The orchestra plays an overture, the music resounds in the hall a bit *unheimlich* simply because the place is so deserted. You have gone to the theater not as a tourist, not as an esthete and critic, but, if possible, as a nobody. . . . As a rule, I sat far back in the box and therefore could not see the second balcony and the gallery, which jutted out over my head like the visor of a cap. All the more magical is the effect of this noise. Everywhere I looked there was mainly emptiness. Before me the vast space of the theater changed into the belly of the whale in which Jonah sat; the noise in the gallery was like the motion of the monster's viscera. (pp. 165–66)

The noise resonates, changing the vast emptiness of the theater into a kind of bodily container, protective and yet threatening at once. Yet what Constantin is trying to forget is even more anxiety producing, as the following apostrophe to the memory of his "unforgettable nursemaid" suggests:

> My unforgettable nursemaid, you fleeting nymph . . . you, my faithful comforter, you preserved your innocent purity over the years, you who did not age as I grew older. . . . Then I lay at your side and vanished from myself in the immensity of the sky above and forgot myself in your soothing murmur! . . . —Thus did I lie in my theater box, discarded like a swimmer's clothing,

stretched out by the stream of laughter and unrestraint and ap-
plause that ceaselessly swirled by me. I could see nothing but
the expanse of theater, hear nothing but the noise in which I
resided. Only at intervals did I rise up, look at Beckmann, and
laugh so hard that I sank back again in exhaustion alongside the
foaming stream.

By itself this was blissful, and yet I lacked something. (p. 166)

In thus responding to the noise and laughter, Constantin has transformed the *Posse* into the same "recollection love" for which he has
castigated in his "young friend" and which he has condemned in
general: "Recollection is a discarded garment that does not fit, however beautiful it is, for one has outgrown it" (p. 132). Alone in his
theater box, oblivious to everything but the noisy laughter that breaks
down all borders and leaves him *beside* himself, he *is* that discarded
garment, which, having severed its connection with the human, can
appear to be exempt from the ravages of time. And yet even such
bliss is not enough for Constantin: "I lacked something." Nor is this
surprising, since he has responded to Beckmann's *Posse* with "recollection's love," which "initially at least makes a person unhappy" (p.
131). This is a love that confirms time as the medium of loss. Repetition, as Constantin understands it, seeks to reverse that movement by
projecting what has been into what will be. Constantin seems to discover the possibility of such a projection in his recollection of a figure
directly across from him:

> Then, in the wilderness surrounding me, I saw a figure that
> cheered me more than Friday cheered Robinson Crusoe. In the
> third row of a box directly across from me sat a young girl, half
> hidden. . . . She was not wrapped in sable and marten but in a
> voluminous scarf, and out of this sheath her humble head
> bowed. . . . When I had watched Beckmann and let myself be
> convulsed with laughter . . . and let myself be carried away . . .
> my eyes sought her, and the sight of her refreshed my whole
> being with its friendly gentleness. . . . She came there, as did I,
> every evening. (pp. 166–67)

Of this vision, nothing will come—nothing except the recollection
we have just read, and the brutal discovery that the recollected experience cannot willfully be repeated. The sight of this young girl, "qui-

etly smiling in childlike wonder," seems to offer Constantin a way out and something to hold onto: a figure that stands out of time in its youthful innocence, a figure also of repetition, for "She came there, as did I, every evening. At times I wondered what could be the reasons for it" (p. 167). Constantin will never find those reasons, just as he will not find the young girl when he returns to the Königstädter Theater in the hopes of repeating his experience. Only through a repetition that is *willed* can Constantin hope to find constancy and continuity in and despite the passage of time: "If God himself had not willed repetition, the world would not have come into existence. . . . Therefore, the world continues, and it continues because it is a repetition" (p. 133).

Thus, the question that has led Constantin to his voyage finally appears with a certain clarity. Not "is" there a repetition, or what it might mean, but rather, can repetition in this sense be willfully brought about? To this question, his experience and experiment provide an equivocal response. This is how he describes his return to the theater:

> No box was available for me alone. . . . There was scarcely a single empty box. The young girl was not to be found, or, if she was present, I was unable to recognize her because she was together with others. Beckmann could not make me laugh. I endured it for half an hour and then left the theater, thinking: There is no repetition at all. This made a deep impression on me. I am not so very young, am not entirely ignorant of life. . . . I did believe, however, that the enjoyment I had known in that theater would be of a more durable nature. (pp. 168–69)

There is no repetition, no "durable" enjoyment, no "recollection projected forwards," not in the theater, at least. But what, then, outside of it? What about at home?

> With these thoughts in my mind, I went home. My desk was in place. The velvet armchair was still there, but when I saw it, I became so furious I almost smashed it to pieces. . . . Of what good is an armchair of velvet when the rest of the environment does not match; it is like a man going around naked and wearing a three-cornered hat.
>
> My home had become dismal to me simply because it was a repetition of the wrong kind. (p. 169)

At his pension Constantin discovers that there *are* repetitions, but "of the wrong kind." Far from procuring the happiness he had hoped for, they call into question the possibility of such happiness. Things can stay the same over time, the armchair for instance. But "what good is a velvet armchair when the rest . . . does not match." The rest—for example, the person who is to sit in that armchair? What good is it if that armchair lasts, endures, stays the same over time, "repeats itself identically," when the person who sits in it does not?

Constantin goes out, to a café he knows, then to a restaurant, then back again to the Königstädter Theater, only to discover, again and again, that "the only repetition was the impossibility of a repetition" (p. 170). And so he gives up on Berlin and decides to return home. "My hope lay in my home." This is the scene of his homecoming; note the shift from present tense to past:

> I arrive. I ring my doorbell. My servant opens the door. It was a moment eloquent with meaning. My servant turned as pale as a corpse. Through the door half-opened to the rooms beyond I saw the horror: everything was turned upside down. I was petrified. In his confusion he did not know what to do, his guilty conscience smote him—and he slammed the door in my face. That was too much. My desolation reached its highpoint, my principles had collapsed. . . . I perceived that there is no repetition. (p. 171)

Constantin could not have been more distraught if his home had been demolished. It is enough that it has merely been turned topsy-turvy in the process of being cleaned by his servant, who has been caught short by Constantin's premature return. Constantin's voyage did not leave the servant enough time. But that is precisely the problem he has to deal with and cannot: there will never be enough time for the kind of repetition Constantin is seeking, the kind that would *give back* rather than *take again*. If Constantin remains true to his name, so does *Gjentagelse*: it takes and takes again, without ever *giving back*:

> How humiliated I was: I, who had been so brusque with that young man, had now been brought to the same point. Indeed, it seemed as if I were that young man myself, as if my great talk, which I now would not repeat at any price, were only a dream

from which I awoke to have life unremittingly and treacherously *retake* everything [*tage Alt igjen*] it had given, without giving a repetition. And is it not the case that the older a person grows, the more and more of a swindle life proves to be? (p. 172)

Different as they may be, the young man and Constantin are impossible to separate, since the "repetition" Constantin is looking for is one that, as he says, would simply repeat recollection forward, as it were, without altering its structure. Constantin's repetition, like the young man's recollection, seeks only to make up for the loss. It expects from life a *fair exchange* and is bitterly disappointed when the books don't balance.

All that is left to Constantin are words whose meanings don't match their sound, the echo of unfulfilled promises and prophecies: in short, the "coach horn" he ironically apostrophizes at the end of his voyage. For the end of the voyage is not the end of the show, but only of a single showing:

> Move on [*Faer fort*], you spectacle [*Skuespiel*] of life—let no one call it a comedy, no one a tragedy, for no one saw the end. Move on, you spectacle of existence, where life is not given any more than money. Why has no one returned from the dead? Because life does not know how to captivate as death does, because life does not have the persuasiveness that death has. (p. 176)

Life cannot hold an audience. Not, at any rate, with the tenacity of the Great Persuader. Only the *Posse* can challenge death, by repeating and rehearsing it in a laughter that cannot be willed, because it is going nowhere.[20]

9

After the End: Adorno

The Art of Reading

A SCENE from *Repetition*, a passage that Adorno considered to be among the most important Kierkegaard ever wrote, can suggest a framework within which to approach Adorno's own work today. To call it a "passage" is misleading, however, since in a certain sense it leads nowhere, neither from nor to any clearly defined place. And yet it doesn't simply stand still, either.

> So I arrived in Berlin. I hurried at once to my old lodgings . . . one of the most pleasant apartments in Berlin. . . . Gensd'arme Square is certainly the most beautiful in Berlin; *das Schauspielhaus* and the two churches are superb, especially when viewed from a window by moonlight. The recollection of these things was an important factor in my taking the journey. One climbs the stairs to the first floor in a gas-illuminated building, opens a little door, and stands in the entry. To the left is a glass door leading to a room. Straight ahead is an anteroom. Beyond are two entirely identical rooms, identically furnished, so that one sees the room double in the mirror. The inner room is tastefully illuminated. A candelabra stands on a writing table; a gracefully designed armchair upholstered in red velvet stands before the desk. The first room is not illuminated. Here the pale light of the moon blends with the strong light from the inner room. Sitting in a chair by the window, one looks out on the great square, sees the shadows of passersby hurrying along the walls; everything is transformed into a stage setting. A dream world glimmers in the background of the soul. One feels a desire to toss on a cape, steal softly along the wall with a searching gaze, aware of every

sound. One does not do this but merely sees a rejuvenated self doing it. Having smoked a cigar, one goes back to the inner room and begins to work. It is past midnight. One extinguishes the candles and lights a little night candle. Unmingled, the light of the moon is victorious. A single shadow appears even blacker; a single footstep takes a long time to disappear. The cloudless vault of heaven looks so melancholy, so dreamlike and so thoughtful, as though the end of the world had come and gone, had already passed, and heaven, undisturbed, was occupied with itself. Once again, one goes out into the hallway, into the entry, into that little room, and—if one is among the fortunate who are able to sleep—goes to sleep.[1]

This passage—which Adorno cites as evidence of the retreat into the inner sanctum of private space, the "interior" that, he asserts, forms the nucleus of Kierkegaard's work—is situated at the problematic but decisive moment when Constantin Constantius returns to Berlin because, as he announces at the very outset of the work, at home he has found himself totally blocked by the question of *repetition*: Is there such a thing, he asks, and if there is, what does it mean? The simplest way to find out, he decides, is for him to go back to Berlin, where he once studied, to see if repetition exists or not.

All of this sounds absurd when retold in this manner, out of all context. And at least part of that absurdity plays an important role in the text as a self-ironizing moment. We will return later to certain aspects of this context. Despite the many important differences in the various positions that Constantin, fictional author and narrator of this text, asserts and assumes, one at least anticipates that which Adorno himself will adopt, and suggests, perhaps, why he was drawn to write on Kierkegaard in the first place. This is Kierkegaard's critique of the subsumptive tendencies of the Hegelian system and, through it, of a certain philosophical rationalism. To be sure, Adorno will sharply criticize what he takes to be the fundamental subjectivism of this critique, which in this respect ultimately falls short of the Hegelian philosophy it is criticizing. For Constantin Constantius, no less than for Theodor W. Adorno, however, the Hegelian notion of universal "mediation" calls for critical scrutiny. Constantin even goes so far to suggest replacing the German term *Vermittlung* by "the good Danish word" that is translated as "repetition," but that actually is far closer to the *literal* meaning of the German *wiederholen*. As discussed in the preceding chapter, the Danish word *Gjentagelse* literally means to *take again*. And indeed, much of Kierkegaard's text remains incomprehensible if one does not refer to this literal meaning. Despite his insistence that one pay close attention to the *Wörtlichkeit* of the text, Adorno himself shows no interest in this "good Danish word," one that points in quite a different direction from the meaning he attaches to "repetition," namely, as that which is eternally the same: *das Immergleiche*. Rather than reflecting upon possible differences in the interpretation of repetition, confronted with what he takes to be Kierkegaard's subjectivist move away from the Hegelian dialectic, Adorno defends the trajectory that leads "from Kant to Hegel," as the following passage demonstrates:

> If, however, the Kantian conception of philosophy as science was first comprehensively formulated by Hegel in the following proposition, "that the time has come for philosophy to be raised to the level of science," his demand for scientific conceptualization does not coincide with the unambiguous givenness of concepts [construed] as bundles of traits [*Merkmaleinheiten*]. The dialectical method, to which, all opposition to Hegel notwithstanding, Kierkegaard's work entirely belongs [*gänzlich zugehört*], has its essence rather in the fact that the elucidation of individual concepts, in the sense of their complete definition, can only be accomplished through the totality of the elaborated system and not in the analysis of the isolated individual concept.[2]

The dialectic thus not only involves an appeal to the whole, to "the totality of the elaborated system," but presupposes its virtual presence, its constant and ubiquitous accessibility. As Hegel puts it, in a celebrated passage from the Introduction to the *Phenomenology of Spirit*:

> If the Absolute could be brought closer to us simply by means of a device [*Werkzeug*], without anything in it being altered, the way a bird is attracted by a decoy, it would—were it not in and of itself with us and did it not wish to be—scorn this trick. . . . Or if the examining of knowledge, which we imagine to be a [kind of] *medium*, teaches us the law of its refraction [*Strahlenbrechung*], it serves no purpose to [try to] subtract it from the

result; for it is not the *breaking* of the ray, refraction, but the ray itself [*der Strahl selbst*] that constitutes knowledge, and to subtract it would leave us nothing but the designation of a mere direction or of an empty place.[3]

"Mere direction . . . empty place": the epitome of abstraction, at least from a Hegelian point of view. Conversely, *concreteness*—a key word in the writings of Adorno—consists essentially in the *growing together* of thought through which knowledge is constituted. Such concretion involves a move beyond the conception of knowledge as a passive *medium* to a conception of knowledge as an active *process of self-constituting*. That the medium itself—for instance, language—could be that active process is a position that the Hegelian tradition tends to reject and to supplant with the notion of mediation. We will return later to this critique of the "medium," which contrasts radically with Benjamin's concern, from his earliest texts on language, with questions involving the medium and mediality. From a Hegelian point of view, however, this supplanting of the medium by the notion of mediation is perhaps the most decisive gain in the move from static Kantian epistemology to the speculative dialectic. And this perspective is still dominant in Adorno's study of Kierkegaard.

Yet if "concreteness" is the result of *mediation*, it is no longer a property of simple sense perception, is never *immediately* given or present *as such*, but must be constructed, configured, construed—through a process that necessarily involves *reading* as much as it involves *interpretation*. Although Adorno tended to keep his distance from the venerable German tradition of "hermeneutics," he nevertheless often found himself obliged to address hermeneutical issues, such as the relation between reading and interpretation. For instance—and it is not just any instance—in the third of his *Studies on Hegel*, entitled, significantly, "Skoteinos or How to Read" ("Skoteinos oder Wie zu lesen sei"),[4] he attempts to outline a strategy for reading Hegel and in the process arrives at a series of familiar problems—or are they paradoxes?

In the realm of great philosophy, Hegel is surely the only instance where upon occasion one literally does not know and cannot decide what is being discussed [*wovon überhaupt geredet wird*] and where the very possibility of such a decision is not guaranteed. . . .[5] [Individual passages] are interpretable through knowledge of the overall Hegelian thrust [*des Hegelschen Gesamt-zuges*] . . . not, however, from the words of the paragraphs themselves. . . . . Nothing can be understood in isolation, everything only with respect to the whole, with the embarrassing difficulty [*mit dem Peinlichen*] that the whole, in its turn, lives only from and in the singular moments [that compose it]. . . . One must, however provisionally, have present to mind in each case what Hegel is after [*worauf Hegel jeweils hinaus will*], elucidating him, as it were, retrospectively [*von rückwärts aufhellen*]. (5:326–27)

The necessary supposition of a pregiven whole in order for individual words, sentences, propositions, and passages to be comprehensible is embarrassing, *peinlich*. And yet the embarrassment cuts both ways, for the whole "is" nothing if separated from the movement of the individual "moments." The whole, or totality, is thus called upon to direct and orient the movement of that which constitutes it. If, as Adorno repeatedly insists, in a quote that he ascribes to Aby Warburg—"God is to be found in details [*Der liebe Gott steckt im Detail*]"—then the problem is to demonstrate, "concretely," just how God can be both "in the detail" and at the same time identical to the whole, to the absolute, which by definition cannot be reduced to any single "detail" but which is everywhere and at all times, *an und für sich schon bei uns.* Or, as Hegel does not say but Adorno writes, in a very different context, to be sure: *allemal.*

It is here that the problem of *reading* rears its ugly head: ugly because, in the eyes of Adorno at least, it cannot solve the problem but at best act it out. Reading, at least reading Hegel, acts out the problem by trying to get at the quintessence of the proper name: One has to know, however provisionally, just what Hegel is *after, worauf er hinaus will,* what Hegel *wants* and *wills,* in order to be able to read his individual words, sentences, and paragraphs. But such knowledge of the whole, of the governing intention or design, depends in turn upon the way one reads those individual words and sentences. There is no simple answer to this hermeneutic dilemma. On the one hand, Hegel "requires repeated reading [*mehrfache Lektüre*]" objectively, and not just in order to habituate the reader. On the other hand, "if one relies entirely on this procedure, one can easily falsify him. One can easily produce that which up to now has been most harmful to interpretation: an empty consciousness of the system, incompatible with the fact that the latter is not supposed to form an abstract and superior concept [*abstrakten Oberbegriff*] but rather to acquire its truth through its concrete moments" (5:328). Hegel's text itself, Adorno makes clear, cannot be taken as a model for resolving this problem because its "concreteness" is often achieved by sleight of hand: "The isolated moments go beyond themselves only by virtue of the fact that the identity of subject and object has already been preconceived [*vorgedacht*]. The relevance of individual analyses is again and again broken by the abstract primacy of the Whole" (5:330).

Such primacy of a whole, which as such remains abstract, should not, Adorno insists, serve as a pretext for simply dismissing Hegel, as has been done in contemporary Anglo-American philosophy. Rather, the problematic relation of whole and part must provoke a new and different kind of reading: one that does not invoke the inevitability of a general understanding in order either to confirm or to disqualify the dialectical movement. This other kind of reading Adorno calls—with a word he surely does not invoke lightly—an *art*: "The art of reading Hegel would have to discern where something new, where content sets in [*wo Neues, Inhaltliches einsetzt*] as distinct from those places where the machine keeps on running, even though it should not be able to continue" (5:330).

The fact that Adorno construes the "new" here in terms of "content," as *Inhaltliches*, a term that is rarely discussed, is, however, the sign of a further problem. How will the borders, without which nothing can be "held-in," be determined? To discriminate between "content" and noncontent requires the same sort of "knowledge" that is in question here. And is the "new" necessarily to be determined as "content"? Does the onset of the new exclude repetition, for instance? Or can repetition be a mode through which the new manifests and articulates itself? I will return to these questions shortly.

For now, let us simply note that Adorno describes two conditions that are necessary, although in tension with one another, for a reading to discern the "new" in Hegel. The first is a certain "immersion [*Versenkung*]" in the text's most minute details; the second is the ability to retain one's freedom and "distance" from them, despite such "immersion." But how does one get absorbed into such "minute" details while at the same time keeping a safe and "free" distance from them? How is such reading possible—if indeed it is possible at all?

Streamers and Rebuses

In order to gather elements in the work of Adorno that might help respond to this question, let us make a detour via another, earlier text, which constitutes a significant "moment" in Adorno's reflections on the question of reading. This text, although published only posthumously, was completed in 1942 as a projected continuation of the chapter in *Dialectic of Enlightenment* entitled "The Culture Industry." In certain respects, the analyses of the "culture industry" can be seen as a sociological anticipation of the later critique of the Hegelian dialectic. In both instances, a general "system" or "scheme" subjugates and subordinates its individual components. To be sure, this analogy, like all analogies, has its limits. Adorno insists that the culture industry can never operate dialectically. Nevertheless, his critique of the culture industry reposes on its *systematic* and *totalizing* character. A question that has since arisen, as a critique of Critical Theory, concerns the extent to which Critical Theory itself, as a systematization of the system of the culture industry, necessarily falls prey to the very tendencies it claims to criticize: the subsumptive tendency of the system. The same question could also be raised with regard to the critique of the Hegelian dialectic, and perhaps even with respect to criticism as such. To the extent that critique is always critique of a system, it always runs the risk of becoming systematic in turn and, hence, of being "overtaken"—in German, Adorno would have written *ereilt*, a favorite expression of his—or contaminated by what it is criticizing. Perhaps this is why the fascination with being *overtaken, ereilt,* is so pervasive in his writings. No simple appeal to the dialectic can serve to "ban"—another favorite word and concept of Critical Theory—this danger if it turns out to be coextensive with the very notion of critique itself.

Be that as it may, from its opening words the analysis of the "culture industry" is concerned with revealing the system dissimulated behind what appears as the anarchy of liberal social relations, including cultural activities. The first sentence of the chapter announces that, contrary to received sociological opinion, the development of modern capitalism does not bring with it "cultural chaos" but rather a highly coordinated and unified system: "Culture today stamps everything with the seal of similitude. Film, radio, magazines all constitute one system. Each segment coheres within itself and with all others."[6] Of course, to be critical, the theoretical analysis of such a system must demonstrate how its unity is anything but simply natural, given, self-identical: how it is a product of historical, conflictual forces and how its operation dissimulates the alternatives upon whose suppression its survival depends. In the posthumously published appendix to "The Culture Industry," entitled "The Scheme of Mass Culture," the word that sums up these suppressed alternatives is *subjectivity*: "It is only insofar as they are subjects that people themselves constitute the limit of reification; hence mass culture must reestablish its hold over them ever anew [*immer aufs Neue wieder sie erfassen*]: the hopeless effort of this repetition is the only trace of hope, that this repetition is in vain, that in spite of everything, people are not controllable."[7] Precisely this motif of repetition, in all of its ambivalence, its despair and its hope, forms the negative backbone of the critique of the culture industry. Let us take a closer look at one such instance.

The contribution of mass culture to the Sisyphean task of monopoly capitalism consists above all in "the fabrication of archetypes," of "archaic symbols [*urzeitliche Symbole*]." Immediately following the text just quoted, we come upon a rather remarkable passage, remarkable not least in appearing to blend the very different scenarios of monopoly capitalism, Nazism, and fascism into a single ritual of reading and writing:

> The dream factory does not so much fabricate the dreams of its customers as disseminate those of its suppliers. . . . In the dream of those who steer the mummification of the world, mass culture is the priestly hieroglyphics [*Hieroglyphenschrift*] that provides the subjugated with images not to enjoy but to read. The authentic [images] of film, but also the inauthentic[8] ones of hit songs and texts, appear so rigid that they are often not even perceived as such, but only as repetitions whose perennial self-sameness [*Immergleichheit*] expresses an identical meaning. The looser the connections between plot and progression [*Handlung und Verlauf*], the more the isolated image [*das abgesprengte Bild*] becomes an allegorical seal [*allegorisches Sigel*]. Optically the flashing, passing images in the movie theater become increasingly like writing. They are grasped, not observed. . . . Thus, the transition from image to writing brought about by the technique of mass artworks consummates the absorption of art through monopolistic practice. (3:332)

Writing absorbs "authentic" imagery, Adorno argues, in the same way "monopolistic practice" absorbs authentic art, in a triumph of self-identical repetition, in *Wiederholungen* as *Immergleichheit*. Despite the terminological borrowings from Benjamin, nothing could be further from the analyses of the *Trauerspiel* book than this equation of "archetype," "archaic symbol," and "allegorical seal [*allegorisches Sigel*]."[9]

Whereas Benjamin presents his elaboration of allegory as an *alternative* to the predominant theory of the symbol as unity of image and meaning, Adorno here collapses the difference into a unity that consummates his critique of the culture industry. The dissolution of narrative-historical continuities is marked by a scripturalization of imagery, which Adorno interprets strictly in terms of reification and ritualization. Reading, in this context, is presented as "deciphering" a fixed code of isolated, abstract "graphic signs [*Schriftzeichen*]," as a more or less mechanical effort to reduce the strange and alien to the known and familiar.

It is undeniable that all reading must include an element of decoding: all reading presupposes reference to a known code, to a relatively closed system; if one doesn't have some knowledge of the system before encountering a text, one cannot read, not, at least, as reading is commonly understood. However—and this is the point of Benjamin's discussion of allegory—the German baroque allegory involves, not a "conventional expression," but an "expression of convention,"[10] which is to say, an expression of the *problematic* status of all such coming together, of all *convenus*, however indispensable such convergence is to all language and culture. As a result, allegory in the German baroque, and perhaps in general, is fundamentally *theatrical*: it involves representations whose referent is necessarily problematic, open, heterogeneous. And theatricality entails first and foremost representation for the other. We will return to this later.

In Adorno's analysis of mass culture, by contrast, the transformation of imagery into allegorical inscription and the ensuing replacement of observation by reading is portrayed as the sign and symptom of the concealed, traumatic core of the culture industry and of the society it helps to reproduce. The breaking of narrative continuity does not merely "isolate . . . individual allegorical gestures," as in film, Adorno argues: it transforms human faces into "culture masks," whose rigid, deathlike traits mark the limits of the unified individual and, perhaps, the limits of subjectivity itself. Such graphic inscriptions encourage both flight into Dionysian self-abandonment (Adorno's example is "dancing to jazz") and its ostensible (but dialectical) opposite, the no less exuberant effort to conform to established social norms.

Adorno concludes his description of the death of imagery at the hands of reading and writing with the following image:

> The streamers that cross high above the cities, whose light obscures the natural night light, announce, like comets, the natural catastrophe of society, its death by freezing [*Kältetod*]. But they do not come from heaven. They are guided from the earth. It's up to human beings to decide if they want to put them out [*sie auslöschen wollen*] and awake from the nightmare, which only threatens to become reality so long as people believe in it. (3:335)

To be sure, this passage—whose voluntaristic tone (It's up to you!) creates as Hollywood an ending as could be imagined—occurs in a text that Adorno himself did not publish and perhaps would never have published in such a form. However, these words were obviously not written casually: they were written to conclude. And the critical perspective they announce seems to consist in the slim hope that "people"—*die Menschen*—may one day finally decide to put an end to the nightmare of reading and writing in order finally to awaken, to open their eyes and see. America, awake out of your bad dream . . . See, and live!

If this passage concludes the supplementary text on the culture industry, other passages in the same text are less "conclusive" and suggest that the nightmare of reading is more complex than appears here at the end. Take the following observation:

> The more the viewer of a film, the listener to a pop song, the reader of detective or magazine stories anticipates the conclusion, the result, the more his attention shifts to the how, from the worthless result to the rebuslike detail, and in the process of this shifting search, the hieroglyphic meaning appears to him in a flash. It articulates all phenomena down to their most subtle nuances according to the simple binary logic of do and don't, and through its consequent reduction of the foreign and the incomprehensible, it catches up with the consumers. (3:333)

What Adorno is describing here is both impressive and puzzling. Impressive, inasmuch as it highlights a tendency that has, if anything, increased in the half century since he wrote: the way interest in the making of films—including their cost, their techniques, and so on—accompanies interest in "content" of the finished product. What is curious, however, is the tendency to condemn critically the shift of interest from theme and content to "rebuslike detail," for attention to detail is what Adorno, as we have seen, would later defend against the Hegelian—and not just Hegelian—tendency to subsume the singular under the general, the nonidentical under the identical. To be sure, not all details are equal, and the "rebuslike detail" referred to here leads to the baleful flash of "hieroglyphic meaning." But why such flashes of hieroglyphic meaning should be so rapidly identified with a "binary logic of do and don't," especially when the hieroglyph involves an enigma, is a question hardly discussed in this text. No room is left for the allegorical resources of writing and inscription, which would question the priestly authority ascribed to "hieroglyphics." Hence, it is only consistent that the dream, which, as Adorno well knew, is a writing system, is also assimilated to the sacerdotal tendencies of the system. In his essay he therefore proposes to resolve the problem by resorting to what only can be described as a surprisingly conventional alternative: either continuing to dream the nightmare of reading or finally deciding to *awake*.[11] It is as though the critical theory of the culture industry were here *ereilt*—overtaken—by the reductive binarism of the system it seeks to criticize.

Allemal Is Not *Immergleich*

To find an alternative, not just to this nightmare, but to the alternative between dream and awakening in which it is inscribed, let us return to Adorno's earlier study of Kierkegaard. There he already finds himself obliged to address the question of reading, albeit in a somewhat different "light." In the process he demonstrates that, whatever his ambivalence toward reading may be, he is far more attentive to its complexities and resources than one might expect, especially in view of passages like the one we have just discussed. Indeed, his book on Kierkegaard begins with a determination of how this author is to be read: not as poetry, Adorno insists, but as philosophy. Why is this distinction necessary? Among other reasons, because of the peculiar and highly distinctive style of writing that characterizes Kierkegaard's texts: "With regard to the claim of being poetry, Kierkegaard's work assumes an ambiguous stance. It is cunningly laid out to anticipate every misunderstanding that inaugurates in the reader the process of appropriating its substance [*Gehalte*]. The dialectic of issues [*Sachen*] is for it at the same time a dialectic of communication" (2:11).

The encounter with the writings of Kierkegaard raises two problems that will turn out to be decisive for all of Adorno's work. The first involves the question of *Gehalt* or, less emphatically, *Inhalt*: the question of *content*. The German word should not be forgotten, however, for it recalls connotations all too easily effaced in English. The root of the words *Inhalt* and *Gehalt* is, of course, the verb *halten*, "to hold," but also "to stop, to halt, to arrest." The action that constitutes "contents" is a *holding action*, an act of *containment*.[12] Given Adorno's constant insistence on the importance of *Inhalt* and *Gehalt* as opposed to mere *form*—and the notion of *Gehalt* emerges in his work to designate the dialectical synthesis of form and content—the following question must be addressed: What are the conditions under which the holding action required to constitute a *Ge-halt* can be effective? For something to be held, the passage of time must be interrupted and suspended. Only by arresting the passage of time can a *Gehalt* be constituted. Since we have seen that the Hegelian notion of determinate negation is not sufficient to legitimate the stoppages that give rise to *Gehalte*, another category must be found to account for what Adorno, in "How to Read Hegel," describes as "the principle of fixation, without which nothing linguistic can be at all [*ohne die kein Sprachliches überhaupt ist*]."[13] Although Adorno sees Hegel's writing as deliberately offering a "provocative challenge" to this "principle of fixation" and hence to language itself, he does not, as we have seen, consider the Hegelian dialectic to be a satisfactory resolution of the problem, perhaps because a holding action is not the same as seizing or grasping; *Halten* is not *Greifen*, *Gehalt* not merely a synonym for *Begriff*. Against the tendency toward dialectical *Aufhebung*, Adorno insists on the necessity of immersing oneself "in details" that precisely are not "resolved" or transcended through "universal mediation" but rather resist, persist, and insist as *das Moment des Nichtaufgehenden*, the moment of that which resists absorption by the mediating movement of conceptualization. To be sure, this does not justify the pure and simple dismissal of conceptual content: rather, it calls for its reconfiguration.

That reconfiguration can take place only in and through a reading process that orients itself, not simply on the concept, however dialectical, but on what Adorno, once again undoubtedly indebted to Benjamin, calls the *name*: "The better procedure would be one that, carefully avoiding verbal definitions as mere constative determinations [*Feststellungen*], shapes [*anbildet*] its concepts to conform as faithfully as possible to what they say in language: virtually as *names*" (5:340).

The problem, Benjamin's argues in his 1916 text "On Language in General and the Language of Man," is that the "pure language" of authentic names, in which language does not merely designate general meanings but creates or recreates that which it singularly distinguishes, disappeared at the very latest with the desire of man to use language as a means, as an instrument of knowledge and, above all, of critical judgment. To *know the difference* between good and evil, even more simply, to *know* the *difference* is to construe it as an object of knowledge. To know the difference, even in order to criticize it, can mean to subordinate its alterity, its nonidentity, to the assimilative acid bath of the familiar, even if the latter is elaborated with the dialectical rigor of fully determined conceptuality. Characteristically, for Adorno this danger appears above all as that of being trapped in language, as a kind of terminological rigor mortis: "Whoever makes himself the slave of his own words, takes the easy way out by shoving them in front of the issues [*vor die Sachen*]. . . . Nevertheless, such a procedure is insufficient, for in empirical languages words are not pure names but always also *thesei*, products of subjective consciousness, and insofar themselves also similar to definitions" (5:340–41).

How, then, can one hope to arrive at a configuration of concepts oriented on the basis of a purity of proper names that is irrevocably gone? The answer is a practice that, it turns out, is not foreign to reading, albeit of the right kind:

A proper linguistic procedure could be compared to the way an emigrant learns a foreign language. [It should be noted that Adorno writes of an *emigrant*, and not an *immigrant*.] He may, impatient and under pressure, operate less with the dictionary than by reading as much as he possibly can. Numerous words will, of course, open up through their context, but remain for a long time surrounded by a halo of indeterminacy, and even subject to ridiculous confusions, until finally, through the plenitude of combinations in which they appear, they unravel entirely [*sich ganz enträtseln*] and better than the dictionary would have permitted. (3:341)

A difficulty in translating the above passage points directly to the key problem: Adorno's appeal to the practical linguistic experience of the *émigré*, rather than of the *immigrant*, an experience involving above all *reading*, culminates in what appears to be the full resolution of the enigma, the puzzle, the *Rätsel* of the foreign word, disclosed through the plenitude, *die Fülle*, of its uses. This pragmatic optimism, however, is called into question by the pragmatic difficulty of idiomatically translating into English the German word used by Adorno to designate this happy end, the word *enträtseln*, literally, "un-riddle, or un-puzzle." I prefer to render it as *unravel*, however, in order to emphasize the paradox that this pragmatist happy ending does its best to conceal. For the "plenitude of combinations" in which a word is used does not merely fix the meaning of a word, it also opens it to constant transformation. Usage may well provide a more reliable way to arrive at the prevailing meaning of words than the dictionary; but it does not resolve the question of reading and interpretation—except insofar as one's object is primarily to avoid being the object of "ridicule." What the appeal to linguistic usage underscores is that the experience of language cannot be confined to grammatical and lexical categories, to definitions, because such experience is intrinsically open. But such openness is not without consequences for the name itself: how "proper" or transparent can a name be that is subject to the unlimitable combinatorics that constitute the experience of language? Is there such a thing as a proper name? This question permits us to return, finally, to Adorno's study of that other *émigré*, Søren Kierkegaard.

Adorno begins his study of Kierkegaard—his second and decisive attempt to acquire the *Habilitation*, without which no academic career would have been possible—by seeking to establish, beyond the shadow of a doubt, that Kierkegaard's text is not *poetical* but *philosophical*, and as such amenable to a philosophical critique. To establish the philosophical nature of the text, however, Adorno has first to deal with the ostensibly literary device of the pseudonyms, which, qua *pseudo*, tend to undercut the power of the proper name to put a definitive and authoritative halt to the dynamics of language, of reading and of writing. Adorno describes the task and its resolution as follows:

Every observation that unqualifiedly accepts the claims of the pseudonyms and takes them as the decisive measure goes astray. They are not figures [*Gestalten*], in whose incomparable being [*Dasein*] intention is densely enclosed. They are entirely abstract-representative figures. This does not mean that criticism could ever neglect their function, taking their opinions to be those of Kierkegaard. Rather, criticism must confront the abstract unities of the pseudonyms with the concrete motifs that are embedded [*eingefaßt*] in the framework of pseudonymity, and then measure the cogency [*Stimmigkeit*] of the context. . . . Critique must first understand the assertions of the pseudonyms in accordance with their philosophical construction, which can be shown at every moment to function as a dominant scheme. What the pseudonyms then say that exceeds the philosophical scheme: their secret and concrete core, falls to interpretation in the literalness [*Wörtlichkeit*] of the communication. No writer uses words more cunningly than Kierkegaard. (2:23–24)

The pseudonyms are, on the one hand, governed by schematic philosophical categories of which, Adorno writes elsewhere, they are the "illustration" (2:14). On the other hand, however, what they say and do is both more and other than what the philosophical scheme prescribes or comprehends. It is here, in this divergence, that "critique" finds its Archimedean point: the point where conceptual-thematic content overflows in and into literal language itself. But if this is the general scheme of how the schematism of the text is to be outwitted, the text itself has, as Adorno knows all too well, already prepared a response: "No writer uses words more cunningly than Kierkegaard." Thus, to trust or take those words at face value, or at any value, is still to run the risk of falling prey to the cunning strategem of the text:

In the labyrinthine lair [*Fuchsbau*] of infinitely reflected inwardness, there is no means of cornering [Kierkegaard; *ihn zu stellen*]—other than taking him at his words, which, planned as traps, ultimately snare the one who sets them. The choice of words, their stereotypical, not always planned recurrence, points toward a tenor [*Gehalte*] that even the most profound of dialectical procedures would rather conceal than reveal. (2:21)

Taking Adorno at his words, here, one would have to wonder about a fox, clever and hunted, laying traps for the hunter and then being caught in them himself. A consoling scenario—for the hunter, at least. But what does it mean to take a text at its word or, rather, at its words? If those words, as the emigrant was to discover, are accessible only through the configurations in which they are used, and if those configurations are *in principle infinite*—each new combination opening possibilities for further use and recombination—then where is the position from which one might *take* the text at its word and thereby *wrest* it away from the "pseudonyms" to whom those words are ascribed? The question grows even more complicated when, as Adorno insists, the very name of the author himself, *Kierkegaard*, must also be read as a "pseudonym": "The interpretation of the pseudonym *Kierkegaard* has to dissect the simulated poetic unity into the polarity of its own speculative intention and that of the literalness that betrays it" (2:21). But how is the literalness, the *Wörtlichkeit*, of the words to be determined, to be read, if those words are all spoken or written by fictional characters, by persona, by pseudonyms whose authority is always relative to their position with respect to other textual elements?

In a short text discussed by Adorno, "A First and Last Explication," "Kierkegaard," apparently finally speaking in his own name, defines his own authorial position in relation to those of his fictional pseudonyms (polyphonic long before Bakhtin introduced the term). Adorno quotes two statements relevant to the problem of authorial voice:

> As a result, I express the desire and the prayer that, should anyone have the idea of citing one of the pseudonymic books, that he should be so kind and do me the favor of citing the name of the pseudonymic author in question and not mine, which is to say, to distribute things among us so that the statements belong in feminine fashion to the pseudonym and the responsibility, civilly, to me.

> What I know about the pseudonyms naturally does not give me the right to affirm or to doubt their reaction, since their significance (whatever it might be in *reality*) absolutely does not consist in making any new propositions, any unheard-of discoveries, or in founding a new party and wishing to "go further," but precisely, on the contrary, in not wanting to have any sig-

nificance, in wanting only to read, at a distance from the remove of double reflection [i.e., that on the object and on the "author"] that singular, originary, and human writing of existence, the ancient text known and transmitted by our fathers, rereading it one more time, if possible in a more interior manner.[14]

This statement of the "author," "Kierkegaard," can of course claim no greater authority than those of the "pseudonyms." But it nevertheless opens a perspective for further consideration: if the significance of the words spoken and written in a text is not reducible to the intention of the speaker or writer, and if the latter is itself part of a larger signifying process, then the process of reading, writing, and interpreting will never be simply distinguishable from the text the way a "subject" seems to be distinguishable from an "object." And then it will not be enough to speak, as Adorno does, of *Wörtlichkeit*. Rather, the notion will have to be supplemented, as Benjamin does in "The Task of the Translator" when he writes of *Wörtlichkeit der Syntax*: literalness of *syntax* as the principle guiding the task of the translator. Syntax here stands for spatial relations that go beyond the rule-governed system of grammar and semantics.

Such syntactical space will never be reducible to the kind of subjective inwardness in which Adorno seeks to trap his prey, "Kierkegaard." We can demonstrate that briefly by returning to the scene from which we set out, in which Constantin Constantius—not "Kierkegaard"—describes the apartment to which he returns after arriving in Berlin. This is the conclusion of Adorno's rather brief commentary to the long scene he quotes, which he considers to be "the most thought-provoking [*denkwürdigste*] passage that Kierkegaard devoted to the interior":

> Out of the half-light of such melancholy emerge the contours of "domesticity," which for Kierkegaard constitutes the arena of existence. It therefore constitutes the contours of his doctrine of existence itself. . . . In the interior, historical dialectics and the eternal power of nature compose their strangely enigmatic image [*ihr wunderliches Rätselbild*]. It must be dissolved [*aufgelöst*] by philosophical criticism, which seeks to attain the real ground of his idealistic inwardness in the historical as well as in the archaic [*Vorzeitlichen*]. (2:69)

Adorno's claim to take Kierkegaard's text at its word seems here to founder on the *parti pris* of the general interpretive argument. He ignores the *literalness of syntax*, which would require one to take into account the context and relations in which the scene is inscribed. To see it as a direct expression of "Kierkegaard's" "doctrine of existence itself" is not just to ignore the wish or "prayer" of the "First and Last Explication," but, more problematically, to ignore the surface facts of the text: the "fact" that the description is that of a pseudonym, a fictional figure, Constantin Constantius, whose return to Berlin and to these lodgings has a very distinct and precise history. It is to ignore that the "interior" being described is not simply "domestic," as Adorno calls it, but that of a rented apartment in a pension and, no less important, of a place to which Constantin *returns*. Adorno completely ignores the incidence of "repetition" in the description, which structurally doubles and breaks open the closed space of any interior, including this one. To see this room as a site of "historical dialectics and the eternal power of nature" is hardly a response to the text's literalness, and even less to its syntax.

To be sure, there can be no reading that is entirely "literal," or even *wörtlich* in the sense Adorno envisages. Every reading, this one no less than any other, must be selective and hence respond, more or less, to preconceived intentions. But the selections and exclusions that underlie all reading must be justifiable in terms of the relations they thereby disclose. Thus, in this particular passage there is a phrase in which Adorno seems uninterested. It sums up the atmosphere of repetition and doubling, of shadows and echoes, and at the same time designates a very important quality of the "interior" with which Adorno is so concerned. It is the phrase: "Sitting in a chair by the window, one looks out on the great square, sees the shadows of passersby hurrying along the walls: everything is transformed into scenic decor" (2:68).

This gives the "interior" a very different aspect from that which Adorno seeks to assign to it: namely, that of a theological cipher or "allegory." What is truly *denkwürdig* about this scene is that in it the spectator, looking out, is described as situated in a kind of *theater*. And the "interiority" of a theater is very different from that of a private home or a domestic house (a fact that worried Plato no end[15]). In a theater, on a stage, as part of a scene, subjects are no longer authentic, no longer at home, no longer fully in control. Inside and outside are no longer simply binary opposites. The space of the theatrical scene, which is not necessarily that of traditional drama, is no longer simply an interior space, since it is always directed outward, away, toward others. As already mentioned, theatricality can even be defined as *representation for others*. In this case, however, dramatic conflict and plot are not its constitutive ingredients.

But if the "interior" is a theater, this endows the description of the night scene outside with a very different resonance from that which Adorno describes. It is not simply the projection of eternal nature upon transient history. Recall the key phrase: "The cloudless vault of heaven looks so melancholy, so dreamlike and so thoughtful, as though the end of the world had *come and gone*, had already passed, and heaven, undisturbed, was occupied with itself." In the German translation cited by Adorno, this phrase reads: "Als ob der Untergang der Welt vorüber . . . wäre." Note the formulation, which literally renders Kierkegaard's Danish ("som var Verdens Undergang forbi"). If we remember Adorno's concluding image in the appendix on the culture industry, it is as though the streamers had finally passed, taking with them the "world" and leaving in its wake, not the alternative of nightmare, on the one hand, and waking reality, on the other, but something very different: a moonlit stage, a "glimmering dream-world," and at the center of the stage a small, candle-lit table, upon which one can write if one cannot sleep.

Adorno stops his reflection with the spectacle itself, that of a sky which, after the downfall of the world, seems preoccupied only "with itself." But the text of *Repetition* continues, describing not just the untroubled spectacle of the sky outside, but the highly troubled response of the spectator within: "One goes out again into the foyer, into the hall, enter a small office, one sleeps—if one is one of those fortunate enough to be able to sleep.—But alas, no repetition was possible."[16] The search for *repetition* will drive Constantin beyond the limits of the home and of all other interiors into the strange space of the Königstädter Theater, which, like every theater—but unlike Adorno's description of the *interior*—is constituted by the intrusion of a certain exteriority.

In the scene from *Repetition* cited by Adorno, "interiority" is not an "image" but an episode in an ongoing scenario. To be sure, the Kierkegaardian scenario is no more continuous than the *Possentheater* that he revisits, in search of "repetition." Not surprisingly, Adorno does not follow him there. For the *Possentheater* was a nineteenth-century version of the kind of mass entertainment that Adorno would associate with the twentieth-century "culture industry." Indeed, in his appendix on that subject, he analyzes a theatrical form that is a distant cousin of the *Possentheater*: the *variété* or variety show. In this connection, Adorno describes, but also criticizes, certain features of this eminently theatrical phenomenon that seem profoundly related to aspects of the media today: the interruption of narrative structure, the implication of the audience in the spectacle, and, perhaps above all, a certain suspension of the linear-teleological movement that Adorno identifies, however dialectically, with historical progress. Adorno himself considers this suspension to reveal the cardinal sin of the culture industry:

> What constitutes the variety act, what impresses the child at its first visit to such a show, is the fact that at one and the same time, both something and nothing happens [*daß allemal zugleich etwas und nichts geschieht*]. Every variety act is actually a waiting. Subsequently it turns out that the waiting for something . . . was actually the thing itself. Applause always [*allemal*] comes a split second too late, when the spectator notices that what he first took to be preparation was already the event [*das Ereignis*], of which he has been, as it were, deprived. In this temporal swindle [*In diesem Betrug um die Zeitordnung*], the trick of the variety show consists in bringing the instant to a halt . . . the symbolic suspension of the process [*des Verlaufs*]. This is why the spectator who always comes late can never be too late: he jumps on as though it were a carousel. . . . The joke is not on the spectator, but on time itself. (3:308)

No matter that Adorno himself concludes this account by assimilating it to a certain domination of nature, which functions through a "technical disposition over time." The "event" of an in-stant that suddenly breaks the continuum of progress and of the kind of history that depends upon such continuity—the event, in which something *happens* without anything *taking place*—stops short and opens out onto a very different dynamic of space and place, time and instant, concretion and abstraction, from that in which critical theory is at home. It is the *uncanny, iterative* space-time of an irreducible theatricality, which is elusive but which, *nevertheless and at the same time—allemal*—must be not just seen but also *read*. In this *allemal* is congealed, not merely the reification, hypostasis, and leveling that Adorno saw as the essence of the culture industry—time as a carousel that returns always the same, *immergleich*—but at the same time, *allemal*, a movement of repetition as alteration and transformation that cannot be reduced to the *Immergleichen. Allemal* is not *immergleich.* But it also leaves no room for the past or future perfect of a dialectic that will always have been the other of what it was.

What Adorno construed univocally as an object of critique, the "ghostly [*gespenstisch*]" spectacle of "the unremitting repetition of the unrepeatable" (3:317), can also operate as the mode in which singularity is articulated. This possibility must be kept open, even if in reality repetition is most often far closer to the self-sameness with which Adorno was obsessed. What Adorno refused to grant to the variety show, although he nevertheless described it, he did accord to the *Posse* in *Repetition.* One of the first readers of Kierkegaard to remark the importance of the *Posse*, Adorno notes:

> The spontaneous intervention of the spectator in the work, which accordingly defines the form of the *Posse*, only apparently derives from the principle of self-centered subjectivism. It turns against the unity of the work [*des Gebildes*], which bears witness to the unity of the subjective synthesis and plays itself out in momentary impulses, which remain as incommensurable with respect to each other as do laughing and melancholy confronted with the *Posse*: responses to the change of images— "situations"—in which "in general" the existence of the *dramatis personae*, like that of the existing person, disappears. What Kierkegaard took license to say about the anarchy of the *Posse* could come to endanger the "hierarchy of the spheres." (2:232)

The inscription of theater as *Posse*, in *Repetition*, undermines any positive "theory," "philosophy," or even religious "dogma" that might otherwise be ascribed to Kierkegaard's texts. But these texts, in their pseudonymic character at least, were designed to comprise, not a "critical theory," but at most, a critical *theater*: one that could not be separated from an experience of reading and repeating.

The notion of the *Immergleich* has served to block the opening to this experience. This cursory attempt to reread Adorno on Kierkegaard, but also Adorno *through* Kierkegaard, suggests that it may be high time to distinguish the pseudo-simultaneity of repetition, as reading, theater, and staging, from the monolithic quality of the *Immergleichen* as the return of the same. What Adorno saw as the ghostly spectacle in which the unrepeatable is incessantly repeated might then turn out to have been nothing more or less than a particularly powerful *pseudonym* for the "nonidentical." Or vice-versa.

10

Psychoanalysis and Theatricality

TO DISCUSS the significance of theatricality for psychoanalysis, and in particular for the thought of Freud, it is first necessary to distinguish what is commonly understood by theatricality from the quite different conception to which Freud appeals. If a certain notion of theater is crucial to Freud in articulating what distinguishes psychoanalysis from previous modes of thought, then this notion itself will have to be understood in a way that diverges from the familiar and still dominant use to which it is generally put.

Two citations can illustrate this use. The first is from the introduction to a book by Joyce McDougall, one of the relatively few analysts to have placed questions of theatricality at the center of her thinking. The passage I want to discuss glosses the title of the book that it introduces, namely, *Theaters of the Ego* (*Théâtres du Je*). McDougall explains the project of this book in the following terms:

> The tragedies of Hamlet, Lear, Richard III . . . entail the history of men confronted by violent forces of their instinctual nature. . . . Traversed by storms of love and of hate, seeking now to seduce and cherish, now to punish and destroy, each man was obliged, from infancy on, to learn how to navigate between the prohibitions and impossibilities of his life. Obliged to invent a solution for each of the inevitable conflicts provoked by his primitive desires, he had to find compromises that satisfied himself as much as others. With all these struggles, and as though with an artistic palette, he sketched the portrait of that person he believed himself to be when he says "I." In fact, this I is a character, an "actor" on the world scene who, in private, in his internal reality, attends a more intimate theater whose repertory is secret. Unknown to him, scenarios are organized, farcical

251

scenes and tragic scenes in search of a place of representation and of action. The director, of course, is the I itself, but the face of the characters, the plot as well as its dénouement, are veiled to him; he does not even know those who are pushing him toward the drama. No warning is given to him that the action is going to begin and that somewhere, in a place of his psyche, a character is moving about—*Seagate*—and wants to enter the stage. . . . And yet it is there, in this interior universe, that the greater part of what is to become his life will be decided.[1]

The second passage is from Freud's "On the History of the Psychoanalytic Movement," and is directed against the conception of the ego he associates with the theories of Alfred Adler. At the center of their divergence stands the interpretation of the ego and its relation to symptom formation. Adlerian theory, Freud argues, overestimates the importance of the ego in this process:

Whereby it entirely overlooks the fact that upon countless occasions the ego merely makes a virtue out of necessity by accepting the most undesirable symptom imposed upon it simply by virtue of the utility attached to it, e.g., when it accepts anxiety as a means of securing something. The ego here plays the ludicrous role of the clown [*des dummen August*] in the circus, who, by his gestures, tries to convince the audience that every change in the circus ring happens as a result of his orders. But only the youngest in the audience are taken in.[2]

Both authors turn to theatrical figures to articulate a situation of conflict, and both focus upon the effects of this situation on a certain "character." However, the way in which this character then is determined is significantly different in each. Although Joyce McDougall also mentions farce, the model of theater for her remains tragedy, and the essence of tragedy is linked to a certain notion of the (Shakespearean) tragic hero: Hamlet, Lear, Richard III. The dramatic conflict is couched in terms that make it an attribute of the conflicted subject itself or, rather, *himself.* The tragic hero is described as a "man confronted by the violent forces of *his* instinctual nature," who "invent[s] solutions to the inevitable conflicts provoked by *his* primitive desires" (my italics), and who has to "find compromises" that will satisfy himself as well as others. It should be noted that, although this account of the tragic hero does not seem to conform very well to the Shakespearean figures named by McDougall, it coincides all the more with a certain modern notion of the autonomous, active subject, struggling to establish control over his destiny.

Freud's account of the Ego is strikingly different. The conflict situation in which it is situated is above all neither of its own making nor even attributable to it. In Freud's description there is no question of ascribing the forces of conflict to the ego as "his instinctual nature" or "his primitive desires"—that is precisely the point, and the joke, if you will: the clown, "stupid August," is stupid precisely insofar as he acts as though he were in control of what is going on. This also determines the kind of theatrical reference that Freud invokes, which is very different from McDougall's, as different as a circus farce is from a Shakespearean tragedy. For McDougall, "conflict" and "struggle" constitute the "dramatic" and hence "theatrical" dimension of psychic activity, centered on the Ego. For Freud, in this context at least, such tragic pretensions are only part of a more general burlesque role that the Ego plays, one that is only indirectly related to its manifest situation. Freud's theatrical references, then, are not defined primarily through conflicts that provoke struggle: rather, they are part of a process of dissimulation, a process that requires others to serve as witnesses. The position of the spectator, then, in this scenario is never simply given or neutral. The function of the spectator, in this passage at least, is to create and confirm a space of deception, and the content of this deception is nothing less than the constitutive axiom or thesis of Western modernity: that of the autonomous, active subject *qua* I, ego, or self-consciousness. For Freud, this scenario, as espoused by Adler, is tantamount to confusing a circus with a tragedy, precisely what McDougall then proceeds to do.

To be sure, her account of the theatrical situation becomes more complicated as the passage proceeds. The cast of characters she assigns to the Ego includes, not just the tragic hero, yet also an "actor" (in quotes in the original: "un acteur"), but one who in addition to acting on the "world stage" is also present at—*assiste à*—"a more intimate theater whose repertory is secret." To complicate matters further, the Ego, which participates as hero, actor, and audience in a secret repertory company and doesn't even know the company it keeps—is above all the company's "director": "le metteur en scène, c'est, bien sûr, le Je lui-même." This director-ego, who is separated from both characters and plot by a "veil," is obliged to stage the play with a cast he does not know and thus begins to resemble Freud's clown, the *dummer August*, while the spectacle he is staging begins to look more and more like a circus than like a tragedy.

Nevertheless, for all of its complexity and subtlety, McDougall's conception of theater is, as the title of her book indicates, informed by the point of view of a *Je*, or "I," that ultimately invests the diverse and conflictual "theater" of the unconscious with an underlying structural coherence and unity. One last citation from her book will indicate how the diversity implied in the notion of theatricality is structurally and methodologically subordinated to the unity of the ego:

> In utilizing this metaphor of theater, I hope to shed light on two aspects of psychic activity: the framework or place where the scene occurs, and the characters that play there. The first aspect relates to the economy of the psyche, the second to its dynamic significance. It is up to the "I" to compose with these elements, *to maintain meaning* and to channel the forces of cathexis. In order to achieve this, he must have both invention and imagination. (p. 11)

Whereas the I thus emerges in McDougall's account as star of the show—its hero and director at once—Freud insists on comparing the Ego to the slapstick clown in the circus, ridiculous but also theatrical in its attempt to create the appearance of being in control. These two conceptions of theater have a long history, going back to the earliest and most influential attempt to articulate a systematic approach to theater, that of Aristotle in the *Poetics*. What we have previously (in Chapter 3) referred to as Aristotle's *synoptic* approach to theater, privileging tragedy and, within tragedy, the unifying function of the plot—*muthos*—has generally been understood as his attempt to rehabilitate *mimēsis*, and in particular, theatrical mimesis, against the Platonic critique elaborated in the *Republic* and the *Laws*. Plato condemns theater as a particularly dangerous form of mimesis, which encourages people to confuse themselves with the parts they play and consequently to forget their proper place in the organization of the *polis*. Against this Platonic verdict, Aristotle defends mimesis and the pleasure it both procures and exploits as a natural and inevitable learning process. In a passage that recalls or, rather, anticipates Freud's argumentation in explaining his move beyond the pleasure principle, Aristotle points to the fact that repetition, even of manifestly unpleasant objects, can be a source of pleasure, and interprets this as evidence of the power and significance of mimesis in human life. This power is related to the pleasure afforded all human beings by the act of *recognition*, even where the objects thereby recognized are repugnant or troubling in themselves:

> There are things that we see with pain so far as they themselves are concerned but whose images, even when executed in very great detail, we view with pleasure. Such is the case, for example, with renderings of the least favored animals, or of cadavers. The cause of this is that learning is eminently pleasurable not only to philosophers but to the rest of mankind in the same way, although their share in the pleasure is restricted, because the reason they take pleasure in seeing the images is that in the process of viewing they find themselves learning, that is, reckoning what kind a given thing belongs to: "This individual is a so-and-so." Because if the viewers happen not to have seen such a thing before, the reproduction will not produce the pleasure *qua* reproduction but through its workmanship or color or something else of that sort.[3]

"Learning," in short, consists in the process of recognition, which in turn entails "reckoning what *kind* a given thing belongs to." Which is to say, being able to put a "given thing" in its proper place by subsuming it under a familiar, generic category, attaching a predicate to it and thus being able to say, "This individual is a so-and-so." This explanation of mimesis as recognition through subsumption of the individual under the generic will turn out to be more important for Aristotelian poetics and its approach to theater than the better-known reference to catharsis, not merely because reference to catharsis occurs only once in the *Poetics*, but also because even that single time makes sense only if one is clear about just what is being "purged." As with Freud's later use of this term, what is being purged is an impurity, a tension, a conflict of some sort. But of what sort? Aristotle's examples in the passage just cited are, as examples almost always are, suggestive and doubtless significant: "least favored animals and cadavers." These examples cite borderline cases of living beings: the animals whose life is most degraded and the physical vestiges of a life that has departed.

However, even such unpleasant examples become sources of pleasure when they furnish occasions for the recognition just discussed. Aristotle speaks of mimesis as a learning experience, but the learning involved in such recognition does not bring anything objectively new. Rather, it merely reconfirms the identity of the learner, who is able to re-identify what he or she has already seen. Learning here is reconfirmation, repetition of the same, recognition. In identifying the other, even others from whom life has departed, it confirms the living self-identity of the one who identifies. Such confirmation is pleasurable, perhaps by suggesting the ability to reckon, not just with the "given thing" at hand, but more generally, with the future.

These considerations inform Aristotle's approach to tragedy in the *Poetics*. Tragedy, he asserts, involves above all the representation upon the stage of an *action* that is complete, unified, and therefore meaningful. Such meaningful representation of action Aristotle designates in Greek as *muthos*, or plot. This is the heart and soul, the goal of tragedy and a fortiori of theater, since tragedy is, for Aristotle, its highest form. However, this formulation of the essence of tragedy calls for further elaboration. To designate tragedy as the representation of a unified and complete action in a plot poses a problem for Aristotle. Given the narrative structure of the plot, this conception of tragedy tends to subordinate tragedy to epic and, indeed, to make it a subspecies of the *epos*. Aristotle, however, insists that tragedy is in its essence both distinct from and at least as valuable as epic poetry, if not more so. Two arguments support his position. First, there is what I have called the *synoptic* argument. Aristotle emphasizes that the didactic value of tragedy is superior to that of the epic by virtue of its compactness and concentration. Tragedy, he insists, should be able to be "taken in at a single view," if not at a single sitting, in contrast to the epic, which is more extended, more dispersed, and therefore less unified. Such a *synoptic* conception of tragedy goes hand in hand with a marginalization, if not devaluation, of everything having to do with mere *opsis*, that is, with the visual, spectacular nature of theater as a scenic medium, rather than with tragedy as its essential manifestation. The optical dimension of tragedy, Aristotle argues, is secondary, instrumental, and does not really pertain to its essence. This is tantamount to asserting that the essence of tragedy is not theatrical, at least insofar as theater remains inseparable from a certain disposition of space, from a locality divided into two interdependent but distinct parts: the space of the stage and that of the audience.

This tendency to subordinate the scenic-medial dimension of theater to its narrative-representational function poses problems in distinguishing theatrical mimesis from that of other media, for instance epic poetry. This may be one of the reasons why Aristotle tries, as it were, to dispose of the question early so that he can get to the points that interest him most, concerning above all the structure of the tragic plot. We will come to that in a moment, but first let us take a closer look at the specific problems Aristotle encounters in his attempt to describe just what distinguishes theatrical representation—which he sees exemplified in *tragedy*—from its rival, epic poetry. In the latter, representation is the result of a narrative discourse, whether this discourse is explicitly enunciated by a narrator who, as Aristotle strikingly puts it, "stays the same [*auton*]," *without changing (kai mē metaballonta)*, or implicit in more directly mimetic forms of narrative, in which the narrated characters speak for themselves, as it were. Epic poetry consists normally of a mixture of these two modes, both of which, however, are sharply distinguished from the theatrical mode of representation, in which—I translate as literally as possible—"all those acting and actualizing in a work, produce the mimesis" (*ē pantas hōs prattontas kai energountas tous mimoumenous*, 48 a 23). If this translation sounds odd, you can safely assume that the Greek isn't too much clearer.[4] The French editors of the *Poetics* note that this "second part of the phrase has generally been considered as corrupted and practically impossible to translate."[5] Is this textual difficulty a mere philological accident or could it be symptomatic of something more significant?

The designation of those producing the mimetic representation on the stage suggests the latter. The term used, *prattontes*, is the gerund of the verb *prattein*, "to act," a word that in its substantive form, *praxis*, will inform Aristotle's entire attempt to account for theater as tragedy. As tragedy, he asserts, theater is above all the representation of a single, complete, and meaningful action on the stage. The heart and soul of tragedy is not the stage but the action, the *praxis* thus represented. However, in order for that representation to be *theatrical*, it must be not just told, but rather *acted upon the stage*. It therefore requires *actors* or, rendering Aristotle more literally, *actants* or *actings*.[6] The reason the noun *acting* is so bizarre, particularly when used in the plural, is that it suggests a multiplicity of elements that themselves seem more like ongoing processes than stable entities. The notion of "actor" is still morphologically individual and hence identifiable with the subject of a single, self-same action or set of actions. Indeed, *prattontes* can refer as easily to the characters represented onstage as to the persons representing, the actors. But *actants* or, even more, *actings* need not refer primarily to persons or even to things. Persons are doubtless required, but qua individuals they need not be the principle of whatever unity may be involved.

This is a notion that is by no means alien to Aristotle. What distances his conception of tragedy from that which has become familiar to us over the past four hundred years is his refusal to place *character* at the center of tragedy. His most emphatic, if not unequivocal, formulation in this regard denies that character, *ethos*, is an indispensable constituent of tragedy. For, he asserts, "a tragedy cannot exist without a plot, but it can without characters" (50 a 23–24). A bit further, he explains this provocative assertion: "But a plot is not unified, as some people think, simply because it has to do with a single person. A large, indeed an indefinite number of things can happen to a given individual, some of which go to constitute no unified event; and in the same way there can be many acts of a given individual from which no single action emerges" (51 a 16–20). This unfounded belief in the unity of an individual's acts or life as a whole is related to a no less credulous overvaluation of "historically given names" in the writing of tragedies, as though such could ground the necessity of the drama.

Aristotle thus marks an irreducible distance from the dominant tendency of "Western" theater in the modern period, a tendency that Artaud was to attack bitterly as psychologistic. Yet despite Aristotle's antipsychologistic emphasis on action as distinct from character, his conception of the unity of the representation of action in the tragic *muthos* seems modeled on the life span of the individual. The tragic plot, Aristotle emphasizes, should be unified and complete in having the tripartite structure of beginning, middle, and end. He associates this, not just with "action," *praxis*, but also with "life," *bios*.[7] Whose life, however, if not that of the heroes represented? There can be only one answer: the life, or afterlife, of the spectators, the audience for whom tragedy, as mimesis, is to be a learning experience that produces recognition and thereby brings the new under the aegis of the familiar, the singular under the cover of the generic.

At the same time, it is this cognitive dimension of *praxis* that the theatrical mode of mimesis tends to undercut. That, I believe, is primarily responsible for the incoherence so often noted in Aristotle's account of the *prattontes*. The unity, completion, and meaningfulness of the tragic action, which, as Aristotle never tires of insisting, should be made accessible to a single, uninterrupted sitting and viewing, tends to dissolve in the face of the *prattontes* acting onstage. First of all, as Roselyne Dupont-Roc and Jean Lallot stress in the commentary to their French edition of the *Poetics*, the word is used in the plural. They consider this to be the decisive element in the passage: "What is essential is that, as a group, [the *prattontes*] divide the *I* among themselves, assuming the discourse as a whole and putting it to work." The French editors formulate this conclusion slightly differently, and that difference underscores an important point. They write not of "putting to work" but of a *mise "en acte."* The Greek word used by Aristotle, *energountas*, can of course mean both. It is related to one of the key words in his entire ontology, *energeia*, which is usually translated "actuality" but which, taken more literally, means the act of "being at work," *en ergon*. Associated with the notion of work is the idea of completion. But what sort of completed work occurs on the stage? It is not just the plurality of actors, of the cast, that is decisive, for that could still be fused into the unity of a work, a tragedy, insofar as it represents a completed and unified action. Between this goal and the *prattontes*, however, a tension subsists. The latter are not just many; they are double. It is difficult to tell if the "actings" apply to the *characters represented* on the stage through their actions, or to the *actors representing* them. Moreover, there is an essential incompletion associated with the gerund that Aristotle employs here: coming from the present participle, its *presence* is that of an indefinitely reiterated movement bounded only by the quasi-simultaneity of its articulation. And yet precisely this precarious presence and simultaneity appear to define the distinctive space-time, the place of theatricality as such. Theatrical representations cannot be framed by a complete, self-contained, meaningful *narrative*, as seems possible in epic poetry, since the actualization of theater involves a temporal repetition that is suspended in a divided space. It is the simultaneity of this division, of actors acting before and to an audience, which both distinguishes theatrical representation from other kinds and makes it difficult for it to be enclosed within the stable structure of a *work*.

This is perhaps why Aristotle is so deeply critical of everything pertaining to the stage, to the theatrical *medium* as such, which he seeks to portray as the merely technical and empirical instrument of a more ideal form of representation, that of tragedy. This is why he spends most of his energy attempting to describe the most effective structure of the tragic plot: the *muthos* through which *praxis* is represented onstage. It is *muthos* that distinguishes tragedy from mere theater and endows it with the completeness of a work. What, then, is characteristic of the tragic *muthos*? Here three elements emerge.

First, there is the general trait that characterizes all tragic plots, insofar as they hope to be theatrical. They all involve some sort of change, in Greek, a *metabasis*. We have already encountered this word, which Aristotle employs to distinguish the two forms of narrative discourse, one in which the narrator stays the same, without changing, and the other in which he metamorphoses into his characters. Plato cited the latter use as evidence of the unreliability and corrupting effects of poetic mimesis.[8] For Aristotle, however, change as such is neither problematic nor interesting, or in any event, not interesting enough to define the essence of effective tragic plots. He is after something else, as his distinction of plots into two general types, "simple" and "complex," suggests. Both types recount situations that change, but in different ways. In simple plots, the changes are predictable, create no surprise, and hence are not very interesting to an audience.

This shows us something about mimesis itself, which leads us to the second element of the tragic *muthos*. To the extent that Aristotle defends mimesis as a learning experience, the recognition to which the tragic *muthos* leads cannot be entirely predictable. Something unexpected must intervene, something whose essential affinity to theater informs the French expression that arose in the eighteenth century to describe an unexpected turn of events, whether onstage or off, which is to say, on other stages. This was, and is, the *coup de théâtre*, which signifies a spectacular turn of events that need not take place in a consecrated theater, since it is the "coup" that makes the theater. Aristotle is perhaps the first to introduce this concept systematically, as one of the traits that distinguish complex tragic plots. He calls it *peripeteia*, and it involves the advent of the unexpected, interrupting intention and expectation and creating the kind of excitement that is characteristic of effective theater. Such instances of *peripeteia* alone, however, even if they are an essential part of effective theater, are not in themselves sufficient to endow it with the status of a valuable *work*.

Without such a *telos*, all that might be left would be the ongoing iterations and gesticulations of the "actants" or "actings" on the stage. There would then be something like pure repetition, not simply of the same, but of the eternally different, one shock following another, surprise piling up on surprise. Something else is clearly required, both to call a halt to this indefinite series of shocks and, in so doing, to endow its repetitiveness with the significance of a genuine *work*.

This third quality Aristotle calls *anagnōrisis*, usually translated as "recognition," signifying, however, not just the repetition or return of cognition after the shock of the unexpected turn, but also the passage from a state of wonder and even ignorance to a state of insight. The best tragic plots, Aristotle insists, are marked not just by the presence of both of these features, *peripeteia* and *anagnōrisis*, but even more by their quasi-simultaneity: "The finest recognition is one that happens at the same time as a *peripeteia*, as is the case with the one in Oedipus." The mention of Oedipus, here and elsewhere in the *Poetics*, reminds us that, despite the length of this apparent digression, we have not wandered very far from Freud and psychoanalysis, to which, in a moment, we will return.

But not before indicating that what informs Aristotle's discussion of complex tragic plots is the way they challenge the conscious, pre-conscious, and perhaps unconscious expectations of the audience. The audience that attended performances of *Oedipus Tyrannos* already "knew" the story, at least in its outlines. They therefore could not have been very surprised by the shocks and surprises that ineluctably drive Oedipus to acknowledge what Tiresias tells him, namely, that "you are the slayer of the man whose slayer you seek."[9] In this respect, Sophocles' audience was not unlike Dora, from whom Freud received one of his earliest lessons in the unconscious, especially when, after repeatedly resisting one of his interpretations, she admitted that she had "known it all the time," just never "thought of it."[10] Oedipus could have said the same, for he too "knew it all the time," he just never "thought of it" that way. Most of the facts of his life were familiar to him, but precisely this familiarity concealed their significance from him. The messenger who brings the news of the death of King Polybus and then seeks to assuage Oedipus' fears by revealing that the king and queen of Corinth, who raised him, were not his true parents, only confirms them. What Oedipus is thereby called upon to "recognize" is the complexly *relational* structure of cognition as such—something that the conqueror of the Sphinx is not in a position to understand at the outset of the play.[11] Cognition is elusive because it is irreducibly relational, involving not something self-contained or *substantial* but rather, in Freudian terms, an *overdetermined network*[12] of relations (Lacan's "signifying chain"). These relations are intrinsically open-ended, but for the singular human being they are also finite. This tension, between a signification that is potentially unlimited and an existence that is finite, informs the Theban trage-dies—and perhaps tragedy itself. "Pity and fear," anxiety and desire, are its most obvious affective consequences. This is why a notion such as "catharsis" can never be sufficient to circumscribe the effects of tragedy, any more than it can circumscribe the workings of the un-conscious. It also indicates why this notion should recur again and again. Oedipus himself uses the word to describe his initial strategy in dealing with the plague. The pollution, the miasma presumed to be the cause of the pestilence, can in his eyes be "purified" only by being *expelled* from the city, as though the opposition of inside versus out-side, self versus other, had any relevance to the problems of Thebes. It is this illusion that the fateful words of Tiresias dispel: "You are the slayer of the man whose slayer you seek." This, however, is the one message Oedipus cannot accept. The problem is *intra muros*, not merely as a Trojan horse brought in from the outside, but because the interior *is* already the outside, just as the ostensible foreigner, Oedipus, is in fact native-born if not bred.

What is at stake, then, in this exemplary tragedy has ultimately more to do with a realignment of topographical notions of *place* than it does with *action*. Indeed, in view of Aristotle's conception of tragedy as the representation of action through plot, what is striking is that the plot of *Oedipus Tyrannos*, as of its sequel, *Oedipus at Colonus*, entails virtually no action at all, nothing except a series of speeches, messages, dialogues—nothing, in short, but language. As for the action, what-ever is relevant occurs offstage—the murder of Laius, the self-blinding of Oedipus. All that is shown onstage are the *effects* of these acts, never the acts themselves.

Where, then, does this leave the *synoptic* understanding that trag-edy, according to Aristotle, is supposed to provide? And what is its relation to the *opsis* that, according to him, is to serve only as its means and neutral medium?

In response, it is important to remember that, although there is no objective action in this play, its plot nevertheless fulfills Aristotle's formal requirements: *peripeteia* and *anagnōrisis*. These are, of course, closer to *parapraxes* than to *praxis*, since they are precisely not the result of conscious intention, will, or expectation. They generally consist in statements that reinscribe events in ways that radically alter their intended, anticipated significance. The possibility of such alteration leads to a double conclusion: first, that the significance of events, persons, and things depends not just on their intrinsic qualities but on their situation, which is to say, on their relation to what is external to them; and, second, that such situatedness can never be internally defined, never finished in the sense of being completed, but only interrupted.

What is interrupted is the expectation of a self-contained story—and a life—that would add up to a meaningful whole. Such a narrative structure is presupposed by Aristotle's demand for a unifying perception capable of synthesizing the diverse elements of the *opsis* into a *synopsis*. This in turn depends on the ability of *anagnōrisis* to reassemble what *peripeteia* has overturned. Only thus can tragic *mimēsis* yield the kind of learning experience upon which Aristotle insists. Learning, for Aristotle, at least in the *Poetics*, is the equivalent of knowing, in the sense of predication: "This individual is a so-and-so."[13] There is, however, a conception of learning that separates it radically from predicative knowledge and it is precisely such a conception that we encounter in the final Chorus of *Oedipus Tyrannos*:

> Sons and daughters of Thebes, behold: this was Oedipus,
> Greatest of men; he held the key to the deepest mysteries;
> Was envied by all his fellowmen for his great prosperity;
> Behold, what a full tide of misfortune swept over his head
> Then learn that mortal man must always look to [*episkopounta*]
>   the final day,
> And call no one happy before he has crossed life's border [*terma tou biou*] free from pain.[14]

Regarding this concluding formulation, Jebb notes that "the use of *episkopounta* is peculiar" and concludes that "the exact sense" must be: "*fixing one's eye on* the final day (as on a point towards which one is moving), *that one should see it*,"[15] However, as *Oedipus at Colonus* will make explicit, the *terma tou biou* is not something that can be "seen," not directly at least. Whence, perhaps, the effort and tension implied in Sophocles' use here of *episkopounta*: the "final day" must be "watched out for," but its "crossing" will never be seen as such.

Not, that is, by the one who "crosses" over. But perhaps by others. This may explain, in part, why one takes such pleasure in seeing the spectacle of such a life *staged*. Whereas "mortal man must always look to the final day," seeing cannot be equated to, or subordinated to knowing. What one "learns" in beholding a tragedy such as *Oedipus* could therefore be that as a mortal being, one always *sees* without *knowing* just what one is seeing. And therefore that the irreducible secret of whatever one sees is that it could mean something entirely different from what one expects. This secret but ubiquitous possibility is not only responsible for the theatrical *peripeteia*—it makes it indistinguishable from the *anagnōrisis* that Aristotle sought to separate from it. The *peripeteia is* the *anagnōrisis*. But that means that what is thereby *recognized* is the possibility of a "turn" whose singularity can never be stabilized or exhausted in a predication, in a "this one is that," which in turn suggests that *anagnōrisis* always contains the possibility of turning out itself to be a *peripeteia*.

This is why the "recognition" of this secret, which is inseparable from a life that is always incomplete, often proceeds by its dissimulation. Thus, theater can create the semblance of a meaningful whole, especially when it displays a story that is ostensibly complete, with "beginning, middle, and end." It does not so much matter what the story portrays, nor if what it portrays involves suffering and death. On the contrary, for those spectators who seem to be "taking it in at a single, uninterrupted glance," the experience, according to Aristotle, can be as pleasurable as the images of lowly animals and corpses. It is the pleasure of recognizing, in the lives of others, what we will never be able to see in our own. The pleasure produced by such recognition is the pleasure of surviving.[16] This is why Aristotle placed so much emphasis on the importance of plot, asserting that it constitutes nothing less than "the goal [*telos*, end] of tragedy, and the goal is the greatest thing of all" (50 a 23–24).[17] Plot alone allows the divergent elements of a fragmentary individual existence to be ordered in a manner that suggests totality, wholeness, and thus meaningfulness—under the condition that the plot as a whole be accessible to an uninterrupted perception. Precisely such accessibility constitutes for Aristotle the privilege of tragedy with respect to epic, which is more extended, less unified, and therefore less intrinsically meaningful.

Nevertheless, the staging of a plot, however unified it may seem, is never as unified and integrated as Aristotle would like to believe. Theater never stages a plot directly precisely *because* it involves staging. It can do without a narrator, but it cannot do without the stage and those who act upon it. The fact that theatrical acting is never the pure representation of acts but rather the actualization of acting upon a stage drives a wedge between "acting" and "action" that remains "active" even in contemporary English. This is even more powerfully at work in Aristotle's Greek when it describes, however ambiguously, how the "acting" of the *prattontes* actualizes nothing so much as the split constitutive of all mimesis. Neither actor nor role can function without the other, but they do not necessarily add up to a whole. That Aristotle is acutely aware of this danger is indicated by his persistent attempt to subordinate everything having to do with the distinctive *medium* of theater, and, a fortiori, of tragedy, to the "goal" of presenting a unified action qua plot.

Thus, Aristotle's *Poetics* constitutes the ambivalent beginning of a powerful tradition that seeks to subordinate the medium of theater to a conception of drama as a poetic genre serving the representation of action structured as a coherent and complete narrative. It is in challenging this powerful tradition that Freud's approach to the unconscious defines itself. This can be demonstrated in two ways: first, by indicating briefly several instances in which Freud explicitly or, more often, implicitly shows how a continuous, coherent narrative functions to conceal the far less coherent, far more disruptive workings of the unconscious; second, by examining one instance in Freud's writing where theatricality and narrative interact to reveal a dimension that he himself might have preferred to ignore, even if, in a certain sense, like Dora "he knew it all the time."

First, then, to indicate how closely Freud's discovery of the unconscious is associated with a move toward a *theatrical* conception of the psyche that implicitly challenges the Aristotelian tradition we have been reviewing, we can begin with *The Interpretation of Dreams*. Lacan was well advised to suggest that the third element of the dream work—in German, *Rücksicht auf Darstellbarkeit*, usually translated as "considerations of representability"—be translated into French as "égards sur la mise en scène [considerations of staging]."[18] Lacan's suggestion was incisive because this aspect of the dream work, like all the others, is theatrical insofar as it is undertaken with the spectator in mind. If the dream must be rendered in what seem to be easily accessible scenes, that is, first, because it is made to provide a certain spectacle for a spectator and, second, because that spectacle must *dissimulate* what it really has to say or to show. This means that it must ultimately conceal *that* it is concealing. The formula that best describes this situation is that the dream is not just a wish fulfillment, nor even a distorted (*entstellte*) wish fulfillment, but rather a distorted wish fulfillment that dissimulates its own distortions.[19] The fact that both of the German verbs Freud uses to describe this double duplicity are derived from the same verb root, namely, *stellen*, "to place," only underscores the theatrical nature of the masquerade. If the initial function of the dream is to protect the sleep of the dreamer, as Freud frequently asserts, it can only fulfill this function by disguising itself, then by *disguising its own disguise*—which is to say, by presenting itself (to the memory of the dreamer) as being perfectly transparent. It is like a mirror on a door that suggests that the door *behind* it is open, while in fact what it shows is only a reflection of what is in front of it.

The dream, however, is not simply a distorting mirror presenting itself to the dreamer as though it were a transparent window. It also addresses the consciousness of the nondreamer, who is (or will be) awake. The latter may be—and in fact to some extent always is—the "same" person, but this person, remembering and retelling the dream, is now in a very different position. She is now a participant through memory and narration, even while experiencing herself as a mere observer. The way the dream creates this impression will be familiar after the discussion of Aristotle's *Poetics*: it creates the illusion of being a more or less unified and coherent spectacle that can be observed and taken in at a single viewing.

It does this through a variety of devices, none of which is more revealing than that designated by Freud as the fourth and last constituent of the dream work, "last" not just because Freud discusses it at the end of the chapter, but, more importantly, because it seems structurally to presuppose the other three. Such an impression, however, may already be part of the self-dissimulation of the dream. Freud reinforces this impression when he designates this component as a "secondary elaboration [*sekundäre Bearbeitung*]" of the dream. Since it is called "secondary," it presumably presupposes a "primary" part of the dream. Freud's discussion reveals that things are not so simple. What secondary elaboration (or "revision," as it is translated in English) does is to "revise" or "work over [*bearbeiten*]" the "rough spots" in the dream, which would otherwise reveal, through illogic and incoherence, its unconscious and conflictual origins. This is how Freud describes its function:

> It fills up the gaps in the dream structure with shreds and patches. As a result of its efforts, the dream loses its appearance of absurdity and disconnectedness and begins to approach the ideal model [*dem Vorbilde*] of an intelligible experience. But such an effort is not always crowned with success. Dreams thus emerge that to superficial observation may seem to be impeccably logical and reasonable; they start from a possible situation, develop it through a chain of consistent modifications, and bring it—although far less frequently—to a conclusion that is neither troubling nor irritating [*zu einem nicht befremdenden Abschluß*]. These dreams are the ones that have been most profoundly worked over by the psychical function that is most akin to waking thought: they appear to have a meaning, but that meaning is as far removed as possible from the real significance of the dream.[20]

This operation of "secondary revision" is, of course, well known. What has been largely overlooked, to my knowledge at least, is that it can accomplish its ends only by revising the dream in a very particular way: namely, so that it appears to be a *coherent and complete narrative*, with beginning, middle, and end, as Aristotle would have said. As Freud writes: Such revisions "start out from a possible situation, develop it through a chain of consistent modifications, and . . . bring it to a conclusion that is neither troubling nor irritating." Freud's term, in German, is stronger: the conclusion to the narrative imposed by secondary revision is, he writes, in no way *befremdend*: which is to say, literally, "alienating, estranging." In short, the *imposition of a narrative continuum* upon the dream makes it familiar, and therefore acceptable to our waking consciousness. Such a continuum tends to assimilate the night dream to a daydream, a fantasy. The difference between daydream and night dream has to do with the positioning of the protagonist. The subject of the daydream or fantasy finds herself confronted with the kind of theater that Aristotle sought to valorize: a spectacle that stages a coherent and complete story. The attractiveness of this form of spectacle, however, is now tied to the desire of the subject to avoid anything that might threaten the unity and stability of its position. Through the continuity of this narrative, the subject is reassured that, despite "constant modifications," it stays the same over time. This is, of course, one aspect of the ego. The ego thus emerges as structurally dependent upon the kind of move we have seen at work in Aristotle's *Poetics*, which could be designated as the *narrativization of the theatrical*, or, to echo the Greek word, its *mythologizing*. The latter term seems preferable, since it distinguishes between narrative in general and the specific kind of self-contained narrative Aristotle associates with the term *muthos*. Thus, what is at stake is not *narrative in general*, but rather a notion of narrative in which "beginning, middle, and end" add up to a meaningful *whole*.

It is precisely this semblance of *wholeness* that secondary revision seeks to associate with the dream. Without it or, rather, since it is never entirely absent, even when it has not fully succeeded, "we find ourselves helplessly face to face with a meaningless heap of fragmentary material," as Strachey translates. Freud's German is less elegant but more powerful: "wie hilflos vor einem sinnlosen Haufen von Inhaltsbrocken"—more literally, "faced with bits of content senselessly piled up."[21]

In short, the model of intelligibility and meaningfulness specific to waking, conscious thought is that of a coherent, consistent, self-contained story, whereas the contrary model of unconscious articulation is that of "bits of content senselessly piled up" without any discernible form or purpose. In this context, another comparison made by Freud seems quite significant. In the dreams that appear to be the most meaningful, "secondary revision has played about with the material the most freely and has retained the relations present in that material to the least extent. They are dreams that might be said to have been already interpreted once, before being submitted to waking interpretation."[22] In short, secondary revision, which operates through the imposition of a continuous, totalizing narrative, is not just a story-teller, it is also an editor and an interpreter, working in ways akin to those we take when we are awake. In this sense it entails a *theoretical* activity as well as a *narrative* one or, rather, an activity in which *narration* and *interpretation* are just two sides of the same effort to impose meaningful form on resistant, conflictual material. Because this tendency is shared both by the unconscious, in its self-dissimulating function, and by theoretical thought, we should not be surprised to find the same struggle going on, not just in the materials described by Freud, but in the very theoretical discourse in which he is analyzing those materials.

This is what we find at work when we move from *The Interpretation of Dreams* to a somewhat later text of Freud's, "The Passing of the Oedipus Complex."[23] This essay seeks to interpret the disappearance of the Oedipus and castration complexes during the "latency" period. Although Freud's account of the latter is well known, a reexamination can be illuminating for the questions we have been discussing. On the one hand, the castration complex involves an experience that Freud describes as being essentially *visual*: the child discovers, with its own two eyes as it were, that significant adult women, such as a nurse or mother, do not possess the male sexual organ, and this discovery has a traumatic effect. As Freud writes, "the observation that breaks the disbelief of the child"—disbelief that the phallus is not universal—"is that of the female genital." According to him, then, a visual perception plays the decisive role in castration. And it does so insofar as it involves a surprise, a sort of *peripeteia*, an unexpected turn of events. All of this is familiar, perhaps over-familiar to anyone who has ever read much Freud. What is less so, however, is this: the initial reaction of the child to its observation of the anatomical sexual difference is to deny it fundamental and lasting value through a device already discussed. The child tells itself, and whomever else will listen, a *story*, precisely the kind of story we have encountered previously, with beginning, middle, and end. It is a story designed to deny sexual difference by subordinating it to sexual sameness or identity. The story is simple and can be quickly paraphrased: Once upon a time, all adults possessed a penis. Now I discover that certain adults (my mother, nurse) do not have one. And if I am not careful, the same thing could happen to me. Beginning, middle, and (possibly catastrophic) end. The averting of this end becomes the burden of "castration anxiety." But the "complex" upon which such anxiety depends has the structure of the self-contained narrative already discussed.

The "threat of castration," which is triggered by reiterated observations but ultimately depends upon a narrative construction, puts an end to the "phallic genital organization" of the child. The child now finds itself in an impasse. If it follows the dictates of its desire and seeks "to take the place of the father" in what Freud calls an "active," "masculine manner," it runs the risk of being punished, that is, castrated, by the one it tries to displace. If, however, it seeks to take the place of the mother, in a feminine manner, it must assume the burden of her "castration." "Castration," here, it should be noted, makes sense *only* within a *narrative* framework that supposes an original, universal identity—"in the beginning was the Phallus"—as the condition of being able to *interpret difference* as a *negative mode of identity.* Thus, anatomical sexual difference, a relationship, is transformed into the negative perception of a *lack* or *absence,* which presupposes that there must have been a penis, "once upon a time." "Castration" is thus not simply a "complex" but above all a *story* the child tells itself in order to protect its narcissism from engaging the challenge of a difference that cannot simply be equated with an object of perception.

In this context, the *Untergang* or "downfall" of the Oedipus complex reveals its significance. Instead of maintaining its position as a detached spectator, at a safe distance from the sights it observes, the child suddenly finds its position invaded, as it were, by the very forces and dangers that it had sought to keep out. From this invasion results the ambivalent instance that Freud will designate the *superego.* Its entry, as it were, into the psychic household of the child marks the downfall of the Oedipus complex and the start of the latency period. But at the same time it marks the emergence of a different paradigm of psychic topology, one that is resolutely *spatial,* involving a multiplicity of relations between "instances" that cannot be reduced to a unified whole, least of all to that of an ego. The ego now comes to designate, not the subject as a whole, but only a particularly ambivalent *part* of it, a *role* it must play. This part or role can no longer be that of a detached observer, since the observation now goes on "within" the space of an irrevocably riven psyche. The psyche has become a kind of "stage" or "arena," a divided site where conflicting forces play themselves out. The ego has now become as much a listener as a viewer, as much a receiver of messages as a teller of tales, and this involves, not just a shift from sight to sound, but, even more significant, a fundamentally different relationship to itself and to others.

The traditional interpretation of vision operates with binary oppositions—inside and outside, here and there, subject and object—that suppose a neutral and transparent space within which each element is positioned as viewer and viewed, spectator and spectacle. The new psychic topography is not binary but ternary: its model is not the daydream but the night dream or the joke, which, Freud insists, is "social" in its appeal to a "third person." Its sociality, however, is also eminently theatrical, insofar as theater exemplifies a triadic relationship in which the "audience" plays an indispensable role. This role, however, remains diverse and heterogeneous in its potentiality. Therefore, the move from a binary to a ternary structure involves a far more radical change than the mere addition of one more element to a structure might suggest. Rather, qua ternary the structure no longer is organized on the basis of an underlying identity. The audience, it turns out, is no more—or less—identical with itself than the "actors" are with their roles.

Another place in Freud's writings where the discovery of difference within the identical links psychoanalysis to theater is the peripheral region known as the uncanny (in German: *das Unheimliche*).[24] The essay bearing that title has remained largely marginal in psychoanalytic literature, a fate for which it was carefully prepared by Freud himself. He broached this topic only with the greatest reluctance, and when he had finally finished his essay on it, it would play no further role in his writings—no obvious, manifest role at least. The essay thus takes on the air of a final *Abrechnung*, one that is also an exercise in exorcism.

Freud seems to have entertained a special relationship to the uncanny. His essay is constructed almost entirely out of stories, and in the process of telling them, it recounts its own autobiographical-philological story as well. The essay begins with a disclaimer: Freud insists that the topic involves an area of experience that has remained very "remote [*abseits liegendes*, more literally, "peripheral"]" for him. It has been a long time, he asserts, since he last "encountered anything that impressed him as being uncanny," and therefore a particular effort on his part is required to enter into the feelings involved (12:230). Ernest Jones, on the other hand, recounts how Freud showed himself to be profoundly fascinated by the uncanny, and how he delighted in telling stories of patients for whom such experiences played a leading role.[25] Prominent among such experiences were those of predictions of death that came true after many years. Perhaps this explains why Freud, having begun work on this essay many years before, appears to have set it aside until he had reached the age of sixty-three. Until he had attained that age, Freud had believed he might die at the age of sixty-two, the year of his father's death. The number sixty-two also crops up in his essay as an example of an uncanny coincidence, without any mention of his own beliefs, of course.

In short, there is good extratextual reason to suspect that Freud, despite his disclaimers, felt himself to be profoundly implicated in the question of the uncanny. Of course, no one knew better than he how such contradictions can become the medium of unconscious articulation. Turning now to the text itself, we find at least two explicitly autobiographical passages, whose implications go far beyond Freud's individual person. In a text that draws most of its material not from the clinic but from fictional narratives, what is striking about these two passages is that they function more in the mode of a *scene* than in that of a story. To be more precise, they begin by telling a story, which soon reveals itself to be more scenic than narrative. The first passage occurs in the context of Freud's discussion of "the repetition of the similar as a source of uncanny feelings" (12:249). Freud admits that not everyone will agree with this and, moreover, that it is not always the case. This is a problem that *haunts* all of Freud's efforts in this essay to analyze the uncanny by means of *examples*: the exemplarity of his examples will repeatedly be called into question. Hence, the recourse to personal, autobiographical experience. One of the most memorable anecdotes that Freud recounts "reminds one of the helplessness of certain dream situations." Here is the story:

> As, once on a hot summer afternoon, I strolled through the unknown, empty streets of a small Italian city, I found myself in an area about whose character I could not long be in doubt. The only people visible were heavily made-up women in the windows of the small houses, and I hastened to leave the narrow street at the next corner. But after I had wandered around for a while, without a guide, I found myself suddenly again in the same street, in which I now began to excite some attention [*Aufsehen zu erregen*], and my hurried departure had as its only result that new detours led me back to the area for the third time. At that point, however, I was seized by a feeling that I can only designate as uncanny, and I was glad when, having abandoned all thoughts of further exploration [*Entdeckungs-reisen*], I found myself back at the Piazza from which I had departed. (12:248)

Freud starts off in the hope of making discoveries, but soon finds himself caught in an infernal repetition that leads him back, again and again, to disreputable figures of desire—figures that, however, share with actresses the quality of being heavily "made up," *geschminkt*, and who offer themselves to be seen, and quite possibly to more than just being seen. The position of the observer is suddenly called into question by the unexpected repetition: the observer ceases to be a casual passerby and becomes himself a character, open to observation as a possible participant, a potential protagonist. The story has become a scenario in which the separation of spectator and actor is undercut by a repetition that undermines all simple linearity.

The second passage, which is not a story but simply a scene, is relegated by Freud quite literally to the margins of his text, since he recounts it in a footnote devoted to the uncanny dimension of the *Doppelgänger.* Freud remembers:

> I was sitting alone in the compartment of a sleeping car when, following a sudden jolt of the train, the door to the adjoining toilette opened and an elderly gentlemen in a bathrobe, wearing a bonnet on his head, stepped into my sleeper. Assuming that he had confused the two doors as he was leaving the toilette and had mistakenly entered my compartment, I leapt up to explain the situation, but immediately had *to recognize*, to my chagrin, that the invader [*Eindringling*] was my own image, reflected in the mirror of the door to the toilet. I still remember that I found the appearance [of the figure] deeply displeasing. (12:262–63 n.)

Here we find the Aristotelian mix of a *peripeteia* associated with an almost simultaneous recognition. The *coup de théâtre*, however, resides in the singular character of that recognition. It is not just that Freud takes his own mirror image for the appearance of someone else, but that, once having recognized his error, he continues to find the image alien, troubling, "deeply displeasing." Like King Oedipus, he would have preferred to have found another instead of himself, and when he is forced to acknowledge the other *as* himself, his self has become irrevocably alien.

The uncanny, which in German refers to the "home" rather than to knowledge, as does the English *canny*, demonstrates how and why the space of a certain familiarity is permeated by the alterity from which it seeks to set itself off. This applies to the *familial* no less than to the *familiar*. In the story that occupies much of Freud's attention in this essay, Hoffmann's tale "The Sandman," the other intrudes in the form of the enigmatic figure of Coppelius, the unwanted but regular visitor in the house of a family he finally destroys. However, Freud's own attempt to appropriate the uncanny for psychoanalysis is overshadowed by a predecessor, who may not have the uncanny stature of Coppelius but who seems to haunt Freud's essay no less than the strange lawyer haunts Hoffmann's story. Although Freud begins by noting the paucity of literature on the uncanny, he nevertheless has to acknowledge at least one significant predecessor, in a certain Ernst Jentsch, who in a previously published article interprets the uncanny as a form of "intellectual uncertainty." Freud rejects this theory as too intellectual, too tied to consciousness, and he seeks to replace it by a more properly psychoanalytic reference to the return of the repressed, in the form of castration anxiety, displaced in Hoffmann's story from the male sexual organ to the eyes. However, every time Freud seeks to identify a motif, a theme, as being an indispensable manifestation of the uncanny, he winds up conceding that his hypothesis cannot be satisfactorily demonstrated. The "return of the repressed," for instance, in the form of ocular anxiety *may be uncanny*, but is not *necessarily* so, for there can be instances of anxieties and of "returns of the repressed" that will not be associated with uncanny situations or feeling. It is as if the uncanny evades every attempt by Freud to bind it to a general characteristic from which it cannot be separated. Freud therefore shifts his focus or, rather, expands it to include not just individual motifs or themes, but the *context in which they emerge* and consequently in which they have hitherto been concealed. He thereby distinguishes two major types of context: the uncanny of lived experience (*Erlebens*) and that encountered in fictional texts. In the latter, he insists, we can best examine the various ways the uncanny is tied, not to an object, but to the manner in which it is presented and, above all, perceived by the reader. An example cited by Freud is the motif of severed bodily members—a head, hands, feet. These *can* be experienced as uncanny, but need not always be so experienced. Only at the very end of his essay does Freud venture an explanation of this curious phenomenon. He does so by comparing two literary texts in which it occurs:

> We asked previously why the severed hand in the "Rhampsenitus's Treasure" does not seem uncanny the way it does in Hauff's "Story of the Severed Hand." . . . The answer is easy

to give. It is that in the former tale we are not focused [*eingestellt*] upon the feelings of the Princess but rather on the superior cunning of the "master thief." The Princess may not have escaped the uncanny feeling, we are even ready to believe that she fainted, but we ourselves feel nothing uncanny since we do not put ourselves in her position but rather in that of the other. (12:267)

The uncanny thus emerges, not as a property of objects or works, themes or motifs, but rather of their *effects*, which in turn depend upon the manner in which they are *positioned* with respect to others and how these others are positioned—in German, Freud's word is *eingestellt*, literally, "placed, accorded, disposed." This sort of reciprocal positioning, however, constitutes an eminently *theatrical* moment, inasmuch as a spectacle can be said to be emphatically theatrical to the extent that it exceeds the narration and representation it contains by presenting them to those others we call "audience," who in fact are as much witnesses as mere spectators or listeners. To the extent that this reciprocal positioning involves the potential recognition of alterity in the recurrence of the same, the uncanny comes into play. To return to the instance cited by Freud: so long as the reader can identify with the "master thief," who seems to be in control, there is no place for the uncanny. This in a certain sense is what happened to Freud himself *after* he had exorcised the uncanny by publishing his essay on it. Psychoanalysis was thus spared further experience of the uncanny, although it is not certain that it has profited from this fact.

Freud's essay, however, suggests that there are other ways in which the encounter with the uncanny can be pursued. One involves precisely the shift we have been discussing, which leads from self-enclosed narrative to the exposure of theater. Theater, in this sense, need be identified neither with tragedy nor even with comedy but rather with *farce*: in German, *Posse*. In a last example I will cite from a text studded with inconclusive and elusive examples, Freud alludes to a well-known piece by the nineteenth-century Austrian playwright Johannes Nepomuk (Nestroy), entitled, hardly by coincidence, *Der Zerrissene* (*The Torn Person*). In the passage quoted by Freud, the main character of the play is on the run because he falsely believes that he has murdered someone: "Suddenly he sees the supposed ghost of his victim rising out of a trap-door whose cover he has just opened, and calls out in despair, 'I only did away with *one*; why this atrocious multiplication?' We know the preconditions of this scene, do not share the error of the 'torn one,' and thus what is uncanny for him is irresistibly comical for us" (12:267).

Nothing less than the tension between the uncanny and the ridiculous delimits the force field alluded to here, which perhaps is—or ought to be—one of the privileged domains of psychoanalysis. It is a field traversed by tales of all sorts, but one that can never be mapped out by them. Which is why it is situated off the beaten track, on the periphery, *abseits*. With respect to this strange field off to the side, tragedy and farce turn out to be two sides of the same play.

11

"The Virtual Reality of Theater": Antonin Artaud

I N A N A G E when the relation of violence to the media has become a widespread concern, the words with which Antonin Artaud introduced his notion of a "theater of cruelty" in the fateful year 1933 acquire a particular resonance:

> The question is to know what we want. If we are prepared for war, plagues, famine, and massacres, we don't even need to say so, all we have to do is carry on. Carry on behaving like snobs, rushing en masse to hear this or that singer, to see this or that admirable show . . . this or that exhibition in which impressive forms burst forth here and there, but at random and without any true conscience of the forces they could stir up. . . .
>
> I am not one of those who believe that civilization has to change in order for theater to change; but I do believe that theater, utilized in the highest and most difficult sense possible, has the power to influence the aspect and formation of things. . . .
>
> That is why I am proposing a theater of cruelty. . . . Not the cruelty we can exercise upon each other by hacking at each other's bodies, carving up our personal anatomies, or, like Assyrian emperors, sending parcels of human ears, noses, or neatly severed nostrils through the mail; but the much more terrible and necessary cruelty which things can exercise against us. We are not free. And the sky can still fall on our heads. And theater has been created to teach us that, first of all.[1]

Artaud's words seem both uncannily appropriate and utterly outmoded. Utterly outmoded in the political and cultural importance he attaches to theater. Uncannily appropriate in his vision of "war, plagues, famine, and massacres" that are the result, not of any special action, but of simply "carrying on" as consumers of "this or that admirable show." Today, where such "carrying on" has itself become the stuff of "reality shows" consumed around the world by TV audiences, the relation between violence, everyday existence, and the media has become all the more obvious—and all the more ominous.

Artaud saw most of this coming. But why, then, should he have proposed, if only for a time, to bring cruelty to the theater? Why bother to theatricalize cruelty rather than just letting it take its course, as indeed it does every day, without requiring any assistance from Antonin Artaud? What claim can this bizarre project of Artaud still make on the attention of those for whom cruelty has become as ordinary, as self-evident, as banal as the evening news? Why bother, then, with a *theater* of cruelty, when cruelty *itself* abounds, offstage as well as on?

> And it will be said that the example calls for the example, that the attitude of healing invites healing and that of murder calls for murder. Everything depends on the way and the purity with which things are done. There is a risk. But it should not be forgotten that if a theatrical gesture is violent, it is also disinterested; and that theater teaches precisely the uselessness of the action which, once accomplished, is never to be done again. (p. 82)

Artaud's defense of a theater of cruelty is not to deny that it *could* incite one to commit the acts it performs. "There is a risk involved, but in the present circumstances I believe it is a risk worth taking" (p. 83). It is here that Artaud's reasoning separates itself from that of apologists for normality: the choice is not between violence and nonviolence, but between different forms and degrees of violence. There will always be a risk involved: the question is which risk is "worth taking." "Everything depends on the way and the purity with which things are done." The "purity" he envisages here is that of a certain instrumentality. Violence on the stage is "pure" in a singular way. Properly performed, namely, *theatrically*, the violent gesture remains *singular.* "Once accomplished," Artaud insists, it can never be identically repeated, above all, not in the world "outside":

> Whatever the conflicts that haunt the heads of an epoch, I defy a spectator whose blood will have been traversed by violent

scenes, who will have felt in himself the passage of a superior
action, who will have seen in extraordinary exploits the extraordinary and essential movements of his thought illuminated as in
a flash. . . . I defy him to abandon himself on the outside to
ideas of war, of revolt, and of dangerous murders. (p. 82)

The spectator of the theater of cruelty envisaged here by Artaud is
one "whose blood will have been traversed by violent scenes." Such
a spectator will have been transformed by what he has witnessed. The
question is: In what way and to what effect? It is curious, symptomatic, and revealing to see how Artaud, to legitimate his notion of
cruelty, is led, here and elsewhere, to appeal to precisely the tradition
he so often attacks: that of an Aristotelian conception of theater. Does
not Artaud's defense of the Theater of Cruelty recall Aristotle's defense of tragedy in terms of *catharsis*, a kind of purgation? Is there not
throughout Artaud's writings on theater an appeal to "action" that
"doubles," as it were, Aristotle's emphasis on tragic mimesis as the
imitation of an *action*, a *praxeōs*? And does not Artaud's emphasis, in
the passages quoted, on a certain pedagogical function of theater also
echo the passages in the *Poetics* in which Aristotle seeks to justify mimesis against its Platonic condemnation by stressing its didactic virtues? Artaud wants his listeners and readers not to forget what theater
above all *teaches*: that we are not free, that the sky can still fall upon
our heads, and, above all, that an action performed on the stage can
never simply be repeated elsewhere.

If theater for Artaud—and not just for him—always involves a
question of "doubles" and of "ghosts," could the Theater of Cruelty
be in some sense haunted by the ghost of Aristotle—the very tradition
against which Artaud rebels? And if this is so, what would it tell us
about the relation of "doubles" and "ghosts" to their "originals," and
hence, about theater as the medium of such duplicity?

It should be remembered, of course, that Artaud—unlike Brecht
for instance—never considered himself primarily "anti-Aristotelian."
Rather, the tradition from which he sought to distance himself was
the modern theatrical tradition that had developed in the West since
the Renaissance, a theater Artaud condemned above all for being
"psychological." This verdict is by no means simply anti-Aristotelian.
In his *Poetics*, Aristotle is unequivocal in insisting that not "character
[*ēthos*]" but rather the action articulated in a narrative plot, a *muthos*,

is the most decisive element in tragedy. It might seem, especially from a contemporary perspective, that it is difficult to speak of *action* without speaking of *actors*. Aristotle, however, insists that the two can and must be separated:

> The greatest of these elements [in tragedy] is the structuring of the incidents. For tragedy is an imitation not of men but of a life, of an action and these . . . include the characters along with the actions for the sake of the latter. Thus the structure of events, the plot is the goal of tragedy, and the goal is the greatest thing of all.
>
> Again, a tragedy cannot exist without a plot, but it can without characters: thus the tragedies of most of our modern poets are devoid of character and in general many poets are like that.[2]

Action can thus do without character but not without plot. With this in mind, we can began to elaborate the manner in which Artaud diverges from the Aristotelian tradition. What is at stake is not simply a question of representation, for Artaud never envisages eliminating or abandoning representation in favor of pure performance (as is evident from his own stagings and proposals for the Théâtre Alfred Jarry). He does insist, however, that the "represented" no longer dominate the practice of theater. This domination, whose theoretical justification goes back to Aristotle, entails two distinct, if interrelated aspects. The first consists in the elevation of "character" and its representation to the predominant theatrical object. Although this focus upon character tends to define post-Reformation theater in the West, it is as alien to Aristotle as to Artaud. The divergence between the two becomes significant only with respect to the second point. It is no accident that Aristotle does not treat theater *as such* in his *Poetics*, but rather only those *forms* of it that he considers most worthy of discussion: in preeminent position, tragedy, and second, comedy. From this choice everything else follows more or less necessarily. Above all, what ensues is the subordination of everything peculiar to theater as a scenic medium to its representational content, which Aristotle identifies, first with a unified action, and then with its narrative representation as plot, *muthos*. Much of Aristotle's discussion of tragedy, therefore, focuses on how effective tragic plots are constructed. Underlying Aristotle's approach to this question is his conception of theatrical mimesis as above all a learning experience, albeit one that proceeds more through feeling, *pathos*, than through conceptual understanding.

We should keep in mind, of course, that Aristotle's discussion of theater in the *Poetics* does not take place in a vacuum but, like much of his thinking, is intended as a response to Plato, in this case to his categorical condemnation of theater and mimesis in the *Republic* and elsewhere. To counteract this verdict, Aristotle in the *Poetics* seeks to defend mimesis by stressing its pedagogical function as an indispensable learning experience, which should be cultivated rather than condemned. This pedagogical bias leads Aristotle to single out tragedy as the most exemplary and worthwhile form of theater.

According to Aristotle, we learn through mimetic behavior and actions. One of these involves the viewing of images. We find it pleasurable to view images that we recognize, he argues. But to *recognize* an image, we must *already know* what it represents. Learning through seeing is an actualization of a knowledge that we already possess, but only virtually. Such actualization consists in an act of judgment that is articulated as a predication: "This one here is a so-and-so." In this act, the encounter with a perceived object becomes pleasurable by permitting the viewer to find the predicates required to subsume the singular manifestation under general concepts.

The construction of plot therefore has to serve this purpose: it must represent the action as a unified and comprehensible whole, with beginning, middle, and end. More specifically, "it must be possible for the beginning and the end to be seen together in one view" (59b). Such synthetic viewing presupposes, however, a certain type of narrative. Artaud singles out this very narrative for criticism:

If people have lost the habit of going to the theater, if we have all finally come to think of theater as an inferior art, as a means of popular distraction, and to use it as an outlet for our worst instincts, . . . it is because for four hundred years, that is, since the Renaissance, we have been accustomed to a theater that is purely descriptive and that recounts psychology. (p. 92)

What Artaud condemns here is, not narrative as such, but the kind of narrative that Aristotle himself rejects: one that subordinates *action* to *character*. Artaud condemns a theater that "recounts psychology," that tells stories whose unity derives from the character of the individual figures involved. But Artaud does not stop there. "Psychology," as he uses the term, does not just designate the state of mind or soul of *individual* human beings or subjects: it goes further, although those readers who have access only to the English translation of *The Theater and Its Double* may have difficulty discerning the direction in which Artaud is moving, for one of Artaud's most powerful formulations is very misleadingly rendered in the published English version. A few lines after the passages just cited, Artaud writes: "If, in Shakespeare, man is sometimes preoccupied with what goes beyond him, *it is always ultimately a question of the consequences of this preoccupation in man, which is to say, [a question of] psychology*" (p. 77, my italics).

As this more literal translation suggests, Artaud criticizes "psychology," not for its individualism, but for its humanism, in the sense of an anthropomorphism that extrapolates from individuals to a general idea of "man," which it then places at the center of the universe, and a fortiori of theater. The English translation, unfortunately, tends to obscure this through a slight but significant error. Instead of translating *l'homme* as "man," it renders it as "a man," and in consequence proceeds to translate the concluding part of the sentence as though it were referring to an individual person or character rather than to "man" in general. Here is the published translation: "If, in Shakespeare, *a man* is sometimes preoccupied with what transcends him, it is always in order to determine the ultimate consequences of this preoccupation *within him*, i.e. psychology" (p. 77, my italics).

What the translation resists here is a critique of psychology directed not just against a form of individualism but against humanism more generally. "Theater" and "cruelty" for Artaud are both inseparably linked with what he at various times refers to as the "inhuman": the "rigor" and "necessity" that he constantly associates with "cruelty" suggest that the forces at work in it cannot be measured in terms of the distinctive traits of modern man: above all, those of self-consciousness, freedom, and autonomy.

All theatrical movements—so the gist of Artaud's critique here— that carry the human subject beyond itself, even in Shakespeare, are ultimately recuperated and resituated once their effects are measured in terms of human beings. That is what "psychology" is all about: it is ultimately concerned, not with individuals, but with making "man" and his consciousness the measure of all things, in particular, the measure of all theater.

It is not, therefore, the theatrical use of narrative elements as such that concerns Artaud, but the dominance of an anthropologically an-chored and teleologically oriented type of storytelling. Why? As long as "man" is essentialized and privileged, the cosmos in which he dwells can be assumed to have a certain stability. With man at the center of the universe, the sky's the limit. But if man can no longer be assumed to provide the governing principle of life and of death, of being and nonbeing, then there is no assurance that the sky will stay put. It "can still fall on our heads," on the part of our bodies com-monly identified with the seat of the distinctive faculty of man: the capacity for reason and self-consciousness, the capacity to know, to learn, and to teach.

"The sky can still fall on our heads"—why should Artaud resort to this formulation to describe what he is after in the notion "theater of cruelty"? It may help to recall once again Aristotle's insistence that a tragic plot should be capable of being "taken in at a single view" (51a).[3] The unity of such a "view" presupposes a stable and detachable *point* of view, a fixed position from which the plot can be taken in as a unified whole. This in turn presupposes a certain arrangement of space: a clear-cut separation, for instance, between stage and audience, actors and spectators. Artaud challenges this stable partitioning of space and the kind of localization it makes possible, thereby continu-ing a tradition that goes back at least to Nietzsche's *Birth of Tragedy* and Kierkegaard's *Repetition*. This emerging conception of a space that is irreducibly theatrical breaks with a tradition that originates not in the Renaissance but in Aristotle's *Poetics*. In reducing theater to trag-edy and comedy, Aristotle's instrumentalization of everything having to do with the scenic medium—*opsis*—includes space and place, local-ization and lighting, and everything connected with *bodies*, masks, and the stage. All of this is considered the mere material conditions of what Aristotle holds to be essential to theater: namely, its representation of action through plot. Through their narrative arrangement in a plot, events and actions are brought together to form a meaningful and intelligible whole.

Precisely such unity, however, is what Artaud's Theater of Cruelty calls into question: unity of meaning, of action, of the subject, and, above all, of time, space, and *place*. This last point is perhaps decisive. What is both explicit and massive in Aristotle's *Poetics*, as well as in the theatrical tradition informed by it, is that everything having to do with the specificity of the theatrical medium, with the *opsis* that Aristotle sought to treat as a mere technical and material accessory, is relegated to instrumental status. *Plot, character, ideas*—their hierarchical sequence may be varied, but these three factors persist in dictating the conception and performance of theater even (and perhaps especially) today. Artaud was not the first to protest against this tradition or to note how it has, effectively, reduced and delegitimized the distinctive resources of theater. But the manner in which he interpreted those resources remains not just unique, but in certain aspects prophetic.

It is here and not in the possibility of *actually realizing* a theater of cruelty on the stage, that the relevance of Artaud's theatrical writings is to be sought. In other words, the *actuality* of the Theater of Cruelty lies not in its practical feasibility but in its *coupling of violence with vituality*—which is to say, in its relation to the future as *risk*. This future can never be risk free. The Theater of Cruelty assumes the risk of this future in a way that not only anticipates but also alters the conception of what today is called "vituality." And in so doing, it has implications for all of the new media that define themselves with reference to this term.

What is "virtualization"? Obviously the term is elusive, and there are many ways of defining it. I will begin by taking one definition that strikes me as particularly symptomatic, if by no means exhaustive, of contemporary usages of the term. It is to be found in a book by Pierre Lévy, entitled *Sur les chemins du virtuel* (*On the Paths of the Virtual*, 1995), whose French text is available for downloading on the Internet.[4] In this book Lévy offers the following approach to the question of virtualization:

> What is virtualization? Not the virtual as a manner of being, but virtualization as a dynamic? Virtualization can be defined as the inverse movement of actualization. It consists in a passage from the actual to the virtual, in an "elevation to potentiality" of the entity under consideration. Virtualization is not derealization (the transformation of a reality into a complex of possibilities), but rather a change of identity, a displacement of the center of ontological gravity of the object being considered: instead of being defined principally by its actuality (as a "solution"), the entity henceforth finds its essential consistency in a problematic field. To virtualize an entity is to discover a general question to which it refers, to transform the entity in the direction of this

interrogation and to redefine the initial actuality as the response to a particular question. (Virt1.htm, 3/8)

"Detachment from the here and now" (4/8), which is another way Lévy characterizes virtualization, is of course in itself nothing new. Indeed, it continues what could be called the "metaphysical" or idealist tendency that has dominated Western thought ever since Plato. And the "dialogical" model of "question" and "answer" invoked by Lévy to define the notion of virtualization also has its origins in the Socratic dialectic, which could be described as an effort to "virtualize" the certitudes that are "actually" taken for granted and thus to reveal problems and questions where before there seemed only self-evident solutions. I emphasize this continuity between the Socratic dialectic and Lévy's definition of virtualization as problematization in order to suggest that Artaud's rejection of the notion of dialogue as an essential element of theater puts him at odds with that tradition. The interpretation of theater as essentially *dialogical* was one of the mechanisms by which Artaud considered Western theater to have been deprived of its specific resources:

> How does it happen that in the theater, at least in the theater as we know it in Europe or, better, in the West, everything specifically theatrical, that is, everything that cannot be expressed in speech, in words, or, if you prefer, everything that is not contained in the dialogue . . . is left in the background? How does it happen that the Occidental theater does not see theater under any other aspect than as a theater of dialogue?
>
> Dialogue—a thing written and spoken—does not belong specifically to the stage, it belongs to books. (p. 37)

Dialogue, as an exchange of questions and answers, is anchored in *meaning*. Meaning, however, at least as traditionally conceived, is considered to be independent of space and of place. Meaning is assumed to *stay the same* no matter *where and when* it occurs. This conception denies the relevance of precisely the factors that Artaud considers specific to theater: "I say that the stage is a concrete physical place that asks to be filled, and to be given its own concrete language to speak" (p. 37).

Despite his attack on verbal discourse, Artaud never dreams of excluding language as such from theater, but rather of restoring its capacity to signify, in short, its *virtuality*. To do this, the tyranny of *meaning* must be supplanted by a language of *signification*: a language, above all, of gesture, intonation, attitude, and movement, but without a recognizable or identifiable "goal." The absence of such a goal would allow the movement of language, its signifying force, to come into its own without being subordinated to a purpose. The incidence of such a language of signification would be inseparable from its location in time and space. At the same time, that location can never be stabilized once and for all. The performance of a gesture on the stage thus remains tied to a *singular* situation. This is why the most concrete manifestation of such a language would be not expression but rather a more or less *violent interruption*. To remain singular, gestures, sounds, or movements must interrupt themselves on the way to fruition. It is as if Artaud sought to separate what Aristotle strove to hold together: *peripeteia* and *anagnōrisis*, fear and pity, emotion and feeling, discharge and purgation, theater and drama, tragedy and the totalizing idea of the hero. The hero stands for the human, and the "human" imposes meaning on all things. If the "goal," as Aristotle states, is "the greatest thing of all," then "man" names the actualization of that greatness, of that "all." "Man" names the being that claims the right to set its own goals, to set goals for all other beings, for being as a whole. Artaud's innovative turn seeks to dehumanize the notion of *peripeteia* and thereby to turn it against its mythological origins. The greatest of myths, in this sense, is that which goes under the name of "man," and Artaud singles out this myth as the greatest obstacle to theater. Against it he seeks to mobilize a certain notion of "things":

> A moment ago I mentioned danger. The best way, it seems to me, to realize this idea of danger on the stage is through the objective unforeseen, the unforeseen not in situations but in things, the abrupt, untimely transition from a thought image to a true image. . . . An example would be the appearance of an invented Being, made of wood and cloth, entirely pieced together [*crée de toutes pièces*], corresponding to nothing [literally: answering to nothing, *ne répondant à rien*], and yet disquieting by nature, capable of reintroducing on the stage a whiff of that great metaphysical fear that is at the root of all ancient theater. (p. 44)

This "invented Being" appears to be a close relative of Kafka's Odradek, from the short text "Cares of a Housefather,"[5] which is theatrical in the same way. Unable to discern in Odradek any sign either of a purpose, *Zweck*, or of its absence, the Housefather is puzzled: "The whole thing looks senseless enough, it is true, but in its way perfectly finished" (p. 160). One never knows where and when one is going to stumble upon Odradek, who has "no fixed residence" and hangs out on the periphery of domestic living space: stairways, halls, attic, cellar. But what really worries the Housefather is that this strange thing may well turn out to outlive him, his children, and even theirs. Things can survive where humans can't. But are they still alive? Were they ever? Where "things" are concerned, life and death are not easy to distinguish. "He does no harm to anyone," concludes the Housefather, "but the idea that he is likely to survive me I find almost painful" (p. 161).[6]

Could the determination of the "goal" as "the greatest *thing* of all" be plausibly interpreted as an effort to avoid such pain? Would what we call *meaning* name yet another such effort? And would the idea of a transparent, cohesive, and coherent narrative mark an attempt to avoid "that great metaphysical fear" in which Artaud saw the primary resource of his Theater of Cruelty, which was also a theater of doubles and of ghosts? For the Theater of Cruelty, not the "goal" of "meaning" or the mythically self-contained plot is "the greatest thing of all," but rather the "great metaphysical fear" itself. And yet, how could such a fear avoid in turn becoming a goal? The goal of the Theater of Cruelty, for instance? Only, perhaps, by being mindful of the singular virtuality of theater, which prevents it from being identically repeatable, generalizable, theorizable, and perhaps even realizable.

This is why such issues cannot, for Artaud, be discussed in abstraction from their scenic singularity. It can also explain why some of the most powerfully *theatrical* articulations in his writing were not written "for" theater, in the sense of "drama" or even "stage." One such instance is his celebrated essay on "The Theater and the Plague." Neither purely theoretical nor purely theatrical, this text demonstrates forcefully what Artaud elsewhere, in "The Alchemical Theater," calls "the virtual reality of theater" (p. 49).

In "The Theater and the Plague," first delivered in April 1933 at the Sorbonne, Artaud recounts the spread of bubonic plague in Marseille in 1720. After a brief discussion of plagues and their possible etiologies, Artaud describes the stages through which the plague passes as it spreads throughout the city. We encounter here an allegory of the origin of theater, which ever since the Thebes of *Oedipus Tyrannos* has been associated with the plague. In Artaud's account the pestilence spreads throughout the city of Marseille in four phases or stages. These mark what can be called a violent *theatricalization* of the *stage* (temporal as well as spatial). As we shall see, this *theatricalization* also involves a kind of *virtualization*, although one that contrasts in certain decisive aspects with virtualization as it is generally understood and practiced today. Let us begin by retracing Artaud's account of the four stages of the plague.

First, as the plague takes hold in the city, there is a progressive collapse of all normal institutions and services, a dissolution of what Artaud in French calls *les cadres réguliers*, the "regular frameworks" that define and maintain social space and time in periods of normalcy: "Once the plague is established in a city, the regular frameworks collapse; maintenance of roads and sewers ceases; army, police, municipality disappear; pyres are lit with whatever arms are available in order to burn the dead. Each family wants to have its own" (p. 23).

Note here how the institution of the family emerges as a response to the crisis, attempting as it were to shore up the social polity on the brink of collapse. But what form does this take? Artaud tells us quite precisely: "Each family wants to have its own"—its own pyre, in this case. Which is to say, each family seeks to maintain or assert its *property rights* with respect to the dead: if not to bury them, then at least to burn them. Although the scourge afflicts everyone collectively, "each family" still "wants to have its own." This type of response is not entirely unfamiliar to us today. But this resurgence of "family values" is soon caught up in the very crisis that brought it forth:

> Each family wants to have its own. Then, with wood, places, and even flames growing rare, family feuds break out around the pyres, soon followed by a general flight, for the corpses have grown too numerous. Already the dead clog the streets, forming crumbling pyramids whose fringes are gnawed at by animals. The stench rises into the air like a flame. Whole streets are blocked by heaps of the dead. (Ibid.)

The orderly, organized space of the city disintegrates, and families contribute to the chaos in their struggle to preserve a minimum of property and propriety—"Each family wants its own." Each succeeds, but not as planned. Each family gets its "own," but what it gets is its own death and disintegration, which rapidly sweep away all possibility of ownership. The first and most significant sign of this disassociation is the *blockage* of the avenues of communication. As a result, habitual movements are no longer are possible. In their stead, a new kind of movement and communication breaks out, and with it, a new arrangement of space and time. This new arrangement ushers in the second stage of the plague:

> Whole streets are blocked by heaps of the dead. At that very moment the houses open up and delirious plague-ridden victims, their minds overwhelmed with hideous visions, stream forth screaming into the streets. The disease [note that Artaud uses a French word here which means not just "disease" but also "evil" and "pain": *le mal*] at work in their guts, spreading throughout their organism, liberates itself in explosions of the spirit. Other plague victims, lacking all bubos, delirium, pain, and rash, proudly observe themselves in the mirror, bursting with health, before falling dead [on the spot], their shaving mugs *still* in their hands, full of scorn for the other victims. (My italics)

This second stage is marked by the implosion of the closed space of domesticity, with houses and homes breaking down and forcing their inhabitants to flee into a space that is no longer either public or private. The orderly, goal-directed movements of organized social life are progressively supplanted by the pointless gestures and explosive spasms of those whose bodies and being have become the staging ground of the plague. What breaks down here is the last vestige of self-control, the faculty of self-consciousness itself. Those who have no visible, outward signs of the plague, and "who, feeling themselves bursting with health [*se sentant crever de santé*]," "burst" indeed, but not with health. Here the *peripeteia* does not interrupt an action or an intention, as envisaged by Aristotle, but rather self-consciousness itself. The abrupt and unexpected turn of events imposes a different temporality: that of the belated reaction. Consciousness cannot keep up with the plague and its effects. People congratulate themselves on having escaped, then drop dead, *still* "full of scorn for the other victims." This belated temporality drives a wedge into the visible. The scene, for all its horror, moves away from drama and tragedy toward comedy and, perhaps even more, toward *farce*. Not only is the consciousness of the characters increasingly inadequate to the situation, the very idea of action, of a plot, begins to disappear. There are acts and agitation, but no unified action: agents, but with no one in command. The lack of visible signs of the plague becomes an invisible sign of its power. Visibility loses all transparency and reflexivity all reliability. The stage is set for what will be the final *coup de théâtre*. But before it can strike, one last desperate effort is undertaken to ward it off. This effort, which brings us to the third stage of the plague, marks the emergence of a certain theatricality:

> Over the poisonous, thick, bloody streams, colored by anxiety and opium, which gush from the corpses, strange figures dressed in wax, with noses long as rods, eyes of glass, mounted on a kind of Japanese sandal composed of double wooden tablets, the one horizontal in the form of a sole, the other vertical, isolating them from infected fluids, pass by chanting absurd litanies whose virtues do not prevent them from sinking into the flames in turn. Such ignorant doctors display only their fear and their puerility. (pp. 23–24)

Such carnivalesque figures, marking the desperate resort to "specialists" to avert the catastrophe, appear in this third stage as a parody of the order they seek to maintain. With their disappearance, however, the last vestiges of propriety, and of property, are condemned. This ushers in the fourth and final stage of the plague, that of the *installation of theater*:

> Into the opened houses enter the dregs of the population, immunized, it seems, by their frenzied greed, laying hands on riches from which they sense it will be useless to profit. It is at that very moment that theater installs itself [*que le théâtre s'installe*]. Theater, which is to say, the immediate gratuitousness that imposes acts that are useless and without profit for actuality. (p. 24).

Acting without actualizing itself, here the *nonperformative* Theater of Cruelty "installs itself," takes its place, as a reality that is irreducibly *virtual*, but in a way that is quite different from the virtualization with which we today are increasingly familiar. However widespread and ubiquitous its effects, virtualization today is almost always and everywhere construed and undertaken from the perspective of *actuality*. Even Lévy, who draws much of his inspiration from Deleuze's seminal discussion of virtuality in *Repetition and Difference*, links virtuality inescapably, if negatively, to actuality. As we have seen, he defines virtualization as a process of de-actualization, which is to say, as an inverted mode of making actual, transforming into acts. In the Theater of Cruelty, by contrast, action can never be measured, either positively or negatively, in terms of actuality. Virtualization, as a defining characteristic of the plague, no longer has any *goal* whatsoever—neither the greatest nor the smallest. On the contrary: what it attacks is not actualization as such, but its specifically modern condition of possibility: *appropriability*. The virtualization that takes place today, in the media and elsewhere, cannot be separated from the economic dictates of what is called *globalization*, which in turn is tied to a very definite, if problematic, goal: that of the *maximization of profit*. Profit, however, entails not just the production of "value" in general, but of value that is *appropriable*. Capital therefore continues to impose its goal upon virtualization, which by and large is permitted to develop only insofar as it serves this particular end.

Artaud's virtual Theater of Cruelty explicitly challenges this goal or *telos*—that of profit and appropriation, in all senses. This is why it is a serious mistake to render, as the published English translation does, the key phrase in this fourth and final stage of the plague, which describes the emergence of theater, as its "birth": "And at that moment the theater is born" (p. 24). Although here as elsewhere Artaud is enormously indebted to the author of *The Birth of Tragedy*, the Theater of Cruelty is still not *born*, not even *stillborn*, if by "birth" is meant the coming into a world of something that was previously absent from it. Theater, like the plague, does not have to *come* into the world: it is always already *there*, albeit often in a dormant manner. Its time is not the linear time of narrative, of plot, of beginning, middle, and end, of before and after. Nor is the time of theater that of production. Theater is not *made*, if by "making" is meant a process of conscious and deliberate construction governed by a design, a plan, an idea or a goal. Least of all is theater *created*, in the sense of a *creatio ex nihilo*. Artaud, as always in decisive moments such as these, is extremely precise in his choice of words. He chooses those whose power over the theater could be dislodged only through a precision that cuts into the specious self-evidence of conventional meaning. What Artaud writes in French to describe the emergence of theater, is that "c'est alors que le théâtre s'installe": it is then, at that moment, "that theater *installs* itself," *takes* its place. To "install oneself," however, is to *take* a place that is *already there*, to occupy it, indeed, to *expropriate* it and, in the process, to *transform* it and oneself as well.[7] That is precisely what theater does when it turns the site into a scene, the place into a stage, and this alteration and expropriation is what makes it *cruel*. What is cruel is the movement of dispossession that is not for profit. A place is robbed of its apparent unity, meaning, propriety. Houses are demolished, the barrier between inside and outside, domesticity and politics, private and public breaks down, just as Artaud envisaged eliminating the partition in theaters between the stage and the audience or, more generally, between the theater and its other. The Theater of Cruelty was to take place in barns and hangars as well as in established "theaters." The audience was to be placed at the center of the theatrical space, but on movable seats, so as to be able to follow a spectacle that was to exploit *all* the dimensions of space, not just that positioned "in front" of the public. The *Vor-stellung*, the German word that signifies both theatrical performance and mental representation, would no longer serve as an alibi by which subjects could hope to exonerate themselves and escape from their involvement in what was necessarily a violation of all constituted legality. The space of the theater would not just be "outside" or "inside"—it would take hold of the border between the two, which is to say, the *body*, whether of humans or of things, and turn it into a *stage* for unheard-of reversals, where sound becomes silence, fluids freeze, and matter is hollowed out.

The "gratuitousness" of the theatrical act, then, is inseparable from the rule of law, which it must presuppose in order to violate, although Artaud always understood the violation to be, paradoxically, prior to any inviolate identity. What it is *not* prior to, by contrast, is some degree of *organization*—organized, delimited spaces: those of domesticity, of propriety, but also of the *polis*, whether as city, state, nation, or even cosmos. At the same time, however, Artaud never left any doubt that the expropriating effects of theater are and must remain violently *virtual*, for it involves a virtuality that does violence to itself: installed on the stage, it is both *here and now* and yet also *there and then*. By being both, it is also neither. Its purity is thus inseparable from the miasma, the plague, the impure: its life inseparable from its death. This is perhaps why such theatricality could never form the programmatic basis for any institutionalized theater. Its spectral virtuality cannot be reduced to any actuality, including that of theater itself. Nor can it be appropriated by any essence, including, first and foremost, that of "man." Not just the idea of man but "his" appearance has long served to justify the possibility of and right to such appropriation. The dismantling of this image of self-containment and of self-contentment forms the primary action of the plague and makes it a powerful allegory of theater—on the condition, however, that we not forget that the plague, and theater, only unleash forces that are *already there*, ready and waiting, if temporarily immobilized:

> The plague takes images that are dormant, a latent disorder, and suddenly pushes them to become the most extreme gestures; and theater also takes gestures and pushes them to the limit: like the plague it reforges the chain between what is and what is not, between the virtuality of the possible and what exists materialized in nature. It recovers . . . all the conflicts that sleep in us, restoring them to us with their forces and giving these forces names that we salute as symbols: and behold, before our eyes a battle of symbols takes place. (p. 37)

The self-containment of the "image" is thus literally pushed to the extreme, where it suddenly reveals itself to be in touch with the other, with what it is not, with the outside. In place of the self-contained image, representing its "content," is revealed the process by which that content was contained: through the arresting of signification as a process that always points elsewhere. This is why the image driven to the "extreme" becomes *gesture*: The gesture points *away*—not, however, toward a goal, the goal that Aristotle called "the greatest thing of all." The goal as end and as purpose has been supplanted by the extreme as enabling limit, though a limit that also disables. At this limit, the limit of gesture and gesticulation, where gesture shades into spasm, stutter, and tic, the Theater of Cruelty *takes place*. But the place it takes can never be fully its own. It must always belong to *another*. This is why its taking place must be conflictual, and why a certain violence and violation are inseparable from the Theater of Cruelty. It is *peripeteia* without end or goal, and therefore produces a theater that must remain virtual.

This is why the "place" or "stage" of the Theater of Cruelty can never be simple or straightforward. It must always be a place of a *singular duplicity*, as in Nietzsche's *The Birth of Tragedy*, which begins

by explicitly asserting the "duplicity [*Duplizität*]," of the great antago-
nistic forces, the Dionysian and the Apollonian, whose struggle it will
then unfold. This Nietzschean *duplicity* foreshadows the "doubles"
and "ghosts" that haunt the Theater of Cruelty. The double and its
shadows replace and supplant the "heroes" of dramatic theater. They
are virtual heroes of a stage that is split and doubled, whose space
Artaud, near the end of his lecture, describes as an "essential separation": "The theater, like the plague, is in the image of this carnage
and this essential separation. It releases conflicts, disengages powers,
unleashes possibilities, and if these possibilities and these forces are
black, it is the fault not of the plague or of the theater but of life"
(p. 31).

Virtualization, then, is not simply de-actualization but "separation." If the theater, like the plague, plays on forces that are already
"there," that is because of this "essential separation" or *separability* of
place "itself." Place as separable is the *stage*. However defined its borders may be, they must still remain in contact with what they exclude
and yet presuppose. Such contact may be temporarily forgotten, excluded from consciousness, but its effects do not disappear. Separation,
in short, does not *dissolve* the relation to the other or to the outside,
nor does it reduce the other to a goal or purpose that would complete
a story and make it intelligible. Rather, separation *communicates* with
that from which it distances itself, even if that communication has to
be "delirious," Artaud's word for describing the spread of the plague
(p. 33).

We can try to ignore such delirium, confine it, shore up the borders
that seem to separate us from it, try to purify and protect our cities
and states by excluding all communication with everything alien. We
can try to forget Artaud's wild warnings and dream of "homeland
security." We can, in short, carry on as we have been doing, label our
fears "terror," and declare war against it. We can do all this, yet violence will still take care of itself—which means, of *us*. Or we can try
to remember that neither violence nor cruelty begins or ends with
Antonin Artaud, who, by placing this word at the center of his discourse on theater, took a risk for which he paid dearly, but one he
thought had to be taken, "in the actual circumstances" (p. 99).

Are those circumstances any less "actual" today?

12

Double Take:
Acting and Writing in Genet's "The Strange Word 'Urb'"

Acting

> In fact, some authorities maintain that that is why plays are called dramas, because the imitation is of men acting [*drōntas*, from *drān*, "do, act"). It is also the reason why both tragedy and comedy are claimed by the Dorians: comedy by the Megarians. . . . They use the names *comedy* and *drama* as evidence; for they say that they call their outlying villages *kōmai* whereas the Athenians call theirs *demes* [*dēmoi*]—the assumption being that the participants in comedy were called *kōmōidoi*, not from their being revelers, but because they wandered from one village to another, being degraded and excluded from the city—and that they call "doing" or "acting" *drān* whereas the Athenians designate it *prattein*.[1]

W H A T   H A S traditionally been called "theater" seems to be in a curious situation today. On the one hand, the emergence of electronically powered techniques of articulation and of transmission appears increasingly to marginalize theater. Insofar as it is considered to be a medium of representation, theater is at an increasing disadvantage with regard to the electronic media. Anything it can represent, film and television can show better, more vividly, more extensively, it would seem. On the other hand, despite such competing media and despite large-scale reductions in government subsidies, theater in its traditional institutional forms persists and in certain areas even flourishes, at least in terms of its ability to attract audiences. Music theater, for instance, whether "musical comedy" or "opera," continues to enjoy considerable popularity, often teaming up with the media to reach audiences that would otherwise remain inaccessible.

The situation is complicated by the very different situations that obtain in different parts of the world. Without even considering the situation of theaters in non-Western countries, sharply divergent tendencies can be observed in countries such as the United States and Germany. In Germany, the extensive network of state-supported theaters, which formerly enjoyed wide access to television, has in recent years been increasingly excluded from the media. Operas, for instance, are no longer broadcast by either of the two national networks, but instead are relegated to regional "third programs." At the same time, despite severe cutbacks, German and French theaters still enjoy state subsidies that would be the envy of their American counterparts. (Of course, there are few American counterparts, in the sense of repertory companies, precisely because of the lack of such subsidies).

The situation is even more complex when one recognizes that the word *theater* is also used in areas that at first sight seem to have little to do with the term's most familiar meaning. A "theater" is not only a place where plays or spectacles are performed: it can also designate a space of action in general, and of hostilities in particular, as in a military "theater of operations." Like dramatic theater, the "theater of operations" designates a space not just of action but also of conflict. Moreover, one of the primary "themes" of classical theater, death, is also a determining factor in military theaters, as well. Finally, as the political and strategic significance of military conflicts becomes increasingly tied to the media, the element of spectacle—or, rather, the presentation of phenomena to a more or less public view—becomes difficult to separate from the purely military dimension of conflict. In this sense, military theaters have also become increasingly spectacular in a traditionally theatrical sense. Given the struggle for subsidies and the highly competitive situation in which drama theaters are forced to operate, their organization, for its part, is becoming increasingly "military" in turn.

Finally, at least one other instance of "theater" is worth mentioning in this context, as much for its differences from the foregoing as for its similarities: what is called "home theater." In "home theater" the entertainment-electronics industry has assembled sets of video, audio, and television equipment designed to reproduce the effects of the movie "theater" within the more restricted space of one's living room or den. With this move—and it remains to be seen just how successful or lasting it will be—theater loses the "public" quality that has distinguished it as the most social of all arts ever since its origins in ancient

Greece. In "home theater" another quality that distinguished theater from the other arts is also lost, or at least radically transformed: its relation to *bodies*. To be sure, the bodies involved were not always or entirely *human* bodies: they could be inanimate bodies—puppets or marionettes, for instance, or even shadows cast on a screen. But a certain assemblage of bodies: whether of actors, puppets, musicians, or spectators, *all sharing the same space*, has always set theater apart from the other arts, such as painting, sculpture, literature, architecture, and music, which could be performed before isolated audiences and in which the mimetic medium did not require the simultaneous presence of actor and audience.

In the electronic audiovisual media of "home theater," by contrast, no such co-presence is either required or possible. Yet "home theater" can be seen as continuing another distinctive feature of theater, the one associated with its etymology, *thea*, *theatron*, the *site* of a *sight*, because "home theater" defines a space in which sights are brought home to a spectator. The space is certainly neither public nor open: it is a contained, interior space with restricted access. Being a "citizen" will hardly be sufficient to gain admission. But neither restricted access to its space nor the quality of the visible as such distinguishes "home theater" from its less domestic predecessors.[2] Rather, what is decisive is the specific configuration of *bodies* and *space*. What sets "home theater" apart from previous dramatic theater are two effects of the electronic media upon which it relies: those of *decorporealization* and *delocalization*. Electricity has no body and knows no locale. In the ideal "home theater," which is often heir to the Bauhaus and Art Deco dreams of a functionalist interior design, the television set and screen ideally disappear into the wall, where they metamorphose into an electronic window that looks not simply outward but inward and at the same time *away*, somewhere else.

This convergence of theater and television, in particular, its effects in disrupting the clear-cut opposition between public and private space, fascinated Genet. In *The Balcony*, for instance, which is set in a brothel, Madame Irma keeps tabs on the goings-on in the different rooms by means of an elaborate system of televisual surveillance, an earlier version of "home video," which, despite its name, includes audio as well. In contrast to the fantasy of being master of one's private space, the studios in *The Balcony* are subordinated to the view of a mistress who knows there is no final mastery, only a constant struggle for control. In its studios, fantasies of mastery and control are played out, but are also controlled and surveyed by means of the television camera, which permits rapid intervention when required.

The Balcony is, as has often been noted, a play about role-playing, theater that reflects on theatricality and reflects it theatrically. "Theatrically" as just used suggests exaggeration, an excess of gesture over signification, of appearance over being. This is one of the reasons why "theater" and "theatricality" have always been regarded with suspicion by guardians of public morals and of political order, from Plato on. Such suspicion, of course, was in turn predicated upon the grudging recognition that the tremendous power of theater could not simply be condemned but would have to be controlled and appropriated by any order that hoped to maintain its stability.

It is this subversive potentiality of theater that interests Genet, and not merely in his writings for the stage. His writing in general, whether explicitly for the stage or not, is per se theatrical, and not just in the sense of being excessive or provocative. His writing is theatrical in a more precise sense that goes back to Aristotle's emphasis on the importance of *peripeteia* in tragedy: that is, of the sudden, unexpected turn of events that interrupts an expectation and gives the material of tragedy, "action [*praxis*]," and its form, that of "plot [*muthos*]" a distinctively theatrical bent.

For Aristotle *peripeteia* consists, not just in a sudden shift of events or in consciousness, but in the supplanting of an erroneous expectation by a more accurate one or, as he puts it, "a shift from ignorance to awareness" (52a). This shift he calls *anagnōrisis*, "recognition." It is not the product of a gradual process of learning but rather consists in a sudden shock: that of recognizing that what one had expected, intended, anticipated does not correspond with what actually has happened.

The English word *recognition* thus tends to gloss over or at least to minimize what is most powerfully at work in *peripeteia* and *anagnōrisis*: the shock of a *double-take*, defined in the 1989 edition of the *O.E.D.* as:

A delayed reaction to a situation, sight of a person, etc. rapidly following an earlier, inappropriate reaction; esp. a procedure in comedy, etc., in which an actor at first reacts unexpectedly or inappropriately to a given situation and then, as if more fully realizing the implications, reacts in an expected or more usual manner. Also, a second, often more detailed, look. Hence double-take, v. intr., to act in such a manner.

Of course, the comic and gestural connotations of the double-take go far beyond such a definition and thus also beyond the immediate implications of Aristotle's theory of *peripeteia* and *anagnōrisis*. Both the notion and the practice of the double-take include an element of self-parody—the implicit suggestion that, having "missed" the point previously, one has no guarantee that this time one is "getting" it right—which would undercut the pedagogical value Aristotle (and much of the theatrical theory and practice that followed) sought to attribute to theater.

Nevertheless, what the Aristotelian emphasis on *peripeteia* shares with the theatricality of Genet's writing, and in particular with his writings on theater—and the juxtaposition of *anagnōrisis* with the self-parodic *double-take* points us in this direction—is a concern with the *spatial*, and in particular *scenic* dimension of theater. To be sure, as we have seen, Aristotle does everything in his *Poetics* to reduce or marginalize whatever might be considered to be specific to the *medium* of theater: spatiality, materiality, visibility—everything having to do with *opsis*, translated, symptomatically enough, by Else as "visual adornment" or "visual effect" (p. 29) whereas Stephen Halliwell, following Ingram Bywater prefers "spectacle" (1450b).[3] Aristotle performs this reduction through two interrelated moves: first, by considering theater primarily as the genre of tragedy (secondarily as that of comedy); and second, by defining this genre as the imitation of an *action*. He thereby reduces the specifically spatial and scenic aspects of theater to the status of mere material accessories and instruments employed to represent something that bears no necessary relation to theater as such, namely, action.[4] Insofar as Aristotle considers the specificity of theater at all, it is strictly identified with the transformation of action into plot. But plot, too, bears no necessary structural relation to the medium of theater as such. This Aristotelian approach to theater, construed in terms of objects and structures that are not themselves specifically theatrical, pervades the Western approach to theater, which initially privileges action and then, increasingly in the modern period, character.[5]

And yet the emphasis Aristotle places upon *peripeteia* and *anagnōrisis* as constituting the decisive qualities of the tragic plot indicates—even against the most explicit intentions of his argument—that "spatial" elements continue to occupy a decisive if concealed place in his thinking about theater, even though he subordinates theater to tragedy and tragedy to action. What do the "brutal arbitrariness and finality" of the "tragic *happening*," as Else puts it,[6] entail if not the interruption of the temporal continuum of conscious intention by something unexpected, something that does not *fit in*—that can not be encompassed, comprehended, *contained* within the preexisting horizon or perspective, whatever these may be? What doesn't fit in, however, *stands out* precisely as a kind of *spatiality*: it makes us aware that our previous frame of reference, the configuration of concepts that we take for granted in perceiving and thinking, our familiar grid, fails *to situate* what is taking place before our very eyes, as it were. The shock that ensues entails, not the elimination of time by space, but the transformation of the way each is construed: space no longer appears to be self-contained, time no longer to be totalizing. Not by accident does Else, in the phrase just quoted, speak of the "particularity" of the tragic *happening* rather than simply of an event or an action, for the gerund here seems best suited to designate the ongoing, open-ended temporality of that which, despite or because of its very proximity, comes as an utter surprise, creating the sense both of wonder and of recognition that marks and divides the double-take.[7]

Although the aim of Aristotle's discussion of *peripeteia* and *anagnōrisis* is clearly to reestablish order and unity in the face of unresolved conflict, his positioning of the unexpected and the unpredictable at the heart of tragic *muthos* indicates just how much the tension between spatial dislocation and scenic reframing remains at the heart of his discussion of theater, despite its being construed primarily as a temporal medium for the sequential representation of meaningful action.

Thus even in Aristotle theater seems inconceivable without a shock that fractures the established grids upon which perception and interpretation depend. Theater, in short, entails not just *space* but, more precisely, its disruption and rearrangement. In other words, *theatricality emerges where space and place can no longer be taken for granted or regarded as self-contained.*

Writing

These allegations of the "Dorians" are neither true nor to the point. "Comedy" is from *kōmos*, "revel," an Attic word, not from *kōmē*, "village," and *drān* is not an exclusively Doric word (it is true that *prattein* is Ionic and Attic).[8]

If Genet's writing is often theatrical, it is so in a sense that both exacerbates and transforms an insight already at work in Aristotle's *Poetics*, albeit, as we have seen, in a highly conflicted manner: an insight into the *disruptive spatiality* of the theatrical. No text of Genet stages such disruptions more powerfully than the short essay published in *Tel Quel* in 1966 and entitled "L'Étrange Mot d' . . ." (translated into English as "The Strange Word *Urb* . . . "). This text, which repeatedly addresses an anonymous addressee (*vous*), resembles in this respect the roughly contemporaneous *Letters to Roger Blin*, written by Genet to the director of the first Paris staging of *The Screens* during the months of rehearsals. Nevertheless, despite this stylistic connection between the two texts, the reasons why Genet decided to publish "The strange word *Urb* . . . " separately seem fairly evident.[9] The text deals with theater, but in a general way, without any explicit reference to *The Screens* or to any other play. Instead, it touches on a number of matters, many of which would seem at first sight to have little to do with theater. These issues, however, turn out to revolve around nothing other than the very dimension of theater that the Aristotelian *Poetics* and the tradition it informs seek to efface: its *spatiality*. Genet's text suggests just why he has felt obliged to downplay everything connected with theater as a spatial, material, even corporeal ritual: The corporeality and materiality that characterize theatrical space involve the relation of society to death—more precisely, to *the dead*. Just as Artaud—to whom Genet here as elsewhere is profoundly indebted, although he does not mention him—in his lecture "The Theater and the Plague" transforms the human body dying of the plague into an extraordinary scene of theatrical *peripeteia*,[10] interrupting not just a single, particular "action" or intention but the very process of living itself, Genet, at the other end of the spectrum, begins, not with the dissolution of society under the impact of a force it cannot control, but rather with its historical tendency to seek protection from such forces by placing them at a distance: a society of exclusion and segregation, seeking to divest itself of its dead as though "of a shameful thought [*comme on se défait d'une pensée honteuse*]." The medium of this attempted divestiture is language: "Whether the strange word *urbanism* comes from one of the Popes Urban or from the City, it will perhaps no longer be preoccupied with the dead. The living will dispose of corpses, surreptitiously or otherwise, as one divests oneself of a shameful thought" (p. 63).

In a certain sense, Genet's essay begins even earlier than these opening lines, namely, with its title, which both repeats (or anticipates) the inaugural phrase and truncates it in a singular fashion: "*L'Étrange Mot d'* . . . " The English translation of this title has the virtue of pointing up what is decisive in the French precisely by omitting it: "The Strange Word *Urb.* . . . " Unable to render the preposition *de*, much less its elided form *d'*, in English, Richard Seaver's translation is compelled to provide a portion of the "strange word" itself: *Urb.* In so doing, he omits in English a certain process of omission itself: an omission that is also an *emission.* The mysterious linkage of word to word is marked in the French by transformation of the preposition *de* into a mere letter: *d'.* What is strange about the word is not just that it is absent, yet to come, but that its place is announced, or taken, by a letter and its punctuation: an apostrophe, indicating the elision, and three dots or points indicating an omission by effectively arresting the phrase in flight. In this sense, the title already says or, rather, *does* it all. In fact it says nothing much, but instead *stages* the process of linkage, coupling, gesturing in all of its enigmatic facticity: "The strange word" in French is not just the word that is missing, the word yet to come, but also and perhaps above all the word that is *already there*, albeit *reduced to an ambiguously literal gesture.* Left hanging, as it were, suspended in the title, the letter *d'* recalls and foreshadows the unruly and unpredictable "war of words" that will later be said to constitute the *attroupement* of language to which the text at its end returns:

> Words. Lived I don't know how, the French language dissimulates and discloses a war waged by words against one another, brothers and enemies, one wresting free of the other or smitten by it. . . . If tradition and betrayal are born of the same original movement and diverge only in order to live singular lives, by what, through the course of language, do they know themselves bound up [*liés*] with one another in their distortion?[11]

Why should a short text that deals primarily with theater and secondarily with death be framed by two such curious encounters with words, by two observations on language? Does the strangeness of language set the stage for the theater? Does it delimit its borders? Could it be that words, at war with one another (at least in French), "know" of their ties to one another precisely in and through their divergences and distortions? What is a "distorted" word? Would *d'* be an example? And what of the *singular lives* of words, which seem to communicate with one another only through their differences? How does such singularity relate to their multiplicity? Can we ever hope to know for sure? What, in the face of such language, and its theater, would it mean "to know"?

If anyone hopes that by means of such a proliferation—or luxuriance—of monsters he will be able to cultivate a coherent discourse [*soigner un discours cohérent*], he is mistaken: at most, he can couple larval and crafty herds like processions of processionary caterpillars, who will exchange ejaculations spawning a carnivalesque litter [*portée*] without real import [*sans portée*], as unimportant as it is inconsequential, descended from the Greek, the Anglo-Saxon, the Levantine, the Arab, the Latin, the Gaelic, from some stray Chinese, three strange Mongolian vagabonds who talk but say nothing, but who by mating reveal a verbal orgy the meaning of which is lost not in the dark night of time but in an infinity of tender and brutal mutations. (p. 73)

If the "meaning" of words, and hence the possibility of understanding them, of making sense in and through language, gets "lost" not simply "in the dark night of time"—that is, not simply through historical change—"but in an infinity of tender and brutal mutations," where does that leave the "singular lives" that the words engaged in those "mutations" are said to lead? Precisely this problematic relation between the singularity of isolated, divergent, and deformed words, on the one hand, and the orgiastic combinatorics of language, on the other, sets the scene and frames the stage for the discussion of theater that remains the primary focus of this short text. But this emphasis upon singularity suggests that no *general* account of the relation of language, meaning, and knowledge will suffice to account for theatricality. For that, we must follow a singular encounter: that with "L'Étrange Mot d'..." We will now return to this opening phrase, taking the liberty, and pleasure, of re-citing it: "Whether the strange word *urbanism* [*urbanisme*] comes from one of the Popes Urban or from the City, it will perhaps no longer be preoccupied with the dead."

For the reader who has been made curious by the truncated, enigmatic title, these first lines provide at least temporary relief: the strange word is spelled out, we recognize it, but it does not, for all of that, appear any less strange or any more transparent: *urbanisme*. Why just *this* word? And what, after all, is it doing *here*? As the worried House-father in Kafka's story can attest[12] and Genet's text confirms, the strangeness of a word is not necessarily diminished by the etymological search for origins that its enigmatic obscurity can easily invite. Knowledge of the past, even if accessible and reliable—*concesso non dato*—does not necessarily provide knowledge of the present, much less of the future. No matter where the "strange word . . . comes from," whether from "one of the Popes Urban or from the City," it still seems strangely out of place at the beginning of a text that is expected to be on anything except urban affairs. Moreover, this word is doubly out of place: not only is its appearance here puzzling, but its linguistic behavior is, to put it mildly, suspect, for it is said that "perhaps" it will no longer "be preoccupied" with the dead. "Perhaps." But, as a critic and biographer of Genet, Jean-Bernard Moraly, has astutely observed: "'A word' (albeit *urbanism*) 'is not preoccupied' with anything. Genet knows that better than anyone else. . . . Rather, it's a deliberate miscue [*un "à côté" voulu*]."[13] In support of this assertion, Moraly cites the following passage from a letter of Genet to Antoine Bourseiller:

> Every theatrical representation, every spectacle is a magic show [*féerie*]. The show of which I speak does not need sumptuous costumes or baroque furniture: it is in the voice that breaks on a word—when it should break on another—but both word and voice must be found; the magic is in a gesture not in place at the right time, in the pinky-finger that's made a mistake [*qui s'est trompé*].[14]

Theater, for Genet, entails not just an *écart*—a deviation from the norm—but something less formal and more violent: what he here refers to as a *cassure*, a break. This is precisely what Aristotle understood as *peripeteia*: an interruption of an intended project, the deviation of a *gesture* that no longer expresses a deliberate, conscious desire but rather the unconscious of the Freudian *Fehlleistung*, "parapraxis, slip." Such "breaks" are always singular, which is why their performance requires not just a general readiness but also the greatest *precision* in the selection of details. That demands both a profound knowledge of tradition (that is, of the determining factors of expectation, of what is likely to be taken for granted) and an acute sense of situation. Only when one is thoroughly aware of what is *expected* can one look for the *unexpected*. It is not enough to state the principle "both word and voice must be found," nor that this is a matter of timing and of spacing in general. Only at a particular time and place—"at the moment"—can a gesture go astray.

The Aristotelian notion of *peripeteia*, then, is continued but also altered: it interrupts not so much the continuity of an *action* (a *praxis*) as the integrity of an *act*. It no longer focuses upon great sequences of events so much as upon minuscule details. Theatrical *acting*, for Genet, breaks, interrupts, suspends the intentional unity of acts prior to any determination or division of these into "mental," "physical," "emotional," "political," and so forth. Theater involves, therefore, neither the constitution of order out of chaos nor the solving of problems. It does not communicate contents or produce positive knowledge. Nor is it "performative" in the sense usually understood, which is to say, that of accomplishing an intention through an act. Rather, by isolating acts and gestures from their intentional context, it points to established frames of reference—and also to the conditions and contexts that those intentions suppose—but only in order to *dislocate* them.[15]

Those conditions and contexts are never simply arbitrary, which is why it cannot be sufficient to describe the mere *fact* of an *à coup*—a jolt—or to speculate about its being *deliberate* (*voulu*). Genet's essay, without elaborating anything like a comprehensive theory of theater—indeed, it explicitly and repeatedly eschews just that—nevertheless points its readers toward the established and problematic *frames* that have to be disrupted if theater is to retain a place in a world increasingly dominated by media whose representational resources far exceed those over which theater traditionally disposes.

Genet was well aware of the threat posed by the media of the nineteenth and twentieth centuries to traditional forms of art. He reacted to this situation, however, much as did Walter Benjamin three decades earlier, judging the challenge posed by the new media to be a salutary one, a necessary impulsion for "art" to change its ways. This meant for Genet above all abandoning the servile project of reproducing a reality from which it held itself to be excluded, and instead concentrating upon elaborating the distinctive reality of its own medium.[16] Like Benjamin, Genet traces this historic challenge to the emergence of photography, which forced painting to look for resources and criteria other than those of "stupidly perceptible similitude [*ressemblance sottement perceptible*]":

> It is possible that, confronted with the results of photography, painters were at first stunned. After they had gotten hold of themselves again, they discovered what painting still could be.
>
> In a like manner, or in a similar fashion, dramatists are stunned by what television and cinema make possible. If they accept to see—in case it can be seen—that theater cannot compete with such excessive means—those of TV and film—writers for the theater will discover the virtues proper to the theater, which, perhaps, derive only from myth. (p. 67)

The "myth" to which Genet refers here has little to do with Aristotelian *muthos*, that is, with a "plot" representing the unity of a *praxis*. Rather, it is related to the *féerie* of the *Fehlleistung*, the slip that escapes the control of the *logos*, of reason, of communicative discourse and consistent argumentation. Here "theater" has something distinctive, perhaps, to defend against the competing media of film and television—something that has to do with an experience of *bodies separating* as they *coexist in a determinate site*.

None of this is explicitly elaborated in "The Strange Word *Urb* . . . " but much of it is adumbrated there, in particular in the opening gambit. The strange word *urbanism* is, in the first clause, linked to a proper name, *Urban*, which is anything but simply proper. It designates no fewer than eight popes of the Catholic Church (hence the qualification whether it comes from "*one* of the Popes Urban." The linking of "proper name" and "common noun" does not eliminate the latter's "strangeness" or clear up its "meaning." Rather, it opens a multiplicity of possible connotations, often at odds with one another. These extend from the proclamation of the Crusades by Pope Urban II, consolidating the position of the Papacy as the leading institution of Western Christendom, to the double schism of the Church, first between East and West, then between Rome and Avignon. The reference to "one of the Popes Urban" thus overlaps in multiple ways with the alternative etymological option, that of "the City." This it reduces to paraphrase, as Seaver does in his translation: simply, "the Latin root of the word *city*." Far more than just "the Latin root," *urbs*, is suggested by "La Ville" in this opening phrase. Also connoted is one particular City, for centuries the capital of Western Christendom, object of struggle involving many of the popes bearing the name *Urban*: the city of Rome. One of the popes bearing the name *Urban*, namely, Urban V, initiated an ambitious project of urban renewal during the three years he was able to reside in the Eternal City before he was forced to return to Avignon in 1370.

"La Ville," then, can refer as much to "the City" of Rome as to the Latin word *urbs*. Indeed, toward the end of this text "Rome" returns in a less universal, less "catholic" context as the site, not of the popes but of a tradition presented as emblematic for the theater envisaged by this text. That is the tradition of the "funeral mime": "Where? Rome, I've read, possessed—but perhaps my memory deceives me—a funeral mime. His role? Preceding the procession, he was charged with miming the most important fact that had composed the life of the dead man when he—the dead man—was living" (p. 72).

We will return to this funeral mime, who, interspersed in a staging of language as a wild war of words, will provide the text with an appropriate finale. But before we reach that part of "the City," we must first return to the essay's opening phrase, which, after naming the "strange word" and offering two possible yet equally enigmatic etymological origins, makes a brief and surreptitious detour via yet another city (Vienna, "qu'il *vienne* d'un pape Urban") before finally arriving at its destination, indeed, at its *raison d'être*: the question of how "urbanism" "is preoccupied," or not, with "the dead": not, it should be noted, with "death" in general, but with "the dead," and more particularly, with their corpses.

The strange word *urbanism* is perhaps going to cease being preoccupied with "the dead." But if this happens, Genet argues, it will put an end to theater. Theater requires a certain proximity to the dead, which is to say, to their mortal remains. To remove those remains from the life of the City, even if they are then recycled as fertilizer for state-run collective farms, for "*kolkhozes* or for *kibboutzim*," is for "the urbanized world to deprive itself of a great theatrical mainstay [*secours*] and perhaps of theater itself" (p. 63).

The strangeness of the word, to be sure, is hardly attenuated by such references to recent history and politics, references that become all the more explicit and insistent as the paragraph unwinds:

All the same, if the cremation takes a dramatic turn [*allure*]—be it that a single man is solemnly burnt and cooked alive, be it that the City or the State should desire to rid itself, at one fell swoop as it were, of another community—the crematorium, like that of Dachau, evokes a very possible future architecturally escaping from time, from the future as well as the past, its chimney constantly maintained by clean-up crews who, around this sex erected obliquely out of pink bricks, sing *Lieder* or whistle tunes from Mozart, servicing the open mouth of this furnace where ten or twelve corpses can be inserted [*enfournés*] at once, a certain form of theater will be able to survive [*se perpétuer*]; but if in the cities the crematoria are hidden or reduced to the dimensions of a grocery-store, theater will die. (pp. 63–64)

Seldom has an "if . . . then" clause been made as interminable a framework for such monstrous thoughts or, rather, scenes. "After Auschwitz," Adorno declared, in a phrase that was to become famous, "there can be no poetry." Genet's implicit response is: No poetry, perhaps, but "a certain theater." Despite its unmistakable historical overtones, this response is anything but simple nostalgia. The Nazi crematoria, for instance, were almost always far removed from urban population centers. Rather, through a series of horrendous but captivating *peripeteia*—but without redeeming "recognition"—the disposition of the bodies of the dead becomes the touchstone for the life or death of theater as Genet conceives it.

But does he "conceive" anything at all? "I offer you this advice without undue solemnity, with the active nonchalance of a child who knows the importance of theater" (p. 64). The curiosity of the reader, whetted by the truncated title, exacerbated by the word that fills in the gap without making it transparent, is finally captivated by a scene that twists and turns on itself: "Cremation" far from the city means the demise of theater, but cremation publicly embraced and celebrated as a phallic and parodic ritual can save theater. Theater requires the proximity of the dead, of their material remains, even if those remains are constantly consumed by fire and volatilized. The "argument" of the "scene" shifts with each new clause while expanding the limits of a sentence beyond what can be taken in at one sitting. (Was it not precisely this that Aristotle demanded of tragedy and that, in his eyes, distinguished it from epic?)[17]

Theater of the Holocaust? Holocaust *as* theater? Not entirely. Rather, the Holocaust as a grisly provocation to rethink the place of theater in relation to the dead—to rethink its strange and ambiguous *corporeality* in relation to corpses: "Do you see what I'm driving at? The theater will be located as close as possible, in the truly tutelary shadow of the place where the dead are kept or of the sole monument which digests them" (p. 64).

Why are the shadows of the crematorium, or of the cemetery, tutelary for theater? Quite simply because they *derange time*: a certain time and a certain history, the time and history whose domination the Popes Urban strove to consolidate. The timeless architecture of the crematorium chimney, for instance, challenges the temporal perspective informed by that "mythical or controversial event also called the Advent [*Avènement*]" (p. 64), which promises the triumph of life over death and the temporal overcoming of time. By contrast, the graves in the cemetery or the crematorium chimney—after its initial exploitation, the crematorium is "dropped" in favor of the cemetery—resist such promises. In place of "the hypothetical Incarnation" they mark the *disincarnation* of physical decay or disintegration. When a city is built around a cemetery, history ceases to be simply the promise of resurrection and serves as a reminder of mortality. It becomes what Benjamin, in his study of the German baroque mourning play, calls "natural history": in a world devoid of grace, it is natural for history to serve as medium for "the production of corpses."[18] In this perspective, an urbanism that continues to be preoccupied with—and by— the dead organizes living space around the possibility of separation and of its correlative, *contact*. This, perhaps, renders this space such a great aid—*un grand secours*—to theater.

In the shadow of the cemetery and of the crematorium, separability and detachment are rendered visible. Hence their importance in situating theater, a theater that is already "detached" by seeking its point of departure, not in any particular object or theme, but in a certain "isolation":

> Th[e] theatrical act cannot be just anything at all, but in anything at all it can find its pretext. In fact, it seems to me that any event whatsoever, visible or not, can, *if it is isolated*, I mean *fragmented in the continuum*, if well handled [*bien conduit*], serve as a pretext or even as the point of departure and arrival of the *theatrical act*. (p. 68, my emphasis)

The fact that "the strange word *urbanism*" starts out, in this text, by preparing to relinquish this *preoccupation* is part of a "history" to which the names of the Urban popes are anything but foreign. The institution and tradition with which they are associated, that of "the Christian West," entails a temporality and spatiality informed by what Genet calls "the Very Debatable Nativity" (*la Très Contestable Nativité*) (p. 65). One of the many ways in which the "urban" culture of the West, which aims to extend its domination over the entire world, has broken with rural traditions—and it is this that is of interest in this text—is by relegating the institutionalized place of the dead to the periphery of social life, concentrated increasingly in cities constructed around monuments to the resurrection and triumph of life rather than memorials to the dead. This separation of church from churchyard marks what can be called a detachment of the living from the dead, if not, indeed, from *detachability as such*. This menaces theater, but the-ater can also respond to it.

The survival of theater, then, depends upon redefining its position with respect to the dead and to their institutionalized place, the ceme-tery. Only in the shadow of the grave can the possibility of detach-ment, and detachment *as the possibility of theater*, perhaps be recovered. To be thus recovered by theater, such detachment must be understood or, rather, *practiced* as an act of disjunction that is something other than a mere moment or station on the way to salvation. In short, such disjunction must be practiced spatially, involving the linkage of theater to a fixed *site*:

> The site. To an Italian who wanted to construct a theater whose elements would be mobile and whose architecture changing, depending on the play to be performed, I replied, even before he had finished his sentence, that the architecture of the theater remains to be discovered, but that it must be fixed, immobilized, so that its responsibility may be recognized: it shall be judged by its form. One can, if one wishes, turn toward the perishable, but only after the irreversible act for which we shall be judged or, if one prefers, *the fixed act that judges itself.* (pp. 65–66, my em-phasis)

The notions of *peripeteia* and *anagnōrisis* echo silently in a passage that once again continues the Aristotelian conception of theater while transforming it. The fixity of theatrical space is the condition of an *act of recognition.* But what is recognized is the *responsibility* of theater itself. Only by immobilizing, by arresting a movement that would otherwise be taken for granted as a temporal transition, does theater become responsible. In what does such responsibility consist? In the obligation to "judge itself." Such self-judgment, we may assume, as in Benjamin's *Trauerspiel,* can only result in a suspended sentence, for the fixity of the theatrical act strikes a counterblow against "the '*coup du calendrier*' that the West seeks to impose upon the entire world" (p. 65). By interrupting that calendar through its "fixity," the theatrical "act" does not merely open the possibility of "a multitude of calendars"—it also introduces "another time . . . having neither beginning nor end" and thus irrevocably at odds with the archeo-teleological time and space that inform Western historical consciousness. At the same time, such a theater finds itself caught in a contradiction. By fixing itself, albeit in the introduction of a new calendar, it also inevitably instantiates itself, thereby furthering the illusion of the very eternity and sameness it seeks to disrupt.

Such a theater can only survive as a parody of itself: neither as tragedy nor as comedy, but rather as farce, as what Kierkegaard describes, in *Repetition,* as *Posse.* The theatrical possibility par excellence, the *Posse* gestures toward a time and space of inauthentic cohabitation, of quasi-simultaneity, of irreducible anachronicity and heterogeneity. In this space of disjunction, the theater and the cemetery mirror each other: "Death would be both closer and lighter, theater graver" (p. 68).

The "tutelary" shadow of the tomb teaches theater to recognize its responsibility as parodic detachment. Theater makes this detachment visible: not the shape of the thing itself, but its *shadow,* not its phenomenality, but its *outlines.* Not bodies, simply, or even corpses, but machines, masks, apparatuses: stage "properties" that belong to no one or to no thing. The funeral mime is an exemplary embodiment of such detachment—and therefore an exemplary theatrical figure:

> And the funeral mime?
> And the Theater in the cemetery?
> Before the dead man is buried, let his corpse be carried to the front of the stage in its coffin; let friends, enemies, and the curious gather in the part reserved for the public; let the funeral mime who preceded the procession divide and multiply himself

[*se dédouble, se multiplie*]; let him become a theater troupe and let him, before the dead and the public, allow the dead to live and die again [*remourir*]. (p. 73)

Theater is the repetition of detachment, of division and of multiplication, by which the singular becomes many and the many singular; the troupe isolated and the isolated a troupe; the dead resuscitated and the resuscitated die again: not to be reborn but to *remourir*. Whether words or mimes, what repeats and reproduces itself never returns as the same. In returning, recurring, repeating, everything detaches itself. That is the death before all death, the detachment that goes on before our eyes. We "know" this all the time and yet, at the same time, rarely *think* of it:

As for me, faced with this enraged herd encaged in the dictionary, I know that I've said nothing and that I never will say anything: and the words couldn't care less.
Actions are hardly more docile. (p. 74)

Unless, that is, the "actions" are those of the funeral mime. His acts are quite special: in a certain sense, they never take place, for they are impossible. That is the *Posse*, the farce that his gesticulation embodies. And with this strange act, which is more a gesticulation than an action, the text, strangely, concludes: "if he wants to make the dead live and die again, [the mime] will have to discover, and dare to say, those dialectophagous words which, before the public, will devour the life and death of the dead" (p. 74). But a funeral mime who would "dare" to say "dialectophagous words" would thereby celebrate his own funeral. Those words would devour him along with the (other) dialects. For a mime that *dares to speak* is no longer a mime—unless, of course, he mimes speaking. Is it such mimicry of language—language as mimicry—that devours "the life and death of the dead" *theatrically*?

There are other reasons. They're subtler. It's up to you to discover them in you without defining or naming them. (p. 69)

13

"Being . . . and eXistenZ": Some Preliminary Considerations on Theatricality in Film

W I T H   T H E advent first of film, then of video, and finally of electronic media and the revolution in transmission that they have brought about, it might seem inevitable that theater should assume an increasingly marginal role, socially as well as aesthetically. The times when theater was a major means either for forging social and national identity or for disturbing it are long past, and although theater survives, its cultural significance seems greatly reduced. Nothing demonstrates this tendency more clearly, perhaps, than the latest invention of the consumer electronics industry: "home theater," which seems designed to absorb the semipublic space of theater into the essentially private space of the home.[1] Such absorption tends to reinforce the traditional aspirations of domestic space to become an autarkical microcosm independent of the outside world. Home theater, which in many ways is the domestic counterpart to the automobile—not least in its exploitation as a preferred site of the consumer electronics industry—appears to provide a window onto the world that lifts, as it were, the home out of the limitations and possible dangers of its immediate environment. If the screen of home theater is a window onto the world, no stone can come flying through it, however large it may be and however global its scope. Rather, in tandem with a sound system designed to surround and envelop the viewer-listener, home theater appears to open the home to the outside world while reinforcing its sense of secure self-containment.

Thus, an experience that formerly required some sort of move beyond private, domestic space and some sort of not entirely controllable social contact is privatized and domesticated. It should be noted that "audio" plays as large a part in this process as the more obvious "video." "Surround sound," "Dolby Digital," and "THX" are only the most widespread brand names for systems of acoustical reproduction and enhancement that bring the cinematic world of sound into the private space of the individual.

This is, of course, only one tendency, albeit one of the most widespread, at work in the extremely complex transformations that the relationship between film and theater is undergoing today. Another is the effort, usually on the part of more or less "avant-garde" theater groups, to adapt cinematic and audiovisual techniques to the stage (in the United States, the productions of the New York–based Wooster Group have been among the most notable). Although such efforts deserve, and are receiving, prolonged attention, I want to address here another aspect of the problem, namely, the strange persistence and, indeed, resurgence of "theatrical" motifs in contemporary cinema.[2] This huge topic has been the subject of book-length studies.[3] Obviously only a very small portion of this complex relationship can be addressed in the space of a single chapter, especially because it is necessary to begin by giving some sort of definition to the most basic terms, whose significance is anything but self-evident. What is meant by *theatrical*? Not just "theater" in the sense previously alluded to. The word itself, in English and other languages as well, has meanings that are by no means limited to the "aesthetic" realm. As already observed, we speak of "theaters of operation" in a military sense, for instance, and the property of "theatricality" need not be tied to "theaters," even in the larger, "metaphorical" sense just alluded to. If one tries to "define" the notion of "theater," and even more that of "theatricality," one immediately comes upon an obstacle to definition that probably communicates with the essence of what one is trying to define: one butts up against the difficulty of finding proper *limits*. This difficulty in finding the limits of the word *theatrical* makes the military use of the word particularly significant, for what allows an area to be designated a "theater" of (military) operations is the importance attached to defining, delimiting, and controlling the space of conflict. In other, more conventional terms, a space or region can be considered to be a military theater of operations when it is about to be transformed from a general *space* to a particular *place*. The transition from *space to place* often depends upon the *intervention* of forces and factors external to the place under dispute. Some such intervention is required to set the frontiers that will retroactively determine space *as* place. A *theater* is thus a locale whose status as determined place depends upon external intervention, and thus upon a relation of forces that can never be "contained" within the place in question. That is the first and perhaps most important trait of the term that the military notion of "theater" brings to the fore. There is, however, at least one other aspect, related to the first. In order for such military "intervention" to be effective, it must be undertaken from a relatively detached and secure position. Only such a position permits the required surveillance—"reconnaissance"—to take place, so that the intervening forces can know just where to intervene. Hence the decisive importance of *reconnaissance* in the planning of military strategies. However, from a military perspective reconnaissance is only a means to the end of the most effective deployment of force. This is peculiar to the military "theater" but not necessarily to theaters or "theatricality" in general.

The nonaesthetic—here, military—use of the word brings to the fore what is perhaps its salient trait, namely, *theater* considered as a *medium in which conflicting forces strive to secure the perimeter of a place in dispute*. "Theater" signifies the *imposition of borders* rather than a *representational-aesthetic genre*. The former focuses upon the *manner* in which a place is *secured*, whereas the latter regards the *place* as already *taken* or *given*, and therefore as a means or instrument of that which is to be *represented*. In respect to its mediality, then, theatricality is defined as a *problematic process of placing, framing, situating* rather than as a process of representation. This aspect is decisive in evaluating the persistence of theatrical modes and motifs in contemporary culture and society in general, and—to come finally to the topic at hand—in cinema in particular.

Having introduced the problem of theatricality in this admittedly very general way, I want now to concretize it by very briefly considering two films.

The first film I want to discuss, all too summarily, is one in which the distinctive temporality of theater—that of the present participle—is already taken up into its title: *Being John Malkovich*. It is no accident that the title links the present participle—and not just any present participle—to what appears to be a proper name: *John Malkovich*. The property and authenticity of that name will be even more emphatically affirmed when the figure, image, and voice associated with it appear in "the title role." Nevertheless, this is not a film about "John Malkovich," in the sense one might have expected. It does not tell the story of the life of a contemporary movie star, even though it does display pictorial evidence of that life: diplomas, high-school photos, and so on. Rather, the name designates a well-known "actor" *acting himself:* "John Malkovich" acting "John Malkovich." The significance of the proper name in this context is anything but simply proper. It is not a linguistic entity designating an extra-linguistic referent, if by the latter is meant someone or something constituted in his or its self-identity independently of all signification. Rather, "John Malkovich" *acting overlaps* with John Malkovich *acted.* Any and all expectations attached to the latter as "person" have less to do with his person as such than with its aura: which is to say, with the curiosity about how something like a "person" or "individual" can possibly relate to the impersonal network that constitutes a Hollywood star.

Yet Malkovich is not just a typical Hollywood star: not just another Tom Cruise or Clint Eastwood (with and against whom he plays in the unforgettable film *Line of Fire*). Why? Because the fascination of *Being John Malkovich* has to do with the way the film *doubles* and thereby *divides* the convergence of image and person that otherwise functions as the condition of Hollywood stardom. One manifestation is Malkovich's *voice:* cultivated in a way that is almost unique among today's Hollywood stars, with a *timbre* that is as aloof and as it is insinuating, as remote as it is seductive, suspending any univocal identification in an indefinite equivocation of gender.

All of this, however, is a preface to the two aspects of the film that are of interest here: first, the motif of the puppets and the puppeteer; second, the fantasy of penetrating the body and soul of John Malkovich, Hollywood star, first in order to watch, then in order to control. I will inverse chronological order of the film by beginning with the latter part first, and ending with the first part last.

Like any good film that plays with uncanny elements, the specific way in which the figures gain access to Malkovich's body has its own distinctive history. In the urban apartment buildings of the forties and fifties, and occasionally even today, the isolation of the American urban apartment dweller was often relieved only by particular kinds of communal "chutes": postal chutes, laundry chutes, or garbage chutes, which became places where otherwise isolated apartment dwellers would occasionally meet and chat. The *déchets* produced by urban life were eliminated from view by being thrown down such communal garbage chutes. From these chutes the sounds of wailing or whistling winds could often be heard. This wind—in the reversed form of suction—sucks various figures in the film deep into the head and soul of the unsuspecting actor. The film celebrates its own "shooting" in the return of this laundry-garbage-postal chute. Whereas the chute served to transport the excesses of urban domestic life *out of* sight and mind, although not necessarily out of hearing, the Malkovich chute transforms its willing spectators *into* sight, mind, and audition. They disappear, first in order to hear and *see* what "John Malkovich" really is—and then, increasingly, to *control* what Malkovich sees and means.

As they do so, the privileged site of the autonomous subject since the Reformation, the individual body—the body understood as *embodied individual*—displays its vulnerability by becoming a *staging area* of a struggle for power and control. The dispossession of the human body is, of course, no new subject in the history of film: Fritz Lang's *Testament of Dr. Mabuse* (1933), Don Siegel's *The Invasion of the Body Snatchers* (1956), and Ridley Scott's *Alien* (1979) all explore fantasies of the vulnerability of the individual body—and hence, of the individual *tout court*—to alien forces that explicitly or implicitly have a political agenda. Against the background of this tradition, it is no doubt significant that the political dimension has disappeared in *Being John Malkovich*. In this film, the "chute" marks the "fall," not just into the body, but simultaneously *of* the body considered to be a self-contained vessel and as the vehicle of a no less self-contained soul. At the same time, by ricochet, the body no longer serves to demarcate the internal self-containment of a subject.[4] Rather, Malkovich's body becomes a kind of apartment house or, better, a dwelling for transients. The body emerges both as a temporary container and as an observation post, something like a loge in a theater. After a period of observation, however, the observation post takes on a more military character—it becomes a forward command post that does not merely observe, but increasingly controls the body it is "in." But its residence in that body is emphatically temporary: the fall *out* (onto the New Jersey Turnpike) is as certain and abrupt as the fall down the chute.

At first, it is this falling-down-and-out and the observations it makes possible that fascinate. Gradually, however, the story*line* takes over, thereby reducing and integrating the distinctively non-narrative, *theatrical* experience. What Benjamin, writing about Brecht's Epic Theater, describes as the actor's ability to "fall out of one's role artistically,"[5] and by implication to "fall" into another one, is increasingly submitted to a narrative logic of identification, power, and control.

317

The latter then culminates in the occupation of Malkovich by "Dr. Lester" (played by Orson Bean) and his crew, who thus hope to postpone their mortality indefinitely—or at least for the duration of a story that can thus come to a proper, meaningful end.[6]

Being John Malkovich thus ends with the good news and happy ending of a collective, conspiratorial fall into grace, one that repeats itself and yet in so doing must try to leave behind the various chutes— garbage, postal, laundry—to which it implicitly alludes. In the process, the open-ended, finite reiterations that constitute the present participle are ironically overshadowed by the ostensible authenticity associated with the proper name and with its vehicle, the individual body. The demand of Hollywood for a meaningful, self-contained storyline is thus fulfilled: the film is not only shot and edited, but also brought to market—that is, "distributed." In the process, however, the "individual" body is revealed to be a highly *divisible* container whose function—as already anticipated by Descartes—remains *essentially* indifferent to that which it contains. The body is thus the site of a struggle for "possession" in which expropriation and reappropriation alternate. The body thus retains certain of its features—name, voice, and figure—while becoming a closed arena (a.k.a. "theater of operations") for ongoing struggles of appropriation. In the end—this end, at least—the organic, human body of "John Malkovich" reveals itself to be not so very different from the mechanical puppets that confront the spectator of this film at its beginning.

The pathos of those puppets, of course, has to do with the fact that they have no "inside" and therefore can "contain" nothing. Their dependence on the outside world, on the strings that tie them to the puppeteer, is visible and undeniable. Such dependence is generally domesticated by being assimilated to a generational immaturity: puppets are for "children," not for "adults." When, however, these puppets display passions and desires that do not conform to the moralistic expectation of youthful innocence, the puppeteer is rewarded by a box on the ears, or on the mouth, by an outraged and indignant parent-spectator, whose avenging blows purport to protect the morality of the child—but also of the adult—from such dubious seductions and contaminations. But the "story" told, mutely, by the puppet show foreshadows that to come in the film "itself." It tells a story of bodies that have no soul, or no one soul, and are not, therefore, self-determining, autonomous, but rather determined by their "ties" to what they are not, in a fixed and yet always changing space. The story of the puppets, by contrast with the storyline to come, will have no promise or consolation, no hope of resurrection or of immortality, because in the world of puppets, at least, life and death are no longer simply mutually exclusive, no longer simply an alternative. The puppets, filmed largely in close-up, are more poignantly moving than the expressive faces of "living" actors. Why? Because their masks and movements reveal a constitutive heterogeneity that the modern conception of the autonomous individual is obliged to deny or combat. The puppets are suspended on threads; their movements come from elsewhere. They *respond*; they do not initiate. The "body" of a puppet, a marionette, is never self-contained, not an organic whole; rather, it *reflects* impulses that come from without. Puppets cannot therefore be said to "act" but at most to *react* to such impulses; their existence hangs on a thread, in all senses. Their movements would be dramatic were they not *removed*; and precisely their *remoteness* constitutes their distinctive *poignancy*. They are touching because in a sense they are already dead, and not yet born. Therein they serve as reminders of the ways in which the animation of the spectators is also suspended between past and future. The more the spectator is drawn into their drama, the more s/he realizes just how much the joke is on him or her, which perhaps explains why an indignant father, confronted by the passion of these puppets, has no alternative but to vent his anger, and presumably his anxiety, upon the body of the puppeteer (John Cusack).

Although they can hardly be said to "act," puppets nevertheless "embody" the essence of the *acting* in which the body itself becomes a stage upon which forces that come from elsewhere play themselves out; such remote bodies are always defined by their relation to the place they occupy without ever possessing. Puppets never take place, and in this they are at odds with *humans* in the specific sense accorded that term by a powerful Western tradition: namely, that of an independent, autonomous, self-conscious subject. Puppets, by contrast, repeat, respond, react, re-move without ever reaching or aspiring to self-consciousness.[7] They are both before and beyond it. Correlatively, their "bodies" never *embody*: not a soul, nor a mind, nor an identity. Their bodies are nonhuman in the extreme, and yet no less "bodily" for it. Their articulations, joints, and members take their cue from elsewhere, and their being, reiterative and inconclusive, always hangs on a thread. Contrary to appearances, the relation of the puppet to the puppeteer is not analogous to that of the creature to the Creator. The puppet is defined, not by its resemblance to the puppeteer, but by the threads that tie it to and remove it from the source of its movement.

This *hanging-on-a-thread* is difficult for Western observers to accept, and yet it is doubtless the source of a fascination that has never entirely disappeared. The puppet, devoid of authenticity, without a soul or a heart, embodies the *division* and *separation* that constitute *acting* as an activity that can only be designated to the present participle, as simultaneous with its enunciation. The "threads" on which its existence "hangs" are the materialization of this simultaneity in its ambivalence: linking and separating at once. These threads remain barely visible in the film, and their shadow remains even when its "plot" seeks to leave them behind.

• • •

The status of the "plot" is also a major issue in the second film I wish to discuss, David Cronenberg's *eXistenZ* (1999). *eXistenZ* addresses many of the problems with which this book has been concerned: the status of narrative, its relation to meaning and, above all, to the medium. The medium here is, of course, film. But the subject matter also involves another kind of medium, namely, the "game." The game concerned, of course, is produced by an age in which biotechnology has developed prosthetic power to the point of decisively blurring the difference between natural and synthetic, objective and subjective. As a result, the "game" of *eXistenZ* is, as its inventor, Allegra Geller, tells audience and future game-players at the outset, "much more than a game . . . " And yet, that "much more" turns out to be strangely—uncannily—familiar: "it's an entire game-*system*." The notion of *system* provides a crucial parameter against which the remainder of the film is mobilized. A "system" consists in a *limited* number of rules that at the same time create an *unlimited* number of possible actions or events. The rules of chess—or, to take the game mentioned in the film, *poker*—are limited, at least at any one time; the "games" made possible by that limited set of rules are not. Although those games must conform to the rules, their possible configurations are unlimited. This is what makes game-playing a question of "strategies" rather than merely of application: that is, of just applying the rules of the game. Such strategies, which negotiate with the aleatory, thus seek to impose a relative order upon the intrinsically unlimited number of games made possible by the rules.

What distinguishes the biotechnological game of *eXistenZ* from other games is, as its name suggests, that its rules are never fully identifiable. Hence, the only "system" that emerges is a certain lack of system. Since, however, the rules of the "game-system" that is *eXistenZ* are difficult if not impossible to discern, the very notion of "game" is called into question. The concept of "game," like that of "fiction," always presupposes its mutually exclusive other: a nonludic "reality" that is self-contained, "natural," nonfabricated, and nonsynthetic. *eXistenZ* calls this enabling other into question by totalizing it. Like the "chute" in *Being John Malkovich*, the individual human bodies of the game-players are opened and attached—"ported"—into an external "game-pod" that looks like a cross between a kidney and a plastic pillow. It is hardly an accident that the scene where the "game-port" is depicted, and installed, occurs at a "gas station" and that the installer (Willem Dafoe, of the Wooster Group) is named, quite simply, "Gas." Individual bodies are plugged into the game (pod) the way automobiles are plugged into gas pumps. What then occurs is both very old and very new. Instead of the machine "tanking up" in order to effect a movement that is still unmistakably *locomotive*—that is, from "place" to "place"—the movement that ensues transforms perception of the entire "world" in which "places" are otherwise situated. Once one is plugged in to the game-pod, what occurs is the most classical and characteristic move of cinema: the sudden "cut" or change of scene, whose abruptness can be gauged only against the constancy of the figure undergoing it. This technique is exploited by Buster Keaton in a celebrated sequence from his film *Sherlock Junior*: Keaton seeks to install himself in one setting, only to find himself suddenly transformed, by the cut, into another.

Such parodic reflection foregrounds the constitutive significance of the "cut" in cinema, a topos highlighted by Vertov and Eisenstein and elaborated by Benjamin.[8] The illusion of a progressive, linear, narrative continuity is sustained by a compositional process that relies upon the intrinsic *discontinuity* of its individual components. The very notion—indeed, term—of *film* can be seen as a reminder of the tension between manifest, surface continuity and dissimulated discontinuity that distinguishes this medium.

This tension is reproduced as *eXistenZ* unfolds. The two main play-ers, Allegra and Ted, are like puppets insofar as they must be attached to an external source, the synthetic game-pod (externalized interior bodily organ), in order to "play." As so often in Cronenberg films, there is even discussion about the reduced importance of "free will," of which, Allegra observes in a Nietzschean vein, there is "just enough to make things interesting." Yet, despite all the talk of obscure and uncontrollable "forces" dominating the game, there remains the expectation of an intelligibility predicated upon individual intention. This is expressed naively by Ted, who remains a hesitant game-player even as he increasingly succumbs to its fascination: "I don't know what's going on. We're both stumbling around together in this un-formed world, whose rules and objectives are largely unknown and seemingly indecipherable, or even possibly nonexistent, always on the verge of being killed by forces that we don't understand."

To which Allegra replies: "That sounds like my game all right!"

Yet in what sense is it "her" game? As it turns out—if, that is, the concluding scene can be taken at face value (and that is, of course, precisely the question)—she is not its creator or inventor but "only" its main player. The "true" inventor of the game, Yevgenji Nourish, is still nourished by the claim to authorial rights over the game. The "anti-game sentiment" that gives *eXistenZ* its dramatic tension, in-deed, its "plot," "surely didn't come from me," he admits. Indeed, such "sentiment" comes from the game-players themselves, whose physical and mental energies are required for the game to function.

Here the structure of the game of *eXistenZ* shows what might be called its true colors,[9] and at the same time demonstrates what might set this sort of "game" apart from what we have been investigating as the medium of "theatricality." Both involve "playing"—whether of "roles" or something else. Both tend to unsettle the dichotomous logic that structures the semantic field in which these terms are gener-ally used.

What distinguishes the playing of this kind of "game" from the play-acting of a theater is that the former conforms to an agonistic logic that is irreducibly binary. However futuristic its biotechnology may allow it to seem, the "game" of *eXistenZ* has one thing in com-mon with the majority of Western games from past centuries: it is played with the expectation of producing *winners* and *losers*. When Allegra explains to Ted that she needs him as her game-partner in order to see if her game has survived the shock of the opening scene, he replies: "How can you expect me to compete with the inventor of the game?" To which she replies, somewhat speciously, "You could beat the inventor of poker, couldn't you?" What is decisive here is not that the "inventor" is the "owner" or master (mistress) of the game—as we will see, this is no longer simply the case—but rather that the game is an activity that allows only one outcome and thereby reduces all differences to the simple alternative *win or lose*, otherwise known as winner take all. Standing alone among the ruins of a savage battle, with machine-guns rattling and bombs exploding, Allegra cries out: "Have I won?"

That is, indeed, the question that this kind of game presupposes and with which it concludes. It is also the question that makes this game so familiar, all of its biomechanical trappings notwithstanding. This is because, as Allegra remarks, "it's a game that everyone is already playing." The name of the game is corporate capitalism. It is a game that overlays competition with complicity, and in so doing relativizes the status of all "proper" names. In the opening scene, the game *eXistenZ* is presented to a selected audience by representatives of its true owner, who is not its inventor but its financer and marketer, "Antenna Corporation." "Allegra Geller" is an employee of this corporation, and the game is its property, not hers (she probably has stock options, or course, which give her a stake in the corporation . . .). At the end of the film, the "same" scene is repeated, but this time the game has changed its name, having now become *transCendenZ*, and its inventor has changed gender, becoming "Yevgenji Nourish," nourished by "Pilgrimàge Corporation." This name is pronounced *pilgri-màge*, as though to emphasize the "I-magical" quality of the modern corporation, which combines bio- with media technology to invest the hallowed goal of capitalism—profit maximization—with a new and quasi-religious fervor.

What distinguishes game-playing from theatrical play-acting is its agonistic principle of winner take all, which is also the logic of the modern corporation. This agonistic logic of the corporation is also resolutely dual or binary, and it informs the ascendance of "drama" into "plot." There is the corporation and its rivals, be they other corporations or anticorporate conspirators. As already discussed, the interruptive function of theatrical gesture is increasingly absorbed into the linear progression of a dramatic plot, in which difference is reduced to opposition and to polar conflict. In *eXistenZ*, such conflict doubles itself. On the one hand, there is the war between "realists" and "gamers." In the eyes of the realists, the game-players, and above all their *inventors*, "deform" reality and must therefore be destroyed. It is suggested, however, that the "realist underground," willing or not, is really a puppet, whose strings are pulled by a competing corporation, "Cortical Systematics." Thus, the violent attempt to liquidate Allegra turns out to be shadowboxing. In the end, Allegra herself, whether she knows it or not, turns out to be yet another "double agent" acting for "the realist underground," that is, for the competing corporation, Cortical Systematics. So much for the possibility of revolt, much less of revolution.

Thus, the "systematics" of this world of corporate capitalism, whether "cortical" or "antenna," inward or outward directed, perpetuates the familiar dualistic logic of profit and loss, winners and losers, exploiters and exploited. It accomplishes this, however, by updating and perpetuating the reduction of theatricality that has been the subject of this volume.

The difference, then, between the "game-system" of *eXistenZ* and a play-acting that does not serve as a vehicle of plot in the Aristotelian, "mythological" sense, resides in the way the "role" is to be played. In *eXistenZ* the frame-setting role is organized in accordance with the dichotomous logic of winner and loser, active and passive. The cast is divided into two main categories: actors and extras. Nowhere are the ethnocentric ramifications of this dichotomy more striking than in the scene in the Chinese restaurant. Ted, the hitherto passive second lead, feels an urge—a "game-urge" Allegra says, encouraging him not to resist—"to kill someone." The "someone" is the Chinese waiter, situated between the passive extra and the active actor. After the murder, the "audience"—and this is the sole scene, apart from the opening and concluding scenes, where an "audience" is shown—stares fixedly, frozen and silent, waiting passively for its "cue," which Ted obligingly gives it, thereby allowing the "action" to resume and the plot to progress.

This freeze-frame audience recalls both Plato's cave dwellers and the spectators presupposed by orthodox Aristotelian theater mythology: an audience that is framed and defined by the self-contained plot, by the *muthos* and its meaning. It is an audience that has no choice but to remain passive, waiting for its cue, or suddenly to spring into action, but in the most destructive way: aiming a revolver and declaiming its intention: "Death to the Demon(ness) . . . " Not for nothing is this theater a (Protestant) church, where the stark interior becomes a setting for a struggle between faith and fanaticism, gods and demons, continued in the Manichean battle between realists and gamers, between the creator and the inventor. While it is characteristic that this opposition should appear to pit symmetrical individual figures against one another, the reality behind the "realists" is the same as that behind the "inventors": the corporation, whether called "Antenna," "Pilgrimàge," or "Cortical Systematics." The "Systematics" is that of the binary logic of appropriation and expropriation: *tertium non datur.*

Except perhaps on the stage; or, rather, *as the stage*: as the "Church" that is anything but the indifferent "setting" of this story. *eXistenZ* reveals its "true" nature as a game being played within the real game of *transCendenZ*. What is perhaps most notable about these names of games, however, is the shift in capitalization. That the "capitals" are no longer at the beginning of the names suggests that these names are no longer "proper," but rather are themselves acronyms of a "systematics" whose logic is open to question—if only because it must be "staged." It must be staged because of the question with which the Chinese game-player confronts his would-be murderers: "Are we still in the game?"

That question remains without an answer. It marks the end of the film, but perhaps not the end of the "game." With this uncertain ending what reemerges is thus the question of the game's *limits*, but now not as a question that can be framed by plot or intention, by determining where the one stops and the other starts. The question now no longer concerns simply beginnings and ends, but rather the *ways* in which plot and intention take place at all. One such way leads from the reconverted church to the gas station, the motel room, and the private house, from the "trout factory" to the Chinese restaurant to the battle scene. These places are almost always "interiors," but at any moment they can be turned inside out. It is the possibility of this *turn-about—peripeteia—*that the move places, or rather *replaces*, on the agenda. That these two names or nouns are both derived from the gerund suggests just how theatrical this agenda remains.

14

"War," "Terrorism," and "Spectacle":
On Towers and Caves

" W A R " **A N D** "terrorism" have traditionally been associated with one another, but to link them both to "spectacle" constitutes a relatively new phenomenon. To "link" does not, of course, mean to *identify*: it does not suggest that war, terrorism, and spectacle are the same. But it implies a necessary relationship among them. And that is new, in a very specific way. War has traditionally been associated with spectacle, with pageantry, parades, and demonstrations of all kinds, but perhaps never in the way we are witnessing it today, when a certain kind of *theatricalization* has come to constitute one of war's most essential components, one not, as in the past, limited primarily to the celebration of its victorious outcome.

To be sure, a certain theatricalization has always played an important part in the conduct of military affairs. Intimidation of the enemy has always been a major goal in combat operations, and reliance on spectacular effects of all kinds has been a long-standing result. In the German *Blitzkrieg*, dive-bombers of the *Luftwaffe* were outfitted with deafening sirens in order to add psychological terror to physical destruction and thus more fully demoralize the adversary. And of course concerted propaganda campaigns also demonstrated the importance of presenting a perspective and narrative of the ongoing struggle that would not be decided by strictly military means.

Yet to understand the distinct role played by theatricalization in conflict resolution today, it is important to take into account the new political and military significance assigned to the notions of "terror" and "terrorism." This may well be the first time in history that the world's reigning power has declared "terror" to be its main enemy— and, moreover, an enemy whose reach is no less global than its own.

On the day following the destruction of the World Trade Center and part of the Pentagon, President Bush proclaimed that the events were "more than acts of terror: they were acts of war," perpetrated by "a different enemy than we have ever faced: this enemy hides in the shadows. . . . This will be a monumental struggle of good versus evil, but good will prevail."[1]

Whether or not the attacks of September 11 changed everything, as is often asserted, is open to question. But they certainly changed the perceptions of those living in the United States who were convinced that "it can't happen here": namely, that organized, mass destruction was something that was exclusively limited to the nightly news. The bombing in Oklahoma City, of course, marked a first breach in this widely held belief. But it could still be regarded as the exception that confirms the rule. That rule, however, collapsed together with the imploding towers on September 11.

One should be as precise as possible here. American society and its media have long been obsessed with violence: The massacres at Columbine High School or of the Branch Davidians in Waco are just two recent instances. But violence in the United States has generally been portrayed, if not always perpetrated, as a *private affair*, done either *by* desperate or deranged individuals, or *against* desperate or deranged individuals. Violence tends to be individualized or, better, *privatized*, as with the Mafia and "organized crime," understood as an extension of individuals, of the family, or of private groups. This is the violence that is demonstrated from morning to evening on the broadcast media, from the reports of mayhem on the highways that accompany the breakfast traffic reports to the incessant series of murders and killings that make up the not so new "nightly news." "Security" has thus for decades been a long-standing preoccupation both of individuals and of the American nation.[2]

What *is* new is the growing efficacy of an organized violence that is no longer simply private or individual, no longer simply "criminal" but rather "terrorist": which is to say, whose goal is to disrupt and destroy the very fabric of society. Of course, this is not absolutely new, far from it. In his message to the special joint session of Congress on September 20, 2001, President Bush himself compared al Qaeda to the Mafia: "Al Qaeda is to terror what the Mafia is to crime. But its goal is not making money; its goal is remaking the world." And he promised: "Our war on terror begins with al Qaeda, but it does not end there. It will not end until every terrorist group of global reach has been found, stopped and defeated." Finally, President Bush emphasized the motif that was to recur again and again in the months and, indeed, years to follow—the absolute uniqueness of this "war": "Our response involves far more than instant retaliation and isolated strikes. Americans should not expect one battle, but a lengthy campaign, unlike any other we have ever seen. It may include dramatic strikes, visible on TV, and covert operations, secret even in success."[3]

The attacks of September 11, 2001, were thus presented to the American public and its representatives by the president as an entirely new and unprecedented phenomenon, one that required an entirely new and unprecedented response. But the "war on terror" that followed was by no means the first such "war" declared by American governments. Following the assassination of President John F. Kennedy, his successor, Lyndon B. Johnson, declared a "War on Poverty," while pursuing the less metaphorical war in Vietnam and Southeast Asia. Succeeding presidents declared a "War on Drugs." And now we have the "War on Terror." As commonly understood, "war" generally implies a conflict between *states*. Notable exceptions, of course, are civil and guerilla *wars*, in which the conflict is not between states but within a single state, or between an occupying power and an irregular resistance. But in all these cases what is at stake is state power—that of an organized polity within a delimited territory. From this point of view, which associates "war" with a constituted "state," "terrorism" can be seen as its excluded other, for what is generally called "terrorism" is the more or less organized use of violence by entities *other than established states*. Terrorism is, of course, never merely a descriptive, constative term: it is an evaluative one. Traditionally, the word has been used to designate a violence considered to be illegitimate, evil, morally reprehensible *because* it is exercised by nonstate organizations, groups, or individuals. The state is thus identified as the guardian of law and order. Where this presumption breaks down, the prevailing conception of terrorism reveals itself to be too simple. Thus, in the years 1940–44, the German occupying power in Europe designated all resistance movements, in France and elsewhere, as "terrorists." Almost every state defends its claim to hold a monopoly of organized violence, in the name of peace and security, by defining the violence of its adversaries—those who do not equate legality with legitimacy—as "terrorist."

In the twentieth century, however, and probably long before, this use of the term became more complicated, as the example of the Nazi occupation suggests. It became increasingly common to designate states themselves as terrorist: Nazi Germany, the Soviet Union under Stalin, and so on. The Israeli government led by Ariel Sharon has designated Yasser Arafat and the Palestinian Authority "terrorist," and Arafat has replied by calling Sharon's Israel a terrorist state. The ETA is a terrorist organization for Spain and France, but a movement of national liberation for segments of the Basque population.

If states are constituted in violence (for instance, through a "revolution") and maintained through the exercise of force, both external and domestic, then the difference between "terror" and "legitimate force" is never simply a neutral assessment, but rather a function of perspective, situation, interpretation, and evaluation. This does not mean that it is entirely arbitrary, of course, but rather that it is always *relational*: a function of its relation to other elements, never simply a judgment that can be self-contained.

American authorities have recently criticized the BBC World Service for its policy of using the word *terrorism* too sparingly, at least by comparison with the American media. But this linguistic restraint is not limited to the Middle East: over the past decades the BBC has rarely if ever referred to the IRA, for instance, as a "terrorist" organization.

Nevertheless, "terrorism" continues to be defined as the enemy of the state *as such*: and if, as Carl Schmitt persuasively argues, the concept of the political is based on the identification of an "enemy," then this discursive practice amounts to nothing less than identifying the terrorist as the *enabling other* of the state: its negative justification. The more powerful the terrorist organization(s), the more powerful the state in its military-political-security functions must become and, correspondingly, the weaker its civilian and civil functions must be made. Such a tendency takes on a special signification in a period when the traditional conception, if not functions, of the nation-state are more in question than at any time probably since its inception. In the post–Cold War period of "globalization" and transnational capitalism, a new "enemy" is needed to consolidate the role and to reinforce the legitimacy of nation-states, which are ever more openly dependent upon, and agents of, transnational corporate interests.[4] Today not just the presidents of universities are primarily fund-raisers rather than policy-makers (at least in the United States): presidents and chief executives of nation-states serve with increasing openness as emissaries and advocates of their country's respective economic interests.[5] Since these interests are also increasingly difficult to identify with the common good of the populations of their respective states, enemies are needed in order to justify the "sacrifices" demanded of populations subjected to increasing social precariousness.

"International terrorism" is at the moment the leading candidate for Public Enemy Number One. But it is an unusual candidate, at least in the forms it has recently assumed. And its unusual quality has to do with the third term, to which I now turn: *spectacle*.

The notion of "spectacle" can help us describe just what is distinctive about "international terrorism" being declared Public Enemy Number One. In order for something to be a spectacle, it must, quite simply, *take place*—which is to say, it must be *localizable*. Whether inside, in a theater (of whatever kind), or outside, in the open, a spectacle must be placed in order to be seen (and heard). But the place and taking place of a spectacle entails no ordinary locality, not at least in the way place has traditionally been defined: namely, as a stable, self-contained container. The stage or scene of a spectacle is never fully self-contained. To function as a stage or a scene, a place must itself take place *in relation to another place*, the place of spectators or audience. The space of a theater is divided into the space of the stage and that of the audience. This makes the place and taking place of a spectacle singularly difficult to pin down, since, as Guy Debord puts it in his book, *The Society of the Spectacle*, "The world the spectacle holds up to view is at once *here* and *elsewhere*; it is the world of the commodity ruling over all lived experience. The commodity world is thus shown *as it really is*, for its logic is one with men's estrangement from one another and from . . . what they produce."[6]

Debord's notion of "spectacle" is an elaboration of Marx's chapter on the "fetish-character of the commodity," in which a social *relation* that is invisible *as such* appears in the form of a self-contained material or natural substance. But Debord's notion of the spectacle foregrounds what is only implicit in Marx: the relation to the spectator (who is, of course, also a listener—an audience). The spectator of the spectacle— which for Debord is always the spectacle of a society determined by the production of commodities—is both separated and isolated: from others, but also from him- or herself. In this context, Debord asserts that "the spectacle is simply the common language that bridges this division. . . . Spectators are linked by a one-way relationship to the very center that maintains their isolation from one another. The spectacle thus unites what is separate, but it unites it only in its separateness" (p. 22).

The spectacle, in being "at once here *and* elsewhere," marks the division of the here and now or rather, more precisely, their separation: the here is not just now, and the now is not just here. At the same time, the spectacle *plays to spectators* who are similarly neither here nor there, or—which amounts to the same—*here and there at once.* The upshot is that such spectators are not just separated from one another, but from themselves, insofar as these "selves" are defined through their position *as spectators.*

Debord's theory of the spectacle and of the spectator gives a certain relief to the deliberately provocative response of Jean Baudrillard to the attacks of September 11. In an article published in *Le Monde* on November 3, 2001, Baudrillard writes:

> All the speeches and commentaries betray a gigantic abreaction to the event and to the fascination that it exercises. Moral condemnation, the sacred alliance against terrorism are in direct proportion to the prodigious jubilation of seeing this global superpower destroyed or better, in some sense, destroy itself. . . . That we dreamt of such an event, that everyone without exception dreamt of it, because no one could not not dream of the destruction of any superpower having attained such a degree of hegemony—this is unacceptable to the Western moral conscience, but it remains a fact, which can be measured precisely by the pathetic violence of all the speeches that seek to erase it.
>
> In the end, it is they who did it but it is we who wanted it.

In the light of Debord's discussion, the voice speaking here—the "we who wanted it"—is the spectator of the society of the spectacle. Some thirty-five years after Debord wrote his book, however, those spectators can be more precisely situated and described: they are television viewers who themselves are sold qua commodities to the advertisers who are the real customers of the national and multinational media. This is, of course, entirely true in the United States and increasingly true in Europe.

Baudrillard's assertion makes sense, I would argue, *only* insofar as it is understood to articulate the position of "spectators," a position that is not the same in Paris as it is in New York, but that nevertheless shares certain general characteristics, which Debord was one of the first to discern. Debord emphasizes that the spectacle perpetuates the separation and isolation of individuals in a commodity society, while seeking to conceal and surmount that isolation. The televisual view of the world propagated by the nightly news, in every country with which I am familiar (a very limited number, to be sure, mainly North America and Western Europe), heightens the *ambivalence* that Debord described but never named as such: that which results when anxieties related to the limitations of physical (and social) existence, involving frailty, vulnerability, and ultimately mortality, are provisionally suppressed through images that position the spectator as an invulnerable and all-seeing survivor: surviving all the catastrophes that constitute the bulk of the nightly news, at least in the United States. The situation of this spectator is akin to that of the child described by Lacan as the mirror stage, characterized by an "imaginary" identification with an image of wholeness. The internal contradiction of such identification is that it institutes an image of unity while occupying two places at once: the desired place of wholeness and the feared place of disunity. In the images of catastrophe that dominate broadcast media "news," disunity is projected into the image itself, while the desired unity is reserved for the spectator off-scene (and for the media itself as global network). To support such identification and the binary opposition upon which its success depends, images must appear to be clearly localizable, self-contained, and meaningful at the same time as they englobe destruction, mutilation, and implosion. They must comprehend the catastrophes that thereby appear to be intelligible in and of themselves, without requiring the spectator to look elsewhere. The spectator thus can sustain the illusion of occupying a stable and enduring position, which allows one to "stay the same" indefinitely. This is the moral of the story, whether it is called "enduring freedom" or "infinite justice." The "War on Terror" is thus conducted in the name of "enduring freedom" as the freedom to remain the same, to keep one's place indefinitely. This is also the message of "infinite justice": to remain indefinitely the same is to pursue the enemy relentlessly, without end, until he is cornered in his innermost redoubts and destroyed. The trajectory that leads from the twin towers to the caves of Toro Bora marks the will to power as a will to endure. This is the not so hidden religious subtext of the ostensibly secular "War on Terror," which is above all a defense and affirmation of "globalization" as the right of the One (superpower) to rule over all the others.

To rule the planet, one must survive. But to survive one must rule. And the rule must serve the one. Which is why the "war against terror" marks the move from the *rule of law* to *the law of the rule.* Or, more precisely, to the rule of rule. "Law" entails "due process," and thus both more and less than undivided rule. It must therefore be subordinated to the law of the rule, in which the suspension of law and the state of exception become the general rule and the principle by which power is exercised.

But in its encapsulated individuality and its claim to indivisible authority, the rule must be constantly renewed, and with it, the state of exception, the emergency, the danger, and the enemy. Because this is an enemy that wears no uniform and never appears as such, it can never be definitively located, "smoked out," and defeated.

Thus "freedom" may be "enduring," but its duration is marked by breaks, interruptions, and the ever-present threat of catastrophe. For the moment, this catastrophe is rendered visible in the spectacle of the twin towers imploding—a phallic fate if ever there was one—and of a portion of the Pentagon in ruins. Broadcast in "real time," this had two effects. On the one hand, it heightened the anxiety of the "break" on which the appeal of consumption is based. Consumer confidence was shattered, at least temporarily, and after a period of mourning the official discourse had to urge all citizens not, as one might have expected, to "get back to work," but to "get back to consuming," and start spending again. The promise of immortality was interrupted, but only to be reasserted for those who would "stay with us . . . after the break." And since such traumatic breaks are the most powerful goad to consume, the basic structure and process were not fundamentally altered. As long, that is, as the putative cause of anxiety could be located *in an image,* confined to a site, a stage. Or rather, to multiple sites and stages, but in succession, one after the other. This is the end of the military response to "terrorism": it must be named (al Qaeda), given a face (Osama bin Laden) and then, above all, *located* (Afghanistan, Tora Bora, Iraq, Sudan, Somalia, etc.): in order then to be depicted, if possible, and destroyed.

On the other hand, when "terrorism" is defined as "international," it becomes more difficult to locate, situate, personify, and identify. Or rather, it can only be located in sequence, one site after the other, not

333

all at once. From this point on, the war on terrorism becomes a scenario, a sitcom that unfolds, step by step and intrinsically without end, in its effort to bring the infinite enemy to "infinite justice." Almost from the beginning of this "war," the Bush administration has asserted that the enemy is "international" in character, neither limited to one person, however important, nor to one state, however nefarious. Thus, the War on Terror, unlike the Cold War, cannot be defined primarily as a war against a single state, the Soviet Union, or against its international emanation, "The Communist Conspiracy." It is not even a war against a single "terrorist" organization, however decentralized, such as al Qaeda. "International Terrorism" englobes all the "rogue" states that for years have been designated by the U.S. State Department as aiding and abetting "terrorism": Iraq, Iran, North Korea, Sudan, Syria, and so on. What characterizes this policy is its continuing effort to tie terrorist networks to nation-states. This identification both supplies and supplants any discussion of other possible "causes," conditions, or ramifications. In this view, all these can be located in the pathological behavior of individual "rogue" states, whose roguishness consists in their refusal to follow the norms of international behavior as laid down by the United States government. (In passing, it should be noted that the political use of the word *rogue* has an interesting history. As far as I can remember, the first time I became aware of the word was in relation to the assassination of President Kennedy, when it was used by investigators—and certainly not by the government—to describe elements of the government ("intelligence" services, military) that might have acted secretly, outside the official chain of command; later the term was used to designate states that did not comply with American expectations of proper political behavior, such as Libya, Cuba, North Korea, and Iraq. In short, from a term designating the disunity of "official" state organizations, it became a designator of abnormal political-state behavior, a symptomatic development, to say the least.

• • •

To conclude: the spectacle, at least as staged by the mainstream broadcast media, seeks simultaneously to assuage and exacerbate anxieties of all sorts by providing images on which they can be projected, ostensibly comprehended, and, above all, *removed*. Schematically, the fear of death is encouraged to project itself onto an image of the other, which as enemy is to be liquidated or subjugated. The viewer is encouraged to *"look forward"* and simultaneously *forget the past*; encouraged to identify with the ostensibly invulnerable perspective of the camera registering as blips the earth-bound destruction tens of thousands of feet below. Such a position seems to assure the triumph of the spectator over the perils of earthbound life. The trails of the B-52s in the stratosphere high above the earth announce the demise of the caves and the second coming of the towers.

If, as Carl Schmitt writes, "the enemy is our own question as figure," then what is new and different about international terrorism is its resistance to figuration. This serves not just to make it the inexhaustible justification of an unending mobilization, but even more, to obscure the extent to which this enemy is indeed *"our* question."[7]

The war against terror thus presents itself as the answer to a question that it does everything not to ask.

15

Stages and Plots:
Theatricality after September 11, 2001

A Discussion with Simon Morgan Wortham and Gary Hall

THE FOLLOWING discussion took place by e-mail during September 2001. On September 11, the World Trade Center in New York was destroyed and the Pentagon badly damaged in a series of well-coordinated attacks. The participants in the exchange obviously felt compelled to respond to these events, although it was envisaged beforehand that the purpose of the interview would be to discuss more generally the work of Samuel Weber. In what follows, therefore, immediate reactions to events as they unfolded contend—perhaps uneasily, but perhaps also productively—with a series of reflections on Weber's thinking, writing, and critical practice over a number of years. What characterizes the discussion overall, both in terms of its "content" and its very "taking place," is perhaps the question of a critical or "theoretical" discourse acting itself out in relation to a series of phenomena, acts, or events to which it feels compelled to respond. It is a matter of judgment whether this distinctive and distinguishing trait of the discussion pulls it apart, or whether in some way it "tears" it or tangles it together. But such a characteristic trait nevertheless engages a whole set of questions and problems (having to do with repetition, singularity, the uncanny, and so forth) which, in turn, might be taken to characterize the work of Samuel Weber in its entirety. Questions and responses are dated to preserve and to highlight the temporal dimension of the "event"—both of the discussion taking place, and the events on a world-scale that this discussion could not help but address.

Simon Morgan Wortham and Gary Hall (September 10, 2001):
Samuel Weber, taking into account a large body of work written over a number of years, the range and scope of your interests is obviously very varied and broad. For instance, you write on psychoanalysis, lit-

erature, philosophy, aesthetics, the media, technics and technology, institutions, and theater. Yet the extent to which certain texts, readings, and critical moves tend to be revisited or replayed on a variety of different occasions is striking. To take just one example, you return more than once to the question of aesthetic and reflective judgment in Kant to show how, in this part of Kant's critical philosophy, cognition and judgment take place on condition of an other. From this point onward, you are able to discuss problems of aesthetic form, of parergon and institution, and of the "fateful and ambiguous legacy" that Kant bequeaths to the institution of the humanities. But this reading also allows you to suggest that such processes or operations of cognition tend to theatricalize knowledge, to transform the grounds of knowledge into a rather more unsteady—or even comedic— platform upon which we witness certain styles of mimicry being performed or staged. Here, then, the ambivalence that attends humanistic knowledge seems to rest upon a question of *theater.* Furthermore, in *Mass Mediauras* the Kantian problem of aesthetic judgment appears to set off your work on Heidegger and his account of the "goings-on" of technics. In this context, technological understanding, activity, and development depend on very ambivalent processes of securing and unsecuring that begin to unravel as man endeavors to "gain a stand" and to "establish himself" by means of the knowledge of beings that Heidegger calls *technē.* Technological man thus orients himself in a way that begins to look rather theatrical and, to go further, perhaps even spectacularly comedic. Such a problem of orientation, then, connects a discussion of technics and technology to problems of cognition and judgment, to questions of aesthetics and form, to the matter of theater, and, indeed, to the problematics of institution.

In returning to a particular text or reading, then, such connections, reorientations, or transformations obviously emerge in a way that powerfully assumes and replays the problematics of repetition and iteration that are discussed in a number of places in your work. Here, the relationship between what is singular and what is universal becomes very complicated, to say the least. Perhaps you might care to say something more explicit about the conceptual grounds of the key "terminology" you deploy: for example, *technics, ambivalence, institution, theater.* Is it at all possible that the re-readings or repetitions that characterize your work rest upon any kind of quasi-transcendental term or terms? Would this be a source of orientation? How else might

337

you describe what is going on when one begins to have the—perhaps uncanny—experience of going over "familiar ground" in your writing?

Samuel Weber (September 10, 2001): Your question, which addresses the "uncanny," is itself not a little uncanny, at least for me. Especially since I'm sure that, however I respond, I won't be able to avoid a certain repetition, and hence, doubtless, a certain "familiarity." Let's hope it's an uncanny one.

Nietzsche—who, together with Kierkegaard, placed the question of repetition, recurrence, *Wiederkehr* on the agenda—writes somewhere that with passing years one finds oneself returning to certain questions that seem to change very little over time. These questions, which function as a kind of bedrock of identity, are more difficult to "lose" than to retain. Whether this "bedrock" becomes a source of strength and discovery or a prison depends on how those questions "return": whether they primarily only "determine," in the simply restrictive sense of setting limits, or whether the limits they trace gesture toward a space not simply contained within the area they demarcate. This is one of the reasons why a sense of the "uncanny"— indeed, an openness to it—is indispensable, if one is to avoid the kind of entropy that a purely obsessive recurrence would entail.

There certainly is a dimension of "familiarity" in my writings, but I try to think of it, to relate to it, as something other than a simple ground. Although I hesitate to limit it to a single name, if I were forced to, I would take the one, or rather, the series you have mentioned and I have begun to extend: "repetition," "iterability," as "uncanny" questions, and as the question of the uncanny.

This set, or series, of related (but not identical) terms marks a certain discovery, an "experience" in the sense of *Erfahrung*, traversal or trajectory, "*peripeteia* without *anagnōrisis*," to vary the Aristotelian formula. Or, perhaps, thinking of Beckett, "*anagnōrisis* as *peripeteia*," a formula for the uncanny recognition of something that, in being the same, reveals itself to be different.

In the course of my thinking, that trajectory begins with Adorno's condemnation of the *Immergleiche*—of that which is "ever-the-same"—as a form of repetition, passes via Freud's "repetition compulsion," which is both "always the same" and yet never entirely appropriable, to Derrida's use of repetition to deconstruct the Husserlian notion of "ideality" as the monological (and prelinguistic) discourse of the soul with itself (in *Speech and Phenomenon*). "Repetition" has, it seems, haunted me for a long time, first in the guise of a polemical object of criticism (Adorno, Marcuse), then as a problematic discovery (Freud) leading to an even more problematic hypothesis ("the death-drive"), and finally—but of course, there is no finality here, only finitude—Derrida's compelling formulation of "iterability" (in "Signature Event Context" and *Limited Inc*) and Kierkegaard's theatricalization of *Gjentagelsen*—"taking again" (*reprise* is the provocative rendering of a recent French translation). "Again," *against*—this recurrence of the motif of "repetition" has been more than a question—rather, a challenge to which I have had little choice but to respond.

A challenge, in the sense of defying whatever I thought I understood of the word, or set of words. Of this challenge, let me just mention two interrelated aspects. First, that, as Kierkegaard—or rather, as Constantin Constantius, the narrative figure who fictionalizes authorship in *Gjentagelsen*—states, repetition, in contrast to recollection (*anamnēsis*), is directed toward the *future*, not toward the past. That certainly doesn't make sense, not at first sight, at least. Which is why it is interesting, and challenges one to think further. *Second*, the *difference*, on which Derrida, in his debate with Searle, insists, between "iter*ability*" and "iteration" (or, if you will, between "repeatability" and "repetition"): the difference between something that simply "is," whose mode of being can be adequately articulated in the present indicative—*iteration*—as an act or occurrence that is present-to-itself, and something that "exists," if it exists at all, as a kind of *possibility* (in *Limited Inc* Derrida calls it a "structural possibility"). A "kind of possibility" in the sense of one that is no longer defined by the oppositional logic of identity, which is to say, as being the opposite of "reality" or "actuality." (The difference between these two terms can be ignored in our context.) What distinguishes iterability from iteration is that it does not necessarily imply the possibility of its enactment: it entails a possibility that is not a subspecies or dialectical other of "reality" as self-fulfillment, actualization, or self-presence. Or, to use a category that has proved useful for me over the years, as a form of *self-containment*. Hence, for Derrida, *iterability*, far from designating a possible realization, is "actually" much closer to "impossibility," inasmuch as its mode of being is such that it never fully "takes place," a process that Derrida early on associates with a certain "theatricality"

339

(my term, not necessarily his): for instance, in his reading of Mallarmé's short text "Mimique" (in "La Double Séance," the "Double Session").

This conjugation of "possibility" and "impossibility" as nonexclusive, indeed, as convergent (although again, not simply identical), is one of the traits or tendencies that I find exemplified in a certain kind of "theatricality." Not necessarily in "theater," and not necessarily in everything that one would call "theatrical," but in the questions and problems, challenges and injunctions that distinguish the history of "theatricality"—if one can speak of such a history in the singular. One of the things that has struck me, in rethinking this history, or certain parts of it, at least, is the link between "iterability," in English at least, and various forms of the present participle, including the "gerund." It is as if the conjugation of possibility with impossibility can be exemplified in what we call "acting" as distinct from "action," "act," or "actual(ity)": *acting* lacks the kind of reality usually associated with the present indicative, and yet it is bound up with "indication"— although it is never simply "present," inasmuch as it is repetitive. At the same time, its *repetition* is also a *rehearsal*—as in French—that is directed not just toward the past but above all toward the future— which, however, it will never fully "attain" (i.e., render present, actualize). This is why it is important to distinguish such iterative theatricality from "performance" and "performative," which often (if not always) imply the realization of an intention, of a purpose.

Understood in this way, such theatricalization could be situated in a series going back at least to Kant's definition of the beautiful as "purposiveness without purpose." The aesthetic judgment of beauty is addressed to something so immediately present that it can never be self-present, never identified. It remains purely indicative, a pointing-toward, a *Zweckmässigkeit ohne Zweck*. But this "pointing toward" turns out, in Kant, at least, to be even more a "pointing away"—away from wherever it is at, and what it seems to be. Kant tries to synthesize this double movement in his notion of "reflective judgment," but the notion only reproduces the split, since it designates a reflexivity that never arrives at its destination: a reflexivity without reflection, one could say, although I doubt that Kant would have been very happy with that formulation. But if one reads the Third Critique closely, one discovers that what Kant is describing or, rather, trying to describe is not a self-contained state but rather closer to the unstable aporia of a unity so self-contained that it tends to dissolve before our very eyes. This is why the "as if" has to intervene so constantly, indeed so obsessively, in that text, creating one parenthetic qualification after another, as Kant literally (or, rather, syntactically) ties himself into knots trying to articulate something in accordance with a logic of identity it tends to undo. Kant's account of the aesthetic judgment of taste is a latter-day version of another of Kierkegaard's favorite anecdotes: that of Cratylus outdoing his teacher, Heraclitus, when he notes that one cannot step into the same river "even once." But Kant doesn't think that he is telling stories . . . or does he?

I haven't touched on the "technical" part of your question. Let me just say that the presentation of iterability that distinguishes theatrical "representation" puts a particular spin on the question of "technics." If one remembers the earlier, pre-Heideggerian definitions of *technē* as involving a prosthetic supplement of an internal lack, then theatrical iterability locates that "lack" in and as the "act" of an "actuality" that must be *repeatable* in order to be *enacted*. The "en-" of "enactment" is thus inseparable from the implicit "ex-" of an iterability that can never be self-contained. "Theatricality" results when the impossibility of self-containment is exposed by iterability as a *scene* that is inevitably a "stage," but which, as such, is determined by whatever surrounds it, by what we call a "theater." More affirmatively formulated, the impossibility of closure opens the scene to a space of alterity that is always *provisionally* embodied in and, even more, *exposed* as an "audience"—singular noun for an irreducibly heteroclite stand-in. The "audience" stands in for the others, those who were and those who will be—and perhaps even more for those who will never come to be. Of course, it is in the nature of our socio-economic system, in an age of "globalization," to do everything possible to appropriate and domesticate such "standing-in" so that it seeks to fulfill itself in and as actual consumption. The audience is thus considered by the commercial media predominantly, if not exclusively, as potential consumers.

SMW and GH (September 10, 2001): Presumably, then, the "age of 'globalization' "—as your work itself would indicate, and as you've perhaps hinted just now—is not and cannot be merely opposed to the issue and effects of "theatricality," in which case the problem of, for want of a better term, the parergon, which seems to re-emerge in the description you've just given of theatricalized space, would also impose itself in any analysis of the globalized, technological age of today?

SW (September 12, 2001): From the point of view I have begun to outline, "theatricality" can provide a particularly interesting way of approaching *globalization*. If one thinks about the word itself, the notion of the world as "globe" suggests two things: first, something visible; second, a sphere, something self-contained. A "world" is not necessarily visible: a "globe" is, at least potentially. It is a visible *Gestalt*. As such, it implies a viewer. But this is no ordinary "globe": it is, as just mentioned, a globe that contains all life as we know it, and, in particular, all human life. *Globalization* in this sense implies totality (although not, in the literal sense, "universality"): it defines the space or site of all options open to life in general, and to human life in particular. As a sphere, it is self-contained, even if it is not all-inclusive. Self-contained also suggests self-sufficient: the globe is the site of a life that can, and must, take care of itself.

And yet, being a visible *Gestalt*, anything that is "global" is also an object of perception and of understanding. An object of consciousness and of cognition. Being the site of all life as we know it—and it is hardly an accident that "globalization" coexists with, and perhaps encourages, a heightened fascination with the "extraterrestrial"—*globalization* names not so much an object as the conditions for all objectification, the conditions of cognition and of action. This is why we speak of "global*ization*" and not just of the "globe" or the "global." "Global war," for instance, is a term that antedates the age of "global*ization*." "Global*ization*" is a *process* by which the world of possibilities is at the same time *totalized* and *restricted*. This is why it serves as an appropriate figure to name a certain *vision* of the *world* in the post–Cold War period. The term *globalization* does not merely emphasize the transnational interdependence of different parts of the world: it implies that there is no longer any alternative to the not so new world order of "late" capitalism and to the relations of power and hierarchies of subjugation that this order entails.

It implies this in a message that may often be transmitted subliminally, but that seeks to eliminate all ambiguity. Nevertheless, *globalization* remains highly ambiguous, as a term and as a process, not so much in its message as in its means of address. *Globalization* does not merely name a worldwide, socio-economic process: it also constitutes an address and an injunction, one that demands a response, which can vary between enthusiastic acceptance, passionate rejection, or resigned indifference, since the primary message conveyed by the word is that there can be no alternative save "fanaticism," "terrorism," and other forms of brutal irrationality. *Globalization*, as embodied in "the media"—television above all, but also to a large extent the print media—is presented as the only game in town or, rather, in the world. This message is reinforced by the very existence and manifestation of the media, which themselves are part and parcel of the globalizing process. Since there is ostensibly no alternative to "globalization," in a world where ostentation and media are inseparable, the only response reserved for the audience is that of acquiescence, if not legitimation, in relation to a process presented as being in any event immutable and inevitable. Nevertheless, the media require this response in order for the process, which claims to be total and yet self-contained, to find its enabling limit. That limit is the acquiescence of the audience, by which the other, and alterity, is placed in the position of the consumer. Everything that globalization is not and cannot be is thus concentrated in and as its audience, which serves as the limit that a capitalism-without-alternative strives both to control and to appropriate.

To use a Derridean term, one might say that the problem of the "parergon" returns today in the form of the theatricalized audience: does it frame the "work" as its intrinsic other, the way the consumer belongs to the process of production as its inner edge? Or does it split and dislocate such a dialectic by exposing that which it delimits to what is irreducibly other? Or does it do both, and if so, in what proportions?

· · ·

To take a horrific instance, one that is all too current at the time we are discussing this, but which will have become a more distant memory by the time our discussion reaches its "audience," or rather readers: Yesterday, September 11, 2001, the World Trade Center was destroyed and the Pentagon badly damaged by what is called, understandably, a "terrorist" attack. The destruction was transmitted, "in real time," by television throughout the world, provoking in the "West" reactions of horror, and in parts of the Near East (and perhaps elsewhere), spontaneous expressions of joy. These two very different responses seem to have nothing in common. And yet they share at

343

least one interpretation of the destruction, which was presumably at the core both of the horror and of the joy: the discovery that no place on the globe could any longer consider itself *safe*, which is to say, *immune* to the violent effects of "globalization." Among the images of the destruction which returned incessantly on the television screen, one seemed to sum up one of the lessons of the horror: a plaque that was all that was left of one of the destroyed buildings, upon which was written "One World Center." Among the countless associations provoked by this inscription was that in today's "One World" the "Center" is no longer safe from the "periphery." The collapse of the two enormous towers, which did not just collapse, but imploded and disappeared into themselves, producing a huge cloud of dust and rubble, which appeared to race toward the camera and, implicitly, toward the millions of viewers all over the world, who sat riveted to their screens in disbelief—all of this exposed the "One World Center" to be as vulnerable as the peripheries. Was I the only viewer who was reminded of Nicholas Meyer's chilling television film "The Day After" (1983), in which the white dust of what was then known as "nuclear winter" covered the condemned survivors of a global nuclear war? Was I the only one for whom the billowing clouds that rose from the collapsing towers recalled the mushroom clouds of previous nuclear explosions? And who then had to acknowledge that the spectacular destruction of September 11 was the result, not of a high-tech explosion, but of a low-tech collision—one that was clearly highly organized, carefully planned, and executed with military precision, but with no technology of its own, only that of the targeted victims?

From this standpoint, at least, September 11 has revealed the vulnerability of the most powerful political and economic structures, in both literal and figurative senses. In doing this it marks the end of an illusion—that of a *locus amoenus* existing at the center of the world system. At the same time, the bad tidings of this revelation have probably also been experienced by many as a confirmation of their most deeply rooted fears, as well as a confirmation of the sense of powerlessness which is one of the primary conditions of being a docile spectator.

The notion of "theatricalization" includes this possibility—that of the docile, reactive, passive, and anxious "beholder"—but it can also reinscribe it in a space that exceeds the frame of spectacle and spectator. The danger is that such "excess" will be experienced only as a source of anxiety and panic, and will thus be rejected and foreclosed by the kind of paranoiac spiral that words such as *terrorism* and *fanaticism* are designed to justify and promote.

SMW and GH (September 15, 2001): An initial reaction to what you've just said about recent events in the United States would be that the value of your remarks *at this time* is certain, even if, as you seem to hint, they are bound inevitably to become an historical artifact, in a sense, a part, however small, of the "events" themselves. This, in turn, might prompt us to wonder about the complicated processes or relationships of partaking, participation, and apartness upon which such a response—perhaps any sort of response—to these "events" inevitably rests. Of course, the terms being used here deliberately recall, recite, or replay key themes and issues within your own work, not least with regard to a whole range of questions having to do with criticism, spectatorship, viewpoint or standpoint, knowledge, judgment, and so on. These questions *install* themselves, one might say, in philosophy and aesthetics, in literary, cultural, and media studies, but also in the realms of politics, technologization, and globalization.

Of course, some might find such reflections or, rather, such self-reflexivity concerning the place or standpoint of any such critical response to move in a direction that becomes self-regarding and, ultimately, a bit detached. On the other hand, by invoking the unstable dynamics of participation and apartness as part of an appeal or injunction that raises once more the question of parergon, limit, boundary, or frame, such concerns could surely be viewed as inseparable from what is most pressing among current international, political issues. Here again, in the very determination of the value or import of the question, the ambivalent interplay of apartness and participation once more imposes itself.

That said, it is also striking that there would seem to be a—perhaps uncanny—link between the question with which we began, concerning the uncanny, the response on your part, and subsequent events that have interrupted or imposed themselves upon this discussion. For instance, there is, in the first place, your awareness that what occurred on September 11, 2001, "will have become a more distant memory by the time our discussion reaches its 'audience', or rather readers"— presumably because this is what has happened to similar events in the past. Immediate responses soon become reconsidered, mediated, overwritten, transformed. There are already claims on the Net that the images to which you refer, of people in the Near East celebrating the attacks on the US, are in fact from old CNN footage dating from 1991. On top of which is the fact that the events themselves resembled the "theatrical" spectacles provided by any number of American films (*Independence Day*, *Mars Attacks*, which themselves link to the "heightened fascination with the 'extraterrestrial'" you speak of)—and one might note reports in the press that the release dates of a number of forthcoming films have been cancelled or postponed due to such similarities (Arnold Schwarzenegger's *Collateral Damage*, for example, which contains scenes of a building in LA being blown up; *Swordfish*, which has a city block being bombed; or *Big Trouble*, which involves a bomb on a plane). All this seems to add up to an uncanny sense, even when watching the events live on Tuesday and being acutely aware of their singularity, that we have been here before; that we are being haunted by a certain repetition which is both "'always the same' and yet never entirely appropriable"—presenting us with a "challenge" to which we have, as you have said, "little choice but to respond."

SW (September 16, 2001): Let me respond, first, to the end of your comment, about the deprogramming of Hollywood catastrophe films, either new ones scheduled to come out in the near future or older ones, which were to be shown on television (several such films will not be shown in the coming weeks as planned on French television). Although I assume that such deprogramming is a fairly general phenomenon, there is perhaps an additional development here in France that is equally significant. The week or so before the destruction of the World Trade Center and the attack on the Pentagon, television viewers in France were treated to a rather unusual advertisement. It showed a worker cleaning the window of a skyscraper, when suddenly a glaring light coming from a mirror far below, in the street, blinds him and also the viewers themselves. The worker loses his balance and falls to certain death. But instead of striking the pavement, his body miraculously hits the roof of a car, a French car traditionally known for the spongy if dangerous comfort of its suspension. The worker is saved.

On September 11, that ad disappeared from television and cinema screens, presumably forever. It was replaced by the sight of other bodies, this time "real ones," falling to their death from far greater heights. One of the effects of this, expected and feared, is a very different kind of "fall" tomorrow, when the American stock exchanges open, for the first time in almost a week. "Consumer confidence," already badly shaken, is expected to be not the least significant of the "collateral damage" caused by the attacks. But was not at least one of the underlying conditions of this "catastrophe" already "mirrored," as it were, in the ad that ran during the week preceding the attacks? If only the miraculous presence of the automobile below could "save" the falling body from the fate visited upon the thousands caught in the upper stories of the two towers of the World Trade Center towers on September 11, what will be the fate of "the fear of falling" to which the advertisement appealed, on the eve of the catastrophe? This ad, like all good advertising, struck a chord, was attuned to the expectations of its audience, even and especially those which are not necessarily conscious or avowed. For instance, the danger that provoked ("triggered") the fall of the window-washer also affected the spectators watching it: like the worker, they too were momentarily blinded by the glare. Where did the glare come from? Watching that ad, one could hardly avoid thinking of a deliberate, malicious, malevolent act: someone manipulating a mirror in order to blind the victim. But the "victim" who is blinded also includes the beholder of the ad, to whom it is addressed. This puts the spectators, as potential consumers, in an "analogous" position to the victim, who is saved by the potential object of consumption, the car.

The spectators watching the ad are, of course, the "commodity" that commercial television sells to its clients, the advertisers. Their sight, and hence their status as spectators, are both "struck" by the same glare that causes the "worker"—the "sight" they are given to see—to fall to an almost certain death. Only the automobile, a specific, distinct automobile, "saves" the worker. By implication—however "ironic" and even silly it may seem—only *consumption* of the commodity in question can "save" the spectator. In 1973, Nissan Motors, then known in the U.S. as "Datsun," launched an immensely successful, if controversial ad campaign under the slogan "Datsun Saves!" The intransitive use of the master word of American advertising raised, for a brief moment, soon to be forgotten, the curtain on the culture of consumption in the U.S. "Datsun Saves!" From what?

From the Fall, which, in the tradition of the religions of the Book, at least, means guilt and death.

This is not the place to develop the links between commodity *consumption*, on the one hand, and the notion of *salvation*, on the other. It may therefore suffice to note that in both what is at stake is *guilt*, on the one hand, and *survival*, on the other. And not just survival, but survival of an *individual* who, otherwise, *qua individual* is condemned to perish. This is also what links the ad I have just discussed to the Hollywood catastrophe films to which you refer, in which, almost always, the threat of disaster is averted or surmounted by the *action* of a single heroic *individual*. Individuals, as a "class," category, or collective, are vulnerable to "terrorists," and only a heroic individual or, less frequently, a small group of individuals can "save" them. The action of an isolated individual redeems individual passivity and vulnerability, in the Hollywood scenarios at least.

September 11 has rendered that scenario obsolete. No Bruce Willis, Arnold Schwarzenegger, Harrison Ford could "save" that day. Whether active or passive, the main role assigned to individuals on that day was that of perishing or running from a danger that could hardly be circumscribed, much less effectively countered: billowing clouds of white smoke sowing panic before their advance (toward the cameras . . .). And the main role assigned to the political embodiment of that sort of individualism was confusion and flight, symbolized by a president of the United States who is warned not to return "home" but instead "flies"—or, rather, is flown—from military base to military base, in an effort to avoid the invisible dangers.

The specter of invisibility persists in the aftermath of the attacks. All major figures of the American government, together with British prime minister Tony Blair, insist that a "war" has broken out. But this war is haunted by enemies who, in the words of President Bush, "believe they are invisible. Yet they are mistaken. They will be exposed and they will discover what others in the past have learned: Those who make war against the United States have chosen their own destruction" (radio address, September 15, 2001).

However, such enemies must first be located in order to be destroyed. And in order to be located, they must be "seen." With astonishing rapidity, an automobile is found with the Koran, flight manuals, maps, and other unmistakable indications. Within two days, pictures and names of the hijackers are flashed across the screens, their whereabouts and histories described in detail. But the direct perpetrators themselves can no longer be seized, much less punished. All the more important, then, to be able to name and depict—that is, *see*—and thus to call to account the mastermind of the destruction. The importance attached to the figure of the individual—above all, to the face, but also to the body once again, as previously in the Gulf War—culminates in the identification of a new, Satanic (Islamic) Anti-Christ. Within hours of the attacks, the bearded figure of "Osama bin Laden" appears on television and computer screens throughout the world as "prime suspect." Somewhat less prominence is given to his writings, with the notable exception of the *fatwa* of 1998, signed by bin Laden but also by a number of other persons, proclaiming that "The ruling to kill the Americans and their allies—civilians and military—is an individual duty for every Muslim who can do it in any country in which it is possible to do it." This phrase is quoted again and again, without any indication that it is part of a larger statement, the remainder of which is almost never cited: "in order to liberate the al-Aqsa Mosque and the holy mosque [Mecca] from their grip, and in order for their armies to move out of all the lands of Islam, defeated and unable to threaten any Muslim." The amputation of the arguments upon which the *fatwa* is based, as well as the focus on a single individual or group, provides the groundwork for the preparation of the Crusade against the Anti-Christ, if not for the War of Civilizations between the Judeo-Christian and Moslem worlds long prophesized by Samuel Huntington.

The notion of a "War of Civilizations"—or rather, of Civilization against the Barbarians—strives to promote the sense of "distance" between friend and enemy so necessary to the detached positioning of the omniscient and secure observer. It also prepares those observers to embrace a solution of the conflict through military intervention. What you refer to as "participation" is acknowledged, but few consequences are drawn from it that might disturb this "friend-enemy" dichotomy. The fact that Western governments, and in particular the U.K. and U.S., have historically sought to defend their interests in the Arab world by supporting authoritarian and often conservative, theological, and political forms of Islam—the Saudi Arabian Wahhabi Islam is probably the most visible instance, but by no means the only one—while often, and concomitantly, weakening secular political governments and groups—is, of course, "acknowledged" but also "isolated," in the Freudian sense—which is to say, cut off from its consequences, some of which we have just experienced, but the most destructive of which may still lie ahead.

This is just one crass instance of how the systematic denial of "participation" in the name of a Manichean dualism of friend and enemy can contribute to the dangerous situation in which we now find ourselves. The forces that fostered the rise of "Islamic fundamentalism" are now obliged to destroy the parts of it that have escaped their control. An old story, but with a new and terrifying twist, since the "center" can no longer take for granted that it will be protected from the events of "the periphery." And it is likely that this all too justified fear will now be exploited to strengthen the very forces and situations that brought it about in the first place.

SMW and GH (September 17, 2001): Coming back to the issue of "globalization," one might wonder what you think of the antiglobalization protestors (of Seattle, Prague, the antisweatshop campaigns directed at the likes of The Gap by students in some universities in the United States, and so forth). In particular, how do these protestors fit into your analysis of American liberal society, for example, in *Institution and Interpretation?* One thinks specifically of the chapter "Capitalizing History," which includes an analysis based on a reading of Louis Hartz's *The Liberal Tradition in America* (1955). Is this "protest" (one is wary of terming something so decentered a "movement") just introducing conflict into a pluralist, nonconflictual space? Or do these protests reveal this space to be conflictual?

If so, is there any extent to which this is a result or an effect of what, in shorthand, might be termed "theory" (in its very broadest conceptualization)—despite Naomi Klein's indirect critique of that in her *No Logo*—given that "theory" "relegitimized" such "conflict," not just "within" fields and institutions, but "of" fields and institutions? Klein interestingly sees what she labels "identity politics," with which she associates "postmodern academics" and the "theory" of Gayatri Spivak, to be the immediate precursor of the antiglobalization protestors: it is against such "identity politics" that the current generation is in part reacting, apparently. Klein is thus just one of those who have recently chastised "theory" (among other things) for "not being political enough," in favor of a concern for the "real," the material, and the economic. But isn't the idea precisely of a re-action to "theory," as well as the notion of theory relegitimizing a certain kind of conflict, bound to create problems for this kind of approach?

SW (September 17, 2001): To create a bridge from our previous discussion to your questions, an article in today's *International Herald Tribune* (hereafter *IHT*) describes al Qaeda (the "Base"), the organization founded by bin Laden and accused by U.S. authorities of being responsible for last week's attacks, as an "example of globalization" (Karen DeYoung and Michael Dobbs, *IHT*, September 17, 2001). The comparison could be illuminating. What the authors have in mind is not just the international scope of the organization but its mode of operation, the relation of the individual, relatively autonomous groups, operating all over the world, to the chain of command, its "base," presumably situated in the Middle East and very likely in Afghanistan. The very notion of "base" seems to change, given that it seems to include alliances of different sorts (tactical, strategic) with other groups not directly linked to bin Laden. The notion of "globalization" thus is associated, not just with worldwide reach, but with an organizational structure in which the relation of "parts" to "whole" is very different from traditional "organic" structures, be they of a traditional military sort or a traditional political-conspiratorial sort (i.e., the "democratic centralism" of revolutionary Communist parties). Such a transformed structure, which permits what is probably an even greater autonomy to the individual units than in conspiratorial groups of the past, is probably itself a response to the changed needs of such groups, faced with the technology of globalization and the new means of surveillance and repression it has developed. Such surveillance is epitomized, on the one hand, by spy satellites that are capable, literally, of surveying the "globe," and, on the other hand, by the network "Echelon," based mainly in the Anglophone countries of the world: the U.S., Great Britain, Australia, New Zealand, and their possessions.

But the comparison becomes truly suggestive when, against this background of commonality, one begins to discern some of the differences between the global quality of an organization such as al Qaeda and what is generally understood, and practiced, as "globalization." Not for nothing was the prime target in the attacks of the past weeks two buildings known as "The World Trade Center." As I have already suggested, the "fundamentalists" are not quite as "fundamental" as this label might suggest. They targeted, and destroyed, the symbol of World Trade: that is, not just of globalization, and not just of American or Western or Judeo-Christian civilization, but of world finance capitalism. This point is being studiously obscured in the American media, although obviously it cannot be entirely ignored. However, there is a rather quick generalization that takes place in this discourse, in which "finance" and "trade" are replaced by "freedom" and "civilization," in order to portray the attackers as "fanatics" and "fundamentalists."

To strike at the World Trade Center and then at the Pentagon (with either the White House or the Capitol as the third intended target) is thus to use certain aspects of "globalization"—the dispersed, decentered, portable, and transportable aspects of its technology—against the primary aim of globalization as it dominates the world today, which is the extraction and appropriation of profit through the production and circulation of commodities. The "religious" program to expel Western infidels from the holy areas of Islam is inseparable from a socio-economic situation caused by a historically specific political relation of forces.[1]

The symbolic significance of the attack on the symbol of global finance, the World Trade Center, together with the symbol of the state institution that maintains the present relation of forces throughout the world, namely, the Pentagon—all of this is, in the words of a French specialist on international law, Professor Brigitte Klein, "breathtaking" in its precision. It is "real" *and* "symbolic," and the "symbolic" element contributes and adds to the "real."

So if the attacks on these symbols were made possible by an organization that shared certain traits with "globalization" and in this sense was indeed "part" of it, they were also clearly intended to call attention to and discredit certain other aspects of the very same process. And yet, another constituent of this "action" clearly distinguishes it from the capitalist mainstream of globalization. This is what is referred to, not accidentally, as its "kamikaze" element: the readiness to give one's life to accomplish one's goal. This is a dimension that, unless I am sorely mistaken, is fundamentally missing from what might be called the mainstream "culture" of globalization, inasmuch, at least, as the dominant aim of that culture—that which determines the primary directions in which it moves—is the private appropriation of profit and the increased level of consumption that appropriation makes possible. This is the point where what has been called a "war of civiliza-tions" may not be an entirely ideological phrase—although it is clearly one that is being used to obscure more than to enlighten.

Let me illustrate what I have in mind by pointing to another ad, this time a full-page ad published in the September 13, 2001, issue of the *IHT* (and doubtless elsewhere as well). The entire background of the page is blue-gray, 75 percent is sky, 25 percent is frozen tundra. On what appears to be the frozen surface of a lake, not far from one of the poles, three tiny figures can be seen, two children and one adult. One of the tiny child-figures appears to be bent forward, skating or skiing, perhaps, in any event poised for something, balancing. S/he is observed, a few feet away, by an adult. A second child is walking toward the two others from the side. High above this scene, two words stand out in large, white type: "We're out." Four inches lower, in much smaller white type, the message: "Vodafone Voice-mail. Get away from it all. Well, for an hour or two." Further down still, the line: "How are you?" And finally, not far from the three small figures, who are enclosed in a bubble, like those in which comic-strip characters speak, the message: "The people you need are only a touch away."

In the immediate aftermath of September 11, nothing, of course, looks or is the same as it might have seemed before. The poignant appeals coming from the cell-phones of those trapped in the burning towers were cries of goodbye, of leave-taking from "the people" who were "only a touch away." But this touch did fulfill the ad's promise: To "get away from it all. Well, for an hour or two." Scarcely an hour was granted those caught in the planes or the towers. Those who were able to get out of the towers may have survived, but none, it is fairly certain, will ever be able to "get away from it all," not even "for an hour or two." And yet, this is precisely what the ad proclaims: "We're out." Who, we? The events of September 11 suggest that it is getting harder and harder "to get out."

Except perhaps for the hijackers. Or the suicide bombers. They are, or will be, "out" and "away from it all"—but not just "for an hour or two." We want to "get away from it all," "get out," for an hour or two—but only before going back "in," presumably refreshed. Those who perpetrate such attacks are ready to go "out" without coming back. Perhaps because they were never "in," or at any rate couldn't stay in. This difference is perhaps one reason why the horrific vision of the towers collapsing inward into themselves, *imploding* rather than *exploding*, is so haunting: the nightmare vision of an immanence disappearing into itself. The attacks were also against the kind of secular "immanence" that those towers both represented and implemented.

This is, of course, a very different rejection from that which led protestors to the streets of Seattle, Prague, and Genoa. Like the conspirators, these protestors were also "decentered." But for the most part they were not organized in secret organizations, and obviously the majority had very different aims. These were informed by notions such as "sustainability of resources" and other "ecological" considerations, as well as the more traditional political values of social and economic justice. Beyond that, given the heterogeneity of the different components participating in the protests, it would be precipitous to relate them to the kind of analysis I sketched out in "Capitalizing History," since we are doubtless dealing with considerable diversity, and hence with very different political and moral perspectives. For instance, the differences among the different "Green" movements, their similarities and divergences with respect to the group "ATTAC,"[2] comprise a vast spectrum of opposition to the reigning form of globalization (but not necessarily to *all* of its aspects, as ATTAC constantly insists). Some of this opposition could no doubt be shown to depend upon the kinds of "naturalizing" that Hartz attributes to the American liberal tradition—but certainly not all of it. It is not, after all, a uniquely American phenomenon. Much would depend upon the way in which these different protests articulate or define their relation to the "future." But this would require minute and detailed analyses, which I can't even begin to attempt here.

As to the "chastising" of "theory" for not being "political enough," it's an all too familiar "logo," an easy enough exercise, especially if one limits oneself to pointing to the distance that separates thinking, of whatever kind, and "action," which is usually considered the sine qua non of the "political." But to do this in the name of something called "the real," "the material," or even "the economic" (and it should be obvious that I much prefer the latter to the former), can also open the door to the worst kind of dogmatism. If "the real" is what resists or, as Freud writes about "reality testing," what returns, remains, then access to it will always be immensely difficult, complex, and never entirely attainable. Conceptual formations such as "the real," which claim both singularity and generality, can become pernicious when they attempt, explicitly or implicitly, to bridge the gap between the two. Suspicion directed at conceptual generality is one of the leitmotifs of modern thought, going back at least to the Scholastics and the struggle of Nominalists against Realists. This assumes a distinctly contemporary cast with the critique of Hegel by Kierkegaard and Marx. Critique, of course, is never enough, and if "theory" means the self-contained study of theoretical utterances, then it should be "criticized." But clearly this is not what most thinkers identified with critical and deconstructive thought of the past decades have done. Almost all have been concerned with the political dimensions, consequences, and conditions of their thinking, and of their *writing*, and the shift from the one to the other is precisely an articulation of this concern. What I have tried to develop concerning the theatrical dimension of inscription, of its propagation and transformation, is an attempt to elaborate this dimension.

It is perhaps worth recalling that there is a difference in being "political" at the level of propositional statements (i.e., making declarations, signing petitions, etc.) and being political at the level of the established codes of articulation to which one is necessarily submitted, but which are also susceptible to change. This is why a certain thinking of virtuality, possibility, potentiality—what in a study of Benjamin I call his "-abilities"—a certain virtualization of conceptualization itself, of "meaning"—can be politically effective, even if it never gets its act together. This doesn't dispense with more conventional forms of "political" analysis and interpretation, much less with "political *action*," but it does affect and possibly transform the grids within which such actions and interpretations must be situated.

SMW and GH (September 18, 2001): It is interesting that you draw to a close the comment you've just made by saying, "There is a difference in being 'political' at the level of propositional statements (i.e., making declarations, signing petitions, etc.) and being political at the level of the established codes of articulation to which one is necessarily submitted, but which are also susceptible to change." Presumably, this statement could be taken to re-mark at least one of the borders or crossroads in our discussion so far. It could be seen as installing itself *in* or *as* one of the places where we find ourselves situated between problems and questions that are ostensibly "philosophical" or "theoretical" in nature, and others that are normally designated "political." Doubtless our exchange has tried to trace, and even *assume*, the very complex traits that tangle together or tear the conflictually riven territory of these supposedly different concerns, "fields," or "disciplines." In this context, we'd risk introducing—in however jarring a way—a question we'd been thinking of asking you beforehand, to see whether it is as far removed as it might seem from the question of "politics" and, indeed, from the politics of "theatricalization," of "propositional statements" and of "codes of articulation."

In your recent work on theatricality as medium, you comment on the way in which the writing of Jacques Derrida explores its own "theatrical quality as a 'staging.'" But what of the performance or performativity that attends your own writing? What of its own "taking place"? Does this open up or open onto a different sort of "theatrical/theoretical" space or (dis-)location? While it can be argued that the tracing out of certain effects of iterability or performativity in— and between—your texts is an indispensable element in the reading of them, some might say that, unlike the Derridean texts that you perhaps tend to privilege in your work (in the more recent material on theatricality, it's Derrida's "The Double Session," while elsewhere, at the end of *Institution and Interpretation*, it's his "Envois") you yourself don't seem to "theatrically stage" the texts you write about. At least, not quite so explicitly. That is, you don't seem to perform or act them out in quite the same way as, say, Derrida does with Mallarmé. Rather, you might appear, to some readers, to remain uncannily the same throughout much of your writing. Do you stop short of retaining your own authorial identity throughout and, if so, how? Would the uncanny experience of the "familiar" in your writing, for example, involve a certain theatricalization, in that we find there (to borrow your own words): "not the communication of something new in the sense of content, but the variation of something familiar through its repetition"? Is your very recognizable style—if we might call it that— the effect of a deliberate strategy on your part? Or is it, as you say in *Mass Mediauras*, in response to a question on the "clarity" of your writing, the result, not of "making or taking decisions but of being taken—even overtaken!—by them"?

This, at any rate, was the question we had in mind. Not for the first time in our discussion, such questions or issues risk seeming quite remote from—and even discontinuous with—the current events with which we are all preoccupied. At first glance, they seem to stand apart and refuse to participate. But the last part of your previous set of remarks, on theatricality and on action and articulation in particular, would seem to allow such concerns to partake of the "political," which otherwise might exclude them. Would you be able at this time, for instance, to reflect further on the (political?) relationship, if there is any, between the kind of acts or "events" with which we are very much concerned now, today, and the kind of act we are engaged in now, over a number of days, in this discussion taking place?

There is another, perhaps related question that we'd like to send you at the same time. It concerns "politics" once more, assuming we can even begin to know what that term means today. The emphasis on institutions and instituting in your work has been presented as a way of making deconstruction "political." (Wlad Godzich offers a reading along these lines in his Afterword to *Institution and Interpretation*, for example.) Indeed, you yourself have argued (in "The Limits of Professionalism") that deconstruction, in what you call "its orthodox form," downplays the forces and powers that maintain certain sets of paradigms, certain authorities and systems. But doesn't this reading (of both your work and deconstruction) rather imply:

a. That other "deconstructions"—those that are not concerned with questions of the institution and instituting, force and power—are not political?

b. That the question of the political, of what the political is and what it is to be political, is decided in advance—thus constituting a limiting of the political, an acceptance of the political as it is institutionally defined—of the sort you elsewhere argue against?

In addition, does the supposed affiliation between "instituting," "institutions," and "the political" as outlined above—and, indeed, the decision about what these terms mean—need to be rethought in light of some of the effects of "globalization" witnessed in the events of the past week?

SW (September 18, 2001): Both of your questions presuppose a consensual understanding of just what is meant by "political." Underpinning such an understanding, I see further questions: Is the political necessarily tied to the state? To society? Is it primarily a question of power? Of the common good? The general will? Community? Is it manifest primarily in "action"? In strategies? In policies? Is it necessarily bound up with *subjects*, in either the philosophical, grammatical, or social senses of the word? What is its relation to spatial and temporal factors: to the organization of space through the assigning of places, and to the organization of time through the regulation of past, present, and future?

Take, once again, the events of September 11. What happened then involved, not only the destruction of specific buildings and people and the more or less immediate aftereffects of that destruction, but its longer-range consequences. The immediate destruction produced images that will haunt us for many years but will also become what Freud calls "screen-memories," blotting out many of the relations that contributed to the actual events, without which they become speciously transparent. In their longer-range ramifications, these events involved a network that, although far less visible, is by no means intangible or unreal. It is, however, more difficult to localize, as the problem of the American response in its "War on Terror" makes clear. Limiting ourselves just to al Qaeda, its "base" also involves a highly complex superstructure or, rather, sub- and infrastructure. The "base" is not identical with those structures, but is also not simply their foundation. That is the problem of the "war" or "crusade" against "terrorism": finding the proper target or targets. Colin Powell and others have compared bin Laden's organization to a "holding"; others, to a "multinational"—but those terms serve more to describe the perspective of those who use them than the very different situation of their adversaries.

Were the events of September 11 "political"? Did they involve "politics"? Much of the official discourse of the American government and much (although certainly not all) of the American media, tend to deny this, at least implicitly. According to this perspective, September 11 was the work of religious fanatics, of resentment, of "evil" in its purest form. It is to be combated militarily, but also morally, in a "crusade" (President Bush) that aims at extirpating its perpetrators, while acknowledging that the struggle may not just be long and complex, but impossible to win. At the same time, this official discourse insists on the term *war* to describe what has happened, as well as the proper response to it. "America's New War" is CNN's heading or title for chapter 2 of its "story." "War" is generally considered to be a "political" phenomenon, but is a "crusade" a "war"? It is true that the two words have been used as equivalents in American discourse of the past few decades: "War on Drugs," "War on Poverty," "War on Crime," and today "War on Terrorism." But such a use employs the word to designate a general mobilization of a nation against an enemy that cannot be identified with a state, and hence is not "political" in the most familiar sense of this word.

The problem in doing "justice" to "the political" is the "cut" required to define the term. "State," "power," "action"—the triad presupposed in most consensual definitions of the term—are notions that operate like "freeze-frame photographs," *Momentaufnahmen* as one says in German, literally, *in-stantaneous*: bringing to a *halt* an ongoing, highly complex, and dynamic *network of relations*, which is constantly evolving and therefore only *provisionally delimitable*. The dilemma of the American response to the attacks of last week illustrates this problem all too well: The "culprits," like many of their victims, are dead. They therefore cannot be brought to justice: only identified, which was accomplished with a speed that is all the more surprising given the apparent lack of preparedness. At the same time, the problem of "terrorism" cannot be limited to al Qaeda, bin Laden, or even Muslim fundamentalism, as the last great attack on American soil in Oklahoma City clearly demonstrated. But how, then, can it be sufficiently delimited to serve as a target of effective action? Are the roots of this "terrorism" "political"? Religious? Economic? Cultural?

To be sure, the discourses of the media, and that of the American government, in no way exhaust the phenomenon of "the political." But they do manifest certain widely held attitudes and conceptions that are by no means foreign to the academy (at least in the United States). Charlotte Raven, writing in the British *Guardian*, touched a nerve when she observed:

> At the root of this (official discourse) is an overwhelming need to control meaning. America can't let the world speak for itself. It was taken unawares last Tuesday and part of the trauma of that event was the shock of being forced to listen to a message that it hadn't had time to translate. The subsequent roar of anger was, amongst other things, the sound of the U.S. struggling to regain the right to control its own narrative.
>
> It did this by declaring war. By this means, Bush ensured that America only had to sit with the inexplicable for a couple of anxious days. After that, the sense, so unfamiliar to them, of not

knowing what had happened or what it meant was replaced by the reassuring certainties of John Brown's body and calls for national unity. By turning what should have been a criminal manhunt into an all-out war, Bush was asserting his right to define America's reality. Instead of submitting to the reality, he created the situation he wanted, fashioning a plausible, beatable enemy. (*The Guardian*, September 18, 2001)

Translating the traumatic into the elements of an all too familiar narrative—Bush describing the "justice" he seeks in terms of a Hollywood Western, "Wanted, Dead or Alive"—condenses a certain conception of "the political": the state, represented by the sheriff, leading the posse, locates the outlaw, neutralizes him, "dead or alive"—and presumably collects the reward. Raven is correct, I believe, to emphasize that a certain narrative is crucial for framing this conception. Only a certain form of narrative allows time and space to be subordinated to meaning as media of self-fulfillment rather than of self-destruction.

The belief that this self-contained narrative, consisting in a continuum of beginning, middle, and end, and providing the sole paradigm of meaning, reality, and identity—a belief that is not limited to the practice or study of literature, but that rather sustains and informs the practices and institutions, the perceptual and conceptual grids of the very "civilization" that erected the twin towers to celebrate, and concentrate, World Trade—is as much if not more a part of "politics" as is the triad of *state, power,* and *action* that constitutes its most obvious and traditional manifestation.

The self-evidence, the self-contained "reality" of this narrative scheme, is challenged, disrupted, and dislocated by many if not all of what are called "deconstructive" texts. Obviously, such dislocation operates in very different ways and to very different degrees. What I have called "theatricalization" is one part of it: by foregrounding the "stage," it resituates familiar narratives so that their framing function is no longer taken for granted. The "scene" is what exceeds any single, self-contained narrative but also enables it to take place. Such *staging* has become fairly evident in the later writings of Derrida, as it did in the later writings of Lacan. But it can be operative without being as obvious or manifest. It is "at work" wherever the established expectations of readers (viewers, listeners) find themselves challenged and in some way forced to adjust, to move, to change. This is obviously a long way from what is generally recognized as effective "political action." But the determination of what is "effective" is never a simple given, just as it is never a simple question of personal preference, never simply aleatory.

With respect to my own writing, it is certainly less "theatrical" than that of either Lacan or Derrida, even if theatricality is more "thematized," more explicitly discussed in my recent work. Perhaps one reason for the difference is that my writing is less rooted in a single discourse and tradition than is Derrida's or Lacan's—or Benjamin's, for that matter. Certain major impulses have come to me precisely from the encounter with *different* cultures and languages: first German, then French, both always interacting with a certain (American) English. Perhaps this is one reason why a certain "intensity" did not develop in the way it has in Derrida's writing, an aspect he has described as his "monolingualism."

If you are asking about this kind of difference, then it is surely not simply a "deliberate strategy" on my part, but something that my experience—trajectory—has imposed upon me. Which doesn't mean that it couldn't change in the future. But certainly that change will never be absolute: it will always be, I fear, more or less recognizable. But with luck, it will not just be "more of the same."

Perhaps this is why one of my next projects, which is already "mired" in repetition, and in a certain sense is therefore anything but entirely "new," involves a "return" to the question of the uncanny, which I began studying some thirty-five years ago, but which only fairly recently I have tried to rethink in terms of a certain theatricality. It is curious that such a significant notion should have received so little attention over the past years. Derrida, once again, seems to be almost alone in his sustained concern for this strangely familiar topic.[3] But even he has *published* relatively little sustained analysis of it so far, although he has discussed it at length in several of his unpublished seminars. I suspect that at least part of the explanation for this benign neglect has to do with the singularly elusive character of the uncanny: Is it a concept, an experience, a feeling? Is it historically conditioned or trans-historical? At any rate, it seems profoundly linked to the end of an epoch obsessed with reflexivity and self-consciousness, while announcing things to come in an as yet undecipherable language.

SMW and GH: A final question, which, given its nature, you may feel unable to answer without referring once more to events of a contemporary nature. In "Force of Law," Derrida names "justice" as the one thing that cannot be deconstructed. In "The Debts of Deconstruction" you seem to add to the list of things that cannot be deconstructed deconstruction's own debts, and furthermore the "question of debt in general." One might wonder where this leaves the question of your own relationship and debts to Derrida and to deconstruction, Beyond this, what then becomes of the relationship of "justice" to "debt"? Is this of special relevance today?

SW: One of the texts I discuss in "The Debts of Deconstruction" is from the *Genealogy of Morals*, where Nietzsche speculates that the stronger a group or "tribe" becomes, the greater its sense of indebtedness to its antecedents. This in turn results in a "fear" of "forefathers," who have become "divinely uncanny and unimaginable." In the end, says Nietzsche, the fear produced by this sense of unrequitable debt transfigures the ancestor into a god. The origin of the gods, then, would "perhaps" be this fear.

But such a birth of the gods out of fear is itself based on the presupposition of an originary *equivalence*, and therefore of a debt that is held to subvene upon a relation that would otherwise be *balanced*. Derrida's notion of "justice" unbalances this balance-sheet of identity, of commensurability. The scales of this justice are not balanced; they are always already tipped, one way or the other, and indeed only thinkable from this situation of imbalance.

Nietzsche's account profoundly modifies our usual conception of debt and its relation to a debtor. We usually think of a debt as something that can and must be "had"—one "has" a debt, it is assignable to a debtor. This debtor in turn is defined by this negative property, "his" (or "her") debt. But debt, as Derrida negotiates it, is not just a debt to another (ego, self): it is that which indebts the self itself to the other. It is, therefore, never something that you can "have," or that can be assigned to you in an unequivocal manner. It is both yours and not yours, *part* of you and that which *parts with* you or, rather, causes you to take leave from, and of, yourself.

There is a word, difficult if not impossible to translate into English, which Derrida uses to describe such a movement, in its irreducibility. In a very long footnote, running across several pages in *Of Spirit*, Derrida demonstrates that Heidegger's notion of thinking as questioning presupposes something that Heidegger calls *Zuspruch* or *Zusage*, a kind of call or appeal. The closest nominal equivalent in English seems to be "appeal," but the German words correspond more closely, perhaps, to the idiomatic phrase "speak to." Thinking as questioning thus never constitutes an absolute beginning or origin, but rather *responds* to an *appeal*. This appeal, as Heidegger formulates it in German (based on the roots *Spruch* and *Sage*), is inseparable from language, understood as a practice or movement, a heightened receptivity, an opening to the other, a *disposition* to *listen, discern, respond*, rather than as an entity or system—understood, in short, as a *saying* rather than as a statement or proposition. At the same time, it antedates, precedes the constitution and acquisition of language as a positive entity. And such a disposition, Derrida argues, involves not simply the assumption of a "debt" but the giving of what he calls—and here we come to that untranslatable word—a *gage*. In English, we would probably have to translate this as a "deposit," or possibly *wager*. The *gage* is thus both a sort of guarantee for the repayment of a debt and a gamble, a promise, an engagement. But there is a difference: the deposit is deposited somewhere, in a safe place. It is a form of *placement*. For Derrida, by contrast, the *gage* whose appeal precedes and permits all questioning says "yes," affirms, but without positing *any thing*. It quite literally, but not idiomatically, de-posits. And it does so by responding to "an event, the memory [*mémoire*] of which precedes all remembrance [*souvenir*] and to *which we are bound by a faith that defies all narrative*."[4]

To be sure, Derrida here is reading, interpreting Heidegger. But at the same time, on the margins of the main text, in this long footnote, he is also *writing*, commenting in the most literal sense: thinking *with*, which means also translating, re-marking, doing *justice* not to "Heidegger" as author, philosopher, or subject, but as a text that is anything but self-identical, harmonious, or self-contained. Derrida's text engages Heidegger by doing justice not to the *spirit* but to the *letters* of his texts, by taking up their challenge, their "gage," without the security of an original, underlying, or overriding meaning. By remarking Heidegger's assertion that "language must already appeal or have appealed to us [*muss sich die Sprache zuvor uns zusagen oder gar schon zugesagt haben*]," *Of Spirit* reshuffles the deck of our usual reading of Heidegger, and of much more, by foregrounding the condition of all *engagement*, political or other, as residing in a certain disposition to assume and respond to the *gage*. There must be a disposition to *engage* that is presupposed by every organization of space and time into places, objects, and, above all, *narratives* "in" which one could place, or deposit, one's *engagement*. There must be an acceptance of "faith" that antedates everything "in" which one could have faith. The *gage* that *vouches for* but doesn't *vouchsafe* entails a faith that *de-fies* the narratives it also makes possible.

Another word for this faith is, perhaps, *justice*. But not "infinite justice" as the unending triumph of Good over Evil. This is precisely the kind of narrative that justice must "de-fy." Today, more than ever, justice demands the de-fiance of all narratives, especially those that seem the most self-evident, the most compelling, and that therefore are perhaps the most dangerous.

Appendix

Other Publications by Samuel Weber dealing with Theater

"Tannhäuser's Start." Program of the Bayreuth Festival, Summer 1987.

"Das Traumspiel: Eine Lektüre." Program, Stuttgart Schauspiel Production of Strindberg's *Dream Play*, October 1987.

"Geschichte, Gestaltung, Geschlecht: Von den Wibelungen zum Ring." In Wolfgang Storch, ed., *Die Nibelungen: Bilder von Liebe, Verrat und Untergang* (Munich: Prestel, 1987), pp. 64–65.

"La Boîte et le balcon: De la technique au théâtre." *Qui parle?* Spring 1989.

Programmheft (Program), Genet's *Le Balcon*. Düsseldorfer Schauspiel, February 1989. (Includes "Über die Treue zum Text" and "Die Wahrheit des Balkons.")

"Theater, Technics and Writing." *1–800*, Fall 1989, pp. 15–19.

"Das Leiden an der Zeit: Gedanken zu *Parsifal*." In Wolfgang Storch, ed., *Les Symbolistes et Richard Wagner* (Berlin: Edition Henrich, 1991), pp. 133–38.

"On the Balcony: The Theater of Technics." In L. Lambrechts and J. Nowe, eds., *Bild-Sprache: Texte zwischen Dichten und Denken* (Leuven: Louvain University Press, 1990), pp. 283–97.

"Taking Place: Toward a Theater of Dislocation." In David J. Levin, ed., *Opera through Other Eyes* (Stanford: Stanford University Press, 1993), pp. 107–46.

"*Nomos* in *The Magic Flute*." Trans. Luke Carson. *Angelaki* 3, no. 2, *The Love of Music* (1998): 61–88.

"Vor Ort: Theater im Zeitalter der Medien." In G. Brandstetter, Helga Finter, and Markus Wessendorf, eds., *Grenzgänge* (Tübingen: Gunter Narr, 1998), pp. 31–51.

"Theater als Übersetzung." In Carsten Ahrens et al., eds. *Axel Manthey: Theater* (Vienna: Residenz, 1998), pp. 247–55.

"Der *Ring* als Dekonstruktion der Moderne: Wagner mit Benjamin."
In Richard Klein, ed., *Narben des Gesamtkunstwerks* (Munich: Fink,
2001), pp. 65–80.
"Exterritorialité et théâtralité chez Benjamin et Kafka." In Peter Hen-
ninger, ed., *L'Exterritorialité de la littérature allemande* (Paris: L'Har-
mattan, 2002), pp. 91–106.

Notes

Introduction

1. Such privileging is at work even today, in the development of a term such as *television* to designate a medium that involves sound as much as sight, and its fascinating power persists in the vogue of what is blithely called "visual culture."

2. Plato, *The Republic*, book 7, trans. Paul Shorey, in Plato, *The Collected Dialogues*, ed. Edith Hamilton and Huntington Cairns (Princeton: Princeton University Press, 1961), pp. 747ff.

3. See the discussion of "Being John Malkovich" in Chapter 13 of this book.

4. On the relation of "medium" and "transparency," see my discussion of Aristotle in "The Virtuality of the Medium," *Sites* 4, no. 2 (2000): 297–317.

5. Nowhere perhaps is the theatrical singularity of the event more clearly staged than in the first act of Shakespeare's *Hamlet*, when the Ghost of King Hamlet pursues his son and the other spectators by moving invisibly under the floorboards of the stage, thereby setting a farcical, undramatic, but eminently *theatrical* counterpoint to his appeal to be remembered—and perhaps to the entire tragic drama that responds to that appeal. I will return to the theatrical significance of "farce" in Chapter 7.

6. J. L. Austin, *How to Do Things with Words* (London: Oxford University Press, 1976), pp. 21–22. See also J. Derrida, *Limited Inc* (Evanston: Northwestern University Press, 1988), pp. 16ff.

7. Ibid., p. 17 et passim. Judith Butler, in a series of incisive and influential writings that build upon Derrida's emphasis on iterability, has shifted the focus of "performativity" from its initial dependence on an informing intention to the social and political *effects* produced by linguistic performances. Noting that "we have yet to arrive at an account of the social iterability of the utterance" (*Excitable Speech: A Politics of the Performative* [New York: Routledge, 1997], p. 150), she sees the direction of such an account proceeding from the insight that "speech is bodily, but the body exceeds the speech it occasions" (p. 156). One question raised by such an assertion is whether

the enabling conditions of such *excess* are to be related primarily to "the body" or to its *situation*, construed as the staging of a theatrical medium, of which, in English at least, the present participle and gerund provide exemplary (although by no means exclusive) articulations. Such an approach is, of course, by no means absent in Butler's work, as when name-calling in hate speech is described as "producing a scene of agency" (*Excitable Speech*, p. 163).

8. Guy Debord, *The Society of the Spectacle*, trans. Donald Nicholson-Smith (New York: Zone Books, 1995), p. 14.

9. "The sun . . . never sets on the empire of modern passivity. It covers the entire globe" (ibid., p. 15).

10. "The spectacle is self-generated, and it makes up its own rules: it is a specious form of the sacred" (ibid., §25, p. 20).

11. "La Double Séance," in: J. Derrida, *La Dissémination* (Paris: Seuil, 1972), p. 220. English translation: "The Double Session," in *Dissemination*, trans. Barbara Johnson (Chicago: University of Chicago Press, 1981), p. 193. Future references to this work, first English, then French, are given in parentheses in the body of the text. The translation has been modified where necessary.

12. This is why "deconstruction" cannot be equated with "criticism" or even with "critical theory" in the strict sense. It is also, however, why it is not "performative," but rather trans- or de-formative. It is the staging of a textual encounter—here, of the *entre*—and hence is *theatrical*. Two recent essays dealing with "The Double Session" make this point in differing ways. Gerald Wildgruber traces a trajectory that leads "From the Notion/Performance of Theater to the Theory of the Text" ("Von der Vorstellung des Theaters zur Theorie des Textes," in G. Neumann, C. Pross, and G. Wildgruber, eds., *Szenographien: Theatralität als Kategorie der Literaturwissenschaft* (Freiburg i. Breisgau: Rombach, 2000), pp. 113–44). Whereas, as his title indicates, Wildgruber reads Derrida's text as moving "from" a notion-performance of theater "to" a "Theory of the Text," Geraldine Harris reads a contemporary play, Rose English's *The Double Wedding*, as a theatrical repetition that, among other things, repeats and transforms "The Double Session" and thereby calls into question the origin of all repetition, including its theoretical origins. Harris notes that the problematic origin of such repetition can be traced back to the Platonic cave, which she justly finds reinscribed in "The Double Session" in the play on *entre* and *antre*: "Throughout 'The Double Session' Derrida constantly plays on the similarity between *entre* and *antre*, which is Latin for 'cave,' so that, like *The Double Wedding*, Mallarmé's 'Mimique' and indeed 'The Double Session' can both be said to start in Plato's cave" (Geraldine Harris, *Staging Femininities: Performance and Performativity* [Manchester: Manchester University Press, 1999], p. 112).

13. Note how, in the following commentary, Derrida resorts to the present participle to describe the singular movement involved: "As pirouette, the dance of the hieroglyph can never play itself out entirely inside. Not simply because of the 'real space, or the scene,' nor because of the point that perforates the page or the illustration of the book, but above all because of a certain lateral displacement: *in turning incessantly* [en tournant incessamment] on its point, the hieroglyph, the sign, the cipher leaves its here, as though not caring [*se fichant*], always here in *passing* from here to there, from one here to another, *inscribing* in the *stigmē* of its here the *other* point toward which it is continually *displacing* itself" (Derrida, *Dissemination*, pp. 241/271–72).

14. Derrida returns to it not often, but at decisive junctures in his argument: first, to describe the Platonic effort to control *mimēsis* by subordinating the *imitant* to the *imité* (p. 190/216); second, to describe the manner in which the "double remark withdraws from the pertinence or authority of truth: not by overturning it but by inscribing it in its play as a piece or a function" (p. 193/220); and finally to describe "what Mallarmé *read* in the libretto (of Paul Margueritte)," namely "the prescription erasing itself, the order given the Mime not to imitate anything that in any way could antedate his operation" (p. 198/225).

15. A relatively recent example is Derrida's elaboration of the notion of the *arrivant*—literally, "the arriving"—in *Aporias* (trans. Thomas Dutoit [Stanford: Stanford University Press, 1993], pp. 33ff). Although this text, which contains a critical reading of Heidegger (and Levinas) on death, does not explicitly link the *arrivant* to a theatrical context, it does define it in relation to a certain experience of space and place, of the threshold as a non-place where identity has not yet become identifiable or nameable: "Since the *arrivant* does not have any identity yet, its place of arrival is also de-identified" (p. 34). The word interprets and transforms the Heideggerian notion of *Ereignis, event*, in terms of taking place and the place thereby taken. But as we will see shortly, the French word *arrivant* could also be read as an elaboration of some of the implications of the German word used by Heidegger to define the "fold"—*Zwiefalt*—to which Derrida here refers, namely, *Anwesen*: oncoming or on-going. Both in German and in French, when the infinitive is used as a noun, it is generally rendered in English by the gerund, a nominalization of the present participle. The clearest—and murkiest—instance of this is *Sein*, "Being," or as I prefer to translate it, "to be." I will explain this choice later.

16. See Chapter 2 of this book.

17. This phrase is both unusual and enigmatic in German: "ohne daß der grammatische Begriff schon eigens in das sprachliche Wissen eingreift" (Martin Heidegger, "Moïra," in *Early Greek Thinking*, trans. D. F. Krell and F. A. Capuzzi [San Francisco: Harper & Row, 1975], p. 86). The translation has been modified. For the translation of *Sein* as "the to be," see Chapter 2, n. 8, below.

18. And a bit later on in the text: "Like modern society itself, the spectacle is at once united and divided. In both, unity is grounded in a split" (Debord, *The Society of the Spectacle*, §54, p. 36).

19. For the record, this word is not to be found in Heidegger's essay, although it is implicit throughout.

20. "Vorliegen-Lassen . . . zum-Vorschein-Bringen" (Heidegger, "Moïra," p. 41).

21. "Der *muthos* [ist] Sage, das Sagen aber das rufende zum-Scheinen-Bringen" (ibid., p. 44). In English, cf. "Hegel's Concept of Experience," in Martin Heidegger, *Off the Beaten Track*, trans. Julian Young and Kenneth Haynes (Cambridge: Cambridge University Press, 2002), pp. 96–97.

22. Heidegger quotes Hegel, who, in passing from Parmenides to Heraclitus, exclaims: "Here we see land; there is no sentence in Heraclitus that I would not have included in my Logic" ("Moïra," p. 32). In his essay, "Hegel's Concept of Experience," Heidegger quotes a similar passage, also from Hegel's History of Philosophy, but this time apropos of Descartes: "Only now do we really come to the philosophy of the new world, which begins with Descartes. With him we enter into a philosophy that is genuinely independent, stands on its own two feet [*selbständig*], which knows that it comes from reason, moving on its own two feet [*selbständig*] and that self-consciousness is an essential moment of the true. Here, we can say that we are at home, and like sailors after long wanderings [*Umherfahrt*] on a stormy sea, we can finally call out, 'land ahoy!' (M. Heidegger, "Hegels Begriff der Erfahrung," *Holzwege* [Frankfurt a. M.: Klostermann, 1963], p. 118).

23. See Chapter 3 of this book.

24. Cited in Pan Xiafeng, *The Stagecraft of Peking Opera* (Beijing: New World Press, 1995), pp. 16–17. Brecht's remarks were occasioned by a tour of the troupe of the famous actor Mei Lanfang, which performed *Fisherman's Revenge* in Moscow in 1935. Mei Lanfang was renowned for playing female roles and was the first to introduce the Peking Opera to foreign audiences. Much of what Brecht saw, therefore, as well as much of what is played today, goes back to innovations introduced by Mei Lanfang, in part in order to accommodate audiences who did not speak Chinese. The role of the "western" audience in determining the theatrical style developed by Mei Lanfang does not, however, negate the importance of the distinctively Chinese traditions these innovations presupposed even while transforming them. Rather, this history of the Peking Opera demonstrates how the theatrical medium is constituted, above and beyond any specific instance, by the interaction of audience and staging.

25. "The custom of the Chinese stage to preserve certain gestures and attitudes of stage figures for several generations of actors seems at first glance a very conservative habit." Brecht argues, however, that this is a specious

impression: the constancy of gesture produces two major effects. First, the gestures are separated from their individual realizations: they are not understood to be the property of an individual, but of a tradition. Second, in defining that tradition, they establish the possibility of altering it. In the West, by contrast, it is far more difficult to transform radically the art of acting, "since it is difficult to transform something that isn't there to be transformed" ("On Chinese Theater," in B. Brecht, *Schriften zum Theater* [Frankfurt a. M.: Suhrkamp, 1963], 4:53–55.

26. Debord, *The Society of Spectacle*, §178, p. 126.

27. Brecht, *Schriften zum Theater*, 4:38 ("Über die Zuschaukunst," "On The Art of Regarding").

28. The Liyuan Theater, its program states, is "jointly run by the Qianmen Hotel and the Beijing Opera Institute of Beijing with the initiation and support of the Beijing Tourism Bureau and the Beijing Cultural Bureau" (*Beijing Opera of China*, program of the Liyuan Theater [Beijing, 1999], p. 73).

29. Although I lack the concepts with which to analyze it, the fascinating intonation of the voice in the Peking Opera derives, in part at least, from a vocal equivalent of such "hollowness" in the abrupt modulations of the voice, recalling to Western ears certain "expressionist" dynamics, for instance in Schoenberg's "Erwartung," although precisely without the expressive "pathos."

30. It should be noted that the etymology of *gerund* a "tense" that is profoundly bound up with theatricality, is from *gerere*, to bear, or be borne along: the movement associated with the verb carries along that which is named by the noun rather than deriving from it.

31. Certain texts on Walter Benjamin's approach to theater that otherwise could and should have been included in this book have been reserved for a book on Benjamin that I am completing and that will appear under the title *Benjamin's –abilities*. For an outline of part of the project of that book, although not including its theatrical dimension, see the article "Benjamin's Style," in Michael Kelly, ed., *The Oxford Encyclopedia of Aesthetics* (New York: Oxford University Press, 1998), 1:261–64.

Chapter 1

1. In various Western languages, including English, *naturalization* is, of course, the political process of giving "aliens" the same rights as "native-born" citizens.

2. An important exception to and critique of such political thought is to be found in the work of Carl Schmitt, who, in *Political Theology* (*Politische Theologie* [Berlin: Duncker & Humblot, 1934]), places the "exception" at the core of his theory of sovereignty. In his *The Concept of the Political* (trans.

George Schwab, foreword by Tracy Strong [Chicago: University of Chicago Press, 1996], p. 27), where he derives the "political" from the friend-enemy relation, Schmitt writes also of political "groupings" (*Gruppierungen*), a term taken over by Benjamin, reader and admirer of Schmitt, to describe the formation of "groupings" through Brecht's "Epic Theater." This term, *grouping*, is thus intended to replace the traditional notion of "audience" (*Publikum*). See W. Benjamin, "Theater und Rundfunk" ("Theater and Radio"), in *Gesammelte Schriften*, ed. Rolf Tiedemann (Frankfurt a. M.: Suhrkamp, 1980), 2.2:775; hereafter *GS*.

3. Plato, *The Laws*, trans. A. E. Taylor, 700 a-d, in Plato, *The Collected Dialogues*, ed. Edith Hamilton and Huntington Cairns (Princeton: Princeton University Press, 1973), p. 1293.

4. Ibid., p. 1294.

5. In his "Critique of Force," Benjamin designates "the setting of limits (borders)"—*die Grenzsetzung*—as the "originary phenomenon of all legislative power [*rechtsetzender Gewalt*]." The rule of law accordingly consists in the setting and maintaining of stable borders. Which is why Carl Schmitt, a decisive source for Benjamin's thinking on violence, emphasizes that the title of Plato's text, *nomoi*, does not simply designate "the laws," as commonly translated and understood, but rather the parceling out and distribution of space. See Carl Schmitt, "Der Nomos der Erde," in *Völkerrecht des Jus Publicum Europaeum* (Berlin: Duncker & Humblot, 1997).

6. Plato, *Philebus*, trans. R. Hackforth, in Plato, *Collected Dialogues*, p. 1131.

7. See the discussion of "pure and impure pleasures" in the *Philebus*, 52c et passim.

8. The power of noise is a persistent motif wherever theatricality, in the strong sense, is involved: see the blaring of the untuned trumpets in Kafka's "Theater of Oklahoma" and Chapter 2 of this book.

9. Plato, *The Laws*, p. 1294.

10. Ibid., p. 1372.

11. One is reminded of Walter Benjamin's account of the tendency of the modern "masses" to break down distance in "bringing closer" all things (*Das Kunstwerk*, *GS*, 1.2:479).

12. Friedrich Nietzsche, *Das Geburt der Tragedie*, §8, in M. Montinari and G. Colli, eds. *Nietzsche Werke: Kritische Gesamtausgabe* (Berlin: De Gruyter, 1972), II.2:56–57 (my translation).

13. Nietzsche's description of the Dionysian *Rausch*, the ecstasy that strives "not only to unite, reconcile, and fuse with the other [*mit seinem Nächsten*], but to become one with it" (I.1:26), renders a *feeling*, a self-perception and desire to overcome the limits and separation of the individual ("Jetzt . . . *fühlt sich* jeder"), but this in no way negates the constitutive reliance of that feeling

upon precisely what it seeks to exclude: separation, individuation, the Apollonian.

14. "The place of a thing is the innermost motionless boundary of what contains it. . . . If then a body has another body outside it and containing it, it is in place" (Aristotle, *Physics*, book 4, 212a).

15. This is why Benjamin, in describing the medially specific form of "collective" called upon to take the place of the ostensibly monolithic "audience" (in German, *Publikum*), resorts to the gerund, in designating it as a *grouping* (*Gruppierung*)—a term that, as noted, is also employed at crucial points by one of Benjamin's major intellectual inspirations, Carl Schmitt. See note 2, above.

16. Joshua Meyrowitz, *No Sense of Place* (New York: Oxford University Press, 1985), p. ix (my emphasis).

17. *On the Genealogy of Morals*, book 2, §7: "In order that hidden, undiscovered, unwitnessed suffering might be banned from the world and honorably negated, one was at the time virtually constrained to discover the Gods, and all the intermediary beings [*Zwischenwesen*] of the heights and depths, in short something that moves around even in hidden places, sees even in the dark and wouldn't miss out on an interesting painful spectacle [*Schauspiel*]. With the aid of such discoveries life was able to . . . justify itself. . . . 'Every evil is justified, whose sight is uplifting for a God.' . . . The Gods as friends of *cruel* spectacles. . . . What ultimate sense did the Trojan Wars and other such tragic horrors at bottom have? There can be little doubt: they were designed as *festival plays* [Festspiele] for the Gods. . . . Virtue without witnesses was entirely unthinkable to this thespian people [*für dies Schauspieler-Volk)*" (Friedrich Nietzsche, *Werke*, ed Colli and Montinari, 2:320–21; my translation).

18. See Chapter 2 of this book.

19. Walter Benjamin, "Was ist episches Theater?" *GS*, 2.2:539; "What is Epic Theater?" (first version), in *Understanding Brecht*, trans. Anna Bostock (London: The Gersham Press, 1977), p. 1 (translation modified).

20. "Cette relation particulière / déroutante et attirante à la fois / entre les vivants et les morts" (Tadeusz Kantor, "Le Théâtre de la mort," in *Le Théâtre de la mort*, ed. Denis Bablet [Lausanne: L'Age d'homme, 1977], pp. 215–24). Kantor links the theatrical function of "the dead" with the use of marionettes in place of "living actors," citing Kleist and the early-twentieth-century English drama theorist and stage designer, Edward Gordon Craig, as antecedents.

21. Benjamin, *GS*, 2.2:536; "What is Epic Theater?" (first version).

22. Ibid., 525.

23. Aristotle, *Physics*, book 4, 3.210a, trans. R. P. Hardie and R. K. Gaye, in Jonathan Barnes, ed., Aristotle, *Complete Works* (Princeton: Princeton University Press, 1984).

24. For an explanation of the translation of *Zustand* as "stance," see Samuel Weber, "Benjamin's Excitable Gestures," in Eckart Voigts-Virchow, ed., *Mediated Drama / Dramatized Media* (Trier: Wissenschaftlicher Verlag, 2000), pp. 15–30.

25. Two of the texts Freud cites, in discussing the "literary" aspects of the uncanny, involve severed hands: "The Tale of the Severed Hand," by Wilhelm Hauff, and a story told by Herodotus, "The Treasure of Rhampsenitus." In the latter narrative, Freud notes, the detached hand does not produce an uncanny effect, whereas in the Hauff story it does (S. Freud, "Das Unheimliche," *Gesammelte Werke* [Frankfurt a. M.: S. Fischer, 1966], 12:259, 267). I have discussed this briefly toward the end of my essay "Uncanny Thinking," which serves as introduction to the second edition of *The Legend of Freud* (Stanford: Stanford University Press, 2000), pp. 1–31.

26. I discuss the significance of touch in connection with Benjamin's theory of translation as "syntactic literalness [*Wörtlichkeit der Syntax*]" in "A Touch of Translation: On Walter Benjamin's 'Task of the Translator,'" in Teresa Seruya, ed., *Estudos de Tradução em Portugal* (Lisbon: Universidade Católica Editora, 2001), pp. 9–24; also published as "A Touch of Translation," in Sandra Berman and Michael Wood, eds., *Nation, Language, and the Ethics of Translation* (Princeton: Princeton University Press, 2004). On touching, see J. Derrida, *Le toucher—Jean-Luc Nancy* (Paris: Galilée, 2000).

27. "There and then" is my, admittedly idiosyncratic, proposal to translate the Heideggerian notion of *Dasein*.

28. See Chapter 13 for a discussion of a few recent instances of this tendency.

29. A recent example has been the development of new audiovisual technologies of reproduction in the consumer electronics industry: recently, techniques of audio-recording, SACD, DVD-A, etc., have been developed in view of the possibility of "copy protection." As technology makes copying easier and more efficient, producers must devise new techniques to keep control of property rights, even at the detriment of the "quality" of the reproduction—such as "watermarking" digital recordings to prevent "pirating." In a discussion of Sony-Philip's SACD, David Rich concludes: "It is likely that SACD was brought to market not as a way of bringing audiophiles closer to the music, but of making digital audio more difficult to copy" (*Stereophile*, November 2000, p. 71).

Chapter 2

1. Martin Heidegger, "The Question Concerning Technology," *The Question Concerning Technology and Other Essays*, trans. and introd. William Lovitt (New York: Harper Torchbooks, 1977), p. 35 (here and throughout,

translations have been modified where necessary to better reflect aspects of the original that are under discussion). Further page references will appear in the text, preceded by QT. For my translation of *das Wesende der Technik* as "the goings-on of technics," see "Upsetting the Setup," in Samuel Weber, *Mass Mediauras* (Stanford: Stanford University Press, 1997), pp. 55–75. The present essay picks up where the earlier one left off.

2. "*Entbergen* connotes an opening out from a protective concealing, a harboring forth," notes the translator, William Lovitt. See QT, p. 11, n. 10.

3. Martin Heidegger, *Der Ursprung des Kunstwerkes* (Stuttgart: Reclam, 1967), p. 67. Further page references will appear in the text, preceded by OA.

4. The same word is used in German to designate the "withdrawal" from addictive habits.

5. Martin Heidegger, *Being and Time*, trans. John Macquarrie and Edward Robinson (New York: Harper & Row, 1962), §§38, 72, pp. 219–24, 424–29.

6. For a Heideggerian reading of the significance of "security" in international relations, see Michael Dillon, *Politics of Security* (London: Routledge, 1996).

7. See Martin Heidegger, *Introduction to Metaphysics*, trans. Ralph Manheim (New Haven: Yale University Press, 1959), chap. 2, "On the Grammar and Etymology of the Word 'Being,'" pp. 52–74. "But the transformation of the infinitive into the verbal substantive further stabilizes as it were the emptiness that already resided in the infinitive: 'sein' [to be] is set down like a stable object. The substantive 'Sein' implies that what has thus been named itself 'is.' Now 'to be' itself becomes something that 'is'"(p. 69).

8. Virtually all translators of Heidegger reject the translation of *Sein* as "to be." "Literally translated, *das Sein* would be "the *to be*," but this would be far too clumsy a rendering" (Translator's Introduction to Martin Heidegger, *Introduction to Metaphysics*, trans. Gregory Fried and Richard Polt [New Haven: Yale University Press, 2000], xi). This clumsiness, however, may be a price worth paying for the recovery of a proximity to contemporary English usage that is totally lost when the decisive Heideggerian distinction between *Sein* und *Seiendes* is made to depend on a stylistic device—capitalization—that has no general currency in contemporary English. Moreover, the English infinitive "to be" has the advantage of connoting the *futurity* of *Sein*, upon which Heidegger places great emphasis. For these reasons, wherever *Sein* is emphatically distinguished from *Seiendes*, I will use *the to be* and *beings* to render that distinction, reserving the word *being* to designate the disjunctive *juncture* of the two. Similarly, for reasons that will emerge at the end of this chapter, I prefer to translate the title of Heidegger's lectures literally, as *Introduction into Metaphysics*.

9. In *Being Singular Plural*, Jean-Luc Nancy radicalizes the Heideggerian

notion of to-be-with (*Mitsein*) elaborated in *Being and Time* by designating the "*with* as the essential trait of being and as its own singularly plural essence" (trans. Robert D. Richardson and Anne E. O'Byrne [Stanford: Stanford University Press, 2000], p. 34). For Nancy, this plural singularity and singular plurality of the *with* implies a disjunctive spatio-temporal simultaneity that calls for "a scenographic praxis" on the part of society, once its collective appearance (*comparution*) is no longer determined as self-expression but as theatrical exposure.

10. "Art is the setting-fast of truth instituting itself in the figure [*Kunst ist das Feststellen der sich einrichtenden Wahrheit in die Gestalt*]" (OA, p. 81).

11. Walter Benjamin, "Franz Kafka," in *Gesammelte Schriften*, ed. Rolf Tiedemann and Hermann Schweppenhäuser (Frankfurt a. M.: Suhrkamp, 1980), 2.2:420; hereafter referred to as GS. Further references to this essay will be given in parentheses in the text. Benjamin had already used the phrase in a text written in 1932, "Theater and Radio," p. 775 of the same volume.

12. "Was ist episches Theater?" ("What Is Epic Theater?"), first version, in Benjamin, GS 2.2:519.

13. Walter Benjamin, *The Origin of the German Mourning Play*, trans. John Osborne (London: Verso, 1985), p. 182.

14. Franz Kafka, *The Man Who Disappeared*, trans. Michael Hoffmann (Harmondsworth, Middlesex: Penguin, 1997).

15. Franz Kafka, *Der Verschollene*, ed. Jost Schillemeit (Frankfurt a. M.: S. Fischer, 1983). Citations in this text refer to the reprint of this edition by Reclam Verlag (Stuttgart: Philipp Reclam, 1997).

16. In a forthcoming book, *Benjamin's –abilities*, I hope to demonstrate that Benjamin should be read above all as a "virtual thinker": a thinker of possibilities whose medium is inextricably bound up with writing as a medium of *signifying* rather than as the production of meaning. Such possibilities cannot be measured in terms of their ability to actualize themselves as comprehension but rather register in terms of their resistance to such expectations. For an initial outline of part of this project, see Samuel Weber, "Benjamin's Style," in *The Oxford Encyclopedia of Aesthetics*, ed. Michael Kelly (New York: Oxford University Press, 1998), 1:261–64.

17. When Benjamin showed his essay on Kafka to Brecht, the latter was openly critical, both of Kafka and of his interpreter. According to the notes Benjamin wrote during his 1934 visit to Brecht in Svendborg, Brecht dismissed his Kafka essay as symptomatic of a more general tendency to "journal jottings [*tagebuchartigen Schriftstellerei*]." By taking Kafka seriously, Brecht argued, Benjamin's essay promoted "Jewish Fascism." Whereas the genuine article looked to "heroism" for a way out of the insecurity of petit-bourgeois existence, Jewish Fascism "asked questions." But both looked to a Führer to provide the answer. See: Walter Benjamin, "Svendborg Diaries," GS, 4:526–

30. For a comprehensive and well-informed discussion of the extremely complex relationship between Benjamin and Brecht, see the excellent study by Nikolaus Müller-Schöll, *Das Theater des "dekonstruktiven Defaitismus"* (Frankfurt a. M.: Stromfeld/Nexus, 2002), pp. 175–230.

18. This would be Benjamin's version of Max Weber's notion of "rationalization."

19. This classical approach to the work of art is of course called into question by the Jena Romantics, in particular by Friedrich Schlegel, whose notion of the "criticizability" of works occupies a central position in Benjamin's thesis "The Concept of Criticism in German Romanticism" (Walter Benjamin, *Selected Writings*, ed. Michael W. Jennings, Vol. 1: 1913–1926, ed. Marcus Bullock and Michael W. Jennings [Cambridge: Harvard University Press, 1996], pp. 116–200). Benjamin contrasts Schlegel's notion of "criticizability" with Goethe's idea of the immanence of the artwork, and then points to Hölderlin as providing a possible way beyond the opposition of classical and romantic conceptions of the work. Benjamin's construction of the German baroque "mourning play" (*Trauerspiel*) as "allegorical" demonstrates a major consequence he will elicit from this problematizing of the work, one that runs through his writings from beginning to end.

20. In an early text, "Typographies," Philippe Lacoue-Labarthe points out the relation between Heidegger's conception of *poēsis* as "a mode of *installation* in general" and *mimēsis*, which Heidegger mistrusts, in the Platonic tradition, as a mode of *disinstallation.* See Philippe Lacoue-Labarthe, "Typographies," in S. Agacinski, J. Derrida, et al., *Mimesis Desarticulations* (Paris: Aubier-Flammarion, 1975), p. 206.

21. "The absolute *arrivant* does not yet have a name or an identity. This is why I call it simply the *arrivant*, not someone or something that arrives, a subject, a person, an individual or a living thing" (Jacques Derrida, *Aporias*, trans. Thomas Dutoit [Stanford: Stanford University Press, 1993], p. 34).

22. It should be noted that in French the verb *arriver* also signifies "to attain a goal or fulfill an intention": the *arrivant* is thus that which is constantly reaching its goal, without ever attaining it.

23. Franz Kafka, *Erzählungen* (Stuttgart: Reclam, 1999), p. 187; "The Next Village," in Franz Kafka, *The Metaphorphosis, The Penal Colony and Other Stories*, trans. Willa and Edwin Muir (New York: Schocken Books, 1948), p. 158. Translation modified.

24. Ibid., p. 43.

25. Derrida relates the *mysterium tremendum* to the trembling of the earth as that "strange repetition that ties an irrefutable past . . . to a future that cannot be anticipated" (*The Gift of Death*, trans. David Wills [Chicago: University of Chicago Press, 1995], p. 54). Derrida traces the motif back to St. Paul's Epistle to the Philippians (2:12).

26. Cited from "Er," "Beim Bau der chinesischen Mauer" ("Constructing the Great Wall of China"), in Benjamin, *GS*, 2.2:435. In *To Be and Time*, §15, Heidegger also cites the example of hammering to illustrate the nature of *Zeug*, "stuff" or, as it is usually translated, "equipment." This nature resides in the relationship "in order that," *um zu*, which, according to Heidegger, pertains to the essence of "hammering." A notion of a "hammering" separated from such a relationship would, for Heidegger, be secondary and derived. This is why Heidegger's discussion of "hammering" is couched in the present indicative and its derivatives, whereas Kafka's account, situating "hammering" in the dimension of desire, tends toward the present participle and toward "becoming" rather than "being" in the sense of "is," as the following assertion demonstrates: "Hammering does not simply have a knowledge concerning the character of the hammer as stuff, but rather has assimilated [*zugeeignet*] this stuff as adequately [*angemessen*] as possible. . . . Hammering itself discovers the specific 'handiness' of the hammer. The mode of being of stuff, in which it reveals itself on its own [*von sich her*], we call 'ready to hand' [*Zuhandenheit*]" (*To Be and Time*, p. 98). In the structure of stuff, which is that of *referring* (*Verweisen*), there lies, according to Heidegger, the reference "of something to something." For Kafka, by contrast, the process of "referring," of *Verweisen*, no longer presupposes that "something," which is why it can be said to be more "real" and yet also "more insane": it is missing precisely the "self" that Heidegger invokes ("Hammering itself discovers"). The reality of the present participle, of the gerund, *Seiend*, cannot be measured in terms of the self of a *Seiendes* as either subject or object. This will lead Kafka to the theater, and perhaps drive Heidegger to avoid it.

27. The noun *act* has been affected by the very spread of theatricality that I am investigating. An "act" can be something that is not "real" or "true," but merely feigned. Yet "action" seems to have retained—for the time being, at least—its value of designating something unambiguously "real."

28. Of course, the two can and do converge, and increasingly do so in American politics, where Ronald Reagan can be identified as the first "acting president" who served his full term while acting the part. Theatrical acting as the way to invulnerability is what the phrase *teflon president* both designates and technologically dissimulates. Vulnerability and mortality thus become "roles" that can be discarded at will, like a bad dream from which one awakes. Could this be the appeal of "politics" in an age of "media"?

29. The standard English translation of this passage can be found in Walter Benjamin, "Franz Kafka," in *Selected Writings*, Vol. 2: 1927–1934, trans. Rodney Livingstone and others (Cambridge: Harvard University Press, 1999), p. 814.

30. The standard English translation can be found in ibid., p. 802.

31. "Hence we conclude that the innermost motionless boundary of what

contains is place" (Aristotle, *Physics*, bk. 4, chap. 4, 212a 20–21, in *The Basic Works of Aristotle*, ed. Richard McKeon [New York: Random House, 1941], p. 278).

32. Kafka, *Der Verschollene*, p. 7.

33. This phenomenon recurs today on a global scale in the remarkable cacophony of boom-boxes, walkmen, and mobile phones, devices that quite literally "drown out" one's relation to the immediate environment and thus make flagrant the indifference to place that is one of the hallmarks of the Heideggerian *Gestell*.

34. Benjamin, *The Origin of the German Mourning Play*, p. 80.

35. In French public television, those who are considered to have "creative" or "artistic" functions, such as directors, are ineligible for long-term contracts and the status of civil servant. Job security is thus considered incompatible with creativity. The Theater of Oklahoma, like most private enterprises today, applies this principle to all labor contracts, whether "creative" or not.

36. S. Freud, "Fetischismus," *Gesammelte Werke* (Frankfurt a. M.: S. Fischer, 1948), 14:316.

37. On July 16 and 17, 1942, the Vichy police rounded up some eight thousand Jews, including over four thousand children, and held them in the Winter Stadium (Vel d'Hiv[er]) in Drancy, a northern suburb of Paris, before deporting them to Auschwitz. The National Stadium in Santiago, Chile, was only one of many stadiums throughout the country that served as mass detention, torture, and execution centers following the coup d'état led by General Augusto Pinochet on September 11, 1973. During the Taliban regime in Afghanistan, public executions and amputations were held in the Ghazi Stadium in Kabul prior to soccer matches.

38. It is unnecessary to insist on the feminine overtones of this darkly glimmering "box," with its "pillars" and "pleats." See "The Meaning of the Thallus," in S. Weber, *The Legend of Freud* (Stanford: Stanford University Press, 2000), pp. 101–20.

39. The same "into" marks the title of Heidegger's lectures, *Introduction into Metaphysics*.

40. Benjamin, "Franz Kafka," *GS*, 2.2:422.

Chapter 3

1. I note in passing that today there is a tendency to assume that any reference to "bodies" necessarily implies *human* bodies, as though the human body were somehow the privileged, exemplary body. This generalized and very deep-rooted assumption must itself be opened to questioning if the relation of "theater" to the "electronic media" is to be productively explored.

2. Aristotle, *Poetics*, trans. Gerald Else (Ann Arbor: University of Michigan Press, 1970), p. 91.

3. To avoid "idealistic" misinterpretation: the "influence" of this theoretical text need not be exercised directly. There is no need for a theatrical director to have "read" the *Poetics* to be "influenced" by the tradition it articulates.

4. Stephen Halliwell translates the beginning of this passage: "They [the Dorians] cite the names [tragedy and comedy] as evidence" (Aristotle, *Poetics*, trans. Stephen Halliwell [Cambridge: Harvard University Press, 1995], p. 37).

5. "There are jests which you would be ashamed to make yourself, and yet on the comic stage, or indeed in private, when you hear them, you are greatly amused by them and are not all disgusted at their unseemliness . . . there is a principle in human nature which is disposed to raise a laugh, and this which you once restrained by reason, because you were afraid of being thought a buffoon, is now let out again; and having stimulated the risible faculty at the theatre, you are betrayed unconsciously to yourself into playing the comic poet at home" (Plato, *Republic*, book 10, trans. Paul Shorey, in Plato, *The Collected Dialogues*, ed. Edith Hamilton and Huntington Cairns [Princeton: Princeton University Press, 1961], p. 606).

6. Sophocles, *The Theban Plays*, trans. E. F. Watling (Harmondsworth, Middlesex: Penguin, 1947), p. 25. Page references to this edition will henceforth be given in the text.

7. Although I cannot go into this in detail, I should note that Hölderlin singles out this point as Oedipus' tragic error, his *hamartia*: "Oedipus interprets the Oracle's message too *infinitely*" he notes in his "Remarks on Oedipus," explaining that Oedipus responds both too generally and too particularly, jumping from the general, the need for purgation, to the particular, the need to identify the impure element as an individual person or culprit. See Friedrich Hölderlin, *Werke und Briefe*, ed. Friedrich Beissner and Jochen Schmitt (Frankfurt a. M.: Insel, 1969), pp. 731–32.

8. Theodor Adorno, "Prolog zu Fernsehen," in *Gesammelte Schriften*, vol. 10.1, *Kulturkritik und Gesellschaft II*, ed. Rold Tiedemann, with Gretel Adorno, Susan Buck-Morss, and Klaus Schultz (Frankfurt a. M.: Suhrkamp, 1997), p. 507.

9. Walter Benjamin, "Theater und Rundfunk" ("Theater and Radio"), in Benjamin, *Gesammelte Schriften*, ed. Rolf Tiedemann and Hermann Schweppenhäuser (Frankfurt a. M.: Suhrkamp, 1980), 2.2:774; hereafter referred to as *GS*. The standard English translation can be found in Benjamin, *Selected Writings*, Vol. 2: 1927–1934, trans. Rodney Livingstone and others; ed. Michael W. Jennings, Howard Eiland, and Gary Smith (Cambridge: Harvard University Press, 1999), p. 584. Future references to this work will include both English and German page numbers, with the English preceding.

10. Benjamin's German formulation, *den Einsatz der lebendigen Mittel*, has been overtaken by history and resonates differently in an epoch that must look back on *Einsatzkommandos*.

11. Benjamin actually refers to the phrase "sacred sobriety," *heilige Nüchternheit*, at the end of his early essay, "Two Poems of Friedrich Hölderlin," *GS*, 2.1, 125–26.

12. Hölderlin, "Remarks," p. 730. The notion of "pure word" here is a forebear of the "pure language" that Benjamin introduces in his early essay "On Language as Such and on the Language of Man,'" in Benjamin, *Selected Writings*, Vol. 2: 1913–1926, ed. Marcus Bullock and Michael W. Jennings (Cambridge: Harvard University Press, 1996), pp. 62–74.

13. "However, in addition to the concept of synthesis, what will become of increasing systematic importance is that of a certain non-synthesis of two concepts in another, since apart from synthesis another relation between thesis and antithesis is possible" (Benjamin, "Über das Programm der kommenden Philosophie," *GS*, 2.1, 166).

14. Jacques Derrida and Bernard Stiegler, *Echographies de la télévision, entretiens filmés* (Paris: Galilée–INA, 1996), back cover text, my translation.

15. Ibid.

16. I return to some of these issues in Chapter 6, below, concerning Benjamin's study of the German *Trauerspiel*, and more extensively in a forthcoming study, *Benjamin's –abilities*, which will discuss the "medialization" of his thinking and writing that allows him to address the "media" in such prescient and challenging ways.

Chapter 4

1. The presidential election of 2000 is only the most recent, and problematic, instance of this tendency, which continues unabated.

2. Ismene reminds Antigone, at the outset, "how our father / Perished in shame and misery" *before* the suicide of Jocasta (ll. 49–50), whereas in the Oedipus plays Oedipus survives Jocasta, goes into exile, and dies peacefully in *Oedipus at Colonus*. Barring a memory blackout on the part of Sophocles, this provides compelling internal evidence that the play was written before the other two. Even more, it indicates the mutability of the myth with respect to its theatrical staging. Throughout this chapter, I have used Sophocles, *Plays*, *Antigone*, trans. R. C. Jebb, introd. Ruby Blondell (London: Bristol Classical Press, 2004); references are given by line number in the text. The play is also available on the Internet at http://www.chlt.org/cgi-bin/ptext?-doc = Perseus%3Atext%3A1999.01.0185.

3. Although *autodelphon* is usually translated without reference to the "brother"—Jebb, for instance, renders it simply as "my own dear sister"—

Notes to Pages 123–33

Nicole Loraux insists that a literal rendition would, in French, be "You are my dearly fraternal head, Ismene [*Tu es ma chère tête fraternelle, Ismene*]" and that "from the very start" Polyneices is present as "the brother who will not be able to be buried" (Sophocles, *Antigone*, trans. Paul Mazon, introd. Nicole Loraux [Paris: Les Belles Lettres, 1997], p. 2, n. 1).

4. To have insisted on the importance of the family is the merit of Jean Bollack: "Neither parricide nor incest constitutes the tragedy, since they are not in themselves tragic events; they also do not constitute the myth, which is above all one of a family, in particular that of the Labdacides. . . . The tragic inscribes itself in the myth, but it is not the myth" (*La Naissance d'Oedipe* [Paris: Gallimard, 1995], pp. 242–43).

5. In Euripides, Laius is said to have abducted the young son of his friend Pelops, Chrysippus, who in shame commits suicide, whereupon his father calls down on Laius the curse that eventually destroys his house (Charles Segal, *Oedipus Tyrannos* [New York: Twayne, 1993], p. 46).

6. G. W. F. Hegel, *Phenomenology of Mind*, trans. J. B. Baillie (New York: Harper & Row, 1967). Page numbers will be given in the text; the translation has been changed where necessary to better reflect features of the original that are under discussion.

7. Cf. A. de Tocqueviille, *Democracy in America* (New York: Vintage, 1945), 2:4: "In most of the operations of the mind each American appeals only to the individual effort of his own understanding. America is therefore one of the countries where the precepts of Descartes are least studied and best applied. . . . It is not only the confidence in this or that man which is destroyed, but the disposition to trust the authority of any man whatsoever. Everyone shuts himself up tightly within himself and insists upon judging the world from there."

8. See Loraux's brief hint in Sophocles, *Antigone*, trans. Paul Mazon, p. 15, n. 16.

9. In book 2, section 7 of *The Genealogy of Morals*, Nietzsche surmises that "in order to abolish hidden, undetected, unwitnessed suffering . . . one was in the past virtually compelled to invent gods and genii of all heights and depths" (*On the Genealogy of Morals*, trans. Walter Kaufman [New York: Vintage, 1969], p. 68).

10. Jacques Derrida, "The Force of Law," in Drucilla Cornell, Michel Rosenfeld, and David Gray Carlson, eds., *Deconstruction and the Possibility of Justice* (New York: Routledge, 1992), pp. 3–67; "Before the Law," in J. Derrida, *Acts of Literature*, ed. Derek Attridge (New York: Routledge, 1992), pp. 181–22. For Derrida, there is not simply a distinction between justice and law, but rather an aporetic relation: "For in the founding of law or in its institution, the same problem of justice will have been posed and violently resolved, that is to say, buried, dissimulated, repressed" (p. 23). Burial is pre-

cisely what Antigone strives to do to serve "justice," even if it means breaking the law proclaimed by Creon.

11. Friedrich Hölderlin, "Antigone," *Werke und Briefe*, ed. F. Beißner and J. Schmitt (Frankfurt a. M.: Insel, 1969), 2:752: "*Mein* Zeus berichtete mirs nicht."

12. Jacques Lacan, *L'Ethique de la psychanalyse* (Paris: Seuil, 1986), p. 324.

13. Not "individual selfhood," as Baillie translates (Hegel, *Phenomenology*, p. 477).

14. Jacques Derrida, *Glas* (Paris: Galilée, 1974), p. 161.

15. *Antigone*, in Sophocles, *The Theban Plays*, trans. E. F. Watling (Harmondsworth, Middlesex: Penguin, 1974).

16. "The feminine element, therefore, in the form of the sister, anticipates and foreshadows most completely the nature of ethical being. She does not become conscious of it, and does not actualize it, because the law of the family is her inherent implicit inward nature, which does not lie open to the daylight of consciousness but remains inner feeling and the divine element exempt from actuality" (Hegel, *Phenomenology*, 476).

17. Jebb adds the following footnote to this speech: "Few problems of Greek Tragedy have been more discussed than the question whether these verses, or some of them, are spurious. Aristotle (*Rhetoric* 3. 16–9) quotes verse 911. . . . Interpolation, then, if such it be, must have been made soon after the poet's death; and has been imputed to his son Iophon (*ho psuchros*), or some other sorry poet, or to the actors. I confess that, after long thought, I cannot bring myself to believe that Sophocles wrote 905–12, with which 904 and 913–20 are in organic unity, and must now stand or fall. . . . The main points (to my mind) are briefly these. (1) The general validity of the divine law, as asserted in 450–60, cannot be intelligibly reconciled with the limitation in verses 905–7. (2) A still further limitation is involved in verse 911 and following. She has buried her brother, not simply as such, but because, while he lived, he was an irreplaceable relative. Could she have hoped for the birth of another brother, she would not, then, have felt the duty to be so binding. (3) The composition of vv. 909–12 is unworthy of Sophocles." What Jebb and so many other commentators overlook is that Antigone never says just *in what the divine laws* might consist. Most commentators simply assume that they consist in the *general* obligation of family members to bury their dead. But in her response to Creon, Antigone is much more specific, referring her obligation to "my mother's son" (ll. 466–74) and thus to the common and irreplaceable parent invoked in her "calculation." It is this law, which is not a law, this "woman's rule," that continues to derange. To Jebb's credit, he concludes his discussion of this passage by acknowledging that "Goethe's wish [that the passage be removed from the text as inauthentic] can never be fulfilled. No one will ever convince everyone that this passage is spurious.

But every student of the *Antigone* is bound to reflect earnestly on this vital problem of the text—the answer to which must so profoundly affect our conception of the great drama as a whole" (Sophocles, *Plays, Antigone*, trans. R. C. Jebb, ed. P. E. Easterling, introd. Ruby Blondell [London: Bristol Classical Press, 2004], p. 263). Although it is over a century since Jebb wrote these words, his conclusion remains at least as timely today as it was in 1900.

Chapter 5

1. Sophocles, *Plays, Oedipus Coloneus*, trans. R. C. Jebb, introd. Ruby Blondell (London: Bristol Classical Press, 2004). References to this text give the line numbers and unless otherwise indicated follow the Jebb translation.

2. Lowell Edmunds, *Oedipus: The Ancient Legend and Its Later Analogues* (Baltimore: The Johns Hopkins University Press, 1985), p. 16.

3. Henry George Liddell and Robert Scott, *An Intermediate Greek-English Lexicon* (Oxford: Oxford University Press, 1975), p. 70.

4. Sophocles, *Plays, Antigone*, trans. R. C. Jebb, introd. Ruby Blondell (London: Bristol Classical Press, 2004).

5. G. W. F. Hegel, *Enzyklopädie der philosophischen Wissenschaften*, §261 (Hamburg: Felix Meiner, 1969), p. 213.

6. Ibid.

7. See Kurt Steinmann, Afterword to his German translation, *Oedipus auf Kolonos* (Stuttgart: Reclam, 1996), p. 115, and Lowell Edmunds, *Theatrical Space and Historical Place in Sophocles' 'Oedipus at Colonus'* (Lanham, Md.: Rowman & Littlefield, 1996), p. 96.

8. At least one commentator has attempted to offer an explanation: "The place of Oedipus' grave had to remain a state secret, and neither the Athenians nor the Thebans were allowed to honor Oedipus's grave, because precisely the absence of such honors to the dead sustained the hatred of the Theban king, buried in foreign earth, against his countrymen and thus guaranteed the Athenians victory over the Thebans" (F. W. Schneidewin-Nauck, 1883, cited in Steinmann, *Oedipus auf Kolonos*, p. 107). But this interpretation lacks any basis in Sophocles' text, in which the very keeping of the secret by Theseus and his "chosen successors" assumes a ritual value and indicates respect for the dead. Schneidewin-Nauck was probably on the right track, however, in seeking to relate the power of the secret to the form of mourning that it permits. What seems to be implied, however, is a change in the kind of mourning rather than its simple absence or presence. We will return to this later. On the relation between the oligarchic movement of the 400 and the notion of the savior, see Edmunds, *Theatrical Space*, p. 145.

9. Karl Reinhardt, *Sophokles* (Frankfurt a. M.: Klostermann, 1947), p. 229.

10. Walter Benjamin, *Das Passagen-Werk*, in Benjamin, *Gesammelte Schrif-*

ten, ed. Rolf Tiedemann and Hermann Schweppenhäuser (Frankfurt a. M.: Suhrkamp, 1980), 5.1:461.

11. Edmunds, *Theatrical Space*, p. 51.

12. Ibid., p. 50, n. 30, quoting l. 138.

13. See Aristotle, *Poetics*, trans. Gerald Else (Ann Arbor: University of Michigan Press, 1970), p. 20.

14. Glossing the local details in the messenger's description of Oedipus' last movements, Steinmann notes: "All of these precise topographical indications are no longer intelligible to us, but the places were, as the scholiast reports, "known to the natives" (Steinmann, *Oedipus auf Kolonos*, p. 108).

15. Edmunds, *Theatrical Space*, p. 91.

16. Ibid., p. 102.

17. Sophocles, *Oedipus Coloneus*, trans. Jebb, p. 21.

18. See also ibid., 269–91, 521ff.

19. In the second chorus from *Antigone*, to which Heidegger has devoted considerable commentary (in *An Introduction to Metaphysics*, trans. Ralph Manheim [Garden City, N.Y.: Doubleday, 1961], chap. 4, "The Limitation of Being," pp. 146–65, and, at greater length, in his 1942 seminar on Hölderlin's poem *Der Ister*, in Martin Heidegger, *Gesamtausgabe*, vol. 53: *Hölderlins Hymne, "Der Ister"* (Frankfurt a. M.: Vittorio Klostermann, 1984), pp. 63–152), the chorus describes man "everywhere setting forth, underway, but with no way out [*pantoporos aporos*]" (*Antigone*, 359).

20. See Jacques Derrida, *Le toucher—Jean-Luc Nancy* (Paris: Galilée, 2000).

21. *Hamlet*, 1.5.91.

22. Leo Meyer, *Griechische Aoriste* (*Greek Aorists*) (n.p., 1879), pp. 124–25.

23. Following and slightly modifying a suggestion of Haun Saussy, the combination of the aorist participle here with a verb in the optative perfect— *memnēisthe*, "may you be mindful of"—suggests a situation that can best be described by varying the Freudian "Wo Es war, soll ich warden" ("Where It was, I shall come to be") to become: "Where *I* was, the memory of my being dead shall come to be."

24. Edmunds, *Theatrical Space*, p. 82.

25. Paul de Man, *The Resistance to Theory* (Minneapolis: University of Minnesota Press, 1986), p. 42: "Hegel, who is often said to have 'forgotten' about writing, is unsurpassed in his ability to remember that one should never forget to forget."

Chapter 6

1. The notion of the Treuga Dei, "truce of God," has been traced back to Aquitaine, where, following a terrible famine in 1033 and the violence and chaos that ensued, the clergy made efforts to prohibit all feuds for a

limited period of a few days, on pain of excommunication. The movement spread first through Burgundy, then through France as a whole, until the Synod of Clermont (1095), under the lead of Pope Urban II, made the Truce of God the general law of the church. The duration of the truce was extended but remained limited to certain holiday periods (Advent to Epiphany, Ash Wednesday to the close of Easter week). (*History of the Christian Church,* vol. 4, *Medieval Christianity,* §78, http://www.ccel.org/ccel/schaff/hcc4.i.vi.vi .html#fnf_i.vi.vi-p11.1). "Admittedly, these rules applied only to conflicts among Christians" (Walter Z. Lacqueur, "Terror's New Face: The Radicalization and Escalation of Modern Terrorism," *Harvard International Review,* http://hir.harvard.edu/articles/?id = 307&page = 5). See also Hartmut Hoffman, *Gottesfriede und Treuga Dei* (Stuttgart: Anton Hiersemann, 1964).

2. Asja Lacis, *Revolutionär im Beruf (Profession: Revolutionary)* (Munich: Rogner & Bernhard, 1971), pp. 43–44. Cited in Walter Benjamin, *Gesammelte Schriften,* ed. Rolf Tiedemann and Hermann Schweppenhäuser (Frankfurt a. M.: Suhrkamp, 1980), 1.3:879–80. (Abbreviated *GS* in later references.)

3. In his "Epistemo-Critical Preface" to *The Origin of the German Mourning Play,* Benjamin designates "allegory" as an "Idea," a term that he takes from Plato and Kant, then reworks to distinguish it from both the empirical given and the theoretical "concept." As an *idea,* Benjamin's notion of the *Trauerspiel* entails what he calls *Darstellung,* which might be translated as "exposition" or, perhaps better, as "staging."

4. For an earlier attempt to discuss Benjamin's relation to Heidegger, see Samuel Weber, "Der posthume Zwischenfall: Eine Live-Sendung," in *Zeit-Zeichen,* ed. G. C. Tholen and M. Scholl (Acta Humaniora: Weinheim, 1990), pp. 181–95.

5. "For all that the increasing worldliness of the Counter-Reformation prevailed in both confessions, religious inclinations did not lose their importance: only a religious solution was denied them by the century, which demanded of them or imposed on them a worldly one instead" (W. Benjamin, *The Origin of the German Tragic Drama,* trans. John Osborne [London: Verso, 1985], p. 79).

6. Cf. *GS* 1.3:888, where Benjamin asserts that works of art are essentially unhistorical and "intensive."

7. See *GS,* 1.3:891–95.

8. It should be noted, in passing, that although Rang's use of this term in a letter to Benjamin is free of any immediate political connotations, this of course does not exclude the question of the political ramifications of such a conception. Rang died in 1924, shortly after writing these letters, while Benjamin was still working on his study. With Rang's death, Benjamin writes Scholem, his book has lost its "true reader" (*GS,* 1.3:883).

9. Quoted in *GS,* 1.3:891. Future references to this source will appear in the text.

10. This is why there can be nothing strictly *individual* in a theater of this kind, something that led Aristotle already to de-emphasize the character of the hero with respect to the "action." See Chapter 3, above.

11. *GS* 1.3:891.

12. The position outlined by Benjamin here seems in large measure to accord with that proposed by Max Weber in his *The Protestant Ethic and the Spirit of Capitalism* (New York: Charles Scribner's Sons, 1958; orig. pub. 1904–5). In that book, Weber emphasizes that Calvinism, rather than Lutheranism, contributed to the evolution of modern capitalism. Luther's attitude toward everyday activity was far too ambivalent, Weber stresses, to encourage anything like the Calvinist "work ethic." Luther, for instance, still understands the notion of "calling" in terms of obedience to a divine ordinance, rather than as a "profession" in the modern sense. (See chap. 3, "Luther's Conception of the Calling: Task of the Investigation," pp. 79–92.) The relation between Benjamin's interpretation of Luther's "storming of the work" and the Calvinist "work ethic" merits further investigation.

13. See the remarkable study by Susan Bernstein, *Virtuosity of the Nineteenth Century: Performing Music and Language in Heine, Liszt, and Baudelaire* (Stanford: Stanford University Press, 1998).

Chapter 7

1. Despite the absence of any direct or explicit indication that Hamlet has succeeded in getting Horatio and Marcellus actually to swear the oath he proposes—in the Quartos and Folio there is neither a stage direction to that effect (this has been "corrected" by subsequent editors) nor any dialogue—most editors seem not to have doubted that the oath is indeed sworn, even if they have to go to great lengths to argue it, as in the following remark by the editor of the Arden edition of *Hamlet*, Harold Jenkins: "When and how many times they swear must, in the absence of a stage-direction, be inferred from the text." Only Dover Wilson, he notes, appears to have envisaged the possibility of the oath having been interrupted by the Ghost. Jenkins counters: "Yet they have placed their hands on the cross of the sword (cf. l. 166) and though the text gives them no word . . . , it subsequently seems to regard them as actually having sworn." He bases this argument on the repetition of Hamlet's injunction to "lay your hands again upon my sword" (1.5.166) or, a few lines later ("But come: / Here as before, lay your hands"). "What I therefore think must happen," Jenkins concludes, "is that the injunction to swear is echoed by the Ghost and obeyed by Hamlet's companions simultaneously." One can only envy Jenkins an ear subtle enough to discern the oath that is, as it were, drowned out by the Ghost's reiterated echoing of Hamlet's injunction, which changes subtly but significantly each time, so that

it becomes increasingly difficult to know just what the terms of this oath actually might be (*Hamlet*, ed. Harold Jenkins [London: Methuen, 1982], p. 459).

2. *Andere Schauplätze*, the term Freud borrows from Fechner to describe the topology of the unconscious.

3. An act or action can be considered finite; *acting*, by contrast, is intrinsically open and indeterminable, determinable only with respect to the space-time of its enunciation.

4. More precisely, perhaps: "here and *wherever*." The force of this "and wherever" can be compared to the vogue in contemporary American slang for what can be called the "terminal *whatever*": that is, the use of the adverbial phrase "or whatever" to conclude an assertion with an interrogative turn. To be sure, the differences between this current American idiom and Hamlet's *et ubique* are at least as illuminating as the similarities. By concluding an assertion with the phrase "or whatever," the speaker disclaims responsibility for the assertion just made. In contrast to such a disclaiming function, *hic et ubique* points to the difficulty of assuming responsibility for words whose effects cannot be unambiguously localized—but it does not attempt to avoid that responsibility.

5. A "stage," as divisible, is also a "stage" in the temporal sense: always on the way to somewhere else. Another indication that time *and* space are both "out of joint," not just in this particular play, but in theater in general.

6. In this context it might be of interest to reread Walter Benjamin's description of what in his writings on the Paris Passages is called the "loquacity of place [*die Kolportage des Raumes*]": the promise of places to tell stories about what has taken place in and around them. The medium as haunted place also suggests a link with the notion of "medium" as intermediary between the living and the dead. Not for nothing is this sort of medium always tied to a particular place and placement: for instance, seated around a table.

7. Carl Schmitt, *Hamlet oder Hekuba: Der Einbruch der Zeit in das Spiel* (Stuttgart: Klett Cotta, 1984), p. 66.

8. Walter Benjamin, *Ursprung des deutschen Trauerspiels*, in *Gesammelte Schriften*, ed. Rolf Tiedemann and Hermann Schweppenhäuser (Frankfurt a. M.: Suhrkamp, 1980), 1.1:318. (Abbreviated *GS* in later references.)

9. Benjamin's German here is, to say the least, unusual but, as usual, significantly so: he begins by describing Hamlet as "Zuschauer von Gottes Gnaden," which Osborne, understandably, translates as "a spectator by the grace of God" (W. Benjamin, *The Origin of the German Tragic Drama*, trans. John Osborne [London: Verso, 1985], p. 158). However, in the following phrase, the third-person plural pronoun, *sie* ("aber nicht was *sie* ihm spielen") seems to have *Gnaden* only as proximate antecedent, which would make the latter a dative plural rather than dative singular and change the meaning to "specta-

tor *of the graces* of God" rather than "spectator *by the grace* of God." In my translation I have chosen to retain both possibilities, since this would reflect the experience of a reader of the German text, who would initially read the phrase as "by the grace of God" and then re-read it as "of the graces of God." The two versions do not exclude each other, since Benjamin seems to be arguing that it is the grace of God that allows Hamlet to become the spectator, not of those "graces" as individual events, but of "his own destiny" as "enclosed in a happening that is entirely homogeneous with his view [*das Geheimnis seines Schicksals* [ist] *beschlossen in einem Geschehen, das diesem seinem Blick ganz homogen ist*]"(*GS*, 1.1.334). The "grace of God" here would thus consist in Hamlet's ability to see (but also to stage) his destiny in a way that allows it to conform to his vision qua spectator. It is the "homogeneity" of the "destiny" of *spectacle and spectator*—in short, of a certain theatrical reflexivity—that is at issue here.

10. Aristotle, *Poetics*, 11 (7), trans. G. Else (Ann Arbor: University of Michigan Press, 1994), p. 30.

11. *King Oedipus*, ll. 1528–30, in Sophocles, *Theban Plays*, trans. E. F. Watling (Harmondsworth, Middlesex: Penguin, 1974), p. 68.

Chapter 8

1. The continued force of this tradition can be seen even in works that explicitly seek to call the tradition into question, such as Jacques Taminaux's *Le Théâtre des philosophes: La Tragédie, l'être, l'action* (Grenoble: Jérôme Millon, 1995), a book for which the "theater" of philosophy is synonymous with tragedy, as indicated by its subtitle: "Tragedy, Being, Action."

2. This is the "good Danish word" that Kierkegaard uses as the title of the study generally translated, in English, as *Repetition*. For reasons that will emerge in the course of this reading, I will often use the Danish term instead of its established English translation.

3. Søren Kierkegaard, *Repetition*, trans. Howard V. and Edna H. Hong (Princeton: Princeton University Press, 1983), p. 131. Page references to this work will be given in parentheses in the body of the text. All translations of this and other works have been modified where necessary to better reflect aspects of the text that are being discussed.

4. Friedrich Nietzsche, *Beyond Good and Evil*, trans. Walter Kaufman (New York: Vintage Books, 1966), §2, pp. 10–11.

5. Plato's *Republic*, trans. B. Jowett (New York: Modern Library, 1982), bk. 3: 393–94, pp. 92–95.

6. Diogenes Laertius, *Lives of Eminent Philosophers*, 6.2.39. Hegel also cites this passage in his *History of Philosophy* (*Hegel's Lectures on the History of Philosophy*, trans. E. S. Haldane and Frances H. Simson (New York: Humanities Press, 1955), 1: 267.

7. In *Beyond the Pleasure Principle*, Freud recognizes that the repetition of traumatic experiences can diminish their pain by submitting them to a certain control of the ego: "It is striking that repetition, the rediscovery of identity, can itself signify a source of pleasure" (Freud, *Gesammelte Werke* [Frankfurt a. M.: S. Fischer, 1967], 12:37). The happiness that Constantin here associates with repetition and that motivates him to seek a confirmation of its reality is of this "egological" nature. What he discovers is that there is repetition, but that it is by no means necessarily a source of happiness.

8. The difference between the Hegelian dialectic and Kierkegaard's way of thinking could be pinpointed as that between the "negation" and the "extreme," which inform the movements of "mediation" and "repetition," respectively.

9. See the Introduction to this volume for a discussion of the significance of this scene for the relation of philosophy to theater.

10. Samuel Beckett, *Endgame* (New York: Grove Press, 1958), p. 74.

11. "Man saetter . . . man betragter . . . man seer . . . man føler en Lyst. . . . Man gjør det ikke, man seer blot," etc. (S. Kierkegaard, *Gjentagelsen*, in *Samlede Vaerkerd* [Copenhagen: Gyldendal, 1962], 5:133).

12. R. Descartes, *Meditations on First Philosophy*, trans. George Heffernan (Notre Dame, Ind.: University of Notre Dame Press, 1990), Second Meditation, p. 113. Future references to this work will be given in parentheses in the body of the text.

13. Nestroy was also a great favorite of Freud and Wittgenstein. Freud's fondness for theater is almost always associated with serious, respectable theater, above all with tragedy, whereas his relation to the *Possen* of Nestroy is largely ignored. See Chapter 10 of this volume for an attempt to demonstrate that the theatricality of psychoanalysis is at least as *possenhaft* as it is tragic.

14. These reflections on the relation of the exception to the rule will provide Carl Schmitt with a methodological conclusion to his discussion of sovereignty at the end of the first chapter of *Political Theology* (Cambridge: MIT Press, 1985), p. 15. For Schmitt, however, the relation between exception and *Posse* disappears entirely.

15. "The historical is always raw material which the person who acquires it knows how to dissolve in a *posse* and assimilate as an *esse*" (quoted in the appendix to *Repetition*, p. 359). *Posse*, possibility, involves the "dissolving" of "raw material," whereas *esse* entails its assimilation.

16. Introduction, *Hegel's Aesthetics*, trans. T. M. Knox (New York: Oxford University Press, 1975), 8.1.c, 1:79.

17. The entire text of *Gjentagelsen* can in this sense be considered to be a *Posse*, as Constantin's concluding Letter shows when it reminds the "reader" that "we are after all *entre nous*. Although you are indeed fictional, you are by

no means a plurality to me but only one, and therefore we are just you and I" (*Repetition*, p. 225).

18. This also describes the style in which the text itself is written: "copious" discussion "of the abstract" interrupted periodically by the "interjection of tangible actuality" (p. 161).

19. Søren Kierkegaard, *Die Wiederholung*, trans. Emanuel Hirsch (Düsseldorf: Eugen Diederichs), p. 37.

20. "Rehearsal" would not be the worst English translation for Kierkegaard's *Gjentagelsen*.

Chapter 9

1. Søren Kierkegaard, *Repetition*, trans. Edward V. Hong and Edna Hong (Princeton: Princeton University Press, 1983), pp. 151–52.

2. Theodor W. Adorno, *Kierkegaard: Konstruktion des Ästhetischen*, in *Gesammelte Schriften*, ed. Rolf Tiedemann (Frankfurt a. M.: Suhrkamp, 1997), 2:9–10. Future page references to this edition will be given in the body of the text.

3. G. W. F. Hegel, Introduction, *Phänomenologie des Geistes*, cited in M. Heidegger, "Hegels Begriff der Erfahrung," in *Holzwege* (Frankfurt a. M.: Klostermann, 1963), p. 106 (my translation).

4. Theodor W. Adorno, *Drei Studien zu Hegel*, in *Gesammelte Schriften*, ed. Rolf Tiedemann (Frankfurt a. M.: Suhrkamp, 1971), 5:326–80. Future references to this work will be given in the body of the text.

5. Adorno gives the following example, from book 2 of the *Greater Logic*: "Becoming in Essence, its reflecting movement, is therefore the movement from nothing to nothing and therein back to itself. Turning-into or coming-to-be suspends and surpasses itself in [its] turn; the other that in such turning-into comes to be is not the nonbeing of a being, but the nothing of a nothing, and this, the negation of a nothing, is what constitutes being.—Being is only as the movement of nothing to nothing, [and only] so is it essence; and the latter does not comprehend movement within itself, but rather is it as absolute semblance itself, pure negativity, which has nothing outside of itself to negate, but negates only its [own] negative, which *is* only in this negating" (G. W. F. Hegel, *Wissenschaft der Logik*, first part, in Hegel, *Jubiläumsausgabe*, ed. Hermann Glockner (Stuttgart: Friedrich Frommann, 1927), 4:493.

6. Max Horkheimer and Theodor W. Adorno, *Dialektik der Aufklärung*, in Horkheimer, *Gesammelte Schriften*, ed. Gunzelin Schmid Noerr (Frankfurt a. M.: S. Fischer, 1987), 5:144.

7. Theodor W. Adorno, "Das Schema der Massenkultur," appendix to Adorno and Horkheimer, *Dialektik der Aufklärung*, in Adorno, *Gesammelte Schriften*, ed. Rolf Tiedemann (Frankfurt a. M.: Suhrkamp, 1997), 3:331. Future page references will be given in the text.

8. This was obviously long before Adorno discovered the jargon of authenticity . . .

9. For a similar, but more interesting and more productive sleight of hand with the same Benjaminian categories, see Adorno's essay on Wagner, *In Search of Wagner* (New York: Norton, 1991), in which the notion of "allegory" is transformed into a *critical* and *geschichtphilosophisches* tool.

10. Walter Benjamin, *Ursprung des deutschen Trauerspiels*, in Benjamin, *Gesammelte Schriften*, ed. Rolf Tiedemann and Hermann Schweppenhäuser (Frankfurt a. M.: Suhrkamp, 1980), 1.1:351.

11. Given the insistent pathos of such admonitions to "awake" in the writings of both Adorno and Benjamin, we should remember that the first line of the Horst Wessel Lied also demands that "Germany awake . . . out of your bad dream!"

12. According to *Duden: Das Herkunftswörterbuch* (Mannheim: Dudenverlag, 1989), "viewed etymologically" *Gehalt* is "the same word" as *Behälter, Behältnis, Aufbewahrungsraum*: that is, as a "container," a place in which things are conserved and saved (p. 224).

13. Theodor W. Adorno, *Drei Studien zu Hegel*, in Adorno, *Gesammelte Schriften*, ed. Rolf Tiedemann (Frankfurt a. M.: Suhrkamp, 1997), 5:351. Future page references will be given in the text.

14. Søren Kierkegaard, "Une première et dernière explication," from *Post-Scriptum aux miettes philosophiques*, trans. Paul Petit (Paris: Gallimard, 1949), p. 425.

15. See Plato's remarks on the corruption of the home by theatrical mimesis in *Republic*, 10.605–6. See also my discussion of these passages in "*Nomos* in *The Magic Flute*," *Angelaki* 3, no. 2 (1998): 61–68.

16. Kierkegaard, *Repetition*, p. 152.

Chapter 10

1. Joyce McDougall, *Théâtres du Je* (Paris: Gallimard, 1982), pp. 9–10 (my translation).

2. Sigmund Freud, "On the History of the Psychoanalytic Movement," *The Standard Edition of the Complete Psychological Words of Sigmund Freud*, ed. James Strachey (London: Hogarth Press, 1953–74), 14: 53; Freud, *Gesammelte Werke* (Frankfurt a. M.: S. Fischer, 1968), 10:97, hereafter *GW*; my translation.

3. Aristotle, *Poetics*, trans. Gerald Else (Ann Arbor: University of Michigan Press, 1970), 48 b 12–19, p. 20.

4. Philologists have often questioned the authenticity of the last two words, *tous mimoumenous*, judging them to be an incoherent scribal addition that renders Aristotle's text incoherent. Whatever their authenticity may be,

however, the fact that someone felt it necessary to add these two words is indicative of the problematic relation of the mimetic to the pragmatic, a relation that Aristotle addresses but by no means resolves.

5. Roselyne Dupont-Roc and Jean Lallot, eds., *Aristote, La Poétique* (Paris: Seuil, 1980), p. 160.

6. To soften the shock of this admittedly bizarre noun, let me recall that Saussure has recourse to a similar gerund in describing the function of language as a system of signs that involves both *signifiants* and *signifiés*. To translate *signifiant* as "signifier" is, of course, to move it away from the present participle and gerund, and consequently to make it more familiar and reassuring. A more idiomatic translation, "agent," suggests that those who are acting are doing so in the service of another subject (although not necessarily an individual or even human one), and since it is precisely the status of the subject that is in question here, "actings," for all of its bizarre and unfamiliar quality, is to be preferred.

7. "For tragedy is the imitation not of men but of a life [*bioū*], of an action [*praxeos*]" (Aristotle, *Poetics*, 50 a 15).

8. Plato, *Republic*, 3.393b–396.

9. Sophocles, *Oedipus Tyrannos*, ed. and trans. R. C. Jebb (Cambridge: Cambridge University Press, 1978), l. 362, 85.

10. Freud, *GW*, 5:218 n.

11. Oedipus' *hubris* consists in seeking to repeat his success with the Sphinx in a situation that is radically different, insofar as it calls, not for a *generic* response, "man," but for a *singular* one, "*this* man, *here*." This response entails acknowledging the implication of the knower in that which is to be known, an implication that excludes any definitive knowledge, as the final Chorus makes clear.

12. Interestingly enough, Freud prefers the notion of "network [*Netzwerk*]" to that of "chain [*Kette*]," doubtless because of the latter's linearity (Sigmund Freud, *Moses and Monotheism* [New York: Vintage Books, 1967], p. 138; *GW*, 16:215.

13. Aristotle, *Poetics*, 48 b 1, p. 20.

14. *Oedipus Tyrannos*, l. 1524–30.

15. Ibid., p. 157.

16. This is also the "pleasure" of watching the nightly news on television, and probably the organizing principle of information as broadcast by the commercial media.

17. In the perspective unfolded by this analysis, it becomes significant that Oedipus does not take his life at the end of *Oedipus Tyrannos*, but instead puts out his eyes. His death will be reserved for *Oedipus at Colonus*, where he will choose a place hidden from all eyes, in order better to keep its secret: a secret, he will claim, that has greater power than armies to save cities from

destruction. Oedipus' insight, which is also his "secret," returns today with a vengeance in the power of the media to keep (the) secret (of) what they ostensibly display.

18. Jacques Lacan, "L'Instance de la lettre dans l'inconscient," *Ecrits* (Paris: Seuil, 1966), p. 511.

19. I have discussed certain ramifications of this in Samuel Weber, *The Legend of Freud*, 2d ed. (Stanford: Stanford University Press, 2000), pp. 104 ff.

20. Freud, *Interpretation of Dreams*, p. 528; *GW*, 2–3:494.

21. Ibid., p. 529; *GW*, 2–3:495.

22. Ibid., p. 528; 2–3:494.

23. Sigmund Freud, *Sexuality and the Psychology of Love* (New York: Collier Books, 1972), pp. 176–82. Future page references will be given in the body of the text.

24. "Das Unheimliche," *GW*, 12:227–68. Future page references to this edition will be given in the body of the text.

25. E. Jones, *Sigmund Freud: Life and Work* (London: The Hogarth Press, 1957), 3:408: "He was fond, especially after midnight, of regaling me with strange or uncanny experiences with patients, characteristically about misfortunes or deaths supervening many years after a wish or prediction. He had a particular relish for such stories and was evidently impressed by their more mysterious aspects. When I would protest at some of the taller stories Freud was wont to reply with his favorite quotation: 'There are more things in heaven and earth than are dreamt of in your philosophy.'"

Chapter 11

1. A. Artaud, "No More Masterpieces," *The Theater and Its Double*, trans. Mary Caroline Richards (New York: Grove Weidenfeld, 1958), pp. 78–79. For this and all other works, the translation has been modified where necessary for the discussion. Future references to this edition will be given in the body of the text.

2. Aristotle, *Poetics*, trans. Gerald Else (Ann Arbor: University of Michigan Press, 1970), 50a, p. 27. Future references to this work will be given by section number (e.g., 50a) in the body of the text.

3. See also *Poetics*, 59b: "It must be possible for the beginning and the end to be seen together in one view."

4. http://hypermedia.univ-paris8.fr/pierre/virtuel/virt0.htm. Document and page references to this work will be given in parentheses in the body of the text.

5. Translated into English by Willa and Edwin Muir as "Cares of a Family Man," in Franz Kafka, *'The Metamorphosis,' 'In the Penal Colony,' and Other Stories* (New York: Schocken Books, 1995), pp. 160–61.

6. I have discussed this text further in Samuel Weber, *Mass Mediauras: Form, Technics, Media* (Stanford: Stanford University Press, 1996), pp. 30–35.

7. Cf. the discussion of "installation" as a theatrical process in Chapter 2 of this volume, "Theatrocracy."

Chapter 12

1. Aristotle, *Poetics*, trans. Gerard Else (Ann Arbor: University of Michigan Press, 1970), 48a-b, p. 19. Further references, by section, will appear in the body of the text.

2. "Home theater" can, however, be seen as the culmination of a specifically modern tradition of theater, going back to the eighteenth century, to the emergence of domestic drama in France and England and of the *bürgerliches Trauerspiel* in Germany.

3. Aristotle, *Poetics*, trans. Stephen Halliwell (Cambridge: Harvard University Press, 1995), p. 53; Ingram Bywater, *Aristotle on the Art of Poetry* (Oxford: Oxford University Press, 1909).

4. *Drama*, to be sure, derives from the Greek verb *drao*, "to do or to act"; but *dramatic* and *theatrical* are not necessarily equivalent terms, as is often supposed—a supposition that continues the Aristotelian tradition of equating the two and thereby marginalizing everything theatrical that is not also dramatic.

5. Aristotle unequivocally emphasizes the decisive structural importance of "action [*praxis*]" as distinct from "character [*ethos*]" in imparting unity to tragic drama, whereas what "characterizes" Western theater since the Renaissance is the increasing emphasis it places on *character* rather than action.

6. Gerard F. Else, note to Aristotle, *Poetics*, p. 9, n. 73.

7. Else himself emphasizes that key Aristotelian terms such as *poiēsis*, "the actual process of composition," and *mimēsis*, which, despite being a noun, is "also active in force," both contain "the same suffix, -*sis*," the Greek equivalent of the English ending "-*ing*." Although Else does not mention it explicitly, the peculiarly "active force" he attributes to nouns such as *poiēsis* and *mimēsis* is related to the dynamics of the gerund and of the present participle: its actuality is all the more immediate and energetic for being, by definition, unfinished and incomplete, and this *ongoing incompletion* distinguishes the gerund from more traditional nouns. (Else refers to "presentation" and "representation" as too static to render what is meant by *mimēsis*; p. 79.) The "presence" of the present participle, by contrast, is tied to the quasi-simultaneity of the process of uttering with the utterance. As a result, such presence is intrinsically open-ended, situated by the split of its articulation and hence never self-contained.

8. Gerard F. Else, note to Aristotle's *Poetics*, p. 85, n. 31.

9. Genet published the text first in *Tel Quel* (1966), then in his *Oeuvres Complètes* (Paris: Gallimard, 1968), 4:9–18. In English, both texts are published in Jean Genet, *Reflections on the Theater*, trans. Richard Seaver (London: Faber & Faber, 1972). Future references to the English edition will be given in the body of the text. All translations have been modified throughout as needed for the discussion.

10. "For if the theater is like the plague, it is not only because it affects important collectivities and overwhelms them in an identical way. In the theater as in the plague there is something both victorious and vengeful: we are well aware that the spontaneous conflagration which the plague lights wherever it passes, is nothing other than an immense liquidation" (A. Artaud, *The Theater and Its Double*, trans. Mary Caroline Richards [New York: Grove Weidenfeld, 1958], p. 27).

11. Genet, *Reflections on the Theater*, p. 73.

12. I have discussed this passage in "The Undoing of Form," in Samuel Weber, *Mass Mediauras: Form, Technics, Media* (Stanford: Stanford University Press, 1996), pp. 30–35.

13. Jean-Bernard Moraly, "Genet urbaniste: Vers un nouveau théâtre sacré," in *Les Nègres au port de la lune: Genet et les différences* (Bordeaux: Editions de la Différence, 1988), p. 184.

14. *Ibid.*

15. On the notion of theater as dislocation, see Samuel Weber, "Taking Place: Toward a Theater of Dislocation," in David J. Levin, ed., *Opera through Other Eyes* (Stanford: Stanford University Press, 1996), pp. 107–43. The conception of theater as interruption and fixation informs Benjamin's reading of Brecht's Epic Theater (Walter Benjamin, "Was ist episches Theater," *Gesammelte Schriften* (Frankfurt a. M.: Suhrkamp, 1980), 2.2:519–39); hereafter abbreviated *GS*. Benjamin locates the "epic" dimension of Brecht's theater in its "interruption of sequences," resulting in a disruption of the "dramatic" progression and opening the way to a theatricality structured in other than narrative (Aristotelian) terms. The decisive concept elaborated by Benjamin is that of the "citable gesture." It is closely related to Genet's notion of the arresting and fixation of the theatrical "act"—just as his conception of the linguistic "war of words" bears a close resemblance to Benjamin's analysis of "allegory" in German baroque theater. The "baroque" dimension of Genet's writing and theater invites comparison with Benjamin's discussion of the German *Trauerspiel*.

16. "With the exception of a handful of paintings—or fragments of paintings—few artists who painted before the discovery of photography have left us any tangible evidence of a vision and a kind of painting freed from the slavish concern with copying natural likenesses. Not daring to tamper with

the face—with the exception of Franz Hals (*The Regents*)—the painters daring enough to serve both the object painted and the painting (Velasquez, Rembrandt, Goya) used as a pretext a flower or a dress" (Genet, *Reflections on the Theater*, p. 67). Benjamin, in "The Work of Art in the Age of its Technical Reproducibility," similarly identifies the *face* as the bastion of "cult value," besieged, he argues, by the new media of "reproducibility" (besieged, but never conquered, like the Alcazar of Toledo in the Spanish Civil War). One finds echoes of similar considerations in the mouth of the Chief of Police, who seeks to create an "image" for himself, in *The Balcony*. I have discussed this play in "On the Balcony: The Theater of Technics," in L. Lambrechts and J. Nowé, eds., *Bild-Sprache: Texte zwischen Dichten und Denken* (Leuven: Louvain University Press, 1990), pp. 283–97.

17. "It must be possible for the beginning and the end to be seen together in one view" (Aristotle, *Poetics*, 59b).

18. Walter Benjamin, *Ursprung des deutschen Trauerspiels*, GS, 1.1:392.

Chapter 13

1. It would be instructive to pursue a comparison between the practice, common in eighteenth- and nineteenth-century bourgeois households, of organizing theatrical representations in the home—"theater" at home"—and "home theater" at the start of the twenty-first century. Without anticipating all the results, one in particular seems relatively clear: the replacement of *staging* and *playing* by *installing* and *receiving*. Although it is still too early to be certain, it seems unlikely that the "interactive" possibilities opened by digitally recorded DVDs will alter the predominantly passive spectator role in electronic "home theater."

2. "From its origins, cinema took over the theaters and turned the public away from living spectacles. It would seem, however, that theater, kicked out the front door, has returned by the window of the screen, by, so to speak, occupying cinema *from within*, through its subjects no less than through the tenacity of dramaturgical forms" (Jacques Gerstenkorn, "Lever de Rideau" ["Curtain Raiser"], in Christine Hamon-Sirejols et al., eds., *Cinéma et Théâtralité*, *Cahiers du Gritec* [Lyon: Aléas, 1994], p. 13). GRITEC is the acronym of the Groupe de Recherches sur l'Interférences du Théâtre et du Cinéma (Research Group on the Interferences of Theater and Cinema), founded in 1991 at the University Lumière (Lyon-2).

3. For instance, Allardyce Nicoll, *Film and Theater* (New York: Arno Press, 1972).

4. Before his God, in the Protestant version.

5. In his essay "What Is Epic Theater?" this is how Walter Benjamin describes the function of the Brechtian actor ("aus der Rolle mit Kunst *zu fallen*,"

my emphasis, W. Benjamin, *Gesammelte Schriften* [Frankfurt a. M.: Suhrkamp, 1980], 2.2:538).

6. The project of Dr. Lester can be seen as an effort to extend the certitude Descartes attaches to the cogito to the *res extensa* that is the body. Descartes, it may be recalled, makes perfectly clear that the certitude of the cogito only obtains during the time of self-consciousness, a time that requires the present participle to be properly articulated: "*I* am, *I* exist: it is certain. But for how long? So long as I am cogitating of course. . . . I am a true thing and truly existing. Yet what kind of thing? A *thinking* thing, I have said [*Dixi cogitans*]" (Descartes, *Meditations on First Philosophy*, trans. George Heffernan [Notre Dame, Ind.: Notre Dame University Press, 1990], p. 105). The present participle, *cogitans*, describes an indefinite period that is present only with reference to its articulation—hence, as self-consciousness, but one that is defined by the simultaneity of act and enunciation. The act can only be considered "certain" so long as it is at least the potential object of an enunciation. That such an enunciation could be of a radically different order from what it enunciates, and that it therefore cannot provide the kind of *evidence* that Descartes assumes it can, is an issue not further explored in the *Meditations*, but one that marks the history of post-Cartesian philosophy. In our film, it returns as the usurpation of Malkovich's body by Dr. Lester and his friends: there may be "self-consciousness" and it may be *thinking*, but it is not necessarily the property of an "ego."

7. This is, of course, one of the main motifs of Heinrich von Kleist's famous essay, "On the Marionette Theater."

8. In 1922 Vertov insisted that "the material" of film was "*the intervals* [the transitions from one movement to another] and in no way the movements themselves" (D. Vertov, "We: Variation of a Manifesto," in *Texte zur Theorie des Films*, ed. Franz-Josef Albersmeier [Stuttgart: Philipp Reclam Jr., 1979], p. 21).

9. Metallic blue—the color of Allegra's boot, in which she carries her "pod," but also of Yevgenji's shirt, as well as of the black (or, rather, blue) board upon which he writes, imparting its hue to the initial scene—is doubtless the dominant color of the film.

Chapter 14

1. Presidential statement following a meeting with his National Security Team, September 12, 2001, http://www.whitehouse.gov/news/releases/2001/09/#.

2. In his remarkable book *Politics of Security* (London: Routledge, 1996), Michael Dillon, one of the organizers of the forum "War, Terrorism, Spectacle" at which this paper was first delivered at the University of Lancaster on

NOTES TO PAGES 328–52

December 15, 2001, argues persuasively, following Heidegger, that the concern with "security" is rooted in Western modernity and the metaphysical tradition from which it emerges.

3. George W. Bush, "Address to a Joint Session of Congress and of the American People," http://www.whitehouse.gov/news/releases/2001/09/print/20010920–8.html.

4. A recent example is "Echelon," the worldwide system of surveillance put into place by the United States, in collaboration with Great Britain and the other countries of the Commonwealth, which apparently has served as much to gather economic information used to advantage American (or British) corporations as to provide political or military intelligence. For details, consult the webpage of "Echelon Watch," a discussion forum sponsored by the ACLU (www.echelonwatch.org).

5. And sometimes even against them. Here a precise analysis would have to bring out the dissymmetry in the respective roles of the hegemonic superpower and the subordinate allied countries. Thus it appears that the Echelon information-gathering system may have been used to help the Boeing corporation compete successfully against Airbus, in which British interests are largely represented.

6. Guy Debord, *The Society of the Spectacle*, trans. Donald Nicholson-Smith (New York: Zone Books, 1995), p. 26. Future references to this work will be given in parentheses in the body of the text.

7. Carl Schmitt, *Theory of Guerrilla Warfare* (Berlin: Duncker & Humblot, 1975), p. 87.

Chapter 15

1. A remark by Professor Robert Precht is worth noting in his context. Prof. Precht served as public defender of one of those accused in the 1993 bombing of the World Trade Center. His conclusion about the state of mind and motivations of those involved in this attack can serve as a valuable warning against easy stereotypes:

> "The things that struck me were the very complicated feelings the people who commit these acts have for America," he said. "Our leaders describe them as evildoers and say they hate everything our country stands for. . . . That was not my experience."
>
> He said several of the defendants admired the US system of government and law and had a real knowledge of American history. But they resented US policies.
>
> The dispute terrorists have with America is really more a political one and has nothing to do with Islamic beliefs, Precht said. Instead, he

said, "these are simply people who develop political agendas and then dress them up in a cloak of righteousness."

("Attacks Remind Professor of 1993," Kathy Barr Hoffmann, AP, Oct. 1, 2001). See also Robert E. Precht, *Defending Mohammed: A Defense Layer's Account of the 1993 World Trade Center Bombing Trial* (Ithaca: Cornell University Press, 1993).

2. ATTAC is the acronym standardly used to designate the original French name of the Association pour une Taxation des Transactions financières pour l'Aide aux Citoyens et Citoyennes (the Association for the Taxation of Financial Transactions for the Good of Citizens), founded in December 1998 and now represented in thirty-three countries, not, however, including the United States.

3. In the time since this interview was held, Nicholas Royle has published a remarkable book-length study of this topic: *The Uncanny* (New York: Routledge, 2003).

4. Jacques Derrida, *Of Spirit*, trans. Geoffrey Bennington and Rachel Bowlby (Chicago: University of Chicago Press, 1989), p. 130, my emphasis.

Index

Acting: and actors, 223, 257–59; and language, 9–10; distinguished from act and action, 75, 116, 188, 340, 388n3. *See also* Aristotle; tragedy

Action (*praxis*): and tragic plot, 24, 99–100, 258; and character 89; in Artaud 279–80

Actors (*prattontes*), as actings, 223, 257–59

Adler, Alfred, 252

Adorno, Theodor W., 229, 308, 338–39; and Benjamin, 237, 241; concept of name, 241–42; culture industry, 235–39, 248–49; 'Prologue to Television', 110; reading of Hegel, 232–34, 239–40; reading of Kierkegaard, 230–31, 239–40, 242–50; tenor (*Gehalt*), 240, 243

Aeschylus, 164

Agon (competition), 163–64, 166, 323

Alien (Scott), 51, 317

Allegory: and mortality, 191; and theater, x, 161–62, 167, 172–74, 176–77, 293; as a mode of perception 161–62; contrast between Adorno's and Benjamin's conceptions of, 237, 246; and the mourning play, x; of theatricality,

28; history as, 178; and fragment, 180

Al Qaeda, 327, 333, 351, 358–59

Anagnorisis, 88, 100, 107, 261–62. *See also* recognition

Antigone (Sophocles), 141, 146; family, 125–29, 131–34; Hegel's interpretation of 124–28, 131–32, 134, 137–38; in relation to other Theban plays, 122–23; *nomos*, 138–40; notion of justice (*Dike*), 132–33, 135

Aorist participle, 156. *See also* present participle

Aristotle, 2, 30, 41, 49, 138; approach to theater: actors, 223, 257–59; catharsis, 255, 279; mimesis, 112, 150, 254, 256, 263, 281; primacy of *praxis* over *ethos*, 89, 116, 258; privileging tragedy, 26, 200, 256–57, 264; unity of plot as *muthos* of *praxis*, 21, 24, 112, 193, 256, 258, 260, 267–68; unity of view (*synopsis*), 89, 99, 101, 254, 256, 266, 283; instrumentality of medium, 100–102, 105; *On the Soul*, 101; *Physics*, 48; *Poetics*, 99–103, 279–81, 283; theory of *peripeteia* and *anagnorisis*, 88, 100, 103, 107, 255–56, 260–61, 263–64, 298–300, 304–5. *See*